Annual World Bank Conference on Development Economics 1995

Edited by **Michael Bruno and Boris Pleskovic**

The World Bank *Washington, D.C.*

Contents

Introduction

Michael Bruno and Boris Pleskovic

Since 1989 the Annual World Bank Conference on Development Economics has provided a forum for debate and the exchange of ideas and information between World Bank staff and development researchers and practitioners from around the world. The conference series reflects the World Bank's strength as a knowledge-based institution as well as a development and a financial institution, ready to share the ideas, knowledge, and experience gained in over half a century of providing advice and technical assistance and disseminating lessons on best practices to nearly 180 countries.

The Bank's knowledge base comes from its research activities and its operational experience and analytical work. The conferences on development economics are another important source of ideas and knowledge, as well as a check on the quality and direction of the Bank's research and operations work. They open the Bank to outside experts who can challenge and expand our knowledge of the theories and practice of development. At the same time the conferences allow Bank experts to challenge or exchange ideas and experience with outside academics. Each year the topics selected for the conference represent new areas of concern or areas we believe will benefit from a review of existing knowledge and identification of the needs for further research.

The seventh conference addresses four themes: revisiting *Redistribution with Growth* (Chenery and others 1974), demographic change and development, aid and development, and fiscal decentralization. The 1995 conference continues the tradition of holding a roundtable discussion related to the subject of the next *World Development Report* (World Bank forthcoming), in this case on second-generation issues in transition economies.

In his opening remarks Gautam S. Kaji, a managing director of the World Bank, notes that the conference has evolved over the years to become the single largest gathering of the development economics community in the world. He emphasizes the Bank's concern not just with the "what" of development but increasingly with the

Michael Bruno is senior vice president, Development Economics, and chief economist at the World Bank. Boris Pleskovic is deputy administrator, Research Advisory Staff, at the World Bank.

Annual World Bank Conference on Development Economics 1995

"how." He links current global economy questions—private capital flows to developing countries; concerns with divergent development trends, especially in Sub-Saharan Africa; links between industrial and developing countries in international trade and economic growth—with the leading topics of the conference. The Bank's main role must remain helping more and more countries, particularly the poorest countries, enter the mainstream of the new global economy. Kaji notes that demand for the Bank's advice is growing more rapidly than demand for our traditional product, our money. Advice and other information-based services are highly knowledge-intensive and draw on the Bank's comparative advantage as a knowledge-based institution. The topics of the conference are all areas where the "how" question is extremely important and where we need to extend the frontiers of knowledge.

In the keynote address Domingo F. Cavallo and Guillermo Mondino reflect on the success of economic reforms in Argentina since 1991. They note that Argentina achieved remarkable economic growth and productivity gains while imposing hard reforms in trade policy and the public sector. The policies that led to the turnaround in the macroeconomic program included a novel stabilization program, far-reaching privatization of state companies, deregulation in many spheres, a reduction in trade barriers, and an overhaul of government spending and taxes. Called the "convertibility plan," the stabilization program introduced important macroeconomic changes. The new currency was fully backed by international reserves. Indexation was dropped completely. Contracts and transactions are free to be carried out in any currency, thereby introducing competition into the monetary side of the economy just as privatization increased competition on the real side. Argentina achieved stability, growth, and (a small) improvement in income distribution within a democratic system. It managed to shock the economy into dynamic growth at relatively little cost. As Cavallo and Mondino point out, these are remarkable achievements, especially since it is often argued that only an autocratic government can impose and maintain the strict policies required to turn an economy around quickly and to hold the course when the pain becomes severe.

Michael Bruno introduces the session on revisiting *Redistribution with Growth,* dedicated to Hollis Chenery. Bruno reminds the audience of Chenery's important contributions to development economics, including the establishment of the intellectual base for research and policy analysis at the Bank. Bruno remarks that Hollis Chenery did more than anyone else to transform the Bank into a knowledge-based institution and that his seminal work on redistribution with growth changed the course of thinking on development, especially on how to help the poor.

Albert Fishlow addresses three questions that are central to economic development: What is the extent and depth of income inequality in developing countries? What policy measures can be adopted to alleviate poverty? What can we learn from recent research on the relevance of inequality to the growth process? Fishlow argues that evidence from the past twenty years shows that income growth can exacerbate inequality. But evidence also shows that economic policies can make a visible difference in lessening or averting inequality. What seems to work best are policies designed to redistribute physical assets, such as land reform, and to promote the rapid accumulation of human capital. Fishlow observes that as income equality improves, poverty falls. Improving the quality of the labor force contributes significantly to higher worker productivity. Modernizing rural technology has the same effect. Reduced pressure from rural migration to cities and towns translates into lower social outlays and lower unemployment. Empirical estimates of new growth models show that income growth and greater equality are positively related. However, this result must be regarded tentatively, particularly because it depends on the inclusion of Latin American countries in the data set. Fishlow concludes that the real task for the future is to ensure that the new consensus on a market-friendly approach to development promotes government activities that reduce poverty and income inequality. One lesson, repeatedly learned, is that equitable development requires adequate resources. To provide the necessary inputs, like education and safety net programs for the poor, countries must develop an increased capacity for public savings.

Pranab Bardhan points out that in the twenty years since the publication of *Redistribution with Growth,* economists have reached a consensus on some issues in poverty research, while others remain contentious. Researchers have learned much about the economic and social relationships that characterize and perpetuate poverty in developing countries. Advances include the development of better ways to measure and identify poverty and closer attention to the problems of particular groups, such as women, who face formidable cultural and economic barriers to advancement. The interrelationships between women's economic and social autonomy and fertility, poverty, and environmental degradation are also better understood. Bardhan argues that these advances in knowledge call for specific policies aimed at poverty. In addition, growth-promoting policies, particularly those that favor labor-intensive industries and allocate resources more efficiently, may substantially reduce mass poverty. There is less agreement about policies related to asset redistribution, such as land reform. Bardhan argues that too much attention has been devoted to showing that faster economic growth will take care of poverty or that the state needs to allocate more resources to welfare programs. Some of this attention should be redirected toward building institutions and organizations at the local level that will better serve the poor. He concludes that community-level institutions can play a vital role in poverty alleviation by coordinating and implementing projects like water management, environmental protection, and regulation of forests and grazing land. Local residents and authorities can often identify cheaper and more appropriate ways of proving basic services. However, national institutions are better able to provide some services, particularly those that require coordination among jurisdictions or administrative sophistication.

Peter Diamond compares what governments tend to do under different systems and what they could do to better provide and regulate retirement income. Diamond notes that the case for mandatory saving rests on the assumption that workers would otherwise save too little for retirement. But an accumulation of savings restricted to use in retirement would not be available for unforeseen needs or opportunities, making such a system inefficient. This problem could be eased through a mandated retirement savings rate lower than is needed to fully finance a comfortable retirement. Diamond distinguishes between defined contribution and defined benefit systems, comparing the systems in Chile and the United States. He argues that any evaluation of a system needs to consider both its benefits and its contribution rates. Different issues matter when creating a new system and when changing a mature system, but politics set the bottom line in any country. It may be easier politically to design a good defined contribution system than a good defined benefit system. If policymakers believe that a well-designed defined benefit system could not be established for political reasons, the country would probably be better off with a defined contribution system. Diamond stresses that the most important criterion is good design and that the World Bank can perhaps be most valuable in identifying good design.

Nancy Folbre asks how economic development affects the organization of family life, the relative power of gender coalitions, and the evolution of economic disadvantages based on gender. Using the concepts of the new institutional economics, Folbre shows that gender-biased policies and property rights reflect the interests of gender coalitions. For instance, men as a group have less to gain economically than women and children from reforms that enforce paternal responsibilities, so it is hardly surprising that women's groups seeking such reforms meet considerable resistance from men. Folbre observes that women have increased their collective bargaining power in some areas more than others. In developing countries they often face a paradox: the same aspects of the development process that increase their economic independence as individuals (expansion of education and wage employment) tend to increase their economic vulnerability as mothers. Under certain circumstances women's groups may correctly calculate that they have more to lose from male-dominated modernization than from male-dominated tradition. She notes that the recent surge in privatization and the dismantling of social safety nets may create unanticipated problems: free markets may provide a good substitute for some previously state-run activities, but they do not provide much support for family life. Childrearing is no longer a remunerative activity, and families and businesses that devote resources to it may have a hard time competing with those that do not. Yet nonmarket work devoted to raising the next generation makes an enormous contribution to economic welfare. Folbre concludes that while some conservatives argue that women have become too powerful, that their independence and self-assertion threaten the viability of the family, it may rather be that women have simply not become powerful enough to persuade men and society to fairly share the costs of rearing the next generation.

In addressing the role of multilateral lending Dani Rodrik argues that the economic rationale for multilateral lending lies in its informational function. Done right, multilateral lending could improve the workings of international capital markets. He observes that multilateral agencies are in a better position than most to collect and disseminate information on the investment environment in different countries since this information is costly to obtain and can be used equally by many potential lenders. In so doing multilateral agencies are well suited to monitoring government policies in recipient countries. As long as multilaterals retain some autonomy from the governments that own them, their interactions with recipient countries can remain less politicized than is possible with government to government links. This gives multilateral agencies an advantage in exercising conditionality on borrowing governments. Rodrik notes that lending is required as an incentive, insofar as policy monitoring and conditionality cannot be adequately performed if they are not backed by loans, but that lending ought to be subsidiary to monitoring and conditionality. Commenting on their information function, Rodrik observes that the World Bank and other multilateral agencies see themselves first and foremost as lenders. Recasting their roles by placing monitoring and conditionally at the top of their agenda would have important repercussions on what they do and how they do it. Rodrik recommends that multilateral agencies disseminate their evaluations of governments' policies, reconsider their rules of secrecy and confidentiality, integrate analytical country work with operational and lending work, and distinguish between good and bad borrowers—and concentrate on the good ones.

Using irrigation systems in Nepal as a case study, Elinor Ostrom found this paradox: "primitive" irrigation systems constructed by farmers outperformed those improved by the construction of modern, permanent headworks funded by donors and built by professional engineering firms. The main reason: the incentives of farmers, villagers, and officials are more important in determining performance than the engineering of physical systems. Ostrom observes that in project planning, most effort focuses on how improving physical capital affects the technical operation of system. But these changes also affect the incentives of participants. When farmers select their own officials to govern and manage an irrigation system, the officials' incentives are closely aligned with those of the farmers and with the system's performance. Many irrigation systems provided by national governments lack any such connection. Ostrom notes that the evidence that farmers can overcome collective action problems when they have sufficient autonomy is consistent with the substantial literature on the capacity of resource users to govern inshore fisheries, mountain commons, grazing areas, and forest resources in all parts of the world. While the difficulties of sustaining long-term collective action are substantial, these high costs can be offset by the benefits of creating local organizations and selecting locals as leaders and rewarding them for their performance. Ostrom recommends that donor agencies deciding where to invest their funds think about investing in countries and sectors where substantial self-organizing activities already exist. If users are willing to invest some of their own resources, an infusion of external monetary capital and the construction of physical capital to complement the institutional capital on the ground may generate much larger returns.

Richard N. Cooper argues that economic growth in developing countries is beneficial to industrial economies. Although the positive effects are likely to be small, they will exceed any negative effects. The trade liberalization that accompanies growth will lift incomes in rich countries both directly and indirectly, through increased saving and investment. Changing patterns of trade will create dislocations in the rich countries, but if the past is a guide, the dislocations will be smaller than those caused by technological change and changes in domestic demand. He observes that increased growth in developing countries, combined with improved capital markets, broadens profitable investment opportunities for savers in industrial countries. Likewise, because output fluctuations in developing countries do not mimic those in industrial countries, they help to stabilize output and employment in industrial countries. Although the stabilizing effect is small, it will grow as the developing economies grow, provided fluctuations in output between the two groups do not become more closely correlated over time. Finally, Cooper argues that economic growth in developing countries will not worsen environmental degradation in the long run. Pollution is likely to increase as growth picks up from low initial levels of income. But as incomes rise, people prefer less pollution-intensive goods and demand environmental improvements. Democracy should evolve according to a similar pattern. Growth involves stress, which could erupt into political violence. However, as countries reach higher income levels, they typically achieve political stability and democracy emerges.

Although countries are moving rapidly toward fiscal decentralization, Vito Tanzi warns that many forces could derail this process. He argues that the institutional and social structures necessary for decentralization may be limited or nonexistent, particularly in developing countries, and that economies that have developed structural fiscal deficits may find it more difficult to adjust. Tanzi recommends that local governments be allowed to levy taxes to finance some of their activities. But it is difficult to assign taxes that will cover a large portion of local government spending. As a result, sharing arrangements have developed. These arrangements often make local governments dependent on the central government, undermining the purpose of decentralization to some extent and constraining the central government's ability to collect taxes. He notes that local governments are often in need of resources beyond those that they receive from the central government and those they raise themselves. They are forced to borrow and often find it difficult to service their loans. The central government is thus pressured to finance these debts, which leads to macroeconomic problems. Tanzi concludes that decentralization is really a contract between the central government and local governments. If the legal aspects are clear, if local governments are given access to necessary resources and have adequate public expenditure management systems in place to control the pace and allocation of spending, and if local bureaucrats are competent, then decentralization can live up to its promise. Otherwise, the results tend to be disappointing.

Also addressing the topic of decentralization, Rudolf Hommes argues that it has both political and practical arguments in its favor. With closer ties to the people, a decentralized government may have access to better information, which would permit more efficient resource allocation. This proximity also allows the community to exert some control over local authorities, strengthening the probability that public officials will work effectively. Hommes discusses several obstacles that stand in the way, drawing on his experience in Latin America. Perhaps the biggest is the cultural conservatism of local communities and the tradition within the central government of monopolizing resources and initiatives. Political problems also present obstacles. The natural tendency of the political system to overspend may be worsened by decentralization or the encroachment of patronage. Conflict may arise between new institutions and congressional or regional electoral barons. Central governments will have to overcome their traditional desire to dominate local jurisdictions to guide reforms without stunting the decentralization process. Hommes points out that the paradox of decentralization is that it demands more central government involvement and more sophisticated political skills at the national level. Central governments must be capable of steering change in the direction of a more democratic and efficient society. But this is a new role for most national governments, which find themselves at the beginning of a steep learning curve. They need to distinguish when to impinge on the autonomy of local governments for the sake of stability and when to refrain from interfering to avoid inhibiting good local government. Reform is irreversible as long as more participatory forms of government prevail.

The roundtable discussion on second-generation issues in transition addresses some of the issues central to the forthcoming *World Development Report 1996*. The panel brings together three experts, each drawing attention to different aspects of the topic. Following a brief introduction by Michael Bruno, Stanley Fischer asks whether macroeconomic policy in transition economies is too tight or too loose and identifies the most serious obstacles to high and sustainable growth. Jana Matesová examines the relationship between mass privatization and restructuring. Susan Rose-Ackerman discusses the growing problem of corruption in transition economies. The presentations were followed by a floor discussion moderated by Michael Bruno.

*　　*　　*

As in previous years, the planning and organization of the 1995 conference was a joint effort. Particular thanks for their support go to Gregory Ingram, the administrator of the Research Advisory Staff; Paulo Vieira Da Cunha; and Mark Baird. We would also like to thank other staff members, in particular several anonymous reviewers; Anupa Bhaumik and Clara Else; and the conference coordinators, Evelyn Alfaro, Mantejwinder Jandu, and Jean Gray Ponchamni, whose excellent organizational skills kept the conference on track. Finally, we thank the editorial staff, especially Meta de Coquereaumont, Paul Holtz, and Patricia McNees.

References

Chenery, Hollis B., Montek S. Ahluwalia, Clive Bell, John H. Duloy, and Richard Jolly. 1974. *Redistribution with Growth*. New York: Oxford University Press.

World Bank. Forthcoming. *World Development Report 1996: From Plan to Market*. New York: Oxford University Press.

The "How" of Development

Gautam S. Kaji

G ood morning and welcome to this conference, the seventh in our annual series. A particularly warm welcome to all our friends and colleagues from outside the World Bank. It is thanks to your participation that this event has evolved over the years to become the single largest gathering of the development economics community in the world, a gathering focused on learning lessons, expanding knowledge, and bringing new ideas to the challenge of development.

As I see it, you are rightly concerned not just with the "what" of development but also with the "how." And in our rapidly changing world the "how" has taken on increasing importance.

We now have enough evidence to say with reasonable confidence that globalization is here to stay. But we need to think more about the implications of that fact— for the Bank and, particularly, for our primary clients, the 4 billion people who live in the world's low- and middle-income countries.

The new global economy presents an array of questions to which we will admit— if we are honest—that we do not have all the answers:

- Yes, private capital flows to developing countries have quadrupled so far in this decade. They are now more than three times the level of aid flows. And yet, as Mexico reminded us, we do not yet know enough about how to manage the volatility inherent in some of those private flows.
- At the same time a very large group of countries has been unable to hook up to the driving dynamics of expanding private capital, trade, and information flows. And some others face a growing risk of marginalization. Real per capita income in Sub-Saharan Africa, for example, is unlikely to grow at more than 1 percent annually over the next decade, compared with more than 6 percent in East Asia. We need to know more about how to reconcile these divergent trends within globalization.
- And likewise, we need to know more about reverse linkages. The links between industrial and developing countries in international trade and eco-

Gautam S. Kaji is managing director, Office of the President, at the World Bank.

Annual World Bank Conference on Development Economics 1995

nomic growth are increasingly clear. It is now estimated, for example, that about 15 million jobs in OECD countries are linked to their exports to developing countries. But big questions remain about what might be called global economic management issues and their impact on different countries. How the G-7 countries manage their economies, for instance, matters much more to developing countries today than it did even a decade ago. How the World Trade Organization functions will make much more of a difference to all countries than how the General Agreement on Tariffs and Trade functioned.

Another issue—and much closer to home—relates to the role of the World Bank. Our main role must remain helping more and more countries, particularly the poorest, join the mainstream of the new global economy: building markets, gaining access to private capital, and reducing poverty. But our future effectiveness is very much linked to the "how" questions:

- How we can do more to leverage our analytical output by improving the dissemination of our cross-country experience and lessons learned.
- How we can do more to bridge the gap between policy formulation and implementation by helping countries establish the institutions, incentives, and rules of the game necessary to make them players in the new global economy.
- And how we can be more agile in recognizing and dealing with the rapid changes in the countries where we work—monitoring developments and helping ensure a more efficient exchange of information between governments and markets.

Because of the enormous increase in private flows, the demand for the Bank's traditional product, our money, is now growing more slowly. At the same time the demand for our advice is growing more rapidly. In fact, there is increasing synergy. For example, our role in helping governments attract private investment and in providing an adequate comfort level for private investors involves both our advice and creative use of our capital base. These kinds of services are highly knowledge intensive and draw on the Bank's comparative advantage as a knowledge-based institution.

Again, the message is that as countries become clearer on the "what" of development, they want to know more about the "how." The Bank's fifty years of experience, our long-term relationship with virtually every developing country, our range of financial interventions, and our research and analytical capacity put us in a unique position to help them with that question. But our effectiveness in doing so hinges on continually replenishing our knowledge base, holding ourselves to the highest intellectual standards, and opening up the institution to the views—and yes, the scrutiny—of the leaders in the knowledge business. That includes many of the people in this room.

You will be grappling with some difficult but very interesting topics over the next two days: the linkages between aid and development, decentralization and development, and demographics and development. These are all areas where we need to extend the frontiers of knowledge, areas where the "how" question looms large. All of us at the Bank look forward to the results of your deliberations.

In closing, I would like to add a personal note on Hollis Chenery, who died eight months ago. Hollis did more perhaps than anyone else to transform the World Bank into a knowledge-based institution. His seminal work on redistribution with growth changed the course of thinking on development—and on how development could be more effectively harnessed to benefit the poor. We who knew Hollis knew him as a man who dedicated his life to the "how" of development—and it is fitting that this conference should honor his contribution.

Keynote Address

Argentina's Miracle? From Hyperinflation to Sustained Growth

Domingo F. Cavallo and Guillermo Mondino

The East Asian miracle is usually identified with high rates of output growth. In some cases this growth was accompanied by rapid and sustained growth in productivity. According to a recent World Bank (1993) study, total factor productivity growth in the most successful East Asian economies ranged from 1.0 percent to 2.4 percent a year over a thirty-year period. In this context Argentina's average total factor productivity growth of 6.5 percent a year during 1990–94 is a remarkable feat. While the jury is still out on whether this rate of growth can be sustained over a much longer period, the growth in productivity is so remarkable that it deserves closer examination. This seemingly miraculous productivity growth inspired the title of this address.

In April 1991 Argentina embarked on a far-reaching program of economic reforms designed to bring inflation down to acceptable levels and to restore growth on a sustainable basis. The program rested on four pillars: opening of the economy, deregulation and reform of the tax code, privatization and elimination of other forms of government interference in resource allocation, and stabilization of inflation and the crucial relative prices. The program is popularly known as "the convertibility plan" thanks to its most notorious and innovative feature: the introduction of a bimonetary currency board.

Notwithstanding its remarkable success in reducing inflation, the program was conceived mainly as a tool to overcome decades of economic stagnation and to regain sustained growth. It is on these grounds that we assess (in preliminary fashion) the accomplishments of the reforms. From the historical and cross-country evidence on productivity growth, we argue that something fundamental has changed in Argentina and that macroeconomic stabilization is a key component of that change. We also consider some other issues—typically overlooked—that are associated with economic reform (such as income distibution and unemployment) and that are important for their impact on social welfare and the development of the coalitions needed to support stabilization.

Domingo F. Cavallo is Minister of Economics, Public Works, and Services of Argentina. Guillermo Mondino is director of the Institute for Economic Research on Argentina and Latin America (IEERAL) of the Mediterranean Foundation.

Annual World Bank Conference on Development Economics 1995

Productivity Growth and Economic Reform

An economy grows because it accumulates factors of production, like physical and human capital, because its labor effort grows, or because it improves the efficiency with which it uses the factors of production. Increases in productivity can result for a number of reasons: a push or shift of the technological frontier, a gradual movement toward the frontier (international best practice), or a reallocation of resources to more efficient uses. In a developing nation any reform that affects the use of factors of production is also likely to alter productivity. For instance, when governments meddle in the allocation of resources through commercial or industrial policies, through changes in incentives (affecting relative prices) to certain types of capital accumulation, or through unstable macroeconomic policies, the rate at which factors are accumulated and the incentives to introduce technological innovations are bound to be affected.

For nearly six decades the Argentine economy experienced continuous deleterious government intervention. Early in the century Argentina's economy had been well-integrated with international goods and asset markets, its relative prices reflecting international scarcities. Per capita income was high, economic growth was strong, and productivity growth was remarkable (figure 1). Then, from the 1930s to the early 1950s Argentina's global integration was severely set back by the Great Depression and World War II. As an adjustment mechanism, Argentina partially closed the economy, initiated some industrial policies, and began to reorganize its labor market. But once the external factors that had prompted these policies disappeared, Argentina never returned to openness, low levels of government interven-

Figure 1. *Total Factor Productivity in Argentina, 1918–94*

Four-year moving average (percentage change)

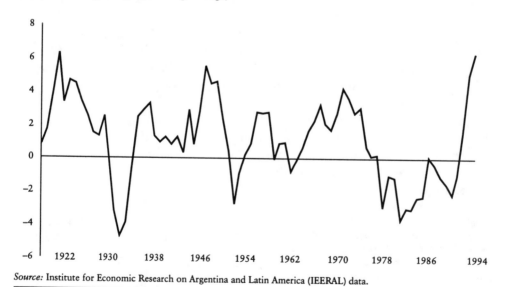

Source: Institute for Economic Research on Argentina and Latin America (IEERAL) data.

tion, and flexible markets. Instead, Argentina experienced a profound move toward import substitution, sectorally biased policies, interventions to affect other relative prices, and overall macroeconomic instability. The interventions and instability had a devastating effect on the efficiency of resource allocation.

Consider the rates of total factor productivity growth for selected periods (table 1).[1] Productivity increased at an average annual rate of 2.3 percent for 1915–30, 1.7 percent for 1930–50, and 2.8 percent for 1960–74. The period from 1975 to 1990 is astonishing, however. Productivity growth plunged by a cumulative 34.3 percent—a loss in efficiency of 2.8 percent a year! This was a remarkable—and remarkably long-lasting—collapse in productivity. Capital accumulation grew by 168 percent between 1960 and 1990, yet output increased only 85 percent, indicating a very low marginal product of capital. Labor productivity, however, as measured by the ratio of GDP to employment, grew by 25 percent during that period. The difference in performance is clearly explained by the artificially low return on capital. It is difficult to imagine that any firm facing world market conditions would undertake a productive investment under those circumstances. Indeed, a large share of aggregate capital accumulation during the period was the product of government fixed capital formation.

Macroeconomic Stability and Growth

Previous research has explained that the very low rate of return on Argentine capital, here identified by the large drop in productivity, was the result of increasing macroeconomic instability, the dramatic detachment from world market conditions, and the substantial drop in the (already low) efficiency of public sector operations. But what explains the recovery of productivity in the 1990s? Recent research shows that productivity growth (both total factor and labor productivity) is closely associated with the macroeconomic environment. For instance, Stanley Fischer (1993) finds that a stable macroeconomic environment is conducive to sustained growth. In particular, the evidence amassed in his and other papers shows that high inflation, large budget deficits, and exchange rate mismanagement all impede growth.

Table 1. *Total Factor Productivity, 1915–94*

Period	Cumulative rate	Average annual rate
1915–30	40.0	2.3
1930–50	40.6	1.7
1960–74	46.4	2.8
1975–90	−34.3	−2.8
1990–94	28.9	6.5

Source: Institute for Economic Research on Argentina and Latin America (IEERAL) data.

To check how important the removal of these impediments is in explaining Argentina's growth performance in the 1990s, we simulated the regressions reported in Fischer's study, using the average inflation rate, the budget deficit (in fact a surplus), the foreign exchange black market premium (none), and the variability of inflation for 1991–94. The regression predicted total factor productivity growth of 2.1 percent a year, well below the observed rates. One reason for the discrepancy is that Fischer's estimates are for a country closer to steady state rather than one in the process of reform. Yet the results suggest that something beyond his measure of macroeconomic stability was operational.

Perhaps Fischer's results do not fully capture the impact of macroeconomic volatility on growth. For instance, one of the most damaging effects of inflation in Argentina was its variability, often associated with repeated government efforts to stabilize the economy using a variety of mechanisms. This series of stabilization attempts, each followed by policy collapse, has had deleterious effects on the level and efficiency of investment and the allocation of resources.

The same argument could be made about the effects of volatility in output and demand (particularly for a relatively closed economy). Ramey and Ramey (1994) present empirical evidence supporting the view that volatility of output is detrimental to growth. Theoretically, there are several mechanisms through which volatility in relative prices (both atemporal and intertemporal) and output could hinder growth. One mechanism is of particular interest for Argentina. When a country precommits to a choice of technology, an increase in volatility leads to lower average output and, through any of the typical endogenous growth mechanisms, the rate of output growth (Ramey and Ramey 1991). The example of technology precommitment we have in mind in Argentina is the inflexibility of labor markets. When it is very costly to hire and fire workers, adjusting the level of production can also be very costly. An economy with a sclerotic labor market is bound to have high average costs of production or low average GNP. There are other arguments that emphasize the increased chance of survival of inefficient firms when uncertainty about relative prices increases. In search-intensive markets with inflation, volatility may increase the market power of firms, allowing those with relatively high costs of production to survive at the expense of the relatively efficient ones. Once again, the link between low productivity and relative price variability and inflation would be established (Tommasi 1994; De Gregorio and Sturzenegger 1994).

To evaluate the importance of this variability (and therefore unpredictability) in relative prices, inflation, and output, we performed a simple exercise. We ran cross-country growth regressions to explain the rate of growth of labor productivity for fifty industrial and developing countries over the period 1960–87. The regressors were level of output per worker in 1960, investment-output ratio, high school enrollment, population growth, and the volatility of the unforecastable component of changes in output growth, real exchange rates, inflation, and the relative price of investment and consumption goods (the data are from Summers and Heston 1991, the IMF, and the World Bank). The unforecastable components were calculated after regressing each variable on itself and on the other three variables lagged one period.

We decomposed the period (before and after 1973) to allow for the general change in exchange rate regimes that took place in 1973. While we held all the parameters to be the same across periods, we allowed the means and variances of variables to change from one period to the next. This technique allowed us to identify much more precisely the effects of volatility on growth.

Beyond the typical results for the importance of investment in physical and human capital, the results show that it is mainly the variability of real exchange rates and inflation that matters (table 2). We found the surprising result that while variability in the real exchange rate does substantial damage to productivity growth,

Table 2. *Cross-Country Growth Effects of Volatility for Fifty Countries, 1960–87*

Independent variable	Regression 1	Regression 2	Regression 3
Y base[a]	−0.298	−0.284	−0.282
	(−3.98)	(−3.77)	(−3.45)
High school enrollment[b]	0.156	0.124	0.156
	(1.72)	(1.40)	(1.82)
Population growth	−0.316	−0.122	−0.244
	(−1.27)	(−0.45)	(−0.76)
Investment[b]	0.65	0.611	0.577
	(5.68)	(5.64)	(4.66)
Output volatility[c]		−1.217	−1.511
		(−0.72)	(−0.88)
Real exchange rate volatility[d]		−1.939	−2.013
		(−3.33)	(−2.31)
Investment–consumption price volatility			0.003
			(−0.72)
Inflation			−0.2
			(−1.77)
Inflation volatility			0.159
			(1.65)
R^2	0.42	0.5	0.48
SSR	5.98	5.05	4.85

Note: Numbers in parentheses are t-statistics; they are heteroscedasticity consistent through a White correction.
a. Level of output per worker in 1960 and 1973.
b. Average for 1960–73 and 1973–87.
c. The unforecastable component of output growth.
d. Changes in real exchange rates.
Source: Authors' calculations based on data from Summers and Heston 1991; IMF; and World Bank.

unforecastable inflation is positively related to growth (though the level of inflation is very detrimental to growth).

Next, we simulated the effect of macroeconomic stabilization by plugging in the realized values of the variables for Argentina in 1991–94. The results, again, fall short of the observed growth in labor productivity. Taking into account the dramatic drop in the volatility of the exchange rate and inflation helps increase predicted labor productivity growth to an average 4.2 percent. Actual labor productivity growth was 6.3 percent (using Argentine national accounts data, not that of Summers and Heston).

Alignment of Relative Prices

These exercises illustrate that although macroeconomic stabilization was an important determinant of growth, other factors must have been operating to produce the healthy recent growth rate in total factor productivity. These factors probably include privatization, deregulation, the opening of the economy, and the substantial drop in the relative price of capital goods.

The literature on economic development has always emphasized the importance of having relative prices aligned with those of the rest of the world. The argument was typically used to point out that substantial static efficiency gains could be achieved through this mechanism. Recently, however, some researchers have gone further to argue that investments in machinery have large growth externalities and should be encouraged (DeLong and Summers 1990; Lee 1994). Since machinery investments in developing countries typically have large imported components, this argument calls for more favorable tariff treatment of capital goods than consumption goods.

There have been large swings in the prices of machinery and other capital goods in Argentina. The relative price of capital goods was very low before the 1930s and then started to rise during the Great Depression (figure 2). Indeed, Diaz Alejandro (1975) and Cavallo and Mundlak (1989) point out that the high price of capital goods helped explain the poor growth performance for the postwar period. The relative price of capital goods remained high until 1985, when a downward trend began. Since 1991 a concerted effort has been made to bring capital goods in line with world prices. The administration has gone a step further and introduced tax incentives to encourage the accumulation of the machinery and equipment shown by international evidence to have large growth externalities. This treatment of capital goods applies across the board, to avoid favoring certain sectors (though the policy is not entirely neutral since it favors capital-intensive industries).

Trade Reform, Privatization, and Deregulation

Argentina drastically reduced trade barriers, eliminating all quotas, taxes, and non-tariff barriers and reducing tariffs and the spreads between them. Argentina's structure of protection now consists of three levels of tariffs, except in a few targeted sectors like the automobile industry, textiles, and paper.

On the export side Argentina eliminated all export taxes and most regulatory institutions. It perfected a mechanism (consistent with the rules of the General Agreement on Tariffs and Trade) to reimburse firms for all indirect taxes incurred in production. To equilibrate the incentives of firms in tradable sectors, exports are subsidized at rates similar to the rate of taxes levied on imports in the sector. Since some protection was viewed as unavoidable during the transition, relative prices between domestic and foreign markets were equalized, so that firms would have the proper incentives to export. Research suggests that exports produce positive growth externalities, and therefore this policy was considered an important building block of the program. The reforms liberalizing trade have operated effectively. Exports grew by 20 percent in 1994 and by nearly 45 percent in the first quarter of 1995, following on three years of relative stagnation (a cumulative growth rate of 6.2 percent from 1991 to 1993).

Perhaps the most dramatic trade reform, however, involves the Mercosur agreement for the creation of a customs union with Brazil, Paraguay, and Uruguay. There are several reasons why Mercosur was actively pursued. First, it expanded the market for Argentine exports. Second, it introduced an important dose of commitment to liberal trade, since any change in tariffs now requires the approval of the other three parties. Third, it created a mechanism for disciplining the countries on their macroeconomic policies, since instability would be severely punished by neighboring countries and capital relocation. There are, however, several problems with the agreement that must be worked out over the next few years, concerning rules of origin, dispute settlement mechanisms, tax subsidies and other fiscal asymmetries, and the common external tariff.

Figure 2. *Relative Prices of Capital Goods in Argentina, 1918–94*

Four-year moving average (ratio to GDP)

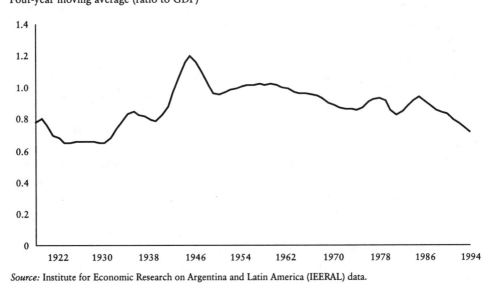

Source: Institute for Economic Research on Argentina and Latin America (IEERAL) data.

Privatizations have given productivity growth a large boost as well. After decades of inefficient investment, deteriorating service provision, and rampant corruption, government-owned corporations were a major stumbling block for the private sector. Privatization was not only fiscally beneficial, since it allowed the government to settle several debts that were fast accumulating, but also productivity enhancing. Investment by privatized firms is very high, accounting for about half of total investment according to some private estimates. Argentina has privatized firms and activities in all areas, from telecommunications and airlines to oil and petrochemicals, water, and sewers. Government business activity has been severely curtailed and will probably be completely eliminated by the end of 1995.

It is this combination of trade reform, privatization and deregulation, and macroeconomic stabilization that lies behind the historically and internationally high rate of productivity growth in Argentina.

The Inflation Stabilization Program

Inflation stabilization programs are typically either money- or exchange rate–based programs. Argentina opted for what is an uncommon combination of the two. The program is not a standard, 100 percent reserves currency board. The convertibility reform introduced a currency that must compete in the market against other currencies.

The idea behind convertibility is theoretically simple and draws on Milton Friedman's concept of the optimal quantity of money. Friedman understood that a monopolist would never set price to equal marginal cost. Rather, with complete disregard for consumer surplus, the monopolist would extract the maximum potential rent. Since money has (basically) zero marginal cost of production, the money monopolist would drive the price to the point where marginal revenue is zero, or the point of maximum seigniorage collection along the Laffer curve. If it were possible to implement a competitive mechanism for issuing money, the price would quickly be forced down to equal marginal cost. Since the price of holding money is the forgone nominal interest earnings, the optimal quantity of money would be reached at the point where inflation was equal to minus the real rate of interest.

The convertibility program had exactly that feature in mind. It allowed for two (or more) currencies to compete against each other in the domestic market. When the program was introduced, many transactions were being carried out in dollars. Rather than forbid their use (doing so had proved futile in the past), the program made all contracts legal and fully enforceable in Argentina, whatever currency they were written in. This freedom to choose the currency to be used in any transaction has dramatic implications. In effect, the government has relinquished its monopoly power over money. Convertibility forces the peso, if it is to be used and held at all, to be price competitive with other currencies of reference. In particular, since the U.S. dollar was in widespread use, it forced the peso to compete against the dollar. In practice, people can purchase anything, anywhere, and at any time in dollars (supermarket purchases, restaurant meals, shoe shines, taxi rides). The market has also chosen to denominate most long-term contracts (particularly loans and rents) in dollars to eliminate any remaining uncertainty.

The second important feature of convertibility, and perhaps the most widely understood, is that the central bank is required by law to hold enough foreign currency or marketable (and liquid) assets denominated in dollars to fully back its monetary liabilities. In other words, every peso that makes up the monetary base has a counterpart dollar resting in the vaults of the central bank. In order to print pesos, the central bank must buy an equal amount of dollars. It is impossible to debase the currency. If the domestic financial market required more liquidity, it would have to provide the central bank with dollars. The only scope left for a marginally independent monetary policy is to conduct open market operations in dollar-denominated securities. Even these are restricted by law to no more than 20 percent of the base; in fact, they represent a smaller proportion of the base. Monetary policy is, then, for any meaningful economic time span, completely subordinated to U.S. monetary policy.

Finally, and perhaps trivially, the rate at which the peso exchanges freely against the dollar has been set at one to one. While this property is inconsequential from an economic perspective, it simplifies calculations, has restored credibility, and provides a clear yardstick for price setting. Argentina does not really have an exchange rate. It has only an accounting rate that allows easy conversion between pesos and dollars. This accounting rate has been set by law, and the government is forced to abide by it.

What most clearly sets the convertibility program apart from other fixed exchange rate stabilization programs is the management of international reserves. In a fixed-rate regime the amount of foreign currency reserves at the central bank indicates the potential sustainability of the plan. The smaller the amount, the more difficult it becomes for the central bank to sustain a fixed parity. But this is not true of the convertibility program. Because for every peso that circulates there must be a dollar waiting at the central bank, the foreign currencies at the central bank are not "reserves" in that they cannot be freely used by the bank. For instance, they cannot be used to cancel foreign debt. The truth is that the reserves are the property of the peso holders. Therefore, when central bank statistics show that reserves are decreasing, they are only showing that people prefer currencies other than the peso for their transactions. In an extreme scenario, economic agents could completely substitute away from pesos and carry out all their transactions in dollars. In this sense, the movements of international reserves or the change in the composition of deposits (according to the currency of denomination) are only the reflection of a continuous currency reform engineered by the private sector. Whether the economy becomes dollarized or not is the choice of private citizens.

Convertibility was remarkably successful in bringing down inflation. Inflation dropped from 30 percent a month in March 1991 to an average of 0.4 percent a month during 1994. This success, plus the elimination of spurious variability in relative prices and, lately, the weathering of the "Tequila" storm, makes it attractive as a potential new variant for the well-developed toolbox of stabilizers. Yet two aspects must be borne in mind when such a program is considered. First and foremost, fiscal discipline is the backbone. Inflation stabilization is impossible without it. Second, the bimonetarism of the economy is important, since that is the strongest disciplinary check on the government. Any attempt to break convertibility would be punished with the sudden elimination of domestic currency demand.

The Social Costs of Reforms

Argentina is one of the few countries that attempted drastic reform under a fully functioning democracy. That adds a new dimension to the social costs since political support for the program must be preserved. The convertibility program was not a costless reform. The costs must be clearly analyzed to avoid drawing the wrong policy conclusions.

Employment and Labor Markets

The first element that stabilizers worry about when considering the costs of their policies is employment loss. Argentina's unemployment rate rose substantially under the stabilization program, from 6.3 percent in 1990 to 12.2 percent in 1994. But the unemployment rate does not reflect a drop in total employment. Rather, it mirrors the large increase in the labor force participation rate. In fact, total urban employment grew by about 515,000 new workers between 1990 and 1994 while the total urban labor supply increased by 1,290,000 people. Whether the increase is due to a reversal of the "discouraged worker" effect or the response to higher potential earnings is still an open issue. Some estimates put the real wage increase (in levels) at close to 30 percent, while others show almost no change. Any tests based on these statistics are bound to be tremendously data dependent.

Not only has the rate of unemployment increased substantially in the last few years, but the average duration of a spell of unemployment has gone up as well (approximated by the ratio of the stock of the unemployed to the inflow of unemployed, which encompasses those who claim to have been searching for work for less than a week). The average duration of unemployment for an unemployed worker in Buenos Aires is now 32.2 weeks, up from 21.7 weeks in October 1989 and 12.9 weeks in 1991. This increase in duration, together with the increase in labor supply (and they are not independent), generates a problem that a reformist government must address. The rapid growth in output and the high levels of capacity utilization are, however, clear indications that pumping up aggregate demand is not the solution.

A better diagnosis of the trends in the labor market is possible after considering the breakdown of unemployment and its duration. The unemployment rate is heavily concentrated among the young (males), the older worker (over 50), and the unskilled (the fraction of the unemployed who have not finished high school is 34 percent higher than that of the labor force as a whole). The largest increases in the duration of unemployment have been among the unskilled (83.9 percent). Increases in duration have also been greater for women (240 percent) than for men (100 percent), and for workers with previous experience (177 percent increase) than for inexperienced workers (4 percent increase, though the duration of unemployment is still longer than for experienced workers). The trends in the labor market are indicative of a workforce that has difficulty reallocating itself between sectors and jobs, because of a mismatch between old skills and new requirements. These trends also suggest a heavily regulated labor market that works against price flexibility and rapid job creation and worker reallocation.

Simultaneously with these trends in employment, the labor market shows a narrowing of the differential in income between skilled and unskilled workers. In October 1989 the hourly compensation for skilled workers was 2.3 times that of unskilled workers. By 1994 the ratio had fallen to 1.76. While the data show a substantial increase in hourly incomes for both groups between 1989 and 1991, the earnings of skilled workers have dropped in absolute values since then, while those of the unskilled have remained flat. As with unemployment and its duration, the market once again seems to be reflecting greater flexibility for those with education than for those without it. To ease the pain of transition, labor markets need to be deregulated to allow for greater mobility among workers.

Income Distribution and Poverty

A related aspect, though typically addressed in a different setting, is the behavior of income distribution. In Argentina income distribution has improved since the beginning of economic reforms and stabilization. The Gini coefficient for the distribution of income in Buenos Aires (close to the country average) has shown a steady decline since 1989, with a 10.7 percent drop in the first two years and a 2.8 percent fall in the next two. Not only did Gini coefficients improve. The share of the population below the poverty line went from an alarming 47.4 percent in October 1989 to a still worrisome but much improved 19 percent. And, finally, not only are fewer households below the poverty line. Those that are poor have also improved their standing. The share of the population at every level of income below the poverty line is smaller today than it was in 1989. For instance, about 5.5 percent of the population earns half the poverty-line income ($82 or less a month); in 1989 the share was 7.0 percent. The moderate increase in real wages for unskilled labor and the disappearance of the regressive inflation tax are responsible for at least some of these improvements in income distribution.

Conclusion

Unemployment and poverty are two issues to which development economists must give top priority. Yet it is not through paternalism, redistribution policies, and macroeconomic expansionism that we will solve those problems. The only way to lift the curse of underdevelopment is by creating the conditions for rapid productivity growth and by letting the benefits spill over to all of society. Argentina's experience with reform, successful stabilization, and rapid productivity growth within a democratic society should be a case study for reformist governments. Argentina has not yet graduated to the status of miracle economy. But can we afford to wait thirty years to evaluate the lessons and correct the mistakes? The poor and unemployed surely do not think so.

Note

1. Our estimates of total factor productivity are calculated using Argentine capital, labor, and human capital elasticities. The parameter estimates are remarkably close to the estimates for industrial countries reported in World Bank (1993).

References

Cavallo, D., and Y. Mundlak. 1989. *La Argentina que pudo ser: Los costos de la represion economica.* Buenos Aires: Manantial.

De Gregorio, Jose, and Federico Sturzenegger. 1994. "Credit Markets and the Welfare Costs of Inflation." NBER Working Paper 4873. National Bureau of Economic Research, Cambridge, Mass.

DeLong, Bradford, and Lawrence Summers. 1990. "Equipment Investment and Economic Growth." NBER Working Paper 3515. National Bureau of Economic Research, Cambridge, Mass.

Diaz-Alejandro, Carlos. 1975. *Ensayos sobre la historia economica argentina.* Buenos Aires: Amorrortu.

Fischer, Stanley. 1993. "The Role of Macroeconomic Factors in Growth." NBER Working Paper 4565. National Bureau of Economic Research, Cambridge, Mass.

Lee, J-W. 1994. "Capital Goods Imports and Long-Run Growth." NBER Working Paper 4725. National Bureau of Economic Research, Cambridge, Mass.

Page, John. 1994. "The East Asian Miracle: Four Lessons for Development Policy." *NBER Macroeconomics Annual.* Cambridge, Mass.: National Bureau of Economic Research.

Ramey, Garcy, and Valerie Ramey. 1991. "Technology Commitment and the Cost of Economic Fluctuations." NBER Working Paper 3755. National Bureau of Economic Research, Cambridge, Mass.

————. 1994. "Cross-Country Evidence on the Link Between Volatility and Growth." NBER Working Paper 4959. National Bureau of Economic Research, Cambridge, Mass.

Summers, Robert, and Alan Heston. 1991. "The Penn World Table (Mark 5): An Expanded Set of International Comparisons, 1950-1988." *Quarterly Journal of Economics* 106: 327–68.

Tommasi, M. 1994. "High Inflation: Resource Misallocations and Growth Effects." University of California, Los Angeles, Department of Economics.

World Bank. 1993. *The East Asian Miracle: Economic Growth and Public Policy.* New York: Oxford University Press.

In Memoriam: A Tribute to Hollis Chenery

Michael Bruno

Hollis Chenery, who died eight months ago at the age of seventy-six, was a commanding figure in development economics for more than twenty-five years, thirteen of which he spent building and running the economics research complex of the World Bank.

Hollis Chenery's best-known pioneering contributions came in two areas. One was the quantitative design of development policy for open economies (I first came to admire and benefit from his seminal work in this area early in my own career). The other was the cross-country analysis of development patterns. In the first area he gave operational content to an approach pioneered by the Nobel Prize–winning economist Jan Tinbergen—and greatly extended it. In the other he built on and significantly expanded an approach initiated by another great Nobel Prize winner, Simon Kuznets of Harvard University.

Hollis made other important contributions as well to a broad range of topics, from constant elasticity of substitution production functions (the "C" in ACMS was Chenery's, along with Arrow's "A," Minhas's "M," and Solow's "S") to economies of scale, the complementarity and timing of investment decisions, investment criteria and shadow pricing, dynamic comparative advantage, and issues of income distribution and growth, the topics to which the commemorative session on *Redistribution with Growth* are devoted.

Hollis came to economics with the practical approach of an engineer (he earned his undergraduate degree in engineering) and a keen awareness of social issues, no doubt bolstered by his wartime experience. Coming out of Harvard with his PhD in 1950, Hollis had his first practical involvement in economic development policy in the postwar reconstruction and development effort, primarily in war-ravaged Italy. He subsequently applied his development policy design skills to the Latin American scene, as well as to other developing regions. Intellectually curious and open-minded, he had little patience for pure doctrinal debates or pure theoretical constructs unless they could be applied to practical policy purposes. He helped build the

Michael Bruno is senior vice president, Development Economics, and chief economist at the World Bank.
Annual World Bank Conference on Development Economics 1995
©1996 The International Bank for Reconstruction and Development / THE WORLD BANK

intellectual bridge between the world of practical policy design and the academic community, a skill that came to the forefront during his tenure at the World Bank.

Hollis came to the Bank in 1970 at the request of Robert McNamara, interrupting a distinguished academic career that had begun at Stanford and continued at Harvard, with several years of exposure to the real world of development as assistant administrator of the U.S. Agency for International Development (USAID). First as economic advisor to the president and then as vice president for development policy he converted a small group of Bank economists into the world's leading research center on economic development. His many institutional accomplishments included setting up the broadly based Bankwide research committee and launching the Bank's flagship publication, the *World Development Report*. He led the research on the set of studies on poverty and distributional issues that evolved into *Redistribution with Growth*. Among his staff he emphasized holding to the highest professional standards in research, while also insisting on their involvement in the Bank's operations work. He left the Bank in 1983, after thirteen very fruitful years, to return to Harvard, where for some years he devoted his intellectual energies to exploring patterns of economic development, much of the work in collaboration with Moshe Syrquin.

I want to end this tribute on a personal note of gratitude. Hollis was my first mentor and tutor in development economics. I met him when I was a very junior economist in the research department of the Bank of Israel in the late 1950s. Hollis was invited to help us design a long-term development strategy under a projected foreign aid constraint (an unlikely job for a central bank today, but common in those days). Soon after his arrival he asked me to construct a quick and dirty 20 by 20 input-output table in a week's time. Hollis was responsible for my first published paper in economics, which I wrote jointly with him, on a two-gap model for Israel— a precursor of work that he and other of his students did along similar lines.

Hollis was also responsible for my enrolling in the doctoral program at Stanford. I experienced first-hand his personal devotion to his students when he and his wife Louise, a southerner like Hollis, extended their warm hospitality to me and my wife and our small baby girl when we stayed at their house during the first week of my visit to Stanford. Very soon afterwards he was called to serve at USAID. During the 1970s and 1980s, when our research and policy activities no longer intersected as much, we continued to meet and talk every now and then. Hollis kept up his keen interest in economic and political developments in Israel and, more generally, the Middle East, and we talked as well about the macroeconomic issues dominating the world scene.

I last saw Hollis at his home in Cambridge, when Lance Taylor and I visited him during the January 1994 annual meetings of the American Economic Association, shortly after his beloved second wife, Mary, died. Mary's death was a terrible blow to Hollis, already weakened by his prolonged illness. Yet he still showed an interest in what we, his former students, were up to, and still warmed us with that friendly Hollis smile. We will all remember him for the great contributions he has made to the profession at large, to the Bank, and to each of us individually. May his soul rest in peace.

Inequality, Poverty, and Growth: Where Do We Stand?

Albert Fishlow

Arguing for the importance of income distribution as a central area of inquiry over the next decade, the article reviews three central questions: the current state of income inequality, whether greater equality is compatible with reduced poverty, and the relationship of inequality to growth. First, the article contends that a complete dismissal of the original Kuznets parabolic relationship between inequality and income may be in error. There is some evidence of its validity when policy is taken into account. Second, it argues that reduced poverty and improved income equality are compatible. Third, it questions the new research findings that show a positive relationship between income growth and greater equality, pointing out that they depend on including Latin America in the general data set.

Income distribution entered the postwar discussion of economic development fairly late. Until the 1960s much of the focus was on industrialization and the need for capital accumulation. It was an era, moreover, of large flows of external assistance, much of it to the European economy, amid the global division between East and West. Not until the mid-1950s did the World Bank turn its focus to the developing countries—and then only gradually.

That early period also saw the end of colonization and the beginning of new national units throughout Asia and Africa. For them economic expansion was a means to political identity. Rapid population growth, associated with steep declines in mortality in most developing countries, demanded that production accelerate to keep pace. Overall, aggregate expansion was much faster than before. And it was accelerating, with per capita growth jumping from 2.4 percent a year in the 1950s to 3.5 percent in 1965–70. Even in Sub-Saharan Africa, which was growing the slowest, per capita growth was 2.3 percent a year.

In that context emerged a new professional interest in income distribution. On the academic side a new series of studies called attention to continuing significant

Albert Fishlow is senior fellow at the Council on Foreign Relations.

Annual World Bank Conference on Development Economics 1995
©1996 The International Bank for Reconstruction and Development / THE WORLD BANK

inequality and the failure of widespread economic growth to remedy the problem (Adelman and Robinson 1989). On the practical side Robert McNamara's policy interest in the subject stimulated the World Bank to produce *Redistribution with Growth* (Chenery and others 1974), an important effort to define new policies and strategies that could increase equity while improving aggregate performance.

Hollis Chenery was the undisputed intellectual leader in this first Bank attempt to deal simultaneously with income distribution and growth, as the title of that 1974 book announced. As Chenery (1992, pp. 399–400) later put it, "This theme began to pervade a substantial part of the Bank's more project-oriented research and, after three or four years, no longer needed much selling in-house. Staff were soon accustomed to the idea that there could be no tradeoffs between growth and the fight against poverty."

The basis of that approach can be stated simply. First, there was acceptance of the Kuznets insight, reinforced by new empirical analysis, that income distribution shows a natural tendency toward greater concentration in a first period. But there was insistence that policy could make a difference. "In several countries, access to modern-sector employment has been improved through education and the rapid demand for labor, while in others land has been redistributed and public investment redirected to offset the initial disadvantages of the poor" (Chenery and others 1974, p. xv). Second, there was insistence on a need for "policy packages," integrated efforts to deal with the target groups, identified as those below a poverty line. Interestingly, these elements have changed little. And third, there was insistence on the compatibility of growth and simultaneous efforts to improve income distribution: "poverty-focused planning does not imply the abandonment of growth as an objective. It implies instead redistribution of the benefits of growth" (Chenery and others 1974, p. xviii).

In the event, distributional issues—soon extending to basic needs, a policy approach emanating from the International Labor Organization and further developed at the World Bank—had only a brief moment at center stage. The rise of oil prices in 1973 set in motion developing countries' excessive dependence on foreign debt, initially cheap but soon impossible to sustain, commanding attention in the 1980s and beyond. Adjustment quickly dominated, and the International Monetary Fund suddenly became a central player in providing assistance to developing countries—something it had not really done before. The balance of payments became the determining factor in policy. Countries were necessarily focused not only on getting their macroeconomies right but also on a whole range of related issues—wage and interest rate policies, government subsidies, and inevitably the role of the state in guiding the development process.

Growth—or its absence—became the burning issue, and since the 1980s the differences in regional performance have been wider than at any time in the postwar period. Africa and Latin America stagnated while Asia moved rapidly ahead. And in the midst of wider democratization, growing concern about the fate of the poor and their future becomes inevitable. With renewed global expansion today, the question of income inequality, and what can be done, again commands serious attention.

In this article I take up three central questions: What is the state of income inequality? What policy measures can support the movement of poor groups out of poverty? Where does recent research on the relevance of inequality to the growth process come out?

The Record

World Development Report 1994 reports in its statistical annex, as it has for many years, data on the measurement of income inequality. Many more countries are represented than in the past, but for twenty-eight of the forty-five low- and middle-income countries the data are for consumption expenditure rather than income (World Bank 1994, p. 244). The story is familiar. The shares of income received by the richest 10 percent of the population in developing countries vary from a high of more than 50 percent in Brazil to a low of about 25 percent in several countries. Including Eastern Europe, and showing the effects of socialist equalization, brings the low average closer to 20 percent. The range among industrial countries is much narrower, concentrated at less than 25 percent. Income inequality is obviously smaller at higher incomes per capita.

Despite serious efforts to collect data on income distribution—by the World Bank through its Living Standards Measurement Survey, by the Economic Commission for Latin America and the Caribbean, and by individual scholars—there are few multiple observations. A comparison of *World Development Report 1980* and *World Development Report 1994* yields only thirteen observations over time, eleven of which show increased income for the poorest 40 percent of the population. In a recent study Fields and Jakubson (1993) could come up with only twenty countries with multiple observations that were fully comparable—and of these, many had few entries. Yet the criteria—basically, comparability over time and the use of a national census or household survey—do not seem excessively rigorous.

For Latin America Altimir (1991) and Morley (1994) have done substantial work using data for the 1980s to assess the effect of that region's dramatic recession on income inequality. Their quantitative results and conclusions differ somewhat. Morley argues that the level of per capita income is key and that the recession was responsible for the poor distributional performance during that tragic decade. Put another way, integration with global markets raised interest rates and required reductions in wages—but continuing growth can make a positive contribution. Altimir emphasizes the regressive effects of stabilization policies that governments were forced to follow and argues the need for much more vigorous policies requiring investment under state leadership. But precisely because of the recession it is difficult to make longer-term comparisons.

The increased, but still largely static, information on income distribution now accumulated does, however, permit more careful analysis of the simple U-hypothesis initially advanced by Simon Kuznets (1955). That concept—that both low-income and high-income countries would have lower inequality because of the greater homogeneity of their labor forces—has been subject to careful, mathematical reexamination in recent years (Anand and Kanbur 1993).

Across developing countries there seems to be little regular variation in equality with income level alone. Thus for recent periods we cannot fit a parabola to the relationship between the income share of the poorest 40 percent and the level of income, as estimated by Summers and Heston (1991) or using more conventional national values. This is true both for a sample of countries similar to that used by Ahluwalia (1976) almost twenty years ago and for a broader one that incorporates more recent entries.

Anand and Kanbur (1993), in the most recent and complete treatment, use different measures of inequality and find three things. First, the different indices yield widely disparate turning points. Second, the statistical results indicated by a strict theoretical derivation are generally poor, especially when only developing countries are considered, and implied restrictions on the arithmetic value of coefficients are not satisfied. Third, the change in relationship between the mean incomes of agricultural and urban labor forces imposes new, and still more rigorous, limitations on the form of the function.

The problem exposed by this analysis, however, seems to have less to do with the inherent consistency of the initial Kuznets hypothesis than with the reality of substantial intervention in the economic system. Policy in individual countries, not explicitly present in the original formulation, does differ widely in the incidence of land redistribution and in the use of the rural labor force. It also varies in urban areas, where employment levels, wage rates, and capital intensity and profitability are much affected by the industrial strategies pursued. Moreover, for most of the developing countries chronicled the share of the population engaged in agriculture has already fallen significantly in recent years, suggesting that many should be on course toward greater income equality.

A slightly more complex statistical relationship, one introducing only two other—though highly relevant—variables to the analysis, allows a partial revival of the Kuznets hypothesis. The two new variables are participation in secondary education—a measure of the social commitment to universal access to education—and a dummy variable indicating whether a country is in Latin America.

These results signal the correct parabolic shape with respect to income both for all countries and for developing countries alone (table 1). (Bulgaria, Hungary, and Poland are excluded.) The results, especially those for developing countries alone, are far from statistical significance. But a clear relationship emerges between inequality and both participation in secondary education and location in Latin America. (More evidence of the second relation appears below in the section on new theoretical advances.)

Clearly, the transformation of economies from low levels of income can create inherent tendencies toward greater inequality. But the record of the past two decades suggests even more strongly that government policies can do much to avert those tendencies.

Milanovic (1994), using the Gini coefficient as his measure of inequality, recently obtained parallel and highly statistically significant results. He derived the Gini coefficient from a variety of sources for some eighty countries. His four key indepen-

Table 1. *Regression Estimates of Inequality*

Variable	All countries (N = 61)		Developing countries (N = 42)	
	Income share of poorest 40 percent	Theil index of inequality	Income share of poorest 40 percent	Theil index of inequality
Constant	36.4	283.7	30.6	303.4
	(2.6)	(8.1)	(1.0)	(3.3)
Income level	−5.64	13.1	−3.7	6.1
	(1.5)	(1.2)	(0.4)	(0.2)
(Income level)^2	0.33	−0.81	0.15	−0.16
	(1.3)	(1.1)	(0.2)	(0.1)
Secondary enrollment[a]	0.065	−0.21	0.09	−0.25
	(2.2)	(2.5)	(2.0)	(2.1)
Latin America	−4.65	14.6	−4.6	13.6
dummy variable	(3.4)	(3.9)	(2.8)	(2.9)
R^2	0.33	0.41	0.26	0.25

Note: Numbers in parentheses are t-statistics. Income level is the logarithm of income reported by the World Bank.
a. Average percentage of age group enrolled in secondary education during 1965–90.
Source: World Bank 1994; World Bank, *Social Indicators of Development* and *World Tables,* various years.

dent variables are the share of employment in the public sector, the share of cash and in-kind social transfers in public expenditures, 1988 real income as estimated by Summers and Heston, and a dummy variable for Asia. He finds the predicted parabolic variation with income, a negative relationship of state employment to inequality, a positive relationship of transfers and social expenditures, and a negative dummy for Asia—that is, less inequality.

Although the diverse origin and timing of the data for the large number of countries included and the inconsistent definition of the transfer variable are cause for some concern, the results—though statistically much better—roughly parallel my own. But I emphasize Latin America's poor distributional performance relative to the rest of the developing world, while Milanovic focuses on Asia's superior performance. The relatively unaltered and high concentration of income in Latin America is a concern. And it is not something deriving only from recent experience.

What to do then? Almost all economists agree that the essential components of policy to improve income distribution are still those advocated by Chenery and his associates some twenty years ago. Perhaps the two most important interventions relate to the distribution of physical assets and the rapid accumulation of human capital.

Of the possibilities for redistribution of wealth, land stands out as the most potent variable used in the past. Land reform, where undertaken, has had a powerful effect on income distribution. The Republic of Korea and Taiwan (China) stand out as the two most obvious cases in which an initial commitment to equalization played a major role, and their experience is being reexamined in an attempt to find ways to generalize it. But the experiences of China and Viet Nam, now showing signs of rapid and vigorous expansion, should not be forgotten. In those countries an imposed equality generated relatively little growth until combined with greater personal incentives and opportunities for improving productivity. Strict communist doctrine did not work, but its initial redistributive measures served as a powerful equalizing device that those countries could later draw on to their advantage.

Where there is a large rural population, productivity and equality are both served by land reform. There is little doubt that the high rates of inequality in Latin America trace back to the initially much higher rates of inequality of land distribution in the region in the nineteenth century and even earlier in some cases. And there can be little question, despite today's dwindling enthusiasm, that fairer allocation of this basic asset can stimulate broadly based development. For many reasons, however, there is seeming reluctance to act—land reform seems to await war or revolution. Yet where land is poorly used and its productivity can be much enhanced, redistribution, even with payment for current capital value, can be quite economical.

Long caught up in the politics of the cold war, land reform initiatives remain relevant, and perhaps more practicable, than they have been for a long time. What must be stressed, however, are the essential additional public inputs required for any distributive policy to be effective. Reallocation alone will not work. It needs to be viewed as a means toward the end of greater efficiency and output.

Human capital is the second area where public actions can make a big difference, an area to which developing countries have made significant commitments over the postwar period. In lower-income countries enrollment in primary school has increased from 54 percent in 1960 to 101 percent in 1991, in secondary school from 14 to 41 percent, and in tertiary education from 2 to 5 percent. In the other developing countries it has gone from 81 to 104 percent, from 17 to 55 percent, and from 4 to 18 percent.

There are two good reasons for countries to have substantially increased their expenditures in this area. First, the social return is quite high. The World Bank finds rates in excess of 25 percent for primary education, 15 to 18 percent for secondary, and 13 to 16 percent for tertiary. There is even a positive relationship with years of schooling: East Asia, with an average of six years, yields a higher increase in GDP for additional investment in education than do other regions (Psacharopoulos 1985, 1994). This reinforces the importance of achieving adequate minimal training—many students in rural areas, through grade repetition and lack of completion, wind up little better for their schooling. Note too that girls' education regularly has an indirect, negative effect on fertility—and positive effects on family health and nutrition.

What is seen for productivity is also seen for income distribution. For a large variety of countries—for which we have some type of decomposition of the sources of inequality—variation in education typically shows up as the principal explanatory variable, accounting for 10 percent to more than 20 percent of observed inequality. Those who are better schooled regularly receive higher incomes, adjusting for age, sector, and so on. Education typically is even more important at the bottom of the income distribution—one recent study finds that those with no schooling have a 56 percent probability of being among the poorest 20 percent, while those with university training have only a 4 percent chance (Behrman 1993). Undoubtedly, education is partly a proxy for other associated factors such as family characteristics, school quality, and labor market characteristics. But its repeated relevance, even discounting some of the gross effects, gives education a crucial policy role in greater distributional equality.

More active participation by government is necessary, particularly at local levels where attendance must be ensured and school quality maintained. Beyond this, curricular reform is in many instances badly required. It does little good to provide standard training that leads simply to the repetition of grades rather than to the acquisition of skills. Whatever the many deficiencies of the formerly communist countries, their record stands out in the speed of achieving universal education. The task remains to show that market-oriented economies can do as well. Also remaining is to ensure that such education in the former communist bloc serves as a productive resource.

Beyond education is a whole range of ancillary activities whose effects are similar in improving the quality of labor: nutrition, health, other social investments. Indeed, for very low-income countries the returns to such outlays may be greater than those from education, precisely because the quantity of education is too slight to have a direct impact. Countries that made early and substantial commitments to universal education have been rewarded by greater equality as growth proceeds. And the social returns to expanded investment in education have permitted simultaneous gains in real product.

Note that this is a generational phenomenon. Today's outlays will have an impact on output that is not immediate and observable, but rather is delayed. That makes it easier for such outlays to be postponed when fiscal stringency is necessary. One of the great tragedies of the 1980s in Africa and Latin America was not only their poor economic performance but also the simultaneous reductions in government expenditures. In many ways it was much easier to cut back in areas that had initially failed to be universal in scope. But this meant shortfalls in reaching the very groups initially excluded from adequate coverage. In most cases private outlays for education, health services, and so on continued, extending the initial divisions between those who were better off and those who had limited initial access—with the effects still to be felt in future decades, even as growth recovers. There has been not only a "lost decade" of growth but also a "lost generation" deprived of skills and the capacity to acquire them.

There is now greater realism in understanding that major efforts to improve distribution of income cannot rely on populist promises of higher wages and extensive direct economic controls and regulations—efforts that are temporary at best. The evidence of failure—in Chile in the 1970s and Peru and Nicaragua in the 1980s—is clear. The initial improvements in distribution through these paths come from arbitrary gains in income, gains that later evaporate as adjustment inevitably occurs. Even without such extremes, policies that rely heavily on subsidies, whether to agriculture or industry, frequently distort incentives and benefit well-placed groups. And the multiplicity of interventions ironically cancels out any real allocation effect that had been hoped for.

Indeed, the triumph of the market is now widely recognized, even where once resisted. (We no longer speak of planning the way we did two decades ago.) But the recognition that markets should play a wider role in the development process is still consistent with important areas of public responsibility. A danger is that the fear of excessive and inefficient government intervention excludes productive investment that can yield growth as well as improve income distribution. The commitment must be not merely to ensure current increases in product, but also to guarantee them through continuing public investment and taxation.

The scope for progressive taxation is necessarily limited when simultaneously advancing private savings and investment. The positive gains from redistribution cannot be assessed without giving attention to potential negative consequences. But equally, the possibilities for using the enhanced revenues productively cannot be ignored. The real challenge is creating an efficient public presence—and nowhere is it more important than in the realm of income distribution.

Poverty Alleviation

Much of the attention in the past fifteen years has turned away from dealing directly with income inequality to the task of reducing poverty. These are not the same objectives. In this effort too Hollis Chenery and the World Bank have led the way. *World Development Report 1980* (World Bank 1980) was centrally directed to the question of poverty, not of income inequality—with four implications. First, such a shift obviously meant more direct concern with those who were worst off, the poorest of the poor. Second, it meant directing attention to the populations of Asia, where incomes were much lower, changing the geographic focus. Third, it meant directing attention to the rural sector, where the poverty burden was larger. Fourth, it reduced the tension between the simultaneous objectives of improving the distribution of income and accelerating growth. Incomes at the bottom could easily increase with greater production—even though the distribution of income remained as unequal as it had been or became even more unequal. Trickle-down effects could still eliminate some poverty.

In many ways dealing effectively with the poor simply means ensuring attention to their problems—and if that is done well, it can simultaneously improve equity. But such a primary emphasis does lead to a different, if not independent, policy approach.

A leading part in the initial effort to focus attention on poverty was played by the "basic needs" approach.[1] This approach emphasized the importance of separating generalized increases in income from the more significant attainment of the requirements for a permanent reduction of poverty—improvements in health, regular access to nutritional food, more education, and better and affordable shelter.

Three arguments were advanced to support this view. First, many poor people are not themselves producers but are part of the dependent population. So, they have no direct earnings of the kind typically evaluated in distribution studies. Second, there is no guarantee that increased income will be spent on essential services. Better medical care may not be available—or safe drinking water or better housing. In such circumstances individuals are nominally better off but lack the basis for permanent improvement. Third, households vary in their ability to spend wisely and effectively. They may irrationally prefer "better" consumption goods that contribute less to welfare than other goods that might serve as inputs to higher productivity.

In the end "basic needs" vanished as a tracking device, perhaps as much because of the difficulties of aggregating them as for any other reason. But the attention that the concept directed—first to the poor, and then to the policies required for improving their lot—has persisted. The United Nations Development Programme's *Human Development Report 1993* is illustrative in distinguishing between income and its potential applications: "The purpose of development is to widen the range of people's choices. Income is one of those choices—but it is not the sum-total of human life" (p. 3). Or to put it differently, the negative correlation between income and poverty does not negate the relevance of public policies directed to improving the lot of the poor.

One consequence of this focus on the poor is the much greater attention to the importance of safety nets to ensure their welfare. As more traditional mechanisms for transfer—such as patron-client or kinship-based systems—have diminished with development, there is a clear role for public intervention. More countries have adopted such programs, some prompted by the absolute declines in income in the 1980s. But these attempts are still partial and inadequate, and in some instances they serve more to ensure survival of a bureaucracy than to direct resources where they are urgently needed.

But safety nets are not the only requirement. *World Development Report 1990*, once again addressing the problem of poverty, adds two more essentials: attention to labor-intensive growth, especially in agriculture (which may also boost exports), and an emphasis on primary education and health, whose relevance to the distribution of income we have already seen (World Bank 1990).

On the first of these—labor-intensive growth—there is little doubt. Poor people, even in rural areas, are food purchasers, and their welfare depends on an adequate local supply. Yet agriculture has frequently been discriminated against in the drive to build up industry, both through inadequate investment in rural areas and through trade protection that levies negative effective tariffs on the sector. The ultimate losers from such discrimination are typically poor people with less preparation and opportunity for other employment.

On the second—primary education and health—I have already commented at length. What may be added here is the importance of ensuring education in rural areas, where poverty is much more pronounced. Having flexible sessions to allow older children to assist with harvests and other economic needs is one possibility. Another general need is improved teaching capability, through better training and salaries for teachers. In too many countries free university education is provided, at great expense, while primary school personnel costs are kept to a minimum to control government outlays. That inevitably results in inadequate preparation at the elementary level, regardless of increases in enrollment statistics.

But a further dimension—recently emphasized by Pranab Bardhan (1994) and stated explicitly in *Human Development Report 1993*—merits discussion. On the one side is the market-oriented approach, with its safety net provisions only for those who fail to be absorbed in productive employment. And on the other is the basic needs emphasis on public intervention on a large scale to meet the unsatisfied needs of the poor for a range of essential services. Bardhan suggests a third alternative, relying on "local self-governing institutions and community involvement to improve the material conditions and autonomy of the poor" (p. 3).

The issue this raises is the capability of the poor to organize their demands effectively and continuously—to some degree the philosophy underlying the poverty program in Mexico and the Grameen Bank in Bangladesh. Equally, such emphasis calls on the state to play a different role—an activist one, but through effective decentralization. Such a restructuring involves important changes, not least in the concentration of public expenditure at the national level; in developing countries decisions and public outlays are most frequently centralized. Pushing local elites beyond their traditional roles as enforcers of a static order is obviously a central and critical requirement.

Community groups, assisted by the recent multiplication of nongovernmental organizations (NGOs), have been an important force in the expansion of local authority. They have been much favored by bilateral assistance programs. In particular, the capacity of NGOs to reach low-income groups, especially in rural areas, deserves emphasis—they now reach an estimated 250 million people. Although still far short of total coverage, the more than doubling in the past decade has been quite impressive. But in the end the issue comes back to central government's capacity to reinforce and sustain effective decentralization. The next decade will test that capability.

There are good reasons to emphasize aiding the poor explicitly as well as reducing inequality generally. Poverty reduction and income growth are not only compatible, but causally related. Improving the quality of the labor force contributes fundamentally to continuing gains in productivity. More adequate rural technologies have the same effect. Reduced pressure from migration to urban areas translates into smaller social outlays and, quite likely, into less total unemployment. The population in poverty is considerable, however—1 billion or more, as estimated by the World Bank. What is worse, even with appropriate policies the poor population in Sub-Saharan Africa continues to expand; simply to stabilize the number of the poor in that region would require realizing a rate of growth in income 2 percentage points higher than predicted over the next several years. This challenge, even in the midst of other pressing development problems, cannot be ignored.

New Theoretical Advances in the Growth-Equality Relationship

Some of the recent gains by economists in the analysis of growth have come from applying new models—the most prominent being the theory of endogenous growth. One part of this neo-Schumpeterian literature starts from external increasing returns that drive continuing expansion. A second emphasizes perfect competition, permitting unlimited accumulation of capital with positive productivity. A third variant goes on to introduce either improved or new goods, invoking fixed costs as the limiting factor. And yet another introduces freer trade as a mechanism for growth, either directly through technological progress or indirectly through the possibility for specialization in intermediate goods.

Some of these efforts have led to empirical estimation. Thus models in which education, for example, plays a key role in explaining sustained growth for a cross-section of countries have become common. Others have related trade policy to long-run growth in similar fashion (Barro 1991; Edwards 1993; Romer 1994). What has been special about this approach is its conversion of theoretical long-term equilibrium conditions to practical application.

Even newer in the recent literature is the explicit addition of political variables as important causal factors. The essence of such political economy is to recognize the important interaction between a willingness to accept less today in return for more tomorrow: democratic voters may be willing to forgo populism now in favor of increased investment and future growth. Thus endogenous growth is combined with endogenous policy in such efforts.

The key result so far—characteristic of recent articles by Persson and Tabellini (1994) and Alesina and Rodrik (1994)—is that inequality is negatively related to growth. Persson and Tabellini find that the effects of equality on growth are not only statistically significant but also quantitatively important. Thus an increase in equality of one standard deviation, changing the income share of the middle quintile of the income distribution by about 3 percent, could increase growth by half a percentage point. Moreover, and powerfully, this relationship seems to hold only for countries that follow democratic policies. For the 40 percent of the sample that do not, inequality is not statistically different from zero. In Alesina and Rodrik the Gini coefficient is a key variable for a larger number of countries, and it turns out to be statistically significant. A one-standard-deviation reduction in the Gini coefficient increases growth by more than 1 percentage point. But Alesina and Rodrik find no difference between democratic and nondemocratic countries.

These findings, and still newer ones in a similar vein, must be regarded as tentative. I maintain this caution despite George Clarke's (1995) recent careful demonstration of the robustness of this result relating inequality and growth. Even he concludes, however, that the relationship between inequality and growth, though statistically significant, is small. And in Birdsall, Ross, and Sabot (1995) a one-standard-deviation change in inequality has much less effect—only 0.32 percentage point. Note, moreover, that the income distribution data in all these studies relate to an early period, the 1950s through the early 1970s, and thus are clearly doubtful. Alesina and Rodrik experiment with a slightly later set of observations—with little difference in the result.

For a somewhat different sample of countries and a slightly different period, I find evidence of no statistical significance for inequality, especially when a dummy variable is introduced for the Latin American observations (table 2). These results run counter to both of these important contributions. I have used observations both

Table 2. *Determinants of the Rate of Growth of Product*

	1976–90		1960–80			
Variable	N = 63	N = 44	N = 46	N = 29	N = 43	N = 27
Constant	−3.16	−2.41	1.37	3.27	2.86	3.11
	(1.1)	(0.85)	(0.88)	(2.01)	(1.87)	(1.79)
Initial real income	−0.00018	−0.00052	−0.00028	−0.00063	−0.00034	−0.00065
	(1.32)	(1.63)	(2.40)	(1.94)	(3.15)	(1.91)
Initial primary enrollment	0.045	0.048	0.039	0.026	0.038	0.027
	(2.91)	(2.75)	(3.34)	(2.15)	(3.50)	(2.09)
Share of income of middle quintile	−0.013	0.052				
	(0.09)	(0.31)				
Gini coefficient			−1.50	−3.44	−3.91	−3.12
			(0.55)	(1.20)	(1.40)	(0.97)
Latin America dummy variable	−2.47	−1.47	−0.84	0.28	−0.76	0.35
	(2.94)	(1.35)	(1.32)	(0.37)	(1.26)	(0.45)
R^2	0.15	0.16	0.16	0.13	0.23	0.12
Constant			2.40	3.46	2.87	3.22
			(1.74)	(2.01)	(1.92)	(1.77)
Initial real income			−0.00030	−0.00059	−0.00032	−0.00062
			(2.89)	(1.71)	(3.07)	(1.73)
Initial primary enrollment			0.036	0.027	0.036	0.028
			(3.45)	(2.13)	(3.37)	(2.10)
Gini coefficient			−3.77	−4.74	−4.45	−4.26
			(1.55)	(1.56)	(1.63)	(1.26)
Latin America dummy variable			−1.58	−0.67	−1.49	−0.56
			(2.78)	(0.86)	(2.53)	(0.68)
R^2			0.29	0.21	0.29	0.18

Note: Numbers in parentheses are t–statistics.
Source: Author's calculations.

for the middle quintile of the distribution (as used by Persson and Tabellini) and for the Gini coefficient (chosen by Alesina and Rodrik). I used more recent data to test the first variable on the grounds that the early information employed is most subject to error. And for the second I used initial measures of inequality dating from the 1960s and early 1970s but extended the analysis to a longer time frame.

In each of the three exercises neither measure of inequality—the share of income in the middle quintile or the Gini coefficient—comes out as a statistically significant variable, whether all countries are used or only developing countries. Moreover, the conclusion is the same whether the Gini coefficients selected by Alesina and Rodrik for Germany, Kenya, and Peru, where there are large differences between possible alternatives, are used or excluded.

One reason for this statistical difference is the inclusion of a separate variable isolating the Latin American countries, as in table 1. In the regressions similar to those of Alesina and Rodrik the Gini coefficient shows up as statistically significant if these countries are not isolated. Yet there seems good reason to separate this group of countries, almost all of which have substantially higher inequality than others with similar incomes outside the region. They are distinctive in the absence of any regular tendency for income distribution to improve with greater prosperity; the evidence offered by Morley (1994), for example, is overwhelmingly of an association between declining income and worsening inequality. Moreover, virtually all these countries have low past savings rates, placing an additional burden on policies designed to foster rapid growth as well as deal with the distribution problem. Clearly, understanding this deviation is crucial for understanding the central process.

In replications of the Persson and Tabellini use of the middle quintile, but for a later period, the results are not statistically significant—regardless of whether the Latin American countries are isolated. Merely substituting later, and presumably more accurate, estimates for inequality is enough to yield results that are not statistically significant.

The new models have additional conceptual issues. The mechanisms through which redistributive policies operated are not specified. The concentration of industrial countries in the sample at one end of the inequality spectrum may make the findings for developing countries more dubious. A further (nontrivial) factor can also be cited. The implicit assumption of equilibrium can hardly be said to hold during an interval in which the debt crisis had already begun and growth was significantly affected. And finally, the model used for the statistical test is still not dynamic and is really only an imperfect model of reality.

Nonetheless, the Persson and Tabellini results—but not those of Alesina and Rodrik or Clarke—support the notion that combining greater equality with democracy may yield higher rates of economic growth. They do so in this case because high income inequality motivates populist policies inimical to the higher rates of investment required to assure adequate growth. In the end that fundamental conclusion conforms to good policy sense rather than depending on scientific demonstration. I cite *World Development Report 1991:* "efforts to improve equity can sit comfortably within reform programs aimed at promoting growth. It is clear, however, that market-distorting and overzealous redistribution can quickly pose overwhelming financial problems. . . . Also, crude transfers through market-distorting interventions almost always end up worsening the distribution of income rather than improving it" (World Bank 1991, p. 139). The difficulty comes in implementation.

Final Remarks

There have been advances in the past two decades in dealing with the continuing problem of economic inequality. There is now much more information available. There is also a recognition that market forces must be capitalized on to ensure a leaner and more effective state presence. Gone is the faith in more complex planning models to regulate and control economic activity. Gone is the commitment to overexpansive public expenditures. But gone too is the view that market forces by themselves could produce a social optimum benefiting all.

Unequal income distribution and its associated poverty problems remain central issues for the future. Other and more immediate adjustment concerns have frequently held sway, with a focus on revamping macroeconomies. Widely recognized today is the need both for restored and continuing economic growth and for renewed attention to the fate of the poor, but the second has not received the priority of the first. Even in democracies, the poor vote less frequently, and even then not always in their material interest.

One task in the future is to ensure that the new consensus on a market-friendly approach to development gives rise to a consensus on state activity, where it is justified. And nowhere is it more justified than in dealing with the problems of poverty and income distribution. Social returns can be enhanced by giving much more attention to education and to equitable rural growth, including through land reform. Safety nets must also become generally accessible. But to make them so will require resources, and inevitably the burden will fall with greater weight on the domestic economy because external public funds simply are not available. That means increasing the capacity for public saving in many countries, especially at the local level.

One of the lessons repeatedly relearned is that the miracle of equitable development requires adequate resources. At a time of increasing convergence in approaches to the poverty problem, and to development generally, it would be tragic to forget this need. It exists just as much for human capital as for physical—as much for social services as for private needs. Investing adequate resources to reduce poverty is an investment for the future, and if it is not pursued vigorously, the democratic tendencies emerging in many developing countries will be tenuous and temporary.

Note

1. See the useful initial summary in *World Development Report 1980* (World Bank 1980), in which various approaches, including basic needs, are discussed. For more recent treatment, see World Bank (1990) and Lipton and Ravallion (1995).

References

Adelman, Irma, and Sherman Robinson. 1989. "Income Distribution and Development." In Hollis Chenery and T.N. Srinivasan, eds., *Handbook of Development Economics,* vol 2. Amsterdam: North Holland.

Ahluwalia, Montek. 1976. "Inequality, Poverty and Development." *Journal of Development Economics* 6: 307–42.

Alesina, Alberto, and Dani Rodrik. 1994. "Distributive Politics and Economic Growth." *Quarterly Journal of Economics* 108: 465–90.

Altimir, Oscar. 1991. "Estabilización y Equidad en America Latina en Los Ochenta." CEPAL LC/R 1132. Economic Commission for Latin America and the Caribbean, Santiago, Chile.

Anand, S., and S.M.R. Kanbur. 1993. "The Kuznets Process and the Inequality-Development Relationship." *Journal of Development Economics* 40: 25–52.

Bardhan, Pranab. 1994. "Poverty Alleviation." Overseas Development Council Occasional Paper 1. Washington, D.C.

Barro, Robert. 1991. "Economic Growth in a Cross-Section of Countries." *Quarterly Journal of Economics* 105: 407–43.

Behrman, Jere. 1993. "Investing in Human Resources." In Inter-American Development Bank, *Economic and Social Progress in Latin America*. Washington, D.C.

Birdsall, Nancy, David Ross, and Richard Sabot. 1995. "Inequality and Growth Reconsidered: Lessons from East Asia." *World Bank Economic Review* 9(3): 477–508.

Chenery, Hollis. 1992. "From Engineering to Economics." *Banca Nazionale del Lavoro Quarterly Review* 183 (December): 369–405.

Chenery, Hollis, Montek S. Ahluwalia, Clive Bell, John H. Duloy, and Richard Jolly. 1974. *Redistribution with Growth*. New York: Oxford University Press.

Clarke, George. 1995. "More Evidence on Income Distribution and Growth." *Journal of Development Economics* 47(2): 403–27.

Edwards, Sebastian. 1993. "Openness, Trade Liberalization, and Growth in Developing Countries." *Journal of Economic Literature* 31: 1358–93.

Fields, Gary, and George Jakubson. 1993. "New Evidence on the Kuznets Curve." Cornell University, Department of Economics, Ithaca, N.Y.

Kuznets, Simon. 1955. "Economic Growth and Income Inequality." *American Economic Review* 65: 1–28.

Lipton, Michael, and Martin Ravallion, eds. 1995. *Handbook of Development Economics,* vol. 3. Amsterdam: North Holland.

Milanovic, Branko. 1994. "Determinants of Cross-Country Income Inequality: An 'Augmented' Kuznets Hypothesis." Policy Research Working Paper 1246. World Bank, Policy Research Department, Transition Economics Division, Washington, D.C.

Morley, Samuel. 1994. "Poverty and Inequality in Latin America: Past Evidence, Future Prospects." Overseas Development Council Policy Essay 13. Washington, D.C.

Paukert, F. 1973. "Income Distribution at Different Levels of Development: A Survey of the Evidence." *International Labour Review* 108: 97–125.

Persson, Torsten, and Guido Tabellini. 1994. "Is Inequality Harmful for Growth?" *American Economic Review* 84: 600–21.

Psacharopoulos, George. 1985. "Returns to Education: A Further International Update and Implications." *Journal of Human Resources* 20: 583–97.

———. 1994. "Returns to Investment in Education: A Global Update." *World Development* 22: 1325–43.

Romer, Paul. 1994. "New Goods, Old Theory, and the Welfare Costs of Trade Restrictions." *Journal of Development Economics* 43: 5–38.

Summers, Robert, and Alan Heston. 1991. "The Penn World Table (Mark 5): An Expanded Set of International Comparisons, 1950–1988." *Quarterly Journal of Economics* 106: 327–68.

UNDP (United Nations Development Programme). 1993. *Human Development Report 1993*. New York: Oxford University Press.

World Bank. 1980. *World Development Report 1980*. New York: Oxford University Press.

———. 1990. *World Development Report 1990: Poverty*. New York: Oxford University Press.

———. 1991. *World Development Report 1991: The Challenge of Development*. New York: Oxford University Press.

———. 1993. *The East Asian Miracle: Economic Growth and Public Policy*. New York: Oxford University Press.

———. 1994. *World Development Report 1994: Infrastructure for Development*. New York: Oxford University Press.

———. Various years. *Social Indicators of Development*. Baltimore, Md.: Johns Hopkins University Press.

———. Various years. *World Tables*. Baltimore, Md.: Johns Hopkins University Press.

Comment on "Inequality, Poverty, and Growth: Where Do We Stand?" by Albert Fishlow

Montek S. Ahluwalia

Albert Fishlow's article presents a succinct summary of what we have learned about inequality and poverty since *Redistribution with Growth* (Chenery and others 1974) was written more than twenty years ago. As one of the coauthors and as one who left research shortly after the book's publication to join the government of India, my comparative advantage obviously lies in presenting some combination of nostalgia about the making of *Redistribution with Growth* and a practitioner's view of its message as it appears today.

To begin with the nostalgia, *Redistribution with Growth* was written in a more innocent world in which growth was taken for granted and the doubts were mainly about whether benefits would be equitably distributed. Several International Labor Organization missions had focused on the problem of worsening unemployment even in situations of reasonable growth. In a celebrated article Fishlow (1972) showed that the distribution of income in Brazil had worsened so sharply in the 1960s that the poor may have become worse off despite impressive growth. In a similar piece on India Bardhan (1973) estimated that the percentage of the rural population below the poverty line increased significantly between 1960 and 1968. At the Institute of Development Studies in Sussex, Michael Lipton, Dudley Seers, and Richard Jolly, all working on different aspects of the development experience, showed that the poor—especially the rural poor—did not benefit sufficiently from growth. Interestingly, these problems received little attention in World Bank research at the time, which focused mainly on trade policy issues, macroeconometric models of the two-gap variety, programming models for agriculture and industry, and, of course, project evaluation methodology.

It was against this background that Robert McNamara, in his 1973 Nairobi speech, placed poverty issues at the top of the World Bank's agenda. That was also the year in which Hollis Chenery began reorienting Bank research to address distributional questions. The process began at a conference organized by Hollis at Bellagio, where a remarkably catholic mix of mainstream and nonorthodox econo-

Montek S. Ahluwalia is secretary of finance in the government of India.

Annual World Bank Conference on Development Economics 1995

mists discussed the relationship among income distribution, poverty, and development in the reflective (if somewhat incongruously patrician) atmosphere of the Rockefeller villa on the shores of Lake Como. Not surprisingly, the papers were too varied to make a good conference volume, so Hollis decided to use the conference as the starting point for a new book. If *Redistribution with Growth* was criticized at the time as a cobbling together of conventional and unconventional wisdom, that is precisely how it began!

Revisiting *Redistribution with Growth,* I am conscious that Hollis himself would have wanted us to be self-critical. Much of *Redistribution with Growth* undoubtedly remains valid, but with the benefit of hindsight one can identify several areas where elaboration and modification of the message are needed.

Defining Distributional Objectives

One of the issues that *Redistribution with Growth* addressed is the need to define the distributional objective more clearly, in particular, to distinguish between inequality and absolute poverty. *Redistribution with Growth* gave primacy to the problem of absolute poverty, and as Fishlow points out, the focus of international discussion in the past fifteen years has shifted entirely to poverty alleviation. Focusing on reducing absolute poverty as a primary objective is undoubtedly correct, but a realistic definition of distributional objectives has to go beyond poverty alleviation to encompass distributional issues affecting nonpoor groups.

Even in countries with severe problems of absolute poverty, nonpoor groups may constitute 65 percent or more of the population. No policymaker can be completely indifferent to what happens to the incomes of such a large part of the population. An increase in inequality may not pose serious problems if the incomes of all groups are growing, even though at different rates. But when inequality increases because the incomes of some groups stagnate or, even worse, decline while the incomes of other groups increase, it is bound to create social tensions even if those hurt belong to the nonpoor groups. Even in the United States concern has been expressed that the benefits of growth in recent years have accrued largely to upper-income groups.

The conclusion is inescapable. Absolute poverty must be the primary focus of distributional concern, but policymakers in democratic societies cannot afford to ignore the distribution of the benefits of growth. Because the number of democracies in the developing world has increased considerably since *Redistribution with Growth* was written, this factor has become all the more important. In fact, many of the distributional issues that can be politically sensitive today arise from the impact of policy on groups above the poverty line. The exclusive focus of the international debate on absolute poverty has its rationale in the perception that the case for international aid in donor countries suffering from aid fatigue can be persuasive only if it is linked directly to the objective of alleviating absolute poverty. Policymakers in developing countries have to address constituencies with much broader distributional concerns.

The *Redistribution with Growth* Strategy

The strategy recommended by *Redistribution with Growth* can also be reexamined in the light of experience. The basic recommendations, later elaborated in World Bank policy, can be summarized as follows:

- The notion of a tradeoff between growth and equality is misleading. Distributional objectives, sensibly defined in terms of improvements in the incomes of the poor and other target groups, should be pursued within the framework of a growing economy.

- Pursuit of growth does not mean pursuit of growth of any kind. Some growth processes are more conducive than others to increases in the incomes of all groups, and the aim of policy should be to promote growth of this kind. Achieving such growth depends on initial conditions—such as concentration of land ownership and distribution of human capital through education—and on policy environments being supportive of employment-generating sectors, especially agriculture and exports. This element of the *Redistribution with Growth* strategy reflected a recognition of the success of the Republic of Korea and Taiwan (China) in stimulating equitable employment-generating growth.

- Pursuit of employment-generating growth must be supplemented by programs aimed at increasing the earning capacity of certain target groups, such as small farmers, landless labor, and the self-employed in the informal sector. This element of the *Redistribution with Growth* strategy was reflected in the Bank's operational policy through its support for poverty alleviation projects.

With the benefit of hindsight it can be said that although the second and third recommendations were meant to be complementary, there was less recognition in *Redistribution with Growth* than there should have been that the second was quantitatively the more important component of the strategy. Greater attention was initially given to targeted programs, in part because of the appeal of direct action to help defined target groups and in part because this element could be more easily linked operationally with the Bank's lending strategy.

It is easy to see why achieving faster growth that generates more employment is quantitatively more important. Shifting to such growth is likely to have a much greater impact on poverty than could any targeted program. The growth component of the strategy might have been inadequately emphasized at the time because the two success stories identified in *Redistribution with Growth* as exemplifying this approach—the Republic of Korea and Taiwan (China), on which Irma Adelman and Gustav Ranis contributed persuasive appendixes—still seemed to be exceptions. Their experience had not yet been replicated in other countries in East Asia. It was only in the late 1980s that the East Asian miracle, characterized by equitable employment-generating growth, began to be generally viewed as a paradigm to be imitated.

There is a second reason why the growth component of the strategy is important: targeted antipoverty programs can be implemented on a significant scale only where the economy has shifted to an efficient, high-growth path that provides the expanded resource base needed to finance these programs. In the absence of an expanding resource base, it is difficult to sustain targeted programs without either risking inflation, which would hurt the poor, or diverting scarce resources from other productive uses, which would lead to the tradeoff with growth that *Redistribution with Growth* categorically rejected.

In retrospect, we can see that *Redistribution with Growth* was too sanguine about the resource constraints developing countries faced. *Redistribution with Growth* was written before the problems that many developing countries have in mobilizing domestic resources, particularly the debilitating drain of a large public sector, had reached the huge proportions they later did. Most observers were also more optimistic then about the external financing situation for developing countries. The heavy burden of debt servicing that was to cripple many countries in Africa and Latin America in the 1980s, at the same time that official flows shrank, had not yet surfaced. Today, with both domestic and external resources under pressure, the importance of efficiency-enhancing elements in any growth strategy looms much larger, as does the need for growth to provide an expanding resource base for financing targeted programs.

Redistribution with Growth was perhaps also overly optimistic about the effectiveness of targeted programs in achieving their objectives. In the twenty years since, vast experience has been accumulated with targeted programs in several developing countries, such as programs aimed at small farmers, employment generation through construction of productive assets in rural areas, provision of credit for microenterprises, and programs providing support for self-help groups. The need for such targeted programs as a complement to a general strategy of employment-generating growth cannot be doubted, especially where significant groups may not benefit directly from accelerated growth for some time.

Many of these programs have been successful and need to be replicated and strengthened. But there are also problems. A common one is top-down designing of programs that does not adequately reflect actual conditions and leads to ineffectiveness. Many income-generating activities have turned out to be unsustainable. Problems of leakages to nontarget groups have been endemic. Implementation capacity on the ground is often weak, especially where beneficiaries are not sufficiently organized or empowered. The solution to these problems clearly lies in much greater attention to project design, greater decentralization of project control, and greater participation by beneficiaries in the design of programs. There is also a growing consensus that active involvement of nongovernmental organizations can improve implementation. Little of this was known at the time *Redistribution with Growth* was written.

Distributional Consequences of Stabilization and Structural Reforms

In recent years the experience of many developing countries with macroeconomic stabilization and structural reforms has raised new concerns about the short-term effect of these policies on income distribution and poverty. These issues were not anticipated in *Redistribution with Growth,* which was concerned mainly with the longer-term effect of different types of development strategies on poverty and income distribution. The debates on the shape of the Kuznets curve, the contrast between the disequalizing growth in Latin America and the more equitable growth in Taiwan (China) and Korea, and the issue of designing strategies to ensure more rapid growth in the incomes of the poor—all relate to long-term processes.

A severe macroeconomic adjustment, which may be required in certain situations, can produce larger changes in income distribution and poverty in a relatively short span of time than were envisaged in the slower-acting, longer-term processes that were the focus of *Redistribution with Growth*. Macroeconomic adjustment typically requires a reduction in aggregate demand, and often this is achieved through large reductions in real wages and thus in the consumption of wage-earning groups in both the formal and the informal sectors. This can hurt the poor but also many non-poor groups.

Structural reforms also have distributional consequences, since they typically involve large shifts in relative prices in favor of some sectors and against others. Trade policy reform may depress wages and employment in highly protected industries that become less competitive while boosting wages and employment in export-oriented industries that become more competitive. Public sector reform may reduce employment in overstaffed public sector units, freeing scarce resources for deployment in other sectors that may well generate more employment or provide services needed by the poor. Conventional measures of income distribution may fail to capture these distributional changes because groups that move down from one decile to another may be "replaced" by other groups moving upward, leaving income shares of deciles (the basis of most distributional measures) unaffected. Similarly, the impoverishment of some groups, moving them below the poverty line, may be offset by the "graduation" of other groups to above the poverty line, leaving the percentage of the population in poverty unaffected. In these situations the measured stability in the traditional indices of distribution and poverty is certainly meaningful in its own context, but if it reflects a process in which large groups experience worsening income it is unlikely to be politically acceptable, even if it is offset by other previously poorer groups experiencing an improvement in income.

Recognition of the distributional consequences of stabilization and reform programs has led to widespread acceptance of the need to incorporate distributional objectives in the design of these programs. Once again priority must go to protecting the poor through appropriate safety nets, but it is unrealistic to suppose that policymakers can stop at that in practice. They cannot ignore significant adverse impacts on the incomes of other groups simply because those groups are above the poverty line.

In practice, these considerations are bound to affect both the pace and the sequencing of policy reforms. Since few countries are likely to have the fiscal capacity to compensate all nonpoor groups that suffer an adverse impact, there will be pressure to moderate the pace of reforms. Trade policy reforms that could hurt employment in some sectors or public sector reforms that may lead to a confrontation with organized labor therefore must be paced to ensure that adverse distributional impacts are kept within tolerable limits. Distributional considerations may also affect sequencing by leading to the delay of reforms expected to have an adverse impact on especially vocal groups and the acceleration of reforms likely to have favorable distributional consequences, especially for groups viewed as particularly important. The optimal package will obviously differ according to country situations, reflecting not only economic circumstances but also political realities.

References

Bardhan, Pranab K. 1973. "On the Incidence of Poverty in Rural India in the Sixties." *Economic and Political Weekly* 245 (February, special issue): 254.

Chenery, Hollis, Montek S. Ahluwalia, Clive Bell, John H. Duloy, and Richard Jolly. 1974. *Redistribution with Growth*. New York: Oxford University Press.

Fishlow, Albert. 1972. "Brazilian Size Distribution of Income." *Papers and Proceedings of the American Economic Association* 62 (May): 391–402.

Comment on "Inequality, Poverty, and Growth: Where Do We Stand?" by Albert Fishlow

François Bourguignon

Albert Fishlow provides a lucid account of the large body of development economics literature that has been exploring the relationship between income distribution and development over the past forty years—since Kuznets's celebrated 1955 paper—but more prominently over the past twenty years—since *Redistribution with Growth* by Hollis Chenery and his associates (1974). I generally agree with Fishlow's views on the subject and with his main conclusions. In particular, I strongly support his idea that—even though it is now commonly held that growth must rely primarily on market mechanisms—some substantial state intervention is necessary for reducing poverty and improving income distribution, both of which may prove to be an efficient growth stimulant in the long run.

I nevertheless would like to go over one important general point that I think is not made in Fishlow's article and that deserves emphasis. I will then consider more technical points related to the evidence he has presented.

Schematically, the postwar history of development can be divided into three periods: intensive growth until the mid- or late 1970s, the debt crisis and adjustment during most of the 1980s, and the recent reactivation of growth. At some time in each period distribution issues came to the fore—though from different, sometimes apparently opposite, perspectives. For lack of time I focus here only on the first and the third periods, although I am convinced that the adjustment episode in the 1980s did much to change our view on the importance of equity for growth.

In the first period the view was that absolute poverty and possibly income inequality would decrease as a result of economic growth—maybe after some turning point had been passed, as in the Kuznets curve tradition. *Redistribution with Growth* did not really challenge the view that income distribution could in some sense be determined by the level of development, but it focused on the need for—and the way to accelerate—the trickle-down process.

The point of view now, more than twenty years later, seems radically different. Growth seems to be back after a long period of crises, and distribution is again seen

François Bourguignon is professor of economics at Ecoles des Hautes Etudes en Sciences Sociales in Paris.
Annual World Bank Conference on Development Economics 1995

as an important dimension of development. But the causality now seems to run in the opposite direction. The reason redistribution matters is not so much that it might reduce poverty at a given level of development. It matters because it might modify, possibly positively, the future rate of growth. The present debate on the relationship between inequality and growth is based on the idea that, through different channels, equality may serve as an engine for growth. But even though *Redistribution with Growth* hinted in that direction, the dominant view at the time was that there was some tradeoff between growth and inequality, at least at the early stages of development.

The view that inequality is mostly determined by the current level of development and the view that it determines the rate of growth are perhaps not contradictory but complementary. They can be seen as partial views of a general equilibrium mechanism in which the characteristics of an economic system determine the current distribution of income along with other current economic indicators, which in turn determine the growth rate and the new characteristics of the economy. In that sense income distribution is both determined by and a determinant of development and growth, except perhaps in the rare case in which the economy has reached some asymptotic equilibrium.[1] The change in view observed in the past twenty years may thus be considered a shift of emphasis on these two complementary aspects of the growth-distribution relationship. Understanding and fully accounting for that complementarity might be the next items on the agenda.

I now turn to some of the empirical issues discussed in the article. I will certainly not enter into a defense of the Kuznets curve here. If there is any parabolic relationship between income inequality and GDP per capita across countries, I agree that it is probably very weak and unstable over time—or that it refers to an extremely long-run view of development and growth that might not be very useful. This is what observation of the growing number of time series on income inequality in single countries suggests. Rarely do these longitudinal data conform to the Kuznets curve hypothesis. On the contrary, they seem to suggest that there is much freedom in the way distribution in a given country may change over time.

That does not mean that there are no fundamental factors that affect income inequality and explain permanent differences across countries. Education is known to do so—as is land distribution. I have shown in previous work with Morrisson (Bourguignon and Morrisson 1990) that in a typical cross-sectional regression for a sample of developing countries, the distribution of land explains 17 percent of the variance in inequality, a figure comparable to that for education and stable over time. Yet the effect of that variable, although significant, is very limited. According to our calculations, increasing the share of land cultivated by small and medium-size farmers by 10 percent—which certainly appears to be a major change—would increase the share of income going to the poorest 60 percent of households by less than 1 percent.

In all cross-sectional exercises there is also a fundamental problem of exogeneity of the explanatory variables. For any significant relationship between X and Y, there will always be a possibility that the relationship is artificially caused by a more fundamental link between both X and Y and a third variable Z. Detecting the risk of such endogeneity bias is sometimes easy. For example, the share of agriculture in GDP is likely to depend, on the demand side, on the unobserved fundamental determinants of income distribution; educational variables may also depend on those determinants. Much more difficult—because of a lack of adequate instruments—is to correct for that bias. For all these reasons we should be extremely careful—even more careful than Fishlow recommends—in using and interpreting the evidence based on cross-sectional regressions.

Recent attempts to relate growth rates—rather than levels—of GDP per capita to income inequality, following the empirical growth literature reinitiated by Barro (1991), also are not immune to these problems. Yet several studies seem to confirm the significance of the statistical link between growth and equality, opening interesting perspectives (Alesina and Rodrik 1994; Birdsall, Ross, and Sabot 1995; Bourguignon 1995; Clarke 1995; and Persson and Tabellini 1994). The recent theoretical literature on the subject points to different justifications of that relationship and its direction (see, for example, Aghion and Bolton 1994; Banerjee and Newman 1993; Bertola 1993). But it is too soon for structural modeling and testing, and data for such exercises are not available.

To illustrate the ambiguity of the apparently significant and positive link between income distribution and growth rates, I refer to recent work in which I ran regressions on growth rates with distribution variables among the regressors (Bourguignon 1995). Unlike Fishlow's table 2 and previous work in this area, I used a structural rather than a reduced form model. The model's structure was inspired by that used by Mankiw, Romer, and Weil (1992) in their well-known empirical work on growth. In the model growth rates depend on initial GDP per capita, the population growth rate, income distribution, and rates of investment in physical and human capital. Theoretical arguments suggest that income distribution affects growth essentially through the accumulation of factors—that is, the rate of investment in physical and human capital—but that the direct effect should be limited.

That is not the case. Even when most of the regressions are properly instrumented, income distribution still has a major effect on growth that does not go through school enrollment and investment rates and that is similar in size to the effect found in other studies—half a percentage point of additional growth for one standard deviation in inequality! Do we really have something new here, or are we facing a large estimation bias? Through which channels could inequality affect growth if not through investment in physical or human capital? This finding, as well as Fishlow's results contradicting those obtained by others, points to the need for much more work in this area.

Fishlow is thus right in recommending caution in the face of this presumed evidence of a positive relationship between income equality and economic growth. Maybe that relationship will suffer the fate of the Kuznets curve—being shown to be weak with respect to estimation periods, data, and accompanying variables. But we may also hope that it will prove to be robust and confirm the intuition developed over the past fifteen to twenty years that reducing poverty and fostering growth are complementary rather than opposing objectives.

Note

1. Models combining endogenous growth and income distribution can be expected to lead to asymptotic equilibriums in which the growth rate and asymptotic distribution of income and wealth appear as functions of the fundamental production and behavioral parameters of the economy. This seems to be the case in models like those of Aghion and Bolton (1994) and, to a lesser extent, Perotti (1993), whereas there seems to be a true causality relationship from distribution to asymptotic growth in models like those of Bertola (1993) or Persson and Tabellini (1994).

References

Alesina, Alberto, and Dani Rodrik. 1994. "Distributive Policies and Economic Growth." *Quarterly Journal of Economics* 104: 465–90.

Aghion, Philippe, and Patrick Bolton. 1994. "The Trickledown Effect and the Relationship between Inequality and Growth." Nuffield College, Oxford, United Kingdom.

Banerjee, Abhijit, and Andrew Newman. 1993. "Occupational Choice and the Process of Development." *Journal of Political Economy* 101: 274–99.

Barro, Robert. 1991. "Economic Growth in a Cross-Section of Countries." *Quarterly Journal of Economics* 106(2): 407–43.

Bertola, Giuseppe. 1993. "Factor Shares and Savings in Endogenous Growth." *American Economic Review* 83(5): 1184–98.

Birdsall, Nancy, David Ross, and Richard Sabot. 1995. "Inequality and Growth Reconsidered: Lessons from East Asia." *World Bank Economic Review* 9(3): 477–508.

Bourguignon, François. 1995. "Growth, Distribution, and Human Resources: A Cross-Country Analysis." In Gustav Ranis, eds., *En Route to Modern Growth*. Washington, D.C.: Inter-American Development Bank, and Baltimore, Md.: Johns Hopkins University Press.

Bourguignon, François, and Christian Morrisson. 1990. "Income Distribution, Development and Foreign Trade: A Cross-Sectional Analysis." *European Economic Review* 34(6): 1113–32.

Chenery, Hollis, Montek S. Ahluwalia, Clive Bell, John H. Duloy, and Richard Jolly. 1974. *Redistribution with Growth*. New York: Oxford University Press.

Clarke, George. 1995. "More Evidence on Income Distribution and Growth." *Journal of Development Economics* 47(2): 403–27.

Kuznets, Simon. 1955. "Economic Growth and Income Inequality." *American Economic Review* 65: 1–28.

Mankiw, N. Gregory, David H. Romer, and David S. Weil. 1992. "A Contribution to the Empirics of Economic Growth." *Quarterly Journal of Economics* 107(2): 407–37.

Perotti, Roberto. 1993. "Political Equilibrium, Income Distribution, and Growth." *Review of Economic Studies* 60(5): 755–77.

Persson, T., and Guido Tabellini. 1994. "Is Inequality Harmful to Growth?" *American Economic Review* 84(3): 600–21.

Comment on "Inequality, Poverty, and Growth: Where Do We Stand?" by Albert Fishlow

Gustav Ranis

A t the outset it is perhaps useful to recall that the concern with equity, whether relative or absolute, is not really a postwar phenomenon but has been a central concern of economists since the beginning of the discipline. Indeed, it would probably be more legitimate to view our early postwar fascination with growth as an aberration. From Smith and Ricardo onward, growth was indeed viewed as a *necessary* instrument for enhancing welfare, but we now know better than our predecessors why it is not *sufficient*. The quality of growth also matters. And that is the issue on which we have focused our attention in recent decades.

Hollis Chenery was a leader in taking up the challenge of Kuznets's 1955 call to arms, and *Redistribution with Growth* (Chenery and others 1974) was the initial salvo. "Redistribution," because it seemed to reinforce the "growth first, distribution later" approach of the early postwar years, was perhaps a misleading label. But Chenery's intellectual leadership, as well as the financial support he brought to bear as chief economist of the World Bank, led the profession to focus increasingly on "distribution with growth."

That is what Albert Fishlow's article does. However, after reviewing the literature, he apparently still seems to accept the basic "inherent tendency" for the infamous inverse U-shaped pattern to hold. As I read the evidence, it suggests that it is time to give a decent burial to that famous "law," which was actually advanced not by Kuznets, who was much too cautious, but by Kuznetsians, who were not. Given the successive writings of Ahluwalia (1976), Anand and Kanbur (1984), Fields and Jakubson (1993), and others, it now seems clear that we need to turn our attention away from the necessity of the inverse U-shaped phenomenon and toward the factors that either enhance or reduce the underlying complementarity between growth and distribution.

Fishlow cites two types of critical interventions, one affecting the initial distribution of physical assets, the other the accumulation and distribution of human capital. Few observers would disagree with the importance of either of these for both growth and equity. But Fishlow gives excessive emphasis to land reform. Given the

Gustav Ranis is Frank Altschul Professor of International Economics at the Economic Growth Center at Yale University.

Annual World Bank Conference on Development Economics 1995

political obstacles he correctly cites, such an emphasis in practice would, if warranted, virtually eliminate the chances for growth with equity in many parts of the developing world, especially Latin America. Recall that in Taiwan (China), for example, where the admittedly very helpful land reforms occurred quite early on (in 1949–51), improvements in both growth and equity became most marked a decade later, during the 1960s. In the early 1960s Taiwan's Gini coefficient was still in the 0.40 range, and it declined to 0.29 only during the high-growth 1960s.

I suggest therefore that Fishlow should have paid more attention to the impact of public policies on the quality of the growth path chosen over time, along with the heavy emphasis he gives to the public goods allocation side of the ledger. The Gini decomposition analysis that my colleagues and I applied to Taiwan (China), focusing on the causes of the high complementarity between equity and growth, points to the important contribution of a more labor-intensive agricultural output mix (from rice and sugar to mushrooms and asparagus), along with the spectacular expansion of labor-intensive rural nonagricultural activities (Fei, Ranis, and Kuo 1979). The analysis overturned two important suggestions by Kuznets. It showed that long before real wages begin to rise the equality of income distribution could improve for rural families, while holding steady for urban families, as a consequence of increasingly labor-intensive technologies, even as industrial output mixes were gradually changing. Moreover, it showed that a reallocation from agricultural to nonagricultural activities does not have to entail a shift from a more equal distribution to a less equal distribution if output mixes and technologies in the nonagricultural sector are becoming increasingly labor-intensive, absorbing the poorest and landless farmers.

We have undoubtedly learned much since Chenery's early efforts about what constitutes an appropriate set of policies to enhance the complementarities among growth, income distribution, and poverty reduction. Yet Fishlow seems to pay relatively little attention to drawing out the alternative combinations and sequencings of macroeconomic and structural adjustment policies that have apparently worked best. The importance of initial conditions, of intersectoral relations, of foreign trade, and of other aspects of the open economy especially come to mind. He might have told us a bit more about what he thinks we have learned, for example, about the importance of early agricultural mobilization, of maintaining labor market flexibility in the industrial sector, of decentralized industrialization, or of a dynamic urban informal sector—or the importance of anything else, for that matter. Such issues could have been usefully addressed—along with his appropriate emphasis on human capital, the initial distribution of assets, and the allocation of public goods. His words of warning about celebrating the absolute triumph of the market are well taken, but letting the pendulum once again swing too far in the opposite direction would be equally mistaken.

Fishlow's emphasis on direct actions by the public sector rather than its indirect influence on the mixed economy's growth path also probably led him to give more credit than deserved to what he calls "socialist equalization." I read the experience of what are now called the transition economies somewhat differently. While income distribution was certainly remarkably equitable in China, Viet Nam, and Eastern Europe, we need to recall the virtual absence of any property income in these formerly socialist societies. Moreover, the unequal distribution of perks and power—now being replaced by greater income inequality in the mixed economy—should also be taken into account.

I have no problem with Fishlow's emphasis on the accumulation of human capital as extremely important for achieving both high growth and equity. But he would probably agree that one needs to disaggregate more than he has done and be more sensitive to the time dimension. In East Asia, and presumably elsewhere, primary education and literacy probably mattered most early on; later, increased emphasis on secondary, especially vocational, education was highly productive; finally, science and technology at the tertiary level became critical. Equity as well as growth was served by the relatively equal, merit-based access to the competitive education system at all levels in these countries. The impact of post–debt crisis adjustment, affecting not only overall expenditure on education but also the public-private composition of education, is, as Fishlow points out, also worth considering. But again, this issue needs to be considered in a disaggregated and time-phased context.

Turning to the state of knowledge on poverty reduction, Fishlow rightly expresses less worry about any tradeoff with growth here; few now doubt the strong complementarity between growth and poverty reduction in all but the most extreme cases (see, for example, Fields 1980). Fishlow discusses the "basic needs" approach, also championed by Chenery, but he does not elaborate on its analytical links to growth and distribution. The weakness of these links is undoubtedly the main reason that the effort to short-circuit income changes in order to move quickly to get specific goods to specific groups proved to be so short-lived.

Today's lineal descendant of that initiative, which goes under the label *human development,* focuses on bottom line measures of welfare and abandons what Amartya Sen (in an oral comment) has termed the "commodity fetish" of the basic needs approach. To my mind, human development as *the* objective—and the financing and input combinations through which progress in this dimension is achieved—lies at the heart of the issue before us. I would argue that we need to move beyond abstract arguments about the quantity of goods provided through the market and through government allocations and focus more on the composition and quality of these allocations—for example, between preventive and curative health or between primary and tertiary education. And we need to examine the feedback from human development to economic development, in all its dimensions, and to the sustainability of progress in the bottom line indicators of welfare.

Fishlow seems to favor alternative institutional delivery mechanisms—witness his endorsement of Bardhan's (1994) suggested "third way," a mix of public sector decentralization and increased reliance on nongovernmental organizations (NGOs). I fully agree on the potential importance of a more decentralized state for achieving both more efficiency and more equity within regions—although achieving equity across regions still requires central government action (Rondinelli, McCullogh, and Johnson 1989; Ranis and Stewart 1994). I also believe that governance and civil society generally warrant more attention. But with respect to reliance on NGOs—currently very much in favor, coincidentally, at a time when public donors are short of resources—I remain somewhat skeptical.

The jury is still out on the sustained effectiveness of NGOs' contribution to societal objectives, given their own bureaucratic foibles and special agendas. Certainly Fishlow's placing Mexico's Solidaridad program and Bangladesh's Grameen Bank in close intellectual proximity does considerable violence. Solidaridad represents precious little grassroots empowerment and a large helping of Institutional Revolutionary Party (PRI) pork, lacking any of the necessary universality, automaticity, and devolution of an efficient infrastructure investment program. The Grameen Bank, by contrast, has proved to be an important and innovative instrument for providing access to credit for the poorest of the poor and thus substantially strengthening the complementarities among the objectives under consideration here.

Any inventory of where we stand today on inequality, poverty, and growth must, of course, include recent efforts to relate our problem to endogenous growth and endogenous policy approaches. Fishlow attempts some of this. For example, I have already expressed the view that, over time, the initial distribution of income and assets may have less impact on the strength of the complementarities among growth, distribution, and poverty reduction than does the choice of an efficiently participatory growth path, including government policies that allocate public goods equitably. Nevertheless, it is difficult to ignore the recent explosion of innovative efforts related to the new growth theory, moving causally from income distribution to growth, as summarized by, among others, Alesina and Rodrik (1994) and Alesina and Perotti (1994).

The general consensus on this score seems to be that the economic channel running from distribution to growth, which itself has alternative branches, is less convincing empirically than the political economy channel. One earlier—by now discredited—branch of the economic channel was that a more equal distribution of income reduces savings rates and thus growth. This is no longer empirically accepted. The present view is that a more equal distribution may generate more domestic demand and that it is less likely to lead to higher taxes, which are inimical to investment. I find it unsurprising that the econometric results for these two propositions are not very convincing; the rejection of supply creating its own demand (Say's law) and the appeal to fiscal disincentive effects, both presumably more relevant to the mature economy, are not persuasive. The argument that credit market imperfections impede the equitable allocation of human capital across the population is well accepted and persuasive, however, if somewhat independent of the initial distribution of income or wealth.

Better results seem to spring from the political economy channel, especially the notion that initial inequality fuels instability and more frequent recourse to populist policies, violating the macroeconomic stability constraint and reducing investment and growth. The poorer the median voter, it is assumed, the more likely that a political equilibrium will be established, yielding more populism and less growth.

I must admit to serious reservations about the wisdom of undertaking cross-country econometric fishing expeditions in either of these channels. Given the well-known large differences in initial conditions and institutions, country-specific historical analysis seems much more promising—as we have painfully discovered with respect to the "patterns of growth" literature of the past. At a minimum, pooling cross-section and time-series data for particular types or groups of developing countries—such as Africa, East Asia, and Latin America—seems indicated. Fishlow appears to be less concerned about this and runs his own rather inconclusive cross-country regressions, though he also deploys a dummy variable for Latin America. Whether endogenous growth and endogenous policy models ultimately prove helpful may well have to be tested in a country-sensitive—or at least typology-sensitive—context.

Fishlow also touches on the post–debt crisis adjustment problem and its impact on growth, poverty, and income distribution, but he neglects the companion issue of inflation. While I can fully understand Fishlow's reluctance to add to the prolific debate on the changing "Washington consensus," the effect of macroeconomic imbalances on inflation—and thus on the ability to achieve growth with equity—also merits attention, as does the need for different types of targeting, safety nets, and so on.

Accepting human development as the underlying objective of all economic activity, with economic development—including the dimensions of growth, distribution, and poverty reduction—as the most important means, seems to me both realistic and promising. This approach should also permit a general equilibrium exploration of the issue. If the bottom line of all development activity is indeed the improvement—per capita and in distributional terms—of some basic quality-of-life composite, it should also be possible to examine the feedback from such improvements for the next year's growth, equity, and poverty performance. In the same vein, it should become possible to trace the links between income-based economic development and bottom line human development and to focus policy on strengthening them.

References

Ahluwalia, Montek. 1976. "Inequality, Poverty, and Development." *Journal of Development Economics* 6: 307–42.

Alesina, Alberto, and Dani Rodrik. 1994. "Distributive Politics and Economic Growth." *Quarterly Journal of Economics* 108: 465–90.

Alesina, Alberto, and Roberto Perotti. 1994. "The Political Economy of Growth: A Critical Survey of the Recent Literature." *The World Bank Economic Review* 8(3): 351–71.

Anand, Sudhir, and Ravi Kanbur. 1984. "Inequality and Development: A Reconsideration." In H.P. Nissen, ed., *Towards Income Distribution Policies: From Income Distribution Research to Income Distribution Policy in LDCs*. Padenburg, The Netherlands: EADI.

Bardhan, Pranab. 1994. "Poverty Alleviation." Overseas Development Council Paper 1. Overseas Development Council, Washington, D.C.

Chenery, Hollis, Montek S. Ahluwalia, Clive Bell, John H. Duloy, and Richard Jolly. 1974. *Redistribution with Growth*. New York: Oxford University Press.

Fei, J.C.H., Gustav Ranis, and S.W.Y. Kuo. 1979. *Growth with Equity: The Taiwan Case*. New York: Oxford University Press.

Fields, G.S. 1980. *Poverty, Inequality, and Development.* New York: Cambridge University Press.

Fields, G.S., and G.H. Jakubson. 1993. "New Evidence on the Kuznets Curve." Yale Economic Growth Center, New Haven, Conn.

Ranis, Gustav, and F. Stewart. 1994. "Decentralisation in Indonesia." *Bulletin of Indonesian Economic Studies* 30 (December): 41–72.

Rondinelli, D., J. McCullogh, and R. Johnson. 1989. "Analysing Decentralisation Policies in Developing Countries: A Political Economy Framework." *Development and Change* 20: 57–87.

Floor Discussion of "Inequality, Poverty, and Growth: Where Do We Stand?" by Albert Fishlow

A participant from Bangladesh asked why there are no theories explaining why countries that demonstrate robust growth also tend to exhibit greater equality. The World Bank has cited shared growth as part of the East Asian miracle but, he asked, what does that mean? Does it mean that putting assets in the hands of the poor makes them more productive, which stimulates economic growth (especially because there are so many poor people)? Is growth more sustainable when the poor have assets that allow them to be productive, which generates demand? The World Bank spent much of the 1980s and early 1990s talking about structural adjustment, one component of which is to shift assets from the public to the private sector. Why, continued the participant, should the structural adjustment model not extend to the redistribution of assets from inefficient productive agents to efficient ones? The Grameen Bank, for example, has helped both alleviate poverty and stimulate village-level productivity by redistributing capital, that is, by getting credit into the hands of the poor. Is the World Bank willing to take the next step and underwrite projects that require land to be taken from unproductive rich farmers and given to more efficient, hard-working households?

François Bourguignon (discussant) responded that it is a mistake to say that limited work has been done on the relationship between income distribution and economic growth. The issue can be addressed through the concept of political equilibrium, for example. Income distribution is basically a measurement, added Gustav Ranis (discussant), whereas growth is basically a theory—and everyone has a pet theory about what causes growth. The challenge, Ranis said, is to measure in a more analytical way the link between growth and income distribution. If a country experiences a prolonged period of economic change, as reflected by poverty indicators or otherwise, development economists should examine that change in terms of the agriculture sector, the labor intensity of nonagricultural activities, and so on. Links should also be forged between growth theory and market activity, whether in terms of income distribution or labor, capital, and credit markets.

This session was chaired by Sven Sandstrom, managing director, Office of the President, at the World Bank.

Annual World Bank Conference on Development Economics 1995
©1996 The International Bank for Reconstruction and Development / THE WORLD BANK

A participant from the World Bank agreed that there are few theories explaining why greater equality is associated with higher growth, but that from an econometrics viewpoint it is likely that variables were missing from the empirical calculations. He guessed that in this case the variable was deregulation, which allowed more flexibility and competition in goods and factor markets and might also have helped to increase growth and decrease inequality.

The speakers had focused on interpersonal disparities and inequities, said Rémy Prud'homme (discussant from another session), but had ignored disparities between regions. Is what they said about interpersonal disparities and growth also true of regional disparities? His sense was that the two were quite different and that disparities between regions, unlike disparities between people, were positively associated with growth. Bourguignon agreed that regional disparities should be taken into account. Moreover, the discussion had been limited to the differences between big and small countries, but big countries (like Brazil, China, and India) are effectively sets of smaller countries, with great inequality between regions. Splitting such countries into regions and reexamining the econometric work might greatly change our view of the world.

A consulting engineer asked Montek Ahluwalia (discussant) what policies and actions the Indian government had taken to reduce inequality. Ahluwalia responded that the policies his government had introduced to spur growth were also designed to remove distortions and generate labor-absorbing growth. Reducing protection of industry, for example, should help agriculture. Thus India's growth-inducing policies were in line with strategies for generating egalitarian growth. India also has targeted interventions, he said. In the past three or four years the government had substantially increased allocations for improving health and human capital and for providing more income support to the poor.

Research on Poverty and Development Twenty Years after *Redistribution with Growth*

Pranab Bardhan

This article starts with a review of some of the broad areas in which research on poverty and development has made significant progress in the past two decades—on the concepts and measures of poverty, on the special problems related to gender, on poverty's interrelationship with the environment and with fertility control, on the effects of growth and direct public action on poverty, on targeting transfers cost-effectively, and on the processes in credit and insurance markets. The second part focuses on more controversial issues, such as the relation between efficiency and equity and the strengths and weaknesses of alternative governance structures in tackling poverty.

Redistribution with Growth (Chenery and others 1974) represented a serious attempt, under the leadership of Hollis Chenery two decades back, to reorient the international development policy discussion toward poverty-focused strategies. This was a time of widespread disillusionment with the trickle-down effects of growth on poverty. While recognizing the need for direct and more active measures of poverty alleviation, Chenery and his coauthors emphasized that, for a lasting impact on poverty, redistributive policies have to be largely consistent with—and conducive to—growth-promoting policies. This emphasis has been amply borne out by the past two decades, and the need for targeting the asset-poor in the rural sector and the urban informal sector is also now widely recognized.

An Overview of Research Progress

This article starts with a brief and selective overview of some of the broad areas in which research on poverty and development since *Redistribution with Growth* has made significant progress.[1]

Pranab Bardhan is professor of economics at the University of California at Berkeley.
Annual World Bank Conference on Development Economics 1995

Concepts and Measures of Poverty

The discussion on the conceptual and measurement aspects of poverty has become much more sophisticated since the early 1970s, when the simple head-count measure using a rather arbitrary poverty line for income or spending was the dominant mode of aggregation. The recent measures are more sensitive to differences in the depth of poverty—as with the poverty gap index—or to inequality among the poor—as with the Foster-Greer-Thorbecke (1984) measure. Even without precise poverty measures or poverty lines, one can draw on stochastic dominance criteria to make unambiguous comparative rankings of poverty if the cumulative distribution function of the living standard indicator in one case lies completely outside that in another (Atkinson 1987). Also very useful in policy debates are exercises in decomposing changes in poverty estimates to quantify the relative importance of growth and redistribution in those changes—as in Datt and Ravallion (1992) for Brazil and India.

The recent literature recognizes the limits of an income-centered or commodity-centered concept of well-being—and the importance of using multifaceted measures of poverty, including those of basic needs (Streeten and others 1981) and human capabilities (Sen 1985). Sen raises foundational issues about the quality of life beyond the possession of commodities (which has only "derivative and varying relevance") and beyond even the utilities generated. But it is not easy to operationalize "capabilities" for measuring poverty, even if we confine ourselves to basic capabilities and human functionings and to minimal partial ordering in poverty evaluations. Also unresolved is the tension between the limits of the mental metric of utilities and of people's ability to define their own well-being (particularly in situations of extreme deprivation, when the deprived internalize the constraints they face) on the one hand, and the occasional paternalism and arbitrariness of (nonwelfarist) judgments on the nature of the "good life" on the other. The nonwelfarist approach has nevertheless focused attention on pro-poor public policies for improving longevity, literacy, basic health and sanitation, basic freedoms, and so on, more than would an income approach or (the usual narrow version of) a utility-centric approach.

Special Problems of Women

The past two decades of research have brought to center stage the problems of special groups, such as women, for whom escape from poverty is particularly difficult.[2] Women face special social and economic constraints in acquiring and using human capital, as the evidence on education shows. In Africa and in West and South Asia more than 70 percent of women 25 years old or older are illiterate. Even for girls in the 6–11 age group, the proportion out of school is above 25 percent in Sub-Saharan Africa and above 15 percent in South Asia (these rates do not include the high absenteeism and dropout rates). Lack of childcare facilities often forces young daughters of poor working women to skip school to take care of their siblings, perpetuating the cycle of low education and low-paid jobs for women from one generation to the next.

The legal and cultural barriers to entering the labor market are often formidable for women, and if they do break in, they are often segregated in casual or dead-end, low-paying jobs. Frequently overworked in domestic chores (including fetching water, firewood, and fodder from long distances), their domestic commitments (and culturally induced low self-esteem) seriously restrict their mobility and ability to seize better work opportunities. Women are often excluded from credit programs because they cannot provide collateral—in South Asia they lack secure property rights to land, and in Africa formal land titling programs have sometimes deprived women of their traditional rights to land. Women's access to extension services is also limited, having particular consequence in Africa, where women are heavily involved in production decisions for some crops. And women lack protection from violence in many societies, further limiting their activity and autonomy.

These considerations have major implications for antipoverty policy. For example, contrary to the so-called unitary household model standard in most of economics, the unequal autonomy and bargaining power of different members of the household may result in underinvestment in human capital for women and even underconsumption on their part. This suggests that the usual public interventions at the household level may be woefully inadequate, calling instead for more effective gender targeting in policy. Similarly, gender equity and efficiency are likely to go together. Better education for women is often associated with better education, nutrition, and health of children (particularly daughters). And better opportunities for outside work for young women can lead to socially more beneficial fertility behavior—through, say, raising the age at marriage.

Fertility Control

Women's autonomy and the expansion of their economic and social opportunities are among the many important aspects relevant to appropriate public policies toward fertility control. Those who oppose fertility control policies point to the fact that a large family may be the voluntary choice of the poor, given their need for extra hands in the family (to earn income and collect nonmarket goods from the village commons) and for old age security. Others point out (see Birdsall 1988 on the general issues here) that childbearing imposes costs on society that are not borne by the family deciding to have the extra child. These costs include the overuse of common property resources, the congestion in such public services as education, health, and sanitation, and the less direct effects of crowding the labor market and depressing wages. In many poor countries these negative effects may outweigh any possible demographically induced improvements in methods of production that some pronatalists point to.

It is also often observed that high fertility is associated with lower parental spending (per child) on education and health, and even if this is voluntary the social consequences are undesirable. Another, less important reason for public policy intervention is that the private market for contraceptive information and services is sometimes underdeveloped—and poor people have more children than they want or would want were they better informed about contraceptive options or better provided with services.[3]

All these suggest active public policies toward fertility control programs for the poor, but success in these programs often depends more on organizational reform and change in social attitudes than on financial resources. Vitally important are a better appreciation, on the part of the family planning authorities, of the complexity of poor families' fertility decisions in the context of a wide range of interrelated household decisions and the need to avoid overly paternalistic or coercive attitudes toward the "fast-breeding, illiterate poor." Above all, as Sen (1994) emphasizes, social investments in education and health care (particularly for women), by expanding choices and enhancing economic security, may be the most effective and sustainable way of controlling fertility in poor families.

Poverty and the Environment

There now is much more awareness of the two-way relationship between poverty and environmental degradation. The poor, particularly in rural areas, depend on local environmental resources—forests, fisheries, grazing lands, irrigating water, and so on. The local commons also provide some insurance for the poor as a fallback source of food and fodder in bad crop years. With the erosion of the local commons—the decimation of forests and grazing lands, the silting and increasing toxicity of rivers and tanks, the depletion of aquifers, and soil erosion and desertification—the life of the rural poor has become more insecure and impoverished, particularly in Africa and South Asia. Poverty estimates based on private consumption expenditure data do not capture this effect, except indirectly through a rise in the prices of such items as firewood. Poverty in turn drives people to desperate short-run mining of land and water and to other intensive resource extraction, straining the already fragile and limited environmental base, sometimes beyond the possibility for repair and renewal.

Some analysts suggest that these problems of overuse and degradation reflect primarily the lack of well-defined private property rights in local common-pool resources. True, private property rights can go a long way toward reducing uncertainty and inducing people to conserve resources and internalize externalities. But privatizing common property resources often disenfranchises the poor. And from the enclosure movement in English history to the appropriation of forests and grazing lands in developing countries by timber merchants and cattle ranchers today, it has been the same sad story. No less bleak is the story of the bureaucratic appropriation by colonial and postcolonial governments of the traditional rights of local communities over these common resources. Sometimes, no longer bound by traditional community norms of regulated use, the dispossessed begin to resort to irresponsible, destructive practices, if they perceive commercial or bureaucratic appropriation as unfair.

Growth Effects on Poverty Reduction

All the foregoing general topics—a broader conception and metrics of poverty, gender, environment, and fertility control—call for special attention to public policies toward the poor. This complements the emphasis that Chenery and his associates put on public policies toward improving the access of the poor to physical assets and human capital. But what about the conventional growth effects on poverty reduction?

In the past two decades of poverty research there clearly is better appreciation of the fact that policies fostering economic growth need not be inconsistent with reducing poverty. In many countries (in East and Southeast Asia, for example) growth-promoting policies have substantially reduced mass poverty. Lipton and Ravallion (1995) report estimates for eight developing countries (Bangladesh, Brazil, Côte d'Ivoire, India, Indonesia, Morocco, Nepal, and Tunisia) that a 2 percent annual rate of growth in consumption per person will typically result in a decline in the poverty gap index of 3 to 8 percent, using local poverty lines and assuming growth to be distributionally neutral.[4] The effects of growth on inequality depends, of course, on the initial distribution of assets, the nature of imperfections in markets (particularly the capital market), the pattern of growth, factor bias in technology, and government policies (on, say, social welfare and openness to international competition).

Some types of growth clearly do not help the poor. The adverse distributional effects of capital-intensive or skill-intensive projects of industrialization and commercialization may delay the decline in poverty of the unskilled and assetless. The centripetal forces of growth with increasing returns may drain resources from backward regions, as economic geographers have repeatedly shown. And large development projects damaging the environment may uproot and disenfranchise sections of the poor from their traditional habitats and their access to common-pool resources. In most of these cases the gainers can afford to compensate the losers—but in the actual political process, they seldom do.

In general, the most important way for economic growth to help the poor is by expanding their opportunities for productive and remunerative employment (including self-employment on farms and in artisan shops). There is also some measure of agreement that policies that contribute to growth by improving the allocative efficiency of resource use (say, by reducing distortions in relative prices, exchange rates, and trade policies) may help the poor. This is particularly so if the traded goods sector is more labor-intensive than the nontraded goods sector and if exports are more labor-intensive than import substitutes (assuming, of course, that the workers have some basic education and skills). Underpricing scarce inputs—such as capital, energy, and environmental resources—often leads to the adoption of capital-intensive and environment-damaging projects that have adverse distributional consequences. Movements of terms of trade in favor of agriculture may help the poor if the sector consists of a large number of small farmers who market a significant part of their output. But if the peasants (including landless laborers) are net purchasers of basic foodgrains and if the wages of agricultural laborers lag behind price rises (as they typically do), some of the poor may be hurt by such a terms of trade change, at least in the short run.

In countries with high and persistent inequality the trickle-down effects of even fairly high rates of growth have been so slow—as in the high-growth phases in

Botswana or Brazil in recent history—that without remedial pro-poor policy actions it will take an unconscionably long time before a sizable dent is made in the backlog of poverty. Even where growth has been associated with substantial reductions in poverty, the association is often mediated by growth-facilitating, pro-poor public expenditure policies (Drèze and Sen 1989).

Then there are the unemployables—the subgroups of the poor who are not helped by the effects of growth on employment opportunities. In this group are the physically disabled, the elderly, the ill, the women overburdened with reproduction and childcare or constrained in joining the labor force (and leaving out those who are often employed but should not be, such as children). Here the policy imperative is appropriate targeted transfers such as food stamps, subsidized food distribution, school lunches, nutrition programs for pregnant and nursing women, basic health care (with emphasis on preventive care for those who are not ill), adequate facilities for primary and secondary education (including financial inducements for children who would otherwise be employed to attend school), and low-cost shelter.

These transfer programs are also important for creating and maintaining a safety net for all poor families. Over the years they have filled the gap left by the decline of traditional patron-client or kinship-based insurance systems for the poor and by the erosion of access to common property resources. The publicly provided minimum economic security program for the poor generally includes targeted income transfer programs (such as the Emergency Social Fund in Bolivia and the National Solidarity Program in Mexico). It also includes public works programs, which provide a necessary income backup for workers in distress and a means for building community capital, as with the Employment Guarantee Scheme in Maharashtra State in India and the Food-for-Work Program in Bangladesh. Other important components are basic education and health care, safe drinking water and sanitation, and some environmental protection measures.

Targeting Transfers Cost-Effectively

The targeting and cost-effectiveness of transfers have been the subject of much discussion in recent years. With structural adjustment programs necessitating large cuts in budgetary subsidies, targeting transfers to vulnerable groups has become even more important, since the leakages from transfer programs to nontarget groups are often considerable. The political and administrative costs of targeting can be significant, however. And because effective targeting through a reliable and cheaply administered means test is infeasible in many contexts, countries need to devise more programs based largely on self-targeting.

For such self-targeting the public distribution of subsidized food could cover only coarse grains, root crops, or other "inferior" goods that the nonpoor usually do not consume. Similarly, public works programs involving heavy manual work are not attractive to the nonpoor. In both cases, however, bogus master rolls still divert some funds to nonpoor middlemen. Subsidizing coarse grains though food stamps is generally preferable to public procurement and distribution (as in India), since the government does not have to be involved in the purchase, transport, and storage of the commodities (a significant part of the budgetary food subsidy in India). To counter the effect of a rise in food prices, as with the food stamp program in Sri Lanka, governments can consider indexing the value of the stamps to the prices of coarse grains or other such goods bought only by the poor.

Rudimentary social services like primary education or basic health care are also usually somewhat pro-poor, as some studies of the incidence of the benefits of public spending on social services suggest. This is presumably because the rich often turn to the private market for primary education and basic health care—and because the poor often have larger families. The distribution of the benefits of public spending for higher education and expensive medical care in urban hospitals is likely to be much more regressive. So the practice of charging low prices across the board for different social services regardless of cost—accompanied by quantity rationing or quality reductions when budgets are tight—has not served the poor either in the quantity or quality of services. High-cost services consumed by the rich are often subsidized more than low-cost services, so selective increases in user fees (with exemptions for the very poor) can serve both efficiency and equity.

When transfer programs are substantial, they have economywide repercussions—depending particularly on how they are financed and how the rest of the economy responds—and these repercussions feed back onto poverty. Several applied general equilibrium models in the recent literature (for example, Narayana, Parikh, and Srinivasan 1991) have tried to trace the quantitative effect of alternative programs for the economy as a whole, for sectors, and for socioeconomic groups. This can be a useful way to provide guidelines for choosing among policy options.

Credit and Insurance Markets

Processes in credit and insurance markets are crucial to understanding the origin and perpetuation of poverty—to see how severe credit market imperfections can cause poverty traps and how lack of access to insurance mechanisms increases the incidence of poverty.[5] Expanding the opportunities for credit can help the poor reap the high potential rates of return from investing in education. It can also make small farmers and artisans more economically viable by allowing them to enlarge their scale of production, to take more risks, and to avoid short-sighted strategies. Chenery states in his introductory chapter to *Redistribution with Growth*: "without a redistribution of at least the increments of capital formation, other distributive measures are not likely to have a lasting impact on the poverty problem" (p. xvii). Imperfections in—and even the nonexistence of—credit and insurance markets and the usually costly private adjustments to those imperfections are also key to understanding the important distinction between transient poverty, caused largely by relatively short-run income variability, and chronic poverty.

Over the past two decades many poor countries have tried to provide subsidized credit to the poor—with mixed results, as with one of the world's largest credit programs for asset-building by the rural poor, the Integrated Rural Development

Program in India. Wealthier borrowers often appropriate the credit subsidies meant for the poor. And the underpricing of credit generally leads to inefficient use of capital. Moreover, having government or semigovernment agencies administering credit weakens the incentives to invest wisely or to repay promptly. Rent seeking and building political connections to get debt relief sometimes become more important than responsible investment behavior.

A fundamental dilemma of the credit market: outside agencies (including government banks) do not have enough local information about the borrower, and monitoring is costly, so they insist on collateral that excludes many of the poor. Meanwhile, local lenders have more personalized information about the borrower, but they often use this informational entry barrier to charge high interest rates. In addition, in rural areas covariate weather risks and sharp seasonality in loan demand and repayment make local deposit banking difficult to develop.

Some Unresolved Issues

Having discussed broad features of poverty issues on which there is some measure of consensus, I turn to approaches and policies that are more often contested—or where unresolved institutional and political economy issues leave considerable scope for further analytical discussion and more empirical work. I shall again be brief, confining myself to broad generalities with varying applicability depending on the historical and institutional context of a country. The territory here is inherently slippery and economists preoccupied with getting the prices right may feel particularly uncomfortable.

Take land reform, an asset-redistributive poverty alleviation measure endorsed by *Redistribution with Growth*. Most major land reforms have taken place in the context of war or social revolution (or threats thereof) and even then have not always achieved much reduction in poverty, as Bolivia and Mexico show. Even in normal times, if (nonconfiscatory) land redistribution is politically feasible, its economic effects on poverty can be ambiguous. In traditional agriculture, where the use of lumpy inputs such as farm machinery is limited, economies of scale are not substantial, and the small farm with a differential advantage in labor cost is often more productive than the large, as evidence from many countries suggests. But the larger farmer may have better access to production credit (particularly significant as purchased inputs become more important in modern agriculture), to information and marketing networks, and to the capacity to diffuse and insure against risk.[6] If these services are not available to the small farmer, land redistribution may not always boost productivity and reduce poverty. The redistribution of land from large to small farmers may also reduce the demand for hired labor (while correcting the underuse of family labor on small farms) and depress the wage rates for landless laborers, particularly if they get no land in the land reform.

In some densely populated poor countries (like Bangladesh), the "surplus" land for redistribution (assuming any reasonable ceiling on large farms) is likely to be far short of what is needed to make a big dent in poverty. Where landlords and large farmers are major providers of credit to poor peasants, vital sources of credit for the intended beneficiaries of land reform may dry up unless there is a simultaneous credit reform. Restrictions on tenancy—without effective ceilings on farm size or progressive land taxes on large holdings—may lead to the eviction of tenants or the conversion of erstwhile tenants into wage laborers on the same farms. As Hayami and Otsuka (1993) point out, such restrictions in the irrigated rice sector in the Philippines closed the possibility for agricultural laborers at the bottom to climb the tenancy ladder. In the Republic of Korea and Taiwan (China), by contrast, tenancy reform has been much more redistributive. There is relative unanimity on the issue of security of tenure, which provides incentives for long-term improvements on the land.

One beneficial by-product of land reform, underemphasized in the usual economic analysis, is changing the local political structure in the village. Redistributive land reform gives more "voice" to the poor and induces them to get involved in local self-governing institutions and in common management of local public goods. Local markets (say, for farm products or credit or water) function more efficiently when the leveling effects of land reform improve competition and make it more difficult for the rural oligarchy to corner markets.

Many regard the political prospects for land reform in most developing countries as bleak—and therefore drop it altogether from the agenda of poverty alleviation. That is not always wise. Some aspects of land reform (like security of tenure) may be easier to implement than others. Besides, in the dynamics of political processes and shifting coalitions, the range of feasibility often changes. And options kept open contribute to the political debate and may influence the political process. Some policy advisers who rule out land reform as politically infeasible are enthusiastic supporters of other poverty alleviation policies that may be no less politically difficult. An example is the strict targeting of food subsidies and thus the cutting of the substantial subsidies to the vocal urban middle classes. In the game of forming political coalitions a radical policy sometimes becomes implementable if it helps cement strategic alliances—say, between groups of the urban upper classes (including white-collar workers) and the rural poor. Compensating for land depends on how willing urban taxpayers are to share the costs of land reform.

Another area of significant divergence in opinion and attitude, despite the measure of consensus noted earlier, is in the basic approach to poverty alleviation itself.

- One approach, popular in some international lending agencies and donor countries, is to rely primarily on market-based growth and then to take care of those who fall through the cracks of the market process with targeted public welfare programs and the provision of infrastructure.
- Another approach is to give much more emphasis to various forms of massive public intervention in directly improving the health, education, and nutrition of the poor.
- A third approach, which has received less attention, is to move some distance away from both state paternalism and the harshness of market processes and instead to rely more on local self-governing institutions and community involvement to improve the material conditions and autonomy of the poor.

Even when the state is obligated to spend a significant part of its budget on antipoverty programs, as in India, too often very little reaches the real poor. The reasons: there is no organized pressure from the intended beneficiaries, and the programs are administered by a distant, uncoordinated, and corrupt bureaucracy unaccountable to the local poor and insensitive to their needs. Even when resources do reach the poor, they often perpetuate a cycle of dependency—and an attitude of malfeasance and opportunism among the poor, with an eye to milking the state cow for its uncertain bounties. Of course, a disproportionate share of the benefits goes to those with the resources, connections, and dexterity to manipulate the milking process and to the large army of middlemen, contractors, officials, and politicians.

The issue is not just the administrative decentralization or better coordination of delivery mechanisms that is sometimes urged. An antipoverty program cannot be effective or sustained, particularly under the usual politics of scarcity, without active and vigilant participation by the poor, demanding the benefits as part of their minimum social and economic rights. But in most parts of the world the poor are much too weak and fragmented to get organized—and even getting organized may not be enough. Take rural West Bengal in India, where under the leadership of a leftist government some institutions of genuine local democracy have spread roots, and groups of the rural poor have been mobilized to demand and get some of the benefits and subsidies flowing from the top—which in other Indian states are often misappropriated by the rich. But these institutions so far have not succeeded in mobilizing their own resources or in launching self-reliant cooperative projects of rural development.

Yet community institutions can do much for poverty alleviation by providing an informal framework for coordinating the design and implementation of projects like water management, environmental protection, prevention of soil erosion, regulated use of forests and grazing land, and the provision of other local public goods. Local information can often identify cheaper, more appropriate ways of providing basic services. There is also scattered evidence that the serious absenteeism of teachers in village public schools and doctors in rural public clinics is significantly reduced when they are made accountable to the local community. Peer monitoring and enforcement of local social sanctions and a common set of norms can also provide the basis for social insurance schemes and group borrowing—as in the widely cited Grameen Bank experiment in Bangladesh, where credit for groups of poor women is organized along lines of joint liability.

Decentralizing or devolving power to a closely interactive and face-to-face local community creates important incentives by placing decisionmaking in the hands of those who have information that others lack—just as private markets do. But as the group borrowing and social insurance schemes suggest, markets sometimes fail as a coordination mechanism when private information renders individual market contracts incomplete or unenforceable. In such situations a local community—if it has stable membership and well-developed structures for transmitting private information and norms among the members—has the potential to provide more efficient coordination.[7]

It is too easy, however, to romanticize the value of the local community as a social and economic organization, as environmentalists, nongovernmental organization (NGO) activists, and other assorted antistate, antimarket social thinkers sometimes do (I am inclined to label the whole group "anarcho-communitarians"). There undoubtedly are many successful local community organizations in different parts of the world, but there are far too many dismal failures to ignore some of the systemic problems.

First, in situations of severe social and economic inequality local institutions can be highly inadequate in helping the poor, as local overlords find it easy to capture the local institutions and the poor are left grievously exposed to their mercies and their malfeasance. (Such capture is more difficult at the national level because the local mafia of different regions may partially neutralize one another.) Appeals to supra-local authorities (such as the national or provincial government) for intervention and protection and relief for the poor are quite common in such cases.

Second, supra-local coordination may become particularly important when the development process has externalities that the decentralized authority of the local community is unable and sometimes even unwilling to cope with. For positive externalities across localities, there may be underinvestment by the local community in infrastructure benefits that would spill over to other communities. For negative externalities, the local control mechanisms may be inadequate—for example, upstream deforestation may cause flooding and soil erosion in downstream communities.

Third, the weak administrative and revenue-raising capacity of community organizations or local administrative units seriously restricts their financial autonomy. While visible benefits and local accountability tend to encourage local resource mobilization, in many countries the geographic concentration of production (caused in part by agglomeration economies) and jurisdictional restrictions leave few elastic sources of revenue with local governments. There is thus a built-in tendency toward vertical fiscal imbalance and dependence on central transfers.

An important contrast comes from China in recent years, where effective fiscal decentralization—Qian and Weingast (1994) call it "market-preserving federalism"—has paved the way for the dramatic success story of township and village enterprises. This in turn has contributed to an unprecedented reduction of poverty in southern China. These enterprises are mostly owned (de jure and de facto) by local governments, and they reinvest a significant part of their profits in building local infrastructure. What institutional mechanisms underpin their success? There is vigorous competition among the enterprises of different localities. The hard budget constraint imposed by central fiscal authorities compels the local governments to raise their own resources. And the local governments are encouraged to do so since they get to keep much of the profits they make. But since this system is inherently biased in favor of localities with better endowments and infrastructure, such "market-preserving federalism" is likely to have worsened the already substantial inter-regional inequality in China.

The advantages and disadvantages of markets and local communities as coordination mechanisms also suggest that we need a more nuanced analysis of the role of the state in poverty alleviation than is usually available from the age-old state versus market debate. To be clearly recognized in this analysis are the limits of the state as an economic governance structure—limits arising from its lack of access to local information and its vulnerability to wasteful rent-seeking processes. But the state is not to withdraw to its minimalist role in classical liberalism. Instead, it is to play an activist role in local participatory development, in supra-local support for raising outside finance, in underwriting risks, in supplying training and extension services, in investing in larger infrastructure, and in coordinating some of the externalities across localities.

This, of course, presumes that the state has some minimum institutional coherence and administrative capacity. In some African countries in recent years even this minimum has been found lacking—and there has been a general unraveling of the state machinery. Civil wars, ethnic strife, and a ruling kleptocracy have decimated the minimum protections and guarantees that a state can provide. The poor have been the greatest victims.

In general, much too often the emphasis is on how faster economic growth mediated through markets and efficient resource allocation will take care of much poverty, or on how the state needs to allocate (and efficiently spend) much larger amounts on various welfare measures for the poor. Our discussion above is aimed at redirecting part of the attention toward building local institutions and organizations that are more sensitive to the needs of the poor and to their opportunities. Some scattered evidence shows that local institutions work better in enforcing common agreements and cooperative norms when the underlying property regime is not too skewed and the benefits are more equitably shared. So, efficiency and equity can go together. Better sharing can facilitate better coordination in organizing access to local public goods, which may in turn boost productivity all around.[8]

We have already referred to cases of how gender equity and efficiency go together and that redistributive land reform can enable the poor to get involved in local self-governing institutions. It is also recognized in the literature on contract theory that there are clear cases of mandated redistribution (such as land reform) that may reduce agency costs. In general, redistributions of property rights—if they align control of noncontractible actions more closely with residual claims over the outcomes of these actions—can also improve efficiency.[9] Similarly, initial inequalities can affect the growth paths through capital market imperfections and resultant occupational choices; and redistribution can help growth by mitigating such capital market imperfections (Banerjee and Newman 1993).

As much of mainstream economics seems obsessed with the equity-efficiency tradeoff and thus with the costs of redistribution, it is important to direct attention to redistributive projects that actually enhance productive efficiency. All this is even apart from the obvious cases of improvement in the conditions of the poor, resulting in reduced crime and political instability, and a healthier and educated workforce that is an asset to producers. In all these respects, redistribution can work hand in hand with growth—as Chenery and his coauthors envisaged two decades back.

Notes

1. For an excellent and relatively comprehensive overview, see Lipton and Ravallion (1995).

2. Other such groups include children, marginalized tribes, and ethnic minorities.

3. Pritchett (1994) provides a convincing demonstration that demand factors in contraceptive use are more important than contraceptive costs or access in explaining variations in fertility rates.

4. For India—the only developing country for which a reasonably long and reliable time series of poverty measures is available—Datt and Ravallion (1994) estimate that measures of absolute rural poverty responded elastically to changes in mean consumption over the period 1958–90 and that the impact of growth was roughly distribution-neutral.

5. For theoretical work along these lines, see, for example, Banerjee and Newman (1993) and Morduch (1994).

6. For a recent overview of these issues, see Binswanger, Deininger, and Feder (1995).

7. For a comparative evaluation of markets, states, and communities in the context of coordination failure, see Bowles and Gintis (1994).

8. For some examples in irrigation, see Boyce (1988) and Bardhan (1993).

9. For examples of this general principle in the theoretical literature, see Bowles and Gintis (1994), Hoff (1994), and Mookherjee (1994).

References

Atkinson, Anthony. 1987. "On the Measurement of Poverty." *Econometrica* 55: 749–64.

Banerjee, Abhijit, and Andrew Newman. 1993. "Occupational Choice and the Process of Development." *Journal of Political Economy* 101(April): 274–98.

Bardhan, Pranab. 1993. "Analytics of the Institutions of Informal Cooperation in Rural Development." *World Development* 21(April): 633–39.

Binswanger, Hans, Klaus Deininger, and Gershon Feder. 1995. "Power, Distortions, Revolt, and Reform in Agricultural Land Relations." In Jere Behrman and T.N. Srinivasan, eds., *Handbook of Development Economics,* vol. 3. Amsterdam: North Holland.

Birdsall, Nancy. 1988. "Economic Approaches to Population Growth." In Hollis B. Chenery and T.N. Srinivasan, eds., *Handbook of Development Economics,* vol. 1. Amsterdam: North Holland.

Bowles, S., and H. Gintis. 1994. "Efficient Redistribution: New Rules for Markets, States, and Communities." University of Massachusetts, Amherst.

Boyce, James. 1988. "Technological and Institutional Alternatives in Asian Rice Irrigation." *Economic and Political Weekly* 23(March): A6–22.

Chenery, Hollis B., Montek S. Ahluwalia, Clive Bell, John H. Duloy, and Richard Jolly. 1974. *Redistribution with Growth.* New York: Oxford University Press.

Datt, Gaurav, and Martin Ravallion. 1992. "Growth and Redistribution Components of Changes in Poverty Measures: A Decomposition with Applications to Brazil and India in the 1980's." *Journal of Development Economics* 38: 275–95.

———. 1994. "Growth and Poverty in Rural India." World Bank, Policy Research Department, Washington, D.C.

Drèze, Jean, and Amartya Sen. 1989. *Hunger and Public Action.* Oxford: Oxford University Press.

Foster, James, Joel Greer, and Erik Thorbecke. 1984. "A Class of Decomposable Poverty Measures." *Econometrica* 52: 761–65.

Hayami, Yujiro, and Keijiro Otsuka. 1993. *The Economics of Contract Choice.* Oxford: Clarendon.

Hoff, Karla. 1994. "The Second Theorem of the Second Best." *Journal of Public Economics* 45: 223–42.

Lipton, Michael, and Martin Ravallion. 1995. "Poverty and Policy." In Jere Behrman and T.N. Srinivasan, eds., *Handbook of Development Economics,* vol. 3. Amsterdam: North Holland.

Mookherjee, Dilip. 1994. "Informational Rents and Property Rights in Land." Boston University, Institute of Economic Development, Boston, Mass.

Morduch, Jonathan. 1994. "Poverty and Vulnerability." *American Economic Review* 84(May): 221–25.

Narayana, N.S.S., K.S. Parikh, and T.N. Srinivasan. 1991. *Agriculture, Growth, and Redistribution of Income: Policy Analysis with a General Equilibrium Model of India.* Amsterdam: North Holland.

Pritchett, Lant. 1994. "Desired Fertility and the Impact of Population Policies." *Population and Development Review* 20: 1–55.

Qian, Yingyi, and Barry Weingast. 1994. "Beyond Decentralization: Market-Preserving Federalism with Chinese Characteristics." Stanford University, Hoover Institution, Palo Alto, Calif.

Sen, Amartya. 1985. *Commodities and Capabilities*. Amsterdam: North Holland.

———. 1994. "Population: Delusion and Reality." *New York Review of Books*, September 22, 62–71.

Streeten, Paul, S.J. Burki, M. Haq, N. Hicks, and F. Stewart. 1981. *First Things First: Meeting Basic Needs in Developing Countries*. New York: Oxford University Press.

Comment on "Research on Poverty and Development Twenty Years after *Redistribution with Growth*," by Pranab Bardhan

Michael Lipton

P ranab Bardhan's article is an excellent, constructive review of many aspects of poverty analysis and policy since *Redistribution with Growth* (Chenery and others 1974). My comments are less about disagreements—I have few—than about recent evidence that strengthens his case or somewhat shifts the emphasis, and the need to set that case in the context of current arguments between two sorts of reformers.

During the 1970s *redistributive reforms* became less effective against poverty because the absence of *market reforms* allowed the rich and the administrators increasingly to capture the benefits of allocations of land, credit, education, and other goods intended for the poor, and reduced the gains to poor people from the benefits of reform that they did manage to obtain—a little land does not do much for you if public policy represses the price of your cash crop. But since 1980 a single-minded concentration on market reforms has similarly become less effective in either promoting growth or reducing poverty, because in the absence of redistributive reforms many poor people are denied basic schooling, health, political influence, and chances to control land and other productive assets.

This constriction of the ability of the poor to operate in the marketplace may help explain why the unprecedented decline in world poverty in 1945–80 appears to have stopped and not to have resumed, though growth has. Denial of market access to the land-hungry, ill-educated "lower 40 percent" impedes not just the reduction of poverty, but also the attainment of efficiency, competition, and growth. Though set up as caricature enemies, redistributive and market reforms need each other if they are to accelerate growth or help the poor.

I consider Bardhan's discussion of poverty measurement and concepts, poverty and demography, poverty and the environment, and gender. I then discuss his reviews of three weapons against poverty: macroeconomic policy, land reform, and civil society and participation.

Michael Lipton is professor of economics at the University of Sussex.

Annual World Bank Conference on Development Economics 1995
©1996 The International Bank for Reconstruction and Development / THE WORLD BANK

Measurement and Concepts

The reason for measuring poverty is to discover how serious it is for different groups (countries, regions, genders, or a population at different times) and to explore causal links between policy and other variables and the seriousness of a group's poverty. There are four main issues.

First, given the poverty line and the unit of measure (for example, real expenditure per adult-equivalent per year), how does one add up the "amount of poverty" of those people, in a country or group, who fall below the line? Bardhan rightly emphasizes the improvement in poverty measures since the simple head counts used in *Redistribution with Growth*. But head counts are still by far the most common poverty measure. While higher-order Foster-Greer-Thorbecke (1984) indicators are clearly preferable, why choose the current favorite, α_2, as the weight given to the severity of poverty? *Any* $\alpha_j > 1$ increases with head count, with intensity of poverty, and with maldistribution among the poor.

Second, what poverty line is appropriate? Stochastic dominance allows us to avoid a choice of poverty line only if we want no more than comparative *rankings* of groups. Even then, if there are several groups to be ranked, stochastic dominance will help only if it applies to all poverty comparisons between two groups. Thus, to allocate resources in ways that reflect needs—or even to assess what has been happening to poverty—a poverty line is usually needed. In and before *Redistribution with Growth*, the poverty lines were indeed arbitrary—and vastly different among countries and periods, making them useless for many purposes.

The current best practice is to use a lower and an upper poverty line. The lower line is the level of private expenditure per person (in 1985 purchasing power parity, or PPP, dollars) at which members of a household can be expected just to meet their food-energy needs—assuming that the household distributes expenditure among uses in a way typical of people at that level of expenditure per capita. (This food-energy method has problems—especially because PPP is estimated at mean national income, not at the mean private expenditure of the poor—but the problems do not, as often alleged, include neglect of nonfood needs; see Lipton and Ravallion 1995.)

Much less objective is the upper poverty line—currently an arbitrary 50 percent above the lower. I suggest instead defining it as the level of real PPP expenditure per capita at which a household's expected net savings (including net investment in human capital) becomes zero.

Third, is there a threshold at the poverty line, and does it matter? Using a sharp poverty line rather than a fuzzy zone makes sense only if there is a threshold. The level of, say, expenditure per person at the line must mark a discontinuity (or at least a point of inflection) in one of two senses: either behavior—for example, the trend in the share of food in expenditure as expenditure rises—changes sharply around the line, or observations—for example, the number of people in the group—are much denser far away from the line than near it.

Fourth, what unit, or units, of measure are sensible—and do they include non-welfarist approaches? Bardhan rightly argues that our units of measure need improvement. Most poverty analyses still measure private consumption per adult-equivalent. We need to add the nonpaid (subsidy) component of collective and state-provided goods. In addition, more panel data are needed to separate chronic from transient poverty; to allow for improvements in longevity, by permitting examination of groups' lifetime poverty indicators; and to clarify the concept of vulnerability—now an unholy confusion among a group's exposure to large or numerous or covariate downside fluctuations, aversion to this, damage from it, and lack of resilience in the face of it.

We also need to measure the relationship between poverty and its ill effects on capabilities (through high infant mortality and illiteracy, for example). All this is useful—but what is useful in poverty analysis is often not nonwelfarist, and what is nonwelfarist is often not useful. *Relative poverty* tends to be a mixture, in need of sorting out, of absolute poverty, low-end inequality, and subjective deprivation. *Self-assessed poverty,* or the change in it, is a valuable research and policy concept, but again not to be confused with food poverty. And *human development indicators* are conflations of items that, though very important in affecting the welfare of the poor (and imperfectly captured in measures of their consumption), are best measured separately: expenditure adequacy indicators (too often measured at the mean of GNP), their consequences for health and literacy, and their values relative to those of good performers.

Demography

Bardhan raises the important issue of the relationship between demography and poverty. (I feel uneasy about rejecting nonwelfarism only when it comes to the relative value of longer life or more people compared with fewer or shorter-lived people less prone to poverty or its ill effects.) Since *Redistribution with Growth* the relationship between large families—through high mortality and even higher fertility—and high risk of poverty has proved to have fewer exceptions than was once believed. Bardhan is right in saying that both publicly subsidized family planning and publicly subsidized measures to encourage poor couples to substitute child quality for quantity—wider female education, better child health care—matter in reducing family size norms, and thus poverty, among the poor. The two approaches are probably complementary, though the second is much more effective.

Environment

Population growth obviously affects the impact of poverty on the environment. Depletion of soil and water resources (rather than pollution or nonrenewable resource issues) appears to be the main environmental threat to the poor. The new institutional economics tends to play down this threat, arguing that population growth and other extra demands for natural resources lead to price changes that induce environment-saving innovations. But this solution does not work so well when real long-term prime interest rates rise from 1.5–2.5 percent, as in the decades before *Redistribution with Growth,* to 4.0–5.5 percent, as in 1980–95. Future economic historians will blame the industrial country policies of 1980–95—which sought to cure inflation but not fiscal deficits and thus deliberately drove up real interest rates—not only for setbacks in the struggle against poverty (transferring income from poor borrowers to wealthier lenders) and environmental depletion, but for "breaking the links" by which poor people's demographic response to poverty would set in motion price changes that reduce environmental threats.

Gender

Poor women's family size norms are usually far smaller than those of their husbands—another reason why gender equality is good for efficiency, not just for equity. Two comments are in order. First, the impetus toward improved conditions for women cannot be provided by markets alone, especially in education, because they respond to existing valuations of—and entry barriers to—women's work. Second, most surveys suggest that females are neither overrepresented in poor households nor (except for young girls in Bangladesh, northern India, and parts of China) exposed to nutritional or health discrimination within the household. Women's poverty appears to consist rather in having to work longer for the same real income (the double day) and—both for this reason and because of educational and job restrictions—being denied access to better-paid work. If women's incidence of expenditure poverty is no more than men's, yet their prospects of escaping poverty are worse, it follows that a higher proportion of female than of male poverty is chronic rather than transient.

Macroeconomic Policy

Bardhan reports the new consensus that reduced market distortions and interventions, especially in foreign trade and exchange, increase allocative efficiency in a way that favors the poor, especially if tradables (particularly exportables) are more labor-intensive than nontradables. But intensive in what sort of labor? Wood (1994) shows that manufactured-export-led growth usually depends on a basically educated work force. Because the poor can usually pay for education only at the cost of worse nutrition, public provision of education is a necessary complement to export-led growth if it is to reduce poverty rapidly. But the main constraint on poor children's education is their parents' need for child labor, to prevent serious and perhaps killing hunger. Therefore, if education is to do its work in remedying poverty, there need to be other ways than child labor for parents to meet basic needs.

Land Reform

Bardhan makes a nuanced case for reviving land reform. When *Redistribution with Growth* was written, this case had to contend with much confused advocacy of two sorts of land *deform.* History has made an overwhelming case against *enforced* collectives and state farming; that case need not be repeated here. The subtler case against restrictions on tenancy is that without effective ceilings on ownership holdings, as in the Republic of Korea and Taiwan (China), they induce evictions and impoverish the poor by discouraging owners from buying their skills as farmers. A more recent land deform, popular in the 1980s, is *enforced* privatization and registration of common-rights land; this does little or nothing for productivity (Migot-Adholla and others 1991) and usually leads to major land transfers from the poor to the nonpoor.

Land reform should be defined as redistribution of land rights to the rural poor. The case for it is even stronger than Bardhan indicates (Lipton 1993). A part of that case is that land reform normally raises total farm output (Binswanger, Deininger, and Feder 1995). There has been much real land reform—often outside the context of war or social revolution—and it has continued in several countries in the 1980s and 1990s. It may have acquired a new lease on life through market-assisted land reform, as in northeastern Brazil and South Africa.

Although, in principle, redistributing land from large to small farmers may reduce the demand for hired labor, in practice, evidence from Bangladesh to Brazil shows that the higher labor demand per hectare on small farms clearly outweighs their lower proportion of labor hired. Moreover, as reform beneficiaries divert family labor to their own land, they reduce the *supply* of hired labor.

It is true that in some densely populated poor countries imposing a reasonable ceiling on the size of farms might not make much of a dent in the poverty of poor peasants. But a policy should not be condemned because it fails to achieve everything. The very size of the poverty problem in such countries means that they need all the dents in poverty that they can get.

Like Bardhan, I have argued that the poor need credit reform and other reforms (of water rights, marketing systems, and so on) to benefit fully from land reform. Such arguments, I now feel, are doubtful. Rural markets, even financial ones, adapt to the new demand structures created by land reform. It is dangerous to make land reform appear to require so many ancillary actions that governments, forced to choose between doing everything and doing nothing, prefer the latter.

Participation

In Bardhan's discussion of the third force—not states, not markets, but civil society, local institutions, and nongovernmental organizations (NGOs)—against poverty, he rightly emphasizes a greater voice for the poor as a benefit of land reform that economic analysis generally neglects. Some of the programs that he discusses—such as Maharashtra's Employment Guarantee Scheme (compare Dev 1994) and Bangladesh's Grameen Bank—have stimulated local groups of the poor, brought together by the schemes, to agitate for their rights (Lipton 1996, p. 58–59).

However, more precise concepts of "civil society" are needed if we are to define its scope and its limits in fighting poverty. Civil society, in Hegel's sense of peacefully contesting organizations and individuals operating in the political sphere, has as a precondition civil society in Hobbes's sense: an implicit contract by which all individuals and groups abjure violence and thereby give the state a monopoly over it. Even Hobbesian civil society has a precondition: a state able to control its own agents. Plainly, the first of these conditions is not met in many developing countries, and the second is not met in several. Participation by the poor would achieve little in Somalia.

Beyond these preconditions for its existence, civil society must be sufficiently strong—in itself and among the poor—if civil associations (in the sense used by de Tocqueville) are to resolve the state-market dilemma in favor of the poor. The dilemma is that state agents, if unconstrained by market forces, arrogate power to themselves; market forces, if unconstrained by the state, arrogate power to victors in the marketplace; yet state agents and marketplace victors, if strong enough, seek to eliminate one another, removing the constraint on abusive power. States and markets need each other, yet subvert or destroy each other—unless constrained from doing so by a powerful, yet competitive, civil society (Lipton 1991). In many countries, such as Kenya, civil society exists but is too weak to fulfill this constraining role.

Hegel had two fears for civil society: that it would stray into the proper preserve of the state—foreign policy—and that it would underrepresent the poor (Avineri 1983). Bardhan's statement that a sustained, effective antipoverty program requires that the poor be active and vigilant assumes that they not only have the skills to organize, but also can meet the costs and take the risks, and that the state (what else?) will protect them against extra-economic coercion rather than siding with their masters. Bardhan's practical suggestions and examples are valuable, and he is fully aware of the dangers of communitarian romanticism.

I am struck by the lack of novelty of several current antipoverty initiatives: peer-monitored local credit is exactly what the Indian primary credit cooperatives—and the Danish cooperatives that inspired them—were supposed to be about in the 1950s, and much of the NGO rural movement reads like a throwback to the 1950s ethos of community development. Even initially, these earlier initiatives seldom reached the poorest, and after a few years they were severely harmed by state co-optation and by private power structures.

Will their modern successors do better? The answer depends crucially on whether they are linked to the acquisition by the poor of performing assets: a little adequately irrigated cropland, a sewing machine or a buffalo (as in the much-derided Integrated Rural Development Program in India), a saleable qualification or skill. To participate, one needs something to participate with.

Conclusion

The reaction against *Redistribution with Growth* has involved the propositions that growth, at least if labor-intensive, does benefit the poor, but that state-sponsored distribution generates not poverty reduction, but growth-reducing economic rents. Bardhan neatly restores the case for systematic antipoverty policy by stressing redistributive projects that may improve productive efficiency—such as land redistribution that reduces agency costs, or the reduction of educational inequalities that waste or misallocate human resources.

Such microeconomic effects probably underlie the cross-national regression results of Birdsall, Ross, and Sabot (1994), Persson and Tabellini (1994), and Clarke (1995). These results show that inequality—by several different measures (including those emphasizing the share of the poorest) and for several different periods and country groups—is robustly associated with substantially *slower* subsequent growth of real GNP per capita. Very few such associations have proved robust in the face of econometric challenge (Levine and Renelt 1992): the only five surviving factors clearly associated with faster subsequent growth are higher shares of fixed investment, better human capital indicators (especially secondary education), lower birthrates and lower death rates (Kelley and Schmidt 1994), and lower inequality between rich and poor. Poverty reduction may be at least as clearly (and importantly) a *cause* of growth as an *effect*. Not only in East Asia do land reform, reduction of child labor, and widely spread education jointly stimulate poverty reduction and then growth.

References

Avineri, Shlomo. 1983. *Hegel's Theory of the Modern State.* London: Cambridge University Press.

Birdsall, Nancy, David Ross, and Richard Sabot. 1994. "Inequality and Growth Reconsidered." St. Anthony's College, Oxford.

Binswanger, Hans, Klaus Deininger, and Gershon Feder. 1995. "Power, Distortions, Revolt, and Reform in Agricultural Land Relations." In T.N. Srinivasan and Jere Behrman, eds., *Handbook of Development Economics,* vol. 3. Amsterdam: North Holland.

Chenery, Hollis B., Montek S. Ahluwalia, Clive Bell, John H. Duloy, and Richard Jolly. 1974. *Redistribution with Growth.* New York: Oxford University Press.

Clarke, George. 1995. "More Evidence on Income Distribution and Growth." *Journal of Development Economics* 47(2): 403–27.

Dev, S. Mahendra. 1994. "Maharashtra's Employment Guarantee Scheme: Lessons from Long Experience." Indira Gandhi Institute of Development Research. Ahmedabad, India.

Foster, James, Joel Greer, and Erik Throbecke. 1984. "A Class of Decomposable Poverty Measures." *Econometrica* 52: 761–65.

Kelley, Allen C., and Robert M. Schmidt. 1994. *Population and Income Change: Recent Evidence.* World Bank Discussion Paper 249. Washington, D.C.

Levine, Ross, and David Renelt. 1992. "A Sensitivity Analysis of Cross-Country Growth Regressions." *American Economic Review* 82(4):942–63.

Lipton, Michael. 1991. "The State-Market Dilemma, Civil Society, and Structural Adjustment: Any Cross-Commonwealth Lessons?" *Round Table* 31(7):21–31.

———. 1993. "Land Reform as Unfinished Business: The Case for Not Stopping." *World Development* 21(4):641–58.

———. 1996. *Success in Anti-Poverty.* Issues in Development Discussion Paper 8. Geneva: International Labour Office, Development and Technical Cooperation Department.

Lipton, Michael, and Martin Ravallion. 1995. "Poverty and Policy." In In T.N. Srinivasan and Jere Behrman, eds., *Handbook of Development Economics,* vol. 3. Amsterdam: North Holland.

Migot-Adholla, Shem, Peter Hazell, Benoît Blarel, and Francis Place. 1991. "Indigenous Land Rights in Sub-Saharan Africa: A Constraint on Productivity?" *World Bank Economic Review* 5(1):155–75.

Persson, Torsten, and Guido Tabellini. 1994. "Is Inequality Harmful for Growth?" *American Economic Review* 84(3):600–21.

Wood, Adrian. 1994. *North-South Trade, Employment, and Inequality: Changing Fortunes in a Skill-Driven World.* Oxford: Clarendon.

Floor Discussion of "Research on Poverty and Development Twenty Years after *Redistribution with Growth*," by Pranab Bardhan

Aparticipant from Bangladesh said he thought that it would have been useful if Bardhan had linked the discussions of land reform and enabling local governments. If you want viable government institutions that have not been appropriated by the rich or the mafia, he explained, you need a property-owning structure that enables the poor to be effective players in the political game. Many of the initiatives by nongovernmental organizations (NGOs)—including the Grameen Bank—have been ineffective because they have been unable to transcend local power structures. For fifteen years, the participant continued, West Bengal has been run by a government that considers itself Marxist. Such a structure could have influenced the local environment in a way that transcended the power of local property owners. The objective of land reform, then, should be to change social structures so that the poor can transcend the immediate, dominant influence of the rich and share access to resources. The purpose of such reform was not simply to increase equality, but to induce transformation. Although some World Bank staff believe that it occupies the middle ground on these issues, most people in developing countries see the Bank on the far right.

Michael Lipton (discussant) said he did not agree that the World Bank was on the far right. He thought that there was a rationale for the Bank's centrist, consensual approach to such issues as land reform. Many people believe that there is a head-on conflict between land reform and property rights and that secure property rights are essential for efficient, market-based capitalist development. Are such complaints about land reform justified? If they are, can they be resolved? If they are not, can they be refuted? South Africa, for example, is considering market-based land reform. This concept, although suspect, is interesting and must be explored.

Before discussing property rights, Lipton continued, it was important to determine whether the property rights were genuine or whether they were property "wrongs." By this he meant that most large landholdings were acquired by conquest and confirmed by bequest, and so do not correspond to income earned by con-

This session was chaired by Ismail Serageldin, vice president, Environmentally Sustainable Development, at the World Bank.

Annual World Bank Conference on Development Economics 1995
©1996 The International Bank for Reconstruction and Development / THE WORLD BANK

tributing to the economy. People who are looking toward redistribution with growth as a means of alleviating poverty in the developing world should closely examine the issue of bequests and inheritance taxes—taxes that are designed not to enrich governments but to redistribute income to the poor. Land reform may be one of the most important ways of achieving the same goal. A participant from the World Bank concurred with Lipton's comments, adding that the Bank's position was necessarily in the center because only there could it learn from both sides.

Also concurring with Lipton's comments, Bardhan said that he generally finds that the people who do not believe in land reform do believe in secure property rights. But securing property rights is often an important part of land reform in developing countries, where many of the poor are insecure tenants. The West Bengal government has tried (with only partial success) to secure the cultivation rights of farmers who have been cultivating the same piece of land for many years without secure property rights. Lack of tenure—not knowing whether you will be around next year—is a disincentive for long-term investment. So there is not always a conflict between land reform and property rights. Bardhan suggested China after 1978 as an example of a massive but generally well-regarded land reform program. Because it happened from the other end—through decollectivization—few people think of it as land reform, despite the fact that the households involved got relatively equal pieces of land and over time their property rights became more secure.

Bardhan agreed that land reform was essential for enabling the poor to participate in local governance. It was true that for full participation in local government you need certain preconditions and that these conditions would not exist in Somalia, for example, for some time. Even in India, although the poor were somewhat organized in West Bengal, the conditions and level of organization are often dismal. But Bardhan was optimistic about the potential of democracy. Even though the poor may not get things done for them, or done in their favor, the power to vote made them more assertive, if only at the voting booth. Even where assets are extremely unequal, everyday forms of resistance develop over time.

Land reform is one means of achieving the initial asset distribution required to get effective income distribution, said a participant from Chile, but privatization is another means of improving income distribution—perhaps not to society's poorest people, but generally. But most privatization in the West has been to friends and relations, responded Lipton. A cynic might say that the problem with privatization is that it is done by the state; certainly West Africa's experience has not been all that different. But privatization can do what the participant suggested, continued Lipton. Land reform in Romania is an interesting example. There, large collective (though not state) farms were given back to individual small family farmers. So it can be done, although it is important to redistribute the water rights along with the land rights.

As for developing local communities' capabilities for delivering better services to the poor, the participant from Chile wondered if the same objective could be achieved more efficiently by having the government subsidize demand through means testing. Chile uses a voucher system to educate the poor and subsidies to house them, and the system works well.

In discussing the efficient functioning of markets, including labor markets, a participant from the International Confederation of Free Trade Unions said that the rights of people involved in those markets should be examined. Someone had mentioned child labor, for example, but discussions of the East Asian miracle generally do not cover basic rights, rights in the workplace, or the rights of the poor. We are not moving quickly toward an equation of competition in which people—especially workers and the poor—are empowered to pursue their best interests. Grassroots efforts to organize workers seem to be the only solution. Individual workers cannot claim their rights or negotiate wages or reduce income inequalities. People should have the right to organize effectively, as the International Labour Organisation conventions guarantee, said the participant. Against that background, she asked Bardhan to clarify the concept of anarchic grouping of NGOs (what he had called "anarcho-communitarianism").

It was true, responded Bardhan, that NGOs and others have tried to organize the poor locally, an effort he supported, but that such efforts had to proceed carefully. In India, for example, despite many decades of attempts at organization, very few poor laborers are organized. Just as there is inequality of assets, so there is inequality of organizational resources. The better workers are the ones who get organized and who get what they demand. Countries often end up with a labor aristocracy, which becomes a tremendously important vested interest group that sometimes blocks reform. Labor organizations often end up supporting workers who are already well-endowed with organizational resources, rather than the poor.

A consulting engineer asked the participants to comment on the problem of infiltration, explaining that as many as 100 million poor people from Bangladesh, Sri Lanka, and elsewhere are believed to have been brought into India by political parties (although they deny it) to register as voters, have settled there, and contribute greatly to India's persistent poverty. Lipton responded that it was a great tribute to India that so many people go there because they are able to live better there. He hoped that India would not adopt the disgraceful policy that his country, Britain, had followed of restricting the immigration of people who want to move in order to work. The more migration there is, the better it is for the poor and for the world. But since few poor people can afford the initial fixed costs and risks of migration, the poorest are not usually the ones who benefit from migration. Bardhan concurred.

Government Provision and Regulation of Economic Support in Old Age

Peter Diamond

There have been major disappointments of expectations of retirement income in both public and private sectors. Governments have contributed to the likelihood of publicly generated disappointments, and they have intervened to affect the frequency and pattern of privately generated disappointments. Nevertheless, both public and private retirement arrangements have contributed to the flow of retirement income of many workers. The concern is to identify mechanisms for government provision and regulation of retirement income that limit such disappointments and to provide retirement income in a manner that adequately balances redistribution and insurance on the one hand and market inefficiencies on the other. The article contrasts approaches built around contribution rates and benefit formulas and discusses striking balances and respecting political forces within each approach. The discussion complements and, in places, criticizes the analysis in Averting the Old Age Crisis *(World Bank 1994).*

My topic is the role of government as provider and regulator of income for the elderly through formal systems. People put forward many arguments for government involvement in the provision of retirement income.[1] While market imperfections and income distribution are generally among the reasons mentioned, the central reason is paternalistic—the belief that left to themselves, many people would not save enough for their own retirement. I begin by considering the economics of mandated savings or contributions (leaving political arguments for later).

The distinction between defined benefit and defined contribution retirement income systems is central. On one side are systems that are organized around formulas relating retirement income flows to individual earnings histories and that also need to determine financing. On the other side are systems that are organized around a contribution rate and that also need to determine the retirement income flows that follow from the individual histories of contribution. Knowledge of how

Peter Diamond is Paul A. Samuelson Professor of Economics at the Massachusetts Institute of Technology.

Annual World Bank Conference on Development Economics 1995

both benefits and contributions are determined is needed in order to evaluate a system. The defined benefit–defined contribution distinction refers not only to the laws and plans of such systems, but also to the mindset of those thinking about them. How defined benefit and defined contribution systems might ideally be used is contrasted with how they tend to be used in practice. Moreover, some important issues vary depending on whether a new system is being created or a mature system is being modified.

Welfare Analysis of Amount and Availability of Mandated Retirement Savings

To begin, let us examine the level of mandated or forced savings. For a simple case, assume that the accumulated savings are available only for retirement income and that the rate of return (adjusted for the value of the insurance provided) is roughly the same as it is outside the mandate. For this purpose it makes little difference whether the funds are invested in the private economy or are bookkeeping entries. For other purposes, this distinction is very important. Now assume that some people save rationally and according to a life-cycle model, while others do no saving whatsoever. Finally, assume that the optimal amount of savings relative to earnings varies in the population over some range, but one that is not too wide. The simplest approach would identify a welfare gain from forcing myopic people to save, provided the forced savings rate were below the amount they would rationally save. In parallel, there would be no effect on rational savers, provided the forced savings rate were below the amount they rationally do save.

Uniform Savings Rate

A major problem with this simple approach is the omission of the multiple reasons for saving and dissaving. A rational saver might devote all of savings first to home purchase, then to education of children, and only later to retirement savings. An accumulation restricted to retirement savings would not be available for unpredicted needs or opportunities. Forcing rational savers to commit their savings to retirement is inefficient. The size of this inefficiency depends on the nature of capital and insurance markets and of government programs to help with home purchase, education, and random calls on wealth, such as unemployment and medical expenses. This analysis suggests that the balance between forcing some people to save too much and allowing others to save too little starts at a lower savings rate than that needed to fully finance an optimal retirement income on average. Use of a forced savings rate that is uniform across all ages compounds this problem. Varying forced savings rates by age (as in Switzerland) might be sensible, although it involves political and administrative difficulties.

With mandated retirement saving both current and accumulated savings are outside an individual's control. Wealth in a mandated account represents wealth that is subject to a capital market imperfection: the inability to use such wealth early. Some such limitation is a necessary part of mandating saving for retirement. But multiple-purpose savings are another option. Withdrawals might be allowed for a variety of purposes, as in Singapore. Evaluations of such proposals need to balance the lower level of forced savings just for retirement with the risk of excessive earlier withdrawals for other purposes. The higher the mandated savings rate, the stronger the economic (and political) case for multiple uses of the accumulated savings. The interaction between withdrawal rules and the politics of programs such as unemployment insurance and medical insurance also needs to be considered. If earlier withdrawals are allowed, such programs could then be restricted to those with low savings accumulations. But this means testing in other programs generates distorting implicit taxes.

Uniform Retirement Age

Mandating retirement savings also raises questions of the vehicle for converting accumulations into retirement income flows and of the minimum age at which such conversion is allowed. The same sort of myopia that justifies mandated saving is likely still to be present (in part) at older ages. For that reason, in some settings the funds are made available only as income flows, not as a lump sum. For the same reason a minimum age is specified at which the funds become available.

Selecting the age when mandated accumulations become available involves a tension between two issues. Some people will myopically choose to consume these funds too soon, just as they would have chosen not to save for retirement. Others will be prevented from making a rational consumption decision by the capital market imperfection of limited or no access to this accumulation. Concern about both of these issues is compounded by the effect of the choice of retirement age on the decision to retire as well as on consumption levels. That is, myopically, some people will inefficiently choose to stop working at the official retirement age because these funds become available, while others, who would rationally stop working before reaching retirement age, will inefficiently continue because of the capital market imperfection.

It is difficult to know how to estimate the balance between these factors at different minimum retirement ages. Declining consumption during retirement might be one sign of too-early retirement. Finding elderly widows in poverty, who (possibly with their husbands) were not in poverty earlier in the retirement period might be another sign. Families with low income whose members work despite poor health just before retirement age might be a sign of too-late retirement. And no matter what age is selected, there will be some inefficiency from the capital market limitation inherent in mandated retirement saving.

Disability insurance is one policy tool to limit the cost of this market imperfection. Adjusting the relationship between the size of the retirement income stream and the age when benefits start is another. This can be done through partial adjustment of benefits on an actuarial basis in a defined benefit system or through tax treatment of withdrawals in a defined contribution system. (Methods of accumulation and of acquisition of retirement income flows are discussed later.) But the concern remains whether, on average, the "wrong" people select early retirement.

Like a uniform savings rate, a uniform retirement age is inefficient. There are systematic differences in life expectancy—by gender, income, education—not just when measured at retirement age but also when measured earlier. Another complication comes from private arrangements that encourage early retirement from a career job without necessarily involving retirement from the labor force. Private disincentives for labor mobility can be efficient or inefficient. In considering such private arrangements, it is useful to know the extent to which they are jointly rational for a firm and its workforce rather than the result of important asymmetries in information and understanding.

Because of these various inefficiencies, there are income distribution implications from mandated savings, even when all the accumulated savings remain the property of the worker. For example, workers with no interest in an estate lose out if they die before reaching retirement age. The likelihood of early death varies, and people with shorter life expectancies may rationally choose to save less and retire early. Thus the inefficiencies in a mandated retirement savings program may be disproportionately concentrated on some groups. In addition, the administrative costs of the program must be allocated among workers in some way, generating an income distribution issue.[2]

Implications of These Inefficiencies

The inefficiencies in mandatory retirement savings make a case for a mandate smaller than the amount (by itself) that provides a "sensible" replacement income rate. With a smaller mandate there will be an uneven pattern of private responses to the need for more retirement income. For example, in the United States, roughly half the workforce is covered by private pensions. An evaluation of the outcome with a smaller mandate needs to recognize the pattern of higher coverage for older workers. It also needs to balance inadequate savings for some without a larger mandate with too large savings for others with a larger mandate.

Basic Systems

In distinguishing between defined contribution and defined benefit systems,[3] it is useful to have real systems in mind. I will contrast some elements of the systems in Chile (primarily defined contribution) and the United States (primarily defined benefit).[4] I choose these because they are well-designed systems. I do not intend to imply that other countries with different administrative capacities or different political structures should not choose other versions.

Generating Retirement Income Flows

A defined contribution system bases retirement income on the history of mandated savings or tax payments. A defined benefit system bases retirement income on a history of earnings within the system, earnings that have been subject to tax. The two systems differ especially strongly during a period of rising taxes. Generating a retirement income flow from mandated savings requires a mechanism for converting the accumulations into retirement income flows.

Chile offers two options, both available on reaching retirement age (whether the worker chooses to retire or not).[5] Under the phased-withdrawal option individuals make monthly withdrawals from their accounts, subject to a maximum allowable withdrawal. Individuals bear some longevity risk, limited by a guaranteed minimum pension, and some rate of return risk on their remaining accumulations. The other option is to purchase an annuity indexed to the consumer price index (CPI). The benefit amount depends on the size of the individual's accumulation, the age when purchasing the annuity, and the terms set by the insurance company selected by the worker.[6]

The U.S. system for generating an annuity differs in a number of ways. Benefits are based on the history of earnings subject to tax, not the history of the amounts of tax paid. Earnings in different years are combined using a wage index rather than an interest rate. The benefit calculation uses the best thirty-five years of earnings, not all years.[7] Earnings histories are converted into income flows using a legislated benefit formula that recognizes the size of the thirty-five-year average indexed earnings and the age when the benefit flow starts. No other individual differences are considered. Benefits are available between ages sixty-two and seventy only when a worker has sufficiently low earnings, perhaps as a result of retirement. After age seventy, benefits are paid without this consideration. There are also legislated differences in the benefit formula across cohorts.

In a defined contribution system the market for annuities has no concern for redistribution. Market forces determine the markup between the expected present discounted value of benefits and the price paid for the annuity. The market is sensitive to interest rates, and the annuity varies with the life expectancy of the worker to the extent insurance companies recognize (and are allowed to recognize) differences in life expectancy. In contrast, a defined benefit system has a legislated formula for determining annuities.

An important element for analyzing an annuity market is the size of the markup over risk-adjusted costs, reflecting how competitive the market is. It is also important to know how life expectancy tables are used in setting prices. Insurance companies will have incentives to try to identify life expectancy differences across people, whether annuity prices vary or not. People who believe that their life expectancy is considerably shorter than the expectancy implicit in the quoted rates will have an incentive to avoid annuities and opt for phased withdrawal. I have heard it argued that removing the phased-withdrawal option in Chile would remove the problem of adverse selection since then everyone would have to purchase an annuity. This argument is based on an idealized market model that assigns each firm a proportionate slice of the market risk. In fact, as we observe with health insurance, companies devote considerable resources to attracting the best risks, given the pricing policy. Thus adverse selection in the sense of inefficient allocations would remain a problem. Further, the ability to decline to purchase an annuity may have a large impact on perceived elasticities of annuity demand and so on equilibrium markups in this market. Some countries have mandated employer-provided pensions rather than individual savings. This arrangement makes it easier to form groups for annuity purchase, considerably reducing administrative costs.

Intergenerational Redistribution

Mortality expectations enter the two systems differently. In Chile the market recognizes differences in life expectancy both within and across generations. In the United States the benefit formula is the same for everyone in a cohort, though the formula does change over time. Sweden's defined benefit system uses intergenerational differences in mortality as a basis for indexing. Another difference arises when a worker dies before retirement age. In Chile the accumulation goes to the worker's estate, partially offsetting the cost of survivors insurance insofar as there are survivors covered by the system. In the United States when a worker dies without survivors recognized by Social Security, there is no return to the worker's estate as a consequence of taxes paid. Instead, the taxes help finance the benefits of those who do reach retirement age. It is important to recognize that many twenty-one year olds will not live to sixty-five. According to the 1990 U.S. life table, 24 percent of men and 14 percent of women age twenty-one will not survive to sixty-five.

It is a central difference that defined contribution systems accumulate taxes while defined benefit systems accumulate earnings. With the common pattern of rising tax rates, a defined benefit system has a strong tendency to redistribute to early retirees. This is a strong tendency, but not a mathematical necessity. The benefit formula could be adjusted as the length of the earnings history grows or as the financing of the system changes. Interestingly, in the United States the shorter averaging period for retirees used when the system was young further increased the redistribution to these retirees.

In principle, a defined contribution system could achieve a similar redistribution by adding government debt to the accounts of early retirees and paying off the debt over time. Chile did this in its transition from a defined benefit to a defined contribution system. Politically, such allocations seem different at a transition than at the start of a new system. Implicit and explicit redistributions are politically different, even when the source of the explicit transfer remains vague, with no plan specifying who in the future will pay for it. Politically, it seems very different whether one is simply applying the "same" benefit formula to different generations or voting a transfer of assets.

I find it interesting that there is a similar issue in corporate pension plans in the United States. It is common to give "past service credits" to older workers when starting a defined benefit plan but uncommon to give assets to older workers when starting a defined contribution plan. The two acts seem different psychologically. When the focus is on a benefit formula, comparing the benefit levels of different workers and recognizing the preplan past seem natural and perhaps fair. When the focus is on accumulations, transfers seem less natural and less fair—starting with the same initial accounts (zero) seems fair.[8]

Different organizing principles highlight different implications of chosen actions, some of which are more likely to trigger reactions. It is not a matter of one system being more "transparent" then another, but of different systems focusing attention on different facets. If it is considered important that people be aware of the benefit-level implications of a retirement income system, then the greater transparency of this dimension of outcomes in defined benefit systems is appealing. If an awareness of the wealth redistribution implications of a system is considered to be more important, then the greater transparency of this dimension of outcomes in defined contribution systems wins out. Indeed, cognitive psychologists and public opinion pollsters find large "framing" effects, with responses being very sensitive to how questions are posed (Tversky and Kahneman 1981; Yankelovich 1991).

It is easy to applaud when the elderly poor receive considerably more than they would receive from programs focused solely on relieving poverty. And it is easy to be appalled when the well-off elderly also get windfalls, often larger windfalls than the poor elderly. What is hard is to decide is whether the combination is better or worse than doing neither, since sometimes those may be the real alternatives. It seems to be the case that a single defined benefit system tends to do better than multiple defined benefit systems in limiting perverse transfers.

Once a defined benefit system is mature, it has far less scope for such intergenerational redistributions. Indeed, the major issue currently is how to make existing systems sustainable given resources and benefit promises. A dislike of the type of intergenerational redistribution that typically happens when starting a new system would be reason to oppose starting a new defined benefit system but would not be a reason to favor change from a mature defined benefit system to a new defined contribution system. Whether such a change helps with the political problem of making an unsustainable system sustainable is a different question, one on which we have little evidence.

Defined benefit and defined contribution systems respond differently to changing circumstances, such as increased life expectancy. With a defined contribution system the adaptation does not require legislation. If the mandated savings rate ceases to be appropriate, the system continues to function, just less satisfactorily. With a defined benefit system benefits and taxes are legislated separately, and legislation is required to bring them back into line when economic or demographic forces have pulled them apart. Because the future is unpredictable, periodic legislation is likely to be needed. Though it is certainly possible to build automatic adjustment into the legislation (as with the adjustment to life expectancy in Sweden), I am not aware of any fully automatic system. Repeated legislation in response to changing circumstances could be good or bad, depending on the quality of the legislative process.

Incentives and Distributions

There is a tension between redistribution and incentives and between insurance and incentives.

Redistribution and Incentives

Whether income provision for the poor elderly happens through an earnings-related retirement income system or a separate safety net, the income going to the poor must be generated from someone at some time. Such revenue gathering necessarily involves disincentives. Similarly, the rules limiting the set of people receiving such transfers also have disincentive effects. That is, revenue generation and payment limitations involve the basic disincentive-distribution tradeoff of tax theory. The question is the best time and place to locate the unavoidable disincentives (and the right size of the redistribution). There is no necessary advantage from separating earnings-related and redistributive pensions in separate programs or pillars; incentives depend on all of the programs that affect the returns to work and saving.

Workers respond to perceived incentives, which are not necessarily accurate. If some young workers myopically apply a high discount rate to future benefits, then future benefits have little current value. This implies a labor market distortion from the payroll tax or mandated savings rate, even if there is a full link between current earnings and future benefits. For such workers weakening the link adds little to the net distortion. A similar result holds for workers who do not believe they will survive to retirement age and place no value on having an estate. It may be, however, that young workers react differently to differently described systems, allowing a potential role for separate pillars, but I am unaware of any direct evidence on the subject.

While distortions necessarily follow from any kind of redistribution, political economy may make the tradeoff worse than it needs to be. This creates a dilemma, one that was well stated by Robert Solow (1980, p. 1) in his presidential address to the American Economic Association:

> Most of us are conscious of a conflict that arises in our minds and consciences because, while we think it is usually a mistake to fiddle the price system to achieve distributional goals, we realize that the public and the political process are perversely more willing to do that than to make the direct transfers we would prefer. If we oppose all distorting transfers, we end up opposing transfers altogether. Some of us seem to welcome the excuse, but most of us feel uncomfortable. I don't think there is any very good way to resolve that conflict in practice.

Insurance and Incentives

In a similar fashion there is a tension between insurance and incentives. There is also an intertwining of these two issues: social insurance affects both redistribution and insurance, as well as incentives. Indeed, insurance is just redistribution viewed from an earlier time.

Consider a forty-year-old female worker who is uncertain about what her life expectancy will be when she retires, say, at age sixty-five. To insure against this longevity risk she could purchase an annuity now when she is forty, or she could join a system in which the conversion between accumulations and annuities at age sixty-five is independent of (or less than fully actuarially dependent on) her life expectancy as measured at age sixty-five. To see the intertwining between this insurance issue and distribution, consider a forty-year-old male worker with the same history of earnings. An annuity purchased at age forty to begin at age sixty-five will be priced differently for him, if prices reflect life expectancy. However, receiving insurance from a system with the same conversion factor for men and women at age sixty-five involves redistribution from male to female workers. Thus providing insurance for longevity risk redistributes toward those who are expected to live longer. It also tends to redistribute to the better off, given the positive correlation between life expectancy and earnings, unless there are offsets in benefit determination. There is one mitigating factor. Having a longer retirement period to finance makes an individual poorer, even if it adds to lifetime utility. That is, annual earnings levels are not a fully satisfactory gauge of the marginal utility of lifetime income.

The 1994 World Bank study *Averting the Old Age Crisis* lists some insurance market issues. "Insurance market failures—adverse selection, moral hazard, and correlations among individuals make insurance against many risks (such as the risks of longevity, disability, investment, inflation, and depression) unavailable" (p. 6).[9] Among the risks noted for defined contribution plans, *Averting* identifies uncertainty about "the duration of working and retirement periods" (p. 83). I discuss two of these risks.

Economists typically see a CPI-indexed annuity as the appropriate form for retirement income.[10] Considering relative incomes and risk sharing, there is also a case for relating annuities to average wages in the economy or to a mix of wages and prices.[11] Another option is indexing annuities to returns on asset portfolios, which would offer some risk sharing of returns.[12] Paralleling the case for mandated savings is a case for mandated annuitization of retirement income. For many people unindexed contracts seem "safer" than indexed ones (Shafir, Diamond, and Tversky 1994). Indexing an annuity, holding its cost constant, lowers initial benefits to finance later ones. It is not clear that people are sufficiently far sighted or free of money illusion to make this choice well. This issue is important when we consider problems of joint life annuities—some people will not look after their dependents adequately.

Another risk is that of a short working life. Disability insurance provides some protection, but disability evaluations are subject to errors. Some people inefficiently stop work to receive benefits, while others are denied benefits and struggle to work or have low incomes. For this second group the problem is compounded by limited access to retirement savings. Other workers without health problems can also experience low earning opportunities relative to their experience and expectations. Bouts of unemployment, working in a declining industry, deteriorating skills, and the like can result in lower lifetime earnings.

Without systematic redistribution rules, defined contribution systems do not provide insurance against randomly lower earnings. Retirement benefits are based on accumulated savings; with a shortened career there is a smaller accumulation and lower benefits. Defined benefit systems can provide insurance against a short career by adjusting the relationship between benefits and the age at which they are claimed. A defined benefit system can decrease benefits for early retirement at a rate that is somewhat less than a full actuarial adjustment for life expectancy. This provides insurance against a short working career at a cost of an implicit tax on work in later years, one that has a deadweight burden. Optimal insurance principles call for balancing insurance provision and the moral hazard problem of this implicit tax. Thus the implicit taxation of work should be neither zero nor 100 percent (Diamond and Mirrlees 1978, 1986).

Insuring against a short career is necessarily intertwined with redistribution to those who have shorter careers even when no uncertainty is involved. With the tendency for workers with higher earnings to have good opportunities to work longer, the result is a redistribution toward lower earners among full-career workers. There is also a countervailing effect in that those with higher incomes can afford earlier retirement, making part of the redistribution perverse. This linking of good and bad redistributions is a recurring issue.

Defined benefit systems base benefits on a specified part of workers' earnings history. In the United States benefits are based on the thirty-five years of the highest wage-indexed earnings. Many defined benefit systems use much shorter averaging periods in determining benefits. Use of a much shorter averaging period causes greater labor market distortions since there is zero marginal benefit in many years and a very large marginal benefit in a few—two sources of inefficiency. (For marginal net taxes in the United States, see Feldstein and Samwick 1992.) A short averaging period is also more susceptible to manipulation and opens the worker to more risk, because benefits are very sensitive to earnings just before retirement. Lack of indexing exacerbates this risk. Though I have seen no analysis of this issue, I expect that the optimal averaging period for a defined benefit system would be close to a full career.

Social Risks

The widespread trend of improvement in mortality rates has not been uniform. Periods of rapid improvement have been followed by periods of slow and even negative improvement. There is heated debate among demographers about the eventual shape of the mortality table and the likely pattern of future improvements. The future course of mortality rates is a major social risk, one that must be borne by some group, however we organize retirement incomes. The futures of wage growth and interest rates are also large societywide risks. Different systems of retirement income provision spread these risks differently.

In a defined contribution system individuals bear the mortality risk up to the time of annuity purchase. Purchases from stock insurance companies place the mortality risk on shareholders (unless there is company bankruptcy or a government bailout). As a societywide risk, the realization of mortality rates will have widespread equilibrium effects. In contrast, purchases from mutual insurance companies, which are "owned" by policyholders rather than shareholders, place the risks on current and future purchasers of insurance. The exact distribution of these risks depends on the practices of the mutual insurance companies (including the accumulation of reserves), the demand behavior of future purchasers of insurance, and the constraints from competition in the insurance market.

Similarly, in the group provision of pension benefits by employers or unions, some risk is shifted to future employees as pension plans change and wages fail to fully offset the changes. This characteristic is clearest in the case of unionized firms, where collective bargaining sets both current wages and current pension benefits. The ongoing health of an industry is an important part of the future development of pension income.[13]

In a government-run defined benefit plan the allocation of risk depends on the workings of the legislative process, for example, with respect to government responses to surpluses or deficits arising from deviations from expected mortality rates. Potentially, the risks can be spread across generations differently than with a government-mandated defined contribution plan. But whether risks are spread through a market mechanism (as with a government-mandated defined contribution plan with market provision of annuities) or a legislative mechanism (through a defined benefit plan that will be modified in the future), it is difficult for individual workers to form accurate perceptions of the risks they bear. Thus government is a device for dealing with the incompleteness of arrangements for the future. But we need to be concerned with the converse as well, which is that the legislative process is itself a source of risk.

Capital Accumulation and Investment Abroad

The link between capital accumulation and the provision of retirement income has several components. One is the degree of funding or, instead, whether wealth is transferred to new retirees when the system is started. Other pieces are private savings and government budget responses to the design of the system.

An immature system that gives high benefits to retirees results in less capital than one that does not. This is not an indictment of such transfers, since they were designed to raise the consumption of the recipients; it is merely to say that providing such consumption reduces capital accumulation. While a funded system results in more capital than the same system without a fund, another question is the impact on capital accumulation of an unfunded system relative to having no system. To the extent that workers would not save on their own, neither taxes paid nor promised future benefits affect savings; consumption is simply transferred from the young to the old. In contrast, to the extent that workers are rational savers, there is a reduction in current savings in response to expected future benefits and to any gain in lifetime wealth. Both types of workers are present in varying numbers in different countries.

Similarly, the impact on government savings depends on how other taxes and expenditures respond to the presence of the retirement income system. In particular, to the extent that funding of the retirement system finances increased government consumption, it does not contribute to capital accumulation.

With funding comes a need for portfolio management. The form that portfolio management takes (private or public, restricted to government debt or invested in private assets) may affect other government expenditures. There is also a need to consider alternative investment strategies. Financing poor investments is worse than financing good ones—it is better to be on the risk-return frontier than inside it. Comparing various portfolio choices on the risk-return frontier requires evaluating general equilibrium risk bearing.

For example, holding government debt rather than private instruments will make more of a difference in a small, segmented capital market than in a large, liquid one. In a large, liquid market any aggregate difference between the two would be slight, arising from small changes in their rates of return. A fall in the rate of return on private investments and a rise in the rate on government debt will affect investment and the government budget. But the long-run aggregate effects of an "open market operation" that replaces government debt with private securities is probably small (Bosworth 1996). In contrast, in a small, segmented capital market investments are more likely to "stay" where they are put—the market adjustments tending to offset the "open market operation" will be smaller.

Returns on a fund portfolio are easy to assess. It is more complex to consider the returns to workers implicit in the retirement income system. In particular, the role of redistribution needs to be recognized. For example, it would be wrong to compare the returns on a mandatory savings pillar, ignoring a separate redistributive pillar, with the returns in a joint savings-redistributive pillar. It is particularly important to include in rate of return calculations any financing of new retirees at the start of the system, since that financing falls on future taxpayers in some form.

One advantage of investment in private assets is the potential contribution to the development of capital markets. This was a major benefit of the Chilean reform. But this capital market development did not follow automatically from the introduction of the privately managed mandatory savings scheme. Extensive development of capital market regulation was a critical part of the privatization. Countries will vary in the extent to which they will benefit from such development. OECD countries would have little or no market development benefit. Some countries would find capital market reform to be beyond their regulatory abilities.

Another issue is whether asset decisions should be made at the individual, group, or country level. The gains from increased choice depend on the extent to which people have different risk preferences and understand the risk-return tradeoffs. In the short run the gains from increased individual choice of asset portfolios are likely to vary with the financial sophistication of the population.

Diversifying assets internationally reduces the dependence of retirement income on risks in the home country. Some international diversification seems good, especially for small countries. The argument from standard finance considerations is that funds should hold "world portfolios."[14] But this argument ignores the impact on the level of capital in the home country. The world capital market is not perfect; the level of investment in a small country depends on where pension funds are invested. There is a cost to foreign investment, paid through the higher rate of return needed to attract foreigners. There is a literature on the optimal degree of openness to capital movements, which I have not studied. My point here is that the pension discussion should recognize these issues. Nevertheless, some significant investment abroad seems valuable for risk diversification, particularly where inflation risk is large.

Actual Markets

It is important to understand how markets actually work, as opposed to how idealized competitive markets are modeled. We think of privatization as a route to greater efficiency and lower costs. Yet a surprising aspect of the Chilean reform has been the high cost of running this privatized system—notwithstanding Beveridge's reference in 1942 to the "markedly lower cost of administration in most forms of State Insurance" (p. 286).

Public or Private

The administrative costs of the new Chilean system include those of the mutual funds that manage the mandatory retirement savings funds and those of the insurance companies that produce disability insurance, life insurance, and annuities.[15] Valdés-Prieto (1994) estimated an average administrative charge per active worker in 1991 of $89.10 a year. This was 2.94 percent of average taxable earnings or nearly a quarter of the 13 percent average charge being paid by Chilean workers to generate the 10 percent mandatory savings rate plus disability and survivors' benefits.

The cost per person is not far from the costs found in other privately managed pension systems, such as private defined benefit pensions in the United States, but it is considerably higher than the administrative costs in well-run, unified government-managed systems. (Note, however, that not all defined benefit systems are well run.) For example, Valdés-Prieto estimates an annual cost for the U.S. social security system of $15 to $20 a person on the same basis. But Valdés-Prieto's estimate includes only a small payment from the Social Security Administration to the Internal Revenue Service to cover payroll tax collection, and it does not follow good accounting practice in measuring of capital costs (Sunden and Mitchell 1994). The costs of running a pension system are neither proportional to average wages nor independent of them. Thus it is not obvious how to compare costs across countries of different sizes and different wages in the absence of an estimated cost function. Nonetheless, however the administrative costs are adjusted, they are much higher in Chile than in the United States.

Apart from any country differences there is the issue of the administrative efficiency of relying on the private market. For example, in the U.S. life insurance industry costs run at 12–14 percent of annual benefits (American Council of Life Insurance 1992), while the Social Security Administration reports administrative costs of less than 1 percent of annual benefits. Even doubling the social security system costs for accounting omissions would leave them well below the private market cost.

Individual annuity markets are generally costly markets. The Chilean experience, as reported in Valdés-Prieto (1994), shows an average spread between the internal rate of return on Chilean indexed annuities (using a government-announced life table for the entire population) and returns on comparable-duration indexed bonds issued by a state-owned commercial bank of 1.27 percent for the eighteen months up to the end of 1991. In the United States Friedman and Warshawsky (1990) find spreads of 2.43 percent and 4.35 percent between the implicit interest rates on nominal annuities (using a life table for annuity purchasers and based on the mean policy for the ten largest insurance companies) and the rates on twenty-year U.S. government bonds and corporate bonds placed directly with insurance companies. The numbers for the United States adjust for improvements in the mortality table, while the numbers for Chile do not, a difference of roughly 1 percent per year.

The annuities market in the United States does not operate like an idealized competitive market with a single price. For the period 1968–83 Friedman and Warshawsky found an average implicit interest rate spread of 1.65 percent between the least and the most expensive of the ten largest companies. This gap varied from 0.75 percent in 1968 to 3.70 percent in 1983. Annuities markets based on individual choice have not generally been considered to work well.[16]

A number of elements contribute to the cost differences between private insurance markets and compulsory government systems. One is the economies of scale that come with a single compulsory system without choice. Another is the differences in direct services provided. For example, Chile's fund managers report on individual accounts regularly, whereas the U.S. Social Security Administration provides statements only on request—though a legislated phase-in of regular reporting will soon increase costs. Private, choice-based systems also bear the costs of competing to attract more customers (advertising, sales personnel). Chile's system has an average of nearly 3.5 salespeople per 1,000 active contributors (Valdés-Prieto 1995); the U.S. Social Security Administration has 0.5 employees per 1,000 insured workers (Sunden and Mitchell 1994). In actual markets demand is much less sensitive to price variation than in idealized competitive models. Thus firms will exercise whatever market power they have. These positive markups allow room for X-inefficiency, and are an incentive for costly spending to attract more customers. Since firms are generally eager to have more business, we can conclude that prices generally exceed marginal costs.[17]

Other contributors to higher costs in private markets are adverse selection and lack of experience in purchasing a product that is difficult to evaluate. Also contributing is the low demand for savings and insurance (the basis for a mandatory program in the first place). The collection of contributions and the delivery of cash benefits are well-defined tasks, more likely to be done efficiently by government than are less well-defined tasks (Wilson 1989). The limited variation in products (associated with limited consumer understanding of and demand for insurance) also keeps the task easy for the government.

Individuals or Groups

Generally, group choice is considerably cheaper than individual choice. For example, in the United States mutual funds aimed at individuals are roughly three times as expensive (relative to assets) as mutual funds aimed at groups and handling large accounts. For that reason a number of countries have mandated employer-provided pensions rather than individual savings. Bateman, Piggott, and Valdés-Prieto (1995) have compared marketing expenses in Chile, which uses individual choice for both accumulation and annuitization, with those in Australia, where the retirement savings mandate is on employers. In Chile nearly 36 percent of the accounting costs of the pension funds are attributed to marketing, while in Australia the share is between 3.2 percent and 6.4 percent. How much of the difference is due to placing the mandate on employers and how much to the nature of regulations in Chile is hard to tell. Employers in Australia set up and run multiemployer funds but do not always employ financial firms to manage them.

Organizing group choice for the annuity market is more difficult because of the greater opportunity for manipulation inherent in the link to employers at the single moment in time when annuities are purchased than the link over time when retirement savings are accumulated. One solution is for the government to organize groups for the purchase of insurance (Diamond 1992). Proposals to reform Chile's annuity market have had rough going, suggesting the difficulty of reforming a system once there are large vested interests.

Political Economy

So far the discussion has considered primarily what can be accomplished with different retirement income systems, not what governments actually do. I turn now to the political economy.

Intergenerational Redistribution

Governments and firms setting up defined benefit systems commonly transfer funds to those nearing retirement age. This redistribution tends to go to both the well off and the less well off; the package may please or displease different people (depending on which effect they weigh more heavily). In addition, defined benefit systems are often set up in a way that is not sustainable, leading to difficult problems of trying to legislate reform and to uncertain and unrealized expectations of workers. Moreover, a defined benefit system will need new legislation from time to time unless it has an automatic adjustment mechanism. These difficulties are a strong argument from a political economy perspective for a defined contribution approach, at least in a society that would have trouble initially in legislating a satisfactory defined benefit system or that expects trouble adjusting it later.

However, once a system has matured and this redistribution is behind it, switching to a defined contribution system will not undo the transfers that have already taken place. Nor will it restore the capital that would have accumulated in the absence of the giveaway. Where transfers are in process but have not yet taken place, they might be lessened by a transition to a defined contribution system—or to a less generous defined benefit system. In considering whether to switch from a defined benefit system to a defined contribution system, a central question is whether such a reform will contribute to the politically difficult act of reducing promised benefits. Workers might be more willing to accept cuts in benefit promises if there were a change in the form of the promise. But an unsustainable defined benefit system could also be reformed by cutting benefits, raising taxes, and indexing promises to costs (for example, longevity) and revenues. The question is whether such an economically viable reform is politically viable, or whether a more radical change would make this difficult political act more palatable. We have little evidence so far on the politics of cutting systems that cost far more than is budgeted, though such experience is likely to accumulate. Whether the lessons can be transferred across countries and across different economic experiences remains to be seen.

Changing from a defined benefit to a defined contribution system requires diverting taxes from financing current benefits to establishing defined contribution accounts. Some other source of finance will be needed to cover the promised benefits that remain. If the other source is current tax revenues, then the transfers to earlier generations are being paid by the generation paying such taxes during the transition—whether this is a good generation to bear this tax burden or not. Alternatively, the transition can be debt financed, by converting the implicit debt of the defined benefit system to explicit debt. Such a conversion alters the growth of the debt and may have indirect consequences—possibly by altering who pays for the transfers that have occurred, possibly by affecting other taxes and government spending, possibly by affecting perceptions in the bond market.

In the United States it is sometimes argued that the current surplus of the social security system is financing the deficit in the rest of the federal budget. It is difficult to evaluate this argument without detailed study of a set of historical examples. To indicate the difficulty, consider that the 1981 Reagan tax cuts that played a major role in generating the country's deficit occurred at a time when social security was in financial difficulty, not surplus. It was 1983 legislation that put social security into short-run surplus, and surpluses have been small relative to the deficit. I think that the difficulty of changing taxes and expenditures has driven the process of attempted deficit reduction in the United States, with social security surpluses having little or no effect. Legislated budget evaluation rules that give a role to social security surpluses are endogenous; one cannot simply look at current rules, given the size of the social security surplus. For example, some in Congress favored a balanced budget amendment that included social security surpluses, but opposed such an amendment if it excluded these surpluses. The endogeneity of budget rules makes it difficult to estimate the link between the funding of the retirement income system and other government actions.

A major question then is whether it is easier to reform an out-of-balance defined benefit system in the context of the larger shrinking or closing associated with starting a defined contribution system. We cannot look to the Chilean reform under a military dictatorship for evidence about reform in a democracy. If a changeover is not particularly helpful in dealing with the difficulties of legislating changes in an unsustainable system, it is not clear what the political economy argument is for encouraging such a changeover. Thus it may be the case that a country that had no defined benefit system in place might want to implement a defined contribution system, whereas if it already had a defined benefit system, it might not want to change.

Intragenerational Redistribution

Defined benefit and defined contribution systems are likely to result in different patterns of redistribution within as well as across generations. The redistribution is likely to be affected by the extent to which distribution issues are concentrated in a single retirement income pillar. In OECD countries, *Averting the Old Age Crisis* observes, the elderly commonly have lower poverty rates than some other segments of the population (figure 3.2, p. 79). In the United States this outcome results from combining redistribution and retirement savings in a single pillar. The impact on poverty of the safety net program for the aged, blind, and disabled, started at the same time as social security, was greatly enhanced by later expansions of social security. Thus there are grounds to worry whether *Averting*'s call for separate pillars is likely to increase the level of poverty among the elderly, perhaps to the level experienced by children. I see little reason to believe that much of the money saved by less redistribution to the elderly will show up as higher benefits for children.

Particularly important for the political economy of redistribution is whether there is a single defined benefit system for the entire economy or separate defined benefit systems for different groups, identified by industry or occupation. Separate systems are much more open to perverse manipulation (redistributing to the well off) and are to be avoided.

Quality of Design and Regulation

By and large, the United States has designed a social security system with a reasonable pattern of benefits and incentives, although there are areas, such as the treatment of single people and one- and two-earner couples, that could stand improvement. However, many countries have designed defined benefit systems with very poor incentive properties. Some of the poorly designed systems are an inheritance from former communist governments, but poor design extends much more widely than that. The design of Chile's defined contribution system is also very good, again with some areas that could benefit from change. Some countries that followed Chile's lead have not done as well in design. It may well be that it is easier politically to design a good defined contribution system than a sound defined benefit system, but there is little evidence. A country that felt it could not design a sound defined benefit system would probably be better off with a defined contribution approach, if that could be well-designed.

Systems are subject to repeated legislative changes once they have been established. Short-term government deficits might lead politicians to reduce benefits in a defined benefit plan (for example, by delaying cost of living adjustments). But retirement income is a poor base for absorbing budget deficit risk. That some retirement benefits flow though the government is not a good reason for them to bear more of the risk of short-term budget deficits than do similar incomes that do not flow through the government. In other words pension incomes should respond to short-term budget risks the same way as other pension incomes do, not the same way as government expenditures in general. It is desirable, then, to insulate social security from short-run fiscal concerns. This can be done by privatizing social security, as in Chile. It can also be attempted by setting up a budget process that distances social security from the rest of the budget.

There is probably value in establishing an institution with professional independence that can affect the dialogue about social security. Having an official actuarial office that is required to report annually and to comment on proposed legislation gives higher political visibility (and presumably strengthens resistance) to changes that may be unsustainable. While it is easy to ignore these pronouncements, they can confer greater political prominence on these long-run issues. A system with privatized management of a separate trust fund also provides a set of professionals ready to comment on proposed legislative changes.

A defined contribution approach does not in itself guarantee that retirement income will be fully insulated from political risk. For example, if unemployment insurance and health and education benefits are cut to deal with a budget deficit, while greater access to defined contribution accumulations is allowed to compensate for some of these cuts, then future retirement income would be exposed to government budget risks.

Sometimes, long-term changes are needed in a retirement savings program. In a defined contribution system promised benefits adjust automatically to the availability of funds, so that no further legislative action is needed to achieve promised benefits. Rather, the promise is elastic. Change is more difficult with a defined benefit system. Although defined benefit systems could have earmarked funds and automatic adjustment, that is not an easy combination to produce. It is also the case, however, that changing circumstances can leave both defined benefit and defined contribution systems ill-suited to the changed circumstances, in the absence of legislation to adjust them.

Another way to influence political outcomes is to change the description of the system in the eyes of the public. For example, the vocabulary of individual accounts has connotations that could affect legislated outcomes in different ways than the terminology of benefit formulas. Referring to social security as a tax-transfer mechanism may make the system more vulnerable than referring to it as an insurance system, in which benefits are earned by paying premiums. A subtler form of pressure resides in the public definition of the budget balance—whether it includes or excludes the social security system. One role for earmarking taxes and having a trust fund is to fortify the sustainability of exclusion. Independent fund management may also add to this sustainability (see Diamond forthcoming). The greater impact of a multipillar system may be that the pillars function differently politically, not that the separation into pillars affects private responses significantly.

Conclusion

This article has explored what can be done with different retirement income systems and what tends to be done in practice. The case for mandatory retirement saving systems rests on the inadequate provision many workers would otherwise make. The inefficiencies associated with mandating such savings suggests the desirability of a lower level of mandate than would, by itself, finance a comfortable retirement. This leaves room for supplementary systems that, for their part, could benefit from regulation. While such systems will be uneven, that is probably better than mandating a high uniform level.

The bottom line for any country contemplating a new retirement saving system or reforming an existing one depends on how the politics are likely to work. The solutions may well be different for new plans than for existing ones. Defined benefit systems have more potential for low administrative costs, more insurance provision, and greater redistribution, both good and bad. But such systems also have a greater risk of poorly designed incentives and require serious recordkeeping. But then mandated private systems also call for administrative expertise.

Similarly, regulating private defined benefit systems is considerably more difficult—and has yielded more unfortunate regulatory side effects—than regulating defined contribution systems. This comparison is somewhat biased, however, given the failure of some defined contribution systems to address the problem of annuity generation. Unless one counts doing nothing as a serious design defect, it is hard to identify poor design where nothing is being done.

But perhaps this is precisely where the World Bank can play its most valuable role, by pushing for good design.

Notes

1. I refer throughout to retirement income, although retirement may or may not be a condition for benefits. The label is shorthand for income for people of "retirement age," although retirement age is a somewhat vague concept, and one that is a policy variable.

2. For example, in the first decade of Chile's new mandated retirement savings program low-income workers had a 7.5 percent real return, while high-income workers had a 10.5 percent real return and pension funds earned 13 percent (Vittas and Iglesias 1992).

3. With limited space, I mostly ignore disability and survivor benefits.

4. My focus is on the earnings-related systems, not the safety nets for the elderly, which both countries have.

5. I ignore the availability of early withdrawal for those with sufficiently large accumulations.

6. For simplicity, I consider a single worker, ignoring issues associated with joint life annuities. There is a large difference in the treatment of dependents between Chile and the United States.

7. Many defined benefit systems use much shorter averaging periods. This major defect is not a necessary part of a defined benefit approach.

8. There is a similar pattern in the voluntary increase in benefits for the already retired. In the United States a significant number of defined benefit plans have increased benefit payments to partially offset

inflation. I am not aware of similar adjustments for those in defined contribution plans (Allen, Clark, and McDermed 1992).

9. The list of definitions includes an incorrect definition of moral hazard on page xxii. Moral hazard arises when insured people do not protect themselves from risk as much as they should given the full social costs with the amount of insurance provided. The book's definition identifies the deviation of protection from that chosen in the absence of insurance as the measure of moral hazard. But social optimality calls for varying the level of protection with the level of insurance. *Averting the Old Age Crisis* attributes to adverse selection the result that "markets break down." Adverse selection can also result in inefficient functioning of active markets.

10. In the U. S. context Feldstein (1987) considered raising real benefits to offset the absence of private CPI-indexed annuities. Crawford and Lilien (1981) argue that rational workers value real annuities above their expected costs, decreasing the implicit net tax on work below the usual measure.

11. A longer life expectancy increases the importance of the choice of index. Similarly, the indexing of disability benefits for young workers should differ from that of retirement benefits.

12. From equilibrium risk-sharing considerations, Merton (1983) has called for indexing to average consumption in the economy.

13. In an idealized competitive model, it is not possible to shift a single firm's pension obligations to its workers. However, in a model where jobs have surpluses above the next best alternatives, such shifting is possible. It is common to suggest that workers do not bear rate of return risks in defined benefit private pension systems. This is only correct if neither wages nor benefit formulas nor firm viability are affected by rates of return. All of these suppositions seem problematic. For a discussion of pensions in terms of risks, see Bodie, Marcus, and Merton 1988.

14. As the finance literature is aware, there are offsetting complications from nontradables and from risky labor income.

15. I do not discuss the cost to employers, which are higher in Chile than they would be if firms sent payments to a centralized collection system, rather than to multiple fund managers.

16. It is curious that *Averting the Old Age Crisis* does not mention the problems with individual annuity markets in making its policy recommendations in chapter 7.

17. *Averting the Old Age Crisis* attributes a decline in administrative expenses relative to assets in Chile to "economies of scale, learning by doing, and competition" (figure 6.1, p. 225). This fails to identify the large fall in administrative expenses relative to assets that would accompany the increase in assets in a new system even if costs per account were unchanged.

References

Allen, Steven, Robert Clark, and Ann McDermed. 1992. "Post-Retirement Benefit Increases in the 1980s." In John Turner and Daniel Beller, eds., *Trends in Pensions 1992*. Washington, D.C.: U.S. Government Printing Office.

American Council of Life Insurance. 1992. *1992 Life Insurance Fact Book*. Washington, D.C.

Bateman, Hazel, John Piggott, and Salvador Valdés-Prieto. 1995. "Australia y Chile: Prevision privada con normas diferentes comparacion de regulaciones y de comisiones de administracion." Working Paper 176. Catholic University of Chile, Santiago.

Beveridge, W. H. 1942. "Social Insurance and Allied Services." Cmd 6404. London: Her Majesty's Stationery Office.

Bodie, Zvi, Alan J. Marcus, and Robert C. Merton. 1988. "Defined Benefit versus Defined Contribution Plans: What are the Real Trade-Offs?" In Z. Bodie, J. Shoven, and D. Wise, eds., *Pensions in the U. S. Economy*. Chicago: University of Chicago Press.

Bosworth, Barry. 1996. "The Social Security Fund: How Big? How Managed?" In Peter Diamond, D. Lindeman, and H. Young, eds., *Social Security: What Role for the Future?* Washington, D.C.: The Brookings Institution.

Crawford, Vincent, and David Lilien. 1981. "Social Security and the Retirement Decision." *Quarterly Journal of Economics* 96: 505–29.

Diamond, Peter. 1992. "Organizing the Health Insurance Market." *Econometrica* 60(6): 1233–54.

———. Forthcoming. "Insulation of Pensions from Political Risk." In Salvador Valdés-Prieto, ed., *The Economics of Pensions: International Experience*. Cambridge: Cambridge University Press.

Diamond, Peter, and James Mirrlees. 1978. "A Model of Social Insurance with Variable Retirement." *Journal of Public Economics* 10: 295–336.

————. 1986. "Payroll-Tax Financed Social Insurance with Variable Retirement." *Scandinavian Journal of Economics* 88(1): 25–50.

Feldstein, Martin. 1987. "Should Social Security Benefits Increase with Age?" NBER Working Paper 2200. National Bureau of Economic Research, Cambridge, Mass.

Feldstein, Martin S., and Andrew A. Samwick. 1992. "Social Security Rules and Marginal Tax Rates." *National Tax Journal* 45(1): 1–22.

Friedman, Benjamin M., and Mark J. Warshawsky. 1990. "The Cost of Annuities: Implications for Saving Behavior and Bequests." *Quarterly Journal of Economics* 105(1): 135–54.

Merton, Robert C. 1983. "On Consumption-Indexed Public Pension Plans." In Z. Bodie and J. Shoven, eds., *Financial Aspects of the U.S. Pension System.* Chicago: University of Chicago Press.

Shafir, Eldar, Peter Diamond, and Amos Tversky. 1992. "On Money Illusion." Massachusetts Institute of Technology, Cambridge, Mass.

Solow, Robert M. 1980. "On Theories of Unemployment." *American Economic Review* 70(1): 1–11.

Sunden, Annika E., and Olivia S. Mitchell. 1994. "An Examination of Social Security Administration Costs in the United States." Pension Research Council Working Paper Series 94-7. Philadelphia.

Tversky, Amos, and Daniel Kahneman. 1981. "The Framing of Decisions and the Psychology of Choice." *Science* 211: 453–58.

Valdés-Prieto, Salvador. 1994. "Administrative Charges in Pensions in Chile, Malaysia, Zambia, and the United States." Policy Research Working Paper 1372. World Bank, Policy Research Department, Washington, D.C.

————. 1995. "Vendedores de AFP: Producto del mercado o de regulaciones ineficientes?" Working Paper 178. Catholic University of Chile, Santiago.

Vittas, Dimitri, and Augusto Iglesias. 1992. "The Rationale and Performance of Personal Pension Plans in Chile." Policy Research Working Paper 867. World Bank, Financial Sector Development Department, Washington, D.C.

Wilson, James Q. 1989. *Bureaucracy: What Government Agencies Do and Why They Do It.* New York: Basic Books.

World Bank. 1994. *Averting the Old Age Crisis.* New York: Oxford University Press.

Yankelovich, Daniel. 1991. *Coming to Public Judgment: Making Democracy Work in a Complex World.* Syracuse, N.Y.: Syracuse University Press.

Comment on "Government Provision and Regulation of Economic Support in Old Age," by Peter Diamond

Nicholas Barr

There are so many good things in Peter Diamond's article that I feel like a kid in a candy store. The richness, diversity, and complexity of different pension arrangements and the great range of economics and finance literature that he draws into the discussion are very evident. With limited space, I concentrate on four key messages for policy design that emerge from his article, all of them inherent in the logic of pensions and therefore transcending the specifics of a particular country or stage of economic development:

- There is no holy grail—no complete, easy solution.
- Effective government is critical whichever approach to pensions is chosen.
- Policy design depends on the starting point.
- The key variable is output.

Message 1: There Is No Holy Grail

Diamond's article reminds us of three sets of problems from which there is no escape: aggregate uncertainty, market imperfections, and the impossibility of distributional neutrality. Policy design, as an inevitable consequence, is a choice among second-best alternatives. Pensions should be designed to respect the economic realities sketched out below and to adopt the imperfections that are least irksome to the electorate of the country concerned.

Aggregate Uncertainty

Diamond refers to "major disappointments of expectation" of retirement income in both public and private sectors. This should not be surprising. From the viewpoint of an individual worker, pensions are a way of exchanging part of her current production for goods produced by the future labor force after her retirement. Pensions thus depend on future output, and future output is uncertain.

Nicholas Barr is professor of economics at the London School of Economics.

Annual World Bank Conference on Development Economics 1995

To compound the problem, this uncertainty is a common risk—that is, one faced by everyone in a given country. Insurance is possible only against individual risks. Given the range of common risks that countries face—declining growth rates in many high-income countries, sharply negative growth rates in the reforming economies of Central and Eastern Europe and the former Soviet Union, and adverse demographic prospects in many countries—it should not be surprising that all pension plans face problems. And as Diamond points out, "The future course of mortality rates is a major social risk, one that must be borne by some group, however we organize retirement incomes. The futures of wage growth and interest rates are also large societywide risks. Different systems of retirement income provision spread these risks differently."

The course of interest rates, particularly the difference between nominal interest rates and the inflation rate, is particularly relevant to pension funds. If one member of a pensioner cohort faces an inflation rate of x percent then so, by and large, do all members of the cohort. Inflation is thus a common risk. Up to a point the problem can be sidestepped: pension funds can often cope with inflation during a worker's contribution years; and internationally diversified funds can resist purely domestic inflation. However, the greater the extent of a common inflationary shock (such as an oil crisis), the less well can funded pensions cope with inflation (Barr 1993, 1994).

Aggregate uncertainty has at least three implications for policy design. First, pension arrangements should be able to adapt to changing output levels in a way that shares burdens between workers and pensioners in a fiscally plausible and electorally tolerable way. Second, and related, pension regimes need to offer pensioners at least some protection against inflation; private pensions may need to operate in partnership with the state for this purpose. Third, and fundamental, even the best-designed and best-implemented pension scheme will not do well if the economy (national or international) in which it operates performs badly. To that extent pension policy cannot be separated from broader policies aimed at encouraging economic growth.

Market Imperfections

Diamond notes the importance of recognizing how markets actually work, as opposed to how idealized competitive markets are modeled. At the World Bank's Fifth Annual Conference on Development Economics, Joseph Stiglitz (1994, p. 20) argued "that financial markets are markedly different from other markets; that market failures are likely to be more pervasive in these markets; and that there exist forms of government intervention that will not only make these markets function better but will also improve the performance of the economy."

Problems are usefully divided into two sorts: imperfect information and transaction costs. Policymakers are impaled on a nasty dilemma. If individuals are allowed unconstrained choice, they may make choices that fail to maximize their long-run welfare, through myopia or for more general lack of information about how well their pension fund is being managed. But if government intervenes by constraining individual choice (for example, the size of the pension contribution or the age of retirement), inefficiency can arise in other ways. As Diamond brings out, a mandated savings system can create inefficiency because it fails fully to respect differences in individual preferences and other relevant differences in individual circumstances.

The ill-effects of poor consumer information are pervasive. As Diamond notes, the incentive effects of institutions are determined not by reality but by people's perceptions of reality. Where there are misperceptions, it is the misperceptions rather than reality that determine behavior. Consumer sovereignty can fail just as government can fail.

Transaction costs constitute the second group of problems. Diamond points out that "the annuities market in the United States does not operate like an idealized competitive market with a single price. . . . Annuities markets based on individual choice have not generally been considered to work well." The reason is twofold. First, information (about the performance of companies, the management of a pension fund, and the like) is a public good, in the sense that the consumption of information by one individual does not reduce the amount available for other consumers. Second, "expenditures on information can be viewed as fixed costs. . . . Markets that are information-intensive are likely to be imperfectly competitive" (Stiglitz 1994, p. 24).

The problem is seen most clearly from the individual perspective. Suppose a market is competitive at the time an individual enters it. However, suppose also, as with pensions, that entry is infrequent or information costly to maintain, so that the transaction costs of monitoring suppliers, and possibly changing from one provider to another, are significant. Thus a market that may be competitive at the time an individual enters it becomes less so over time. The cause of the problem is the cost of acquiring information and the fact that, because of information's public good attributes, the individual is often unable to appropriate all the benefits of new information.

In addition to the costs of acquiring information are the separate costs of administering pensions. Diamond points out that individual pensions generally have higher costs than more aggregate arrangements, such as occupational or state schemes, which are able to exploit administrative economies of scale. It should therefore be no surprise, as Diamond notes, that the administrative costs of the Chilean scheme are broadly on a par with the costs of private systems elsewhere. This is not an argument against individual pensions, merely a reminder to take account of all costs and benefits in assessing different arrangements.

For these and other reasons the microeconomics of pensions is more complex than that for the generality of commodities. A major implication for policy design is the need for regulation, not least to protect consumers in an area too complex for them to protect themselves. Such financial market regulation exists in all Western economies and is wholly necessary.[1] As Diamond makes clear, however, regulation will itself create inefficiency. Policy design, again, is a matter of second-best choice.

The Impossibility of Distributional Neutrality

Other things being equal, actuarial insurance has no systematic redistributive effects, except from those who are ex post unlucky (they die young) to those who are ex post lucky. However, as Diamond points out, other things are not always equal, so that insurance can have unintended redistributive consequences. Providing insurance "tends to redistribute to the better off, given the positive correlation between life expectancy and earnings, unless there are offsets in benefit determination." A similar problem, through the same mechanism, can arise for administrative costs, which can bear disproportionately on lower earners. Policy designers may or may not wish to take cognizance of these effects. They should at least be aware of them.

Message 2: Effective Government is Critical

This is true whichever approach to pensions is adopted.

Government Failure Harms Both State and Private Schemes

The problem of government failure is most obvious in the case of defined benefit state schemes built on fiscally irresponsible promises, coupled with an inability to collect contributions. Results include inflationary pressures and political instability.

Private pension funds, however, are also vulnerable. At the macroeconomic level, fiscal imprudence often leads to a loss of control of the money supply and to inflation, which can decapitalize private funds. At the microeconomic level, the inability to regulate financial markets creates inequity and may also squander the efficiency gains that private pensions are intended to engender.

Effective Government Assists Both State and Private Schemes

Government failure is not inherent. Diamond concludes that the U.S. social security system has a reasonably good pattern of benefits and incentives. More generally, governments throughout the OECD are putting into place cost-containing measures to prepare for demographic changes (United Kingdom Department of Social Security 1993).

Government capacity, similarly, assists private schemes. Diamond points out that one advantage of investment in private assets is the potential contribution to the development of capital markets, as occurred in Chile. But he also notes that capital market development in Chile was not automatic, but required "extensive development of capital market regulation." In other words the benefits of the Chilean privatization depended critically on the fact that the Chilean government was (and remains) effective.

The key message for policy design is the importance of finding ways to help government to be effective with respect to macroeconomic policy, pension system design, and the design and enforcement of regulation.

Message 3: Policy Design Depends on the Starting Point

Reform, in other words, depends on the initial conditions. Again, this applies equally to state and private schemes. Diamond argues that at least so far as economic rationality is concerned, the case for introducing a defined contribution scheme into a country with no (or little) pension provision does not necessarily hold for a country that already has a mature defined benefit scheme: "A dislike of the type of intergenerational redistribution that typically happens when starting a new system would be reason to oppose starting a new defined benefit system but would not be a reason to favor change from a mature defined benefit system to a new defined contribution system."

As mentioned, one of the major benefits of pension reform in Chile was the push it gave to capital market development. A move to funded pensions elsewhere would not necessarily have similar benefits, for instance in countries that already have well-developed capital markets or in those that lack the institutional capacity to implement the necessary regulation (the issue of government capacity again).

There is a more general point. Policy design should take explicit cognizance of the constraints, or lack of them, that countries face. Kopits (1993, p. 23) points to "societies where the extended family . . . still operates rather actively as an informal social security scheme, obviating the urgent introduction of large-scale public pensions and assistance schemes." Countries differ both in their institutional capacity and in the extent to which governments are able politically to maintain support for policies, like pensions, that have a long-term time horizon.

Message 4: The Key Variable Is Output

From the perspective of the economy as a whole, pensions are a device for dividing output between workers and pensioners. Thus what matters is output. If we think that the combined demand of workers and pensioners is (or will be) too high, for instance because of the demographic prospects or because of rash promises by government, the solution is to bring demand and supply into balance. This can be done by reducing the demand of pensioners (through lower pensions) or of workers (through higher contributions).

Alternatively, on the supply side, both workers and pensioners can have the consumption they currently expect, so long as output rises sufficiently to maintain average consumption. In theory, this involves either or both of two strategies. Output per worker can be increased by increasing the quantity and quality of capital and the quality of labor. The number of workers can be increased by increasing labor force participation by those of working age, raising the retirement age, and importing labor.

In practice, policies to increase output could therefore include:
- Taking measures to increase the stock and quality of capital.
- Increasing investment in labor through education and training.
- Increasing labor force participation, for instance through reduced unemployment and improved child care facilities.

- Raising the retirement age; in the West a two-year increase for men (from sixty-five to sixty-seven) with no increase in pensions is an implicit reduction in benefits of about 15 percent, but with the advantage that it works by reducing the average duration of retirement rather than by reducing living standards in retirement.[2]
- Importing labor through immigration.

Pension schemes offer individuals a measure of certainty about their future, but no pension arrangement, state or private, can insure against common shocks. The future is full of uncertainties—about rates of inflation, output growth, birth rates, and the like—that affect pension schemes just as they affect most other institutions. The tension for retirement income schemes is that the capacity to adapt—a desirable feature in the face of uncertainty—is also a capacity to be subverted by weak government. Pensions, like the rest of the economy, are therefore best served not only by good design but also by the whole range of policies intended to encourage economic growth. To echo Diamond's conclusion, this is one of the World Bank's central purposes.

Notes

1. The effectiveness of such regulation is under continuing review, for instance in the United Kingdom in the wake of the Maxwell imbroglio (see United Kingdom Pension Law Review Committee 1993) and in the United States after the savings and loan scandal.

2. Policies of this sort have already been announced in the United Kingdom and the United States for the years after 2000.

References

Barr, Nicholas. 1993. *The Economics of the Welfare State.* Stanford, Calif.: Stanford University Press and Oxford: Oxford University Press.

———. 1994. *Labor Markets and Social Policy in Central and Eastern Europe: The Transition and Beyond.* New York: Oxford University Press.

Kopits, George. 1993. "Reforming Social Security Systems." *Finance and Development* 30 (June): 21–23.

Stiglitz, Joseph E. 1994. "The Role of the State in Financial Markets." In *Proceedings of the World Bank Annual Conference on Development Economics 1993.* Washington, D.C.: World Bank.

United Kingdom Department of Social Security. 1993. *Containing the Costs of Social Security—The International Context.* London: Her Majesty's Stationery Office.

United Kingdom Pension Law Review Committee (the "Goode Committee"). 1993. *Pension Law Reform.* Volume 1, Report; volume 2, Research. CM 2342-I. London: Her Majesty's Stationery Office.

Comment on "Government Provision and Regulation of Economic Support in Old Age," by Peter Diamond

Estelle James

I agree with Peter Diamond's analysis on many key points. Retirement age and mandatory contribution rates should be chosen carefully, with the contribution rate set on the low side to accommodate diverse preferences. Some countries will benefit from the development of a funded, privately managed pillar more than others. International diversification of investments is desirable, but to different degrees for different countries, and indexation to the world portfolio is probably not optimal. Having separate noncompeting plans for different occupations and industries is usually not efficient. And political economy or political psychology issues are probably central to the choice of pension system. In fact, as I argue below, differences in assumptions about political economy and political psychology issues probably account for most of the differences economists have about pension policy recommendations. Thus, although I concentrate my remarks on areas of disagreement, that should not obscure the considerable agreement between us.

There is an important methodological difference between Diamond's article and *Averting the Old Age Crisis* (World Bank 1994). Diamond discusses pension system choice from a theoretical perspective, using Chile and the United States to illustrate particular points. *Averting the Old Age Crisis* is grounded in empirical analysis of many countries, guided by theory. This difference in emphasis is important because the political economy issues are crucial and we do not yet have an adequate understanding of how governments behave or how citizens make collective choices. So from a theoretical point of view, anything can happen, depending on your assumptions. But when we looked at the empirical evidence, we found consistent problems in many countries at all stages of economic development and with different types of political systems. The broad range of this experience led us to believe that a pension system should be designed to be more immune to these effects. At the same time the political economy underpinnings of our recommendations should clearly be investigated further.

Estelle James is lead economist, Policy Research Department, Poverty and Human Resources Division, at the World Bank.

Annual World Bank Conference on Development Economics 1995

Diamond's article and *Averting the Old Age Crisis* also have important substantive differences. Diamond emphasizes the distinction between defined benefit and defined contribution, while *Averting* emphasizes the distinction between fully funded and pay as you go. It seems to me that Diamond confuses some of the consequences of these two properties of pension plans. Publicly managed defined benefit plans have historically been pay-as-you-go or only partially funded (the same is true of employer-sponsored defined benefit plans in the absence of regulation)—but this connection is not inherent.[1]

As an example of this confusion, Diamond points out that employers and governments have been willing to give the first cohorts of retirees under defined benefit plans large income transfers. He attributes this willingness to the psychology of defined benefit plans—people perceive the benefits under such plans and so they want to equalize them. It seems more plausible to me that the giveaways common under defined benefit plans derive from their pay-as-you-go status. Today's politicians and corporate managers can reap the good will that comes from promising benefits without having to worry about the costs, which come due much later. Employers in the United States largely stopped the giveaways under defined benefit programs once legislation required full funding after 1973. The changing attitude toward these transfers to the older generation probably stemmed from simple economics rather than psychology: in the short run pay-as-you-go hides real costs while full funding requires you to face up to the costs as well as the benefits from the start.

The emphasis on pay-as-you-go versus funding is crucial because it leads directly to the major rationale for a multipillar system—a rationale that Diamond overlooks—the economic and political advantages of having a large, funded, privately managed component of the old age security system. But this component cannot do the whole job. A publicly managed tax-financed component is also needed, to provide a social safety net. And that is why we end up with a multipillar system. My remaining comments elaborate on this theme.

Averting the Old Age Crisis examined how pay-as-you-go systems actually work in the real world. We found them commonly beset by political economy problems—when politicians have to worry about getting elected next year, their time horizon grows very short. Therefore, pay-as-you-go systems were often designed to yield short-run advantages without a careful analysis of long-run costs, for example, promising overgenerous benefits and early retirement ages that are inefficient and not sustainable in the long run. The implication that contribution rates would have to rise steeply as populations age was simply not taken into account. Intergenerational transfers were often not well thought out (if at all), and the "giving" generation had no voice in the decision.[2] Old age security programs were not used to augment long-term national savings, even in countries where that is a goal, nor was investment finance used as a mechanism to increase pension size or lower required contributions. To avoid such problems, *Averting* recommended that a substantial part of a country's old age security system be fully funded.

And because we observed many problems in countries with public management of pension reserves, we recommended that fund management be decentralized and competitive, though regulated. Again, the experience of many countries shows that publicly managed funds earn lower returns than privately managed funds. During the 1980s, for example, public funds in many countries lost money because their investment choices were very restricted by the government—funds were often required to lend the bulk of their reserves to the state or to state enterprises at interest rates below the rate of inflation—while private pension funds typically had a wider range of investment options.[3]

We concluded that a privately managed, funded pension pillar should handle much of peoples' mandatory retirement savings (in countries where financial markets and the government's regulatory capacity are adequate for this job). Domination of investment discussions by political objectives would be avoided, allowing for the most productive allocation of capital and encouraging the development of financial markets. (Even Singapore, which has one of the better publicly managed plans, is introducing greater decentralization and individual control over investments, for these reasons.)

Why is this one pillar not enough? One reason is that some people earn very low lifetime wages, not enough to keep them above the poverty line after they retire as well as before. Also, investments may fail for some people, even if investment options are regulated by government. We need a second pillar to provide a social safety net. Since this pillar involves redistributions to low-income groups, it must be managed by the government. It should be tax-financed, out of payroll taxes if coverage is limited and out of general revenue taxes once coverage becomes close to universal. Since different managerial and financing mechanisms are involved for the funded privately managed pillar and the redistributive publicly managed pillar, a multipillar system is required.

A multipillar system also has the advantage that it provides valuable risk diversification for individuals, another factor Diamond does not mention. Retirement plans can span sixty or more years from the time a person enters the labor force to the time he or she dies, and we cannot know in advance all the surprises the world will hold and whether those surprises will favor a publicly managed plan tied to wage growth or a privately managed plan tied to the interest rate. The best way to insure in a very uncertain world is to diversify—don't put all your nest eggs in one basket. High-income people do this all the time on a voluntary basis. We are saying that low-income people should also be given the benefits of diversification by building it into the mandatory plan.

This brings me to my next point, on the distributional issue. Diamond asserts, largely on theoretical grounds, that a single-pillar system will redistribute to the poor and alleviate poverty better than a multipillar system and that giving less to the old would not necessarily mean giving more to children, who are the highest poverty group today. But he does not present any facts to prove these assertions. Looking at the empirical evidence led us to the opposite conclusions in *Averting*.

The mandatory, pay-as-you-go, publicly managed pension systems in the Netherlands, Sweden, the United Kingdom, and the United States show little if any lifetime redistributions from those with high permanent incomes to those with low permanent incomes (despite much rhetoric to the contrary). One important but nontransparent reason: high-income people live longer and so collect their annual benefits for more years. In the first generations of pension programs poverty among the old was reduced, primarily because of the large transfers from the young generations, rich and poor, to the older generations, rich and poor. Because benefits tend to be earnings-related, the biggest transfers in the early generations often went to high-income retirees. In the future this intergenerational transfer will become negative instead of positive, so the system will not alleviate old age poverty unless the public benefits are more narrowly directed to the poor. Meanwhile, the high and regressive payroll taxes paid by low-wage workers today to partially finance these transfers to the old contributes directly to the poverty of young families and their children.[4] If the public pillar had the more limited objective of providing a social safety net and assisting low-income families, it would be easier to keep track of whether it was accomplishing this goal.

In general, when a system is complex, nontransparent, and serves multiple purposes, it is likely to be easier for middle- and high-income families to figure out the system and use it to their advantage. (The underlying assumption here is that those in the upper-income brackets are not "tricked" by the current murky systems into redistributing more than they would in a transparent system. This is a political psychology issue about which we do not have firm information—but we do have evidence that high-income people have not, in fact, been tricked into redistributing under the current system.) The goal of poverty alleviation is especially important now, since income polarization has increased in all high-income countries and the size of the group of low-wage earners or unemployed workers at the bottom of the income distribution has increased. We may well see an increase in child poverty and a resurgence of old age poverty in these countries unless we develop a public pillar that is more redistributive in both its benefit and its contribution structures. This redistributive pay-as-you-go pillar in turn requires a second pillar that is funded, in which middle- and high-income people save for their own old age.

Diamond argues that the rationale for using a funded plan as part of a multipillar system is much greater in immature systems than in mature systems, where the giveaway to the first cohorts of retirees is already a sunk cost. However, we at the World Bank must remember that virtually all of our client countries, except for the transition economies, have immature systems. In almost all of these countries less than half the labor force is covered. More than half of all old people in the world and more than two-thirds of all young people live in countries with immature pension systems. In these countries the costs of a pay-as-you-go system are not sunk, because the system will gradually extend its coverage, increasing the transfer and the public pension debt. We argue that these countries should carefully consider the negative consequences for economic growth and equity before they incur these costs.

As for mature systems, for the most part they fall into one of two categories. One group includes countries that are in serious and immediate financial trouble and that are facing formidable political obstacles to pension reform, such as countries in Eastern Europe. The other group includes countries where trouble is looming but is not immediate, such as the United States. These countries need to ask themselves a series of revealing questions: will a switch in systems help them to raise taxes or reduce benefits to meet the growing burden of their aging populations? Will it increase national saving, where that is a goal? Will it direct redistribution more closely to lower-income groups, an especially important goal in view of the increasing polarization of wages in all high-income countries? Should the funded pillar be mandatory or voluntary? And how can the transition be tailored to a country's needs and circumstances, while keeping disruptions to a minimum?

In *Averting the Old Age Crisis* we argue that it would be least disruptive for high-income countries to plan for the impending financial problem now, and to take gradual steps to avoid it, instead of waiting for the crisis to hit. We suspect that an increase in contribution rates will be more politically acceptable and less economically distortionary if it goes into peoples' own retirement savings accounts. This would increase national saving, and the individual accounts would be used to top up retirement income as the old age dependency rate (the ratio of retired to working-age people) rises and public pensions are cut. And we recommend that public benefits be cut by raising the retirement age to match increases in longevity and by flattening out the benefit structure, so that the cuts come at the top rather than at the bottom end.

The retirement age required to receive full benefits could be gradually raised and possibly indexed to longevity. People who wish to retire at the previous retirement age could do so, at a benefit rate that is reduced on an actuarially equivalent basis to take into account the additional years of collecting pensions and the reduced years of making contributions. A proposed reform in Sweden incorporates this idea. Diamond argues for a less-than-actuarial reduction on insurance grounds, but the counterargument is that once disability and unemployment coverages are taken into account as observable conditions for which special programs exist, any additional early retirement is largely voluntary. That is, the decision to retire early is subject to great moral hazard problems, so it may not be an insurable risk. Our evidence is that, in fact, men have been withdrawing from the labor force at an earlier and earlier age, despite improvements in longevity and health. Access to pensions that have not been reduced on an actuarially equivalent basis may be part of the reason.

Once these steps have been taken to avoid the impending pension crisis, we will have the beginnings of a multipillar system—a privately managed savings pillar and a more limited redistributive public pillar. (On economic grounds we think the private funded pillar should be mandatory and large relative to the public pay-as-you-go pillar. But on political grounds many countries with mature systems may choose to make it voluntary, encouraged by tax incentives, with limited coverage, retaining a relatively large public pillar.)

One of the most controversial issues in pension finance concerns administrative costs, which are said to be higher in decentralized systems such as that in Chile than in centralized systems such as that in the United States. It is true that marketing costs are higher in the Chilean scheme than in the U.S. social security system; in general a market system entails some marketing costs. But I believe that Diamond overstates the real cost differential between the U.S. and Chilean schemes.

His numbers include an imputation for the future cost of annuities that many retirees will, in fact, choose not to buy. He omits the costs of collection and administration in the United States, which are borne by the Internal Revenue Service rather than the Social Security Administration. And he ignores the investment function carried out by the mandatory scheme in Chile but not in the United States. In the United States many people voluntarily pay mutual funds administrative fees to invest in stocks and bonds, so they clearly value this function. When we add in the annual fee that the average U.S. investor pays for an amount of private investment equivalent to that of the average Chilean, the cost disadvantage of Chile's system is largely eliminated. Another way of putting this: an evaluation of costs must consider services and benefits as well. The average Chilean would probably want to keep the services provided by the privatized pension plan rather than shift to a public pay-as-you-go system, despite the marketing costs this might save (James and Palacios 1994).

As Diamond points out, private annuities markets are known to be complex and are said to be prone to market failure (see discussion in Chapter 6 and Issue Brief 10 of *Averting the Old Age Crisis*). However, the simple fact of the matter is that we do not know how they would operate if they were mandatory and a major part of an overall retirement saving system instead of being voluntary and crowded out by large mandatory public annuities. The paper by Friedman and Warshavsky (1990) that Diamond cites does not tell us this because it applies to the United States, where public pensions are mandatory, and so the leftover demand for annuities is small and highly income elastic. Since high-income people have longer expected lifetimes, and Friedman and Warshavsky do not use income-specific mortality tables, their analysis may substantially understate the implicit rate of return and overstate the spread.

In the multipillar system we propose, part of the demand for annuities would continue to be met by the public pillar. Annuities would also be offered through the private pillar. Without denying the problems, there is also a possible advantage to a private annuities system: it forces discussion of whether price differentiation by socioeconomic status, occupation, race, or gender is to be allowed, so that an explicit decision will replace the implicit redistribution—from poor to rich, from construction worker to school teacher, from blacks to whites—that takes place when everyone is put into the same annuity pool at the same price, as in public systems. (Again, this raises the political economy issue of whether such discussions are good because they allow more deliberate decisions, or bad because they tend to be divisive.)

In view of the annuity market problems, some people might wish to take their retirement income from the private pillar in the form of gradual withdrawals. Shanghai and Mexico are considering an interesting variation on this theme. In Shanghai workers who reach retirement age would be required to spread withdrawals over an expected lifetime (about eighteen years in Shanghai). If retirees die before the end of the eighteen years, a portion of the remaining accumulation would go into a publically managed fund that would be used to pay pensions to those who live longer than eighteen years. In Mexico workers can spread their withdrawals over an expected lifetime but must supplement this with private insurance that pays them an annuity if they live longer than expected. In both countries the dependence on private annuity markets is reduced, while retaining longevity insurance and private management of most money in the funded pillar.

Obviously, there are many remaining problems and possible solutions, so this remains a fertile area for ongoing research.

Notes

1. For example, since 1973 U.S. employer defined benefit plans have been required to be fully funded; Sweden and some cities in China are considering the introduction of notional defined contribution accounts that are essentially pay-as-you-go. In the past when governments tried to fund defined benefit plans, they either dissipated the funds with loss-making investments or found themselves subject to political pressures to increase benefits, which used up the funds and effectively turned the plans into pay-as-you-go.

2. Diamond argues that these intergenerational transfers were intentional, but I know of no evidence showing that the transfers were publicly discussed or that careful long-term simulations of the winners and losers were carried out. At any rate the young (the losers) certainly did not participate in this discussion, since they were not yet voters—many had not yet been born.

3. It is sometimes suggested that this directed investment of public funds has a distributional effect (it is like a tax on workers and future pensioners) but that it has no effect on capital allocation. The argument is that government would issue the same amount of debt in any case, so someone in the economy would end up holding that debt, and the rest of the country's savers would hold private assets. This is another political economy issue—do governments borrow more because they have exclusive access to publicly managed pension funds? We do not have a definitive answer to this question, but two points seem relevant. First, private investors might not hold government debt for long if the returns were largely negative, and if government had to pay a much higher—and transparently so—interest rate, pressure might build to constrain its spending. And second, if pension fund assets become a large part of the country's financial assets—as they would if they were mandatory—they would exceed 100 percent of GNP and therefore would exceed the conventional debt in most countries. In that case the use of these funds would be bound to affect the country's total capital allocation. If the funds are publicly managed, they will increase either government debt or public holding and control over private debt and equity.

4. The U.S. Department of Labor has suggested a redefinition of income that would take these high regressive social security taxes into account and that would directly increase the measured poverty rates among young families with children. The wage-earners in many of these families will never live long enough to collect the pension benefits for which they are paying. A cut in the payroll taxes of low wage-earners would reduce child poverty, a change that could be kept revenue-neutral by raising the ceiling on taxable earnings at the top end. Both of these moves are consistent with the more redistributive role we recommend for the public pillar.

References

Friedman, Benjamin M., and Mark J. Warshavsky. 1990. "The Cost of Annuities: Implications for Saving Behavior and Bequests." *Quarterly Journal of Economics* 105(1): 135–54.

James, Estelle, and Robert Palacios. 1994. "Comparing Administrative Costs of Pension Schemes." World Bank, Policy Research Department, Poverty and Human Resources Division, Washington, D.C.

World Bank. 1994. *Averting the Old Age Crisis.* New York: Oxford University Press.

Comment on "Government Provision and Regulation of Economic Support in Old Age," by Peter Diamond

Salvador Valdés-Prieto

The central issue in current discussions of pension policy is whether traditional state-run defined benefit systems, most of them financed on a pay-as-you-go basis, should be replaced with privately operated and funded defined contribution systems. *Averting the Old Age Crisis* (World Bank 1994) proposes a three-pillar policy that in effect espouses the introduction of privately managed defined contribution systems and a reduction in the size of public defined benefit systems. Peter Diamond offers a critique of this policy recommendation, on which I comment.

Immaturity, Politics, and the Three Pillars

Some countries have an immature defined benefit system, meaning that the first generation of workers that will have rights to a full pension once coverage has stabilized has not yet retired. I understand Diamond's policy framework for this set of countries to be as follows. For political reasons related to framing effects, defined benefit systems have a strong tendency to redistribute in favor of the generations of workers alive before the system matures. Societies that like this type of redistribution should thus favor starting a defined benefit system. Those that dislike this type of distribution should propose a defined contribution system. Diamond writes that the two systems are equally nontransparent; it is just that one focuses on benefits while the other focuses on contributions.

I agree that in a defined benefit system political attention focuses on whether the "same" benefit formula is being applied to different generations, with little attention devoted to differences in the contributions required from each generation. However, in a defined contribution system the focus is on contributions and benefits simultaneously. I disagree with the suggestion that defined contribution systems focus solely on contributions. As a close observer of the Chilean defined contribution system, I can report that the center of public discussion of most reforms has been whether they will improve benefits. That the contribution rate will remain constant is taken

Salvador Valdés-Prieto is professor of economics at the Catholic University of Chile.

Annual World Bank Conference on Development Economics 1995

for granted. That seems to be the case in Malaysia and Singapore as well. A defined contribution design reduces framing effects and allows the polity to focus on the system as a whole. Only the defined benefit system suffers from framing effects that induce uninformed policymaking.

A side issue is that during the immature phase of a system the poor will receive considerably less under a defined contribution system than under a defined benefit system. Of course, so will the rich of the original generation. Some people may still prefer the defined benefit system if they value the transfers to the poor more than they dislike the even larger transfers to the rich. This argument for a defined benefit system does not take into account the fate of the future poor. Once the defined benefit system matures, many generations of the poor will have to bear large taxes to finance the transfers paid to both poor and rich retirees who were alive during the immature phase. Current proposals in the United States to withdraw support for the poor young while most pensioners enjoy a comfortable standard of living may be an example of this problem.

Now consider a multipillar policy—which I define as the coexistence of a defined benefit and a defined contribution system—for countries with immature systems. From the perspective of avoiding framing effects in pension policymaking, this proposal seems unwise. The defined benefit pillar is a clear political winner over the defined contribution pillar, because the defined benefit pillar allows politicians to please today's voters at the cost of future generations. An alternative approach is a single defined contribution pillar plus redistribution, in which a mandatory defined contribution pillar is supplemented by taxes, transfers, and monitoring institutions that redistribute toward the elderly poor.

Consider a country at an early stage of an immature defined benefit system, with a low contribution rate that yields a cash surplus, as happened by 1992 in El Salvador, which had a contribution rate of 3.5 percent, and in Colombia, which had a contribution rate of 6.5 percent. In those countries stopping the growth of the defined benefit pillar requires a gradual reduction of legislated benefits to a level that can still be financed by this low contribution rate once the system matures. This level of benefits will be quite low, so there will be demand for a supplement, which can be met by mandating the gradual introduction of a new defined contribution pillar alongside the (smaller) defined benefit pillar.

Such a policy freezes intergenerational redistribution at the current level without rolling it back, so there are no fiscal transition costs. Instead, the originally scheduled increase in contributions to the defined benefit system are channeled to a new defined contribution system, while the benefit promises of the defined benefit system are reduced and those paid by the defined contribution system take over. Adopting the multipillar approach in the middle of the introductory phase has much smaller fiscal costs than a later rollback.

However, such a multipillar approach may be a political nonstarter because it dashes the expectations of today's voters that they will receive large intergenerational transfers. It may also violate legally sanctioned property rights. In addition, the stability of the reform is questionable. Framing effects continue to favor a reverse reform, in which contributions to the defined benefit system are raised while contributions to the defined contribution system are scaled back. This approach allows politicians to please current voters, as happened in Argentina and Chile in the early 1950s.

Diamond points out that the central question is how a reform will contribute to the politically difficult act of reducing promised benefits to future retirees who are alive today. I would add the question of how to design a system that permanently reduces the likelihood at some later date of politically expedient acts to increase promised benefits to the generations that currently vote. Diamond asks whether a more basic change that aims directly at the framing effects associated with defined benefit systems may make today's workers more willing to accept the loss of the intergenerational transfer they had expected, while also preventing future relapses.

The evidence from democratic political systems is limited. The Colombian reform of 1994 opted for the multipillar solution, but many observers fear back-sliding. The public institution that manages the defined benefit pillar has been allowed to advertise on the radio about the superior benefits it offers current generations, which of course come from the system's growing coverage and therefore from intergenerational redistribution.

The United Kingdom introduced an earnings-related defined benefit system in 1978 called SERPS. But reforms in 1988 and 1995 changed course, dramatically reducing SERPS benefits in relative terms in favor of the growth of personal pensions. In this case the policy shift seems permanent because voters are frightened about long-term fiscal stability. They have been reminded that such factors as increasing longevity and lower birthrates will make the future fiscal cost of a defined benefit system extremely onerous. Argentina seems to have introduced a multipillar system in 1994, but the 16 percent tax rate associated with the defined benefit pillar coupled with low benefits suggests that this pillar is just a cover for a large earnings tax to finance the transition.

Two countries have followed the approach of a single defined contribution pillar plus redistribution. In democratic Chile (after 1989) a relapse to a defined benefit system appears unthinkable, because the old defined benefit system is associated with patronage practices and the new defined contribution system has delivered more than was expected. Peru chose the same design in its 1993 reform, but the authorities' unwillingness to face the full fiscal costs has reduced the credibility of that reform.

While the evidence accumulates for or against a multipillar system on one side and a single defined contribution pillar plus redistribution on the other, I suggest that the World Bank should favor any reform in countries with immature retirement systems that limits intergenerational redistribution led by framing effects.

Countries with Mature Systems

There is a large set of countries with mature defined benefit systems, from Japan, Western Europe, and (maybe) the United States to China and countries in Eastern Europe and the former Soviet Union.

The first task is to make these out-of-balance defined benefit systems sustainable. This seems to call for major reductions in benefits. The critical problem is that, as the private sector grows in Eastern Europe, the former Soviet Union, and China, collecting contributions has become a major fiscal problem. An urgent role for the World Bank in these countries is to help them design and implement tax administration and collection systems that work in a private economy. The option of outright default on pension commitments, which occurred in practice in Russia, is inequitable and unsustainable. Of course, benefits should be streamlined, health and housing benefits must be separated from pensions, and egregious redistributions should be stopped. My point is that reducing benefits will not solve the fiscal problem but preventing a drop in contribution coverage might.

However, this is not true for countries with a mature system that is not currently out of balance. Countries in that position can consider an overall pension reform of a different type, by replacing hidden pension debt with explicit government debt, hidden labor taxes with explicit labor taxes, and the traditional defined benefit pension system with a three-pillar system or with a single defined contribution pillar plus redistribution. Note that the replacement of implicit with explicit debt occurs gradually over a forty-year period, so there would be no dramatic impact on financial markets (Valdés-Prieto 1996). Why adopt such a reform, which does not increase national savings? Because it offers potentially significant efficiency gains.

One gain from such a reform that is especially attractive for small countries is that it allows international diversification of pension assets, a feature absent from state-run pay-as-you-go systems. For large countries like China and Russia, the most important gain from such a reform may be a boost to the development of domestic capital markets. For large countries that already have a capital market, gains may come from improvements in the quality of pension legislation once the framing effects in the treatment of shocks such as an increase in life expectancy are eliminated, and from reductions in the labor market distortions associated with defined benefit systems, such as limited labor mobility and large implicit taxes on formal labor contracts.

On the other hand if this type of reform implants a simplistic defined contribution design, it may sacrifice valuable risk-sharing features of the defined-benefit design. My view is that it is possible to create designs that continue to be actuarially fair but nevertheless provide partial or total insurance for longevity risk, lifetable risk, short working life risk, and other risks while relying on heavy holdings of corporate and government debt and international diversification to limit investment risk. Inflation risk can be eliminated with indexed bonds and deposits, as Chile has shown (less than 5 percent of pension funds are invested in nominal debt securities).

The other problem with this reform is that it requires somebody to decide where to invest the explicit assets, which may be substantial. That is where privatization comes in, as it allows decentralized investment decisions and forces politicians who want to use the funds to face a market test: the securities they issue must compete with those issued by the private sector and by other governments. Private provision of pension services has two other impacts worth mentioning. First, it enhances private sector development, which is an important concern for the World Bank. It is private provision that brings capital market development, with its positive spillover effects on the growth prospects of other parts of the private economy. Second, existing private pension systems are more expensive to operate than existing well-run state systems, although some claims in this area have been exaggerated. The World Bank could play an important role in this area by supporting research and promoting the international exchange of best practices.

Two Design Issues

One design issue relates to privatizing the provision of pension services, which Diamond reports to be a costly option from a regulatory and administrative perspective. One such area is the regulation of commissions. In a recent study I argue that the large number of salespeople hired by Chilean pension fund managers derives in part from misguided price and tax regulations (Valdés-Prieto 1995). One regulation prohibits fund managers and members from agreeing on even limited exit charges to cover some of the cost of processing exit from a fund. (Chileans are free to switch fund management companies.) The absence of exit charges subsidizes switches between fund managers and makes salespeople too "efficient." Another regulation prohibits fund managers and members from agreeing on commissions that are smaller than listed commissions. This tilts bargaining power toward fund managers and prevents large savings in marketing costs by rendering group plans and group negotiations useless (see the recent comparison of systems in Australia and Chile by Bateman, Piggott, and Valdés-Prieto 1995). A third regulation exempts commission payments from personal income tax. In a system of mandatory contributions with a fixed total number of members, this exemption reduces the elasticity of demand to commissions as perceived by individual pension fund managers. The lower price elasticity allows higher margins, which in turn increases the equilibrium number of salespeople.

The available data show that administrative charges are higher in private pension markets, but the magnitude is unclear. Chilean fund managers that provide services to workers charged an average of $51.60 a year per contributor in 1992. Thirty percent of net commission income in 1994 went to pay the salaries of the salesforce. By comparison, the average cost per pensioner or worker in the government-managed defined benefit system in Chile, which serves workers who chose to remain in the old system, was $40.80 in 1993 (Reid and Mitchell 1995). This government-managed system was created in 1979 from the merger of twenty-two separate institutions. It has received technical and financial assistance from the World Bank to invest in modern information systems and to help it focus management efforts on performance.

Now consider the cost of serving pensioners in the United States. Dividing the portion of administrative costs devoted by the Social Security Administration to pensioner services (Sunden and Mitchell 1993) by the number of pensioners yields

$47.50 per person in 1990, in 1992 dollars. Spreading this cost over the average active life yields an annual figure in the $15–$20 range. This may be compared with the $130.90 per year of active life that U.S. life insurance companies charge for group annuities, on the same basis, and the $320.90 per year they charge for individual annuities (Valdés-Prieto 1994a). This difference is much larger and certainly justifies Diamond's worry about the costs of annuity markets relative to the costs of a well-run public pension program.

A second design issue concerns the contribution rate. Diamond shows why it is desirable to keep the size of contributions to mandatory retirement income systems small. I recently proposed a plan for a flexible contribution rate that would reduce some of the problems Diamond mentions (Valdés-Prieto 1994c). The core idea is that each worker who voluntarily contributes additional sums to the mandatory old age account for four years becomes exempt from further mandatory contributions. Workers who save a bit more than the mandatory amount at middle age, when credit constraints cease to bind, thereby demonstrating that they are not myopic, would be free to allocate their past and future savings as they see fit. The sacrifice of temporarily locking up voluntary savings in an old age account would be compensated by the gain from achieving the freedom to use all the funds later on to finance health emergencies, children's college expenses, or other life-cycle or investment needs. There is a wide-open field for World Bank research on improving the design of retirement income policy around the world.

References

Bateman, H., J. Piggott and S. Valdés-Prieto. 1995. "Australia y Chile: Previsión privada con normas diferentes." Working Paper 176. Catholic University of Chile, Santiago.

Reid, Gary, and O. Mitchell. 1995. "Social Security Administration in Latin America and the Caribbean." World Bank, Latin American and the Caribbean Technical Department, Washington, D.C.

Sunden, A., and O. Mitchell. 1993. "An Examination of Social Security Administration Costs in the United States." Latin America and the Caribbean Regional Office, World Bank Technical Department, Washington, D.C.

Valdés-Prieto, Salvador. 1994a. "Administrative Charges in Pensions in Chile, Malaysia, Zambia, and the United States." Policy Research Working Paper 1372. World Bank, Policy Research Department, Macroeconomics and Growth Division, Washington D.C.; also in Spanish in *Cuadernos de Economía* 93 (August): 185–227.

———. 1994b. "Earnings-Related Mandatory Pensions: Concepts for Design." Policy Research Working Paper 1296. World Bank, Policy Research Department, Poverty and Human Resources Division, Washington D.C.

———. 1994c. "La obligación de cotizar: una alternativa de solución." *Administración y Economía UC.* Bulletin of the Faculty of Economics and Management, Catholic University of Chile, Santiago.

———. 1995. "Vendedores de AFP: ¿Producto del mercado o de regulaciones ineficientes ?" Working Paper 178. Catholic University of Chile, Santiago.

———. 1996. "Financing a Pension Reform toward Private Funded Pensions." In Salvador Valdés-Prieto, ed., *The Economics of Pensions: Principles, Policies, and International Experience.* Cambridge: Cambridge University Press.

World Bank. 1994. *Averting the Old Age Crisis.* New York: Oxford University Press.

Floor Discussion of "Government Provision and Regulation of Economic Support in Old Age," by Peter Diamond

L ike the World Bank study *Averting the Old Age Crisis,* Diamond's presentation was fascinating and filled with insight, said Willem Buiter (discussant from another session). However, the works share a weakness: an overly technocratic approach to designing systems of economic support for old age and a downplaying of intergenerational conflict about distribution. Yes, it matters whether something is funded or unfunded, is a defined benefit or a defined contribution, is single pillar, multipillar, or no pillar, but none of this makes the intergenerational conflict go away. A large, mandated, funded, privately managed component of the system can still be raided by a government that has distributional objectives, using ordinary tax instruments. So if there is no consensus within society on intergenerational distribution, the pension reforms being discussed are of little value.

Incentives to stimulate private savings usually take the form of tax-exempt or tax-deferred savings, said a participant from the World Bank, and the income from compound interest could take decades, under generations of government. How can we ascertain politicians' commitment to resist the temptation to tap into potential tax revenues part way through that savings cycle? The participant had a similar concern about corporate pension plans. For any mature pension system, it is inevitable that the government will introduce complex laws about compliance, with requirements corporations might see as prohibitive. Knowing that a particular mechanism might not provide adequate retirement income, the corporations might adopt alternative mechanisms and shy away from providing the best pension plan. Finally, she observed that pension plans cannot be designed in isolation: the definition of retirement income should be expanded to include the costs of medical care as an essential component of net income requirements.

Both participants are essentially asking the same question, said Nicholas Barr (discussant): What guarantees that the government will keep its greedy paws off pension funds? And the answer is, you cannot necessarily trust governments. Governments can misbehave if they want to, no matter what type of pension arrangement is in

This session was chaired by Jessica P. Einhorn, senior vice president and treasurer, at the World Bank.
Annual World Bank Conference on Development Economics 1995
©1996 The International Bank for Reconstruction and Development / THE WORLD BANK

place. If a Machiavellian government wants to get its hands on pension funds or private wealth, it can do so by printing a lot of extra money, generating plenty of inflation, and benefiting from the yield of the inflation tax. And since no pension arrangement is safe from the government, the key political question to ask is how to strengthen government capacity. Diamond had made Barr realize that the lesson from Chile and East Asia is that successful reform rests on two legs: the capacity of both the private sector and the government must be developed. The question is, what can the World Bank do to help governments introduce better, more consistent policies?

Estelle James (discussant) agreed that bad governments could wreck anything. So could polarized societies. But she believed that some systems make it easier for governments to misbehave. Systems that set up checks and balances between countervailing powers make it harder for governments to be irresponsible. She believed a funded, decentrally managed but regulated system was more immune to irresponsible behavior than either a pure pay-as-you-go scheme or a publicly managed funded scheme. James agreed that it was important that the definition of retirement income include income to cover medical care because both private and social health spending were clearly age-related; you cannot discuss aging without discussing health problems. And while Diamond spent a lot of time discussing what adequate retirement income would be, that amount depends on whether people are paying for their own health care.

True, a funded pension system could be raided through taxes, said Salvador Valdés-Prieto (discussant), but that was true of any form of capital. Even land could be redistributed to friends of public officials. The issue really was what the World Bank could do to improve the political design of systems, to make them more transparent. Making systems transparent enough so that intergenerational transfers can be identified reduces the probability of a large tax on capital and, in countries that already have a large tax on capital and a mature defined-benefit system, introduces the possibility of eliminating the tax.

Diamond responded that he did not think the conflict was intergenerational. In his experience raids on funds happened because there were alternative uses for current resources. He believed that if the United States had large mandated individual accounts like Chile's, the amounts in each account would be viewed as a basis for means testing for other programs. Unemployment insurance benefits, for example, or medical subsidies for the poor might become available only after individuals had used up their retirement account—in lieu of having Medicare or another system that extended to younger people. The conflict is over how the funds will be used, and these funds are more vulnerable to means testing considerations partly because there are well-documented amounts in them. There is a risk to any capital, as Valdés-Prieto said, but these funds are more vulnerable than others.

As for the problem of regulating private plans, Diamond responded that there is lots of room for private corporate plans and that overregulation is less likely if the type of plan allowed is restricted. The relative harm inherent in defined benefit or defined contribution plans is different for corporate plans than for government plans. Diamond saw little merit in corporate defined benefit plans, which are governed by complex rules; worker mobility makes it difficult to evaluate them for individual employees. He would not be unhappy to see a tax in transition economies favoring (in the sense of allowing room for the creation of) defined contribution plans and banning defined benefit plans for corporations. The main problems are information problems and potential fraud.

Diamond asserted that single-pillar systems have better redistributional effects, said James, but she knew of no facts to support that view. In the current systems, for example, there is no evidence of lifetime redistribution from people with high permanent incomes to people with low permanent incomes. There is some intergenerational redistribution from the young (both rich and poor) to the old (both rich and poor), but the largest transfers go to the old people whose pensions are higher because their incomes were higher. James then cited an article that she had seen in the New York Times that said high social security taxes on young families were contributing to increasing youth poverty in the United States.

A participant who had worked on *Averting the Old Age Crisis* disputed Diamond's claim that elderly populations in OECD countries have lower poverty rates than other segments of the population. This finding was true for eight OECD countries for which they had reliable data, but in Germany and the United States poverty rates were higher for the elderly than for other parts of the population. Diamond had also said that in the United States the lower poverty rate among the elderly was attributable to the presence of both redistribution and retirement income provision within a single pillar. But the countries in which the elderly have lower poverty rates are those that have well-defined redistribution pillars—Canada, the Netherlands, and Sweden. In light of these errors, the participant wondered if Diamond still considered the U.S. system to be well-designed.

Diamond responded that he had intended to say that the elderly in OECD countries have lower poverty rates than some other segments of the population, not all other segments. As for whether the U.S. system was well-designed, that had to be answered in the context of U.S. politics. It seemed to him that it was important to ask how much redistribution could be expected in a country with the politics and attitudes of the United States. There is no way to draw conclusions about structure based on a comparison of, say, U.S. and Swedish structures; the Swedes can be expected to achieve more redistribution no matter what kind of structure they have. But the U.S. social security system has succeeded in driving down poverty among the elderly. Diamond said that he had not claimed that the redistribution was good because it all went to the poor. He had explicitly noted that redistribution was always mixed—some going to people you would like to see getting more and some going to people you would prefer did not get more. He had said that the United States gave away much larger sums to the well-off elderly than to the poor elderly. But some might prefer such an arrangement to one that leaves the elderly—particularly those who lived through the Great Depression—with less money overall. Diamond had not decided whether it was a good or a bad result; he simply emphasized that it was an important issue.

Engendering Economics: New Perspectives on Women, Work, and Demographic Change

Nancy Folbre

Rent-seeking coalitions based on gender create a gender bias in social institutions that influences market outcomes. How does economic development, which involves substantial relocation of economic functions from the family to the market and the state, affect the behavior of gender coalitions and the evolution of gender bias? Economists will not be able to adequately answer this question until they develop a broader research agenda and begin to collect more systematic data on institutional bias, the organization of nonmarket work, and the distribution of resources within the family.

engender. v. 1. To give rise to. 2. To procreate.
—American Heritage Dictionary, third edition

Gender is now a popular, indeed indispensable, word in the development vocabulary. Most major international organizations, including the United Nations and the World Bank, have special units devoted to research and policy formulation on women's issues. A growing official literature describes the importance of moving from models of "women in development" toward models of "gender and development," signaling a new emphasis on analyzing men's roles as well as women's.[1] A widespread consensus on the benefits of investing in women's education has radically altered public policy in many parts of the world. Yet discussions of gender have remained segregated within special reports or specific policy initiatives, having relatively little impact on the mainstream discourse of development economics.

There are many good reasons to focus on women. Women generally have lower incomes and less leisure time than men, and seldom have equal opportunities to develop their capabilities. Investments in women's human capital typically yield a greater rate of return in labor productivity, child health, and family welfare than investments in men's human capital (Subbarao and Raney 1993). But apart from

Nancy Folbre is professor of economics at the University of Massachusetts at Amherst. The author thanks Martha Chen for helpful suggestions on an earlier draft, and Elissa Braunstein for research assistance.

Annual World Bank Conference on Development Economics 1995

these practical benefits lies the possibility that the growing literature on women's productive and reproductive work will offer important insights into the development process itself. "Engendering" economics—forcing it to explain the role gender plays in economic life—could help us better understand the evolution of social institutions and how they shape market outcomes.

This article uses the concepts of the new institutional economics to illustrate differing approaches to women and development and to explain the theoretical significance of recent empirical research on women, work, and demographic change. The central hypothesis is that rent-seeking coalitions based on gender create a significant gender bias in social institutions, which strongly influence market outcomes. In turn, economic development, which involves a substantial relocation of economic functions from the family to the market and the state, affects the behavior of gender coalitions and the evolution of gender bias. This process could be better understood if economists paid more attention to institutional bias, the organization of nonmarket work, and the distribution of resources within the family. These issues are explored by considering four separate but related topics: property rights over land; explicit and implicit contracts governing intrafamily distribution; other institutional influences on the labor market, including government policies toward benefits and pensions; and estimates of the value of nonmarket work.

Gender Bias and Distributional Coalitions

> In most cases, people do not perceive themselves to be rent seekers. . . .
> —*Anne Krueger (1974)*

Much of the recent research on women, gender, and development focuses on gender bias, a term used to convey the notion that social institutions do not treat men and women in a welfare-neutral way. The problem emphasized is almost always male bias, and explanations for this bias fall into two categories (Kabeer 1994; Moser 1993). The women in development approach, the first to emerge in the literature, is an application of modernization theory. It treats the marginalization of women during development as an oversight that can be remedied by better incorporating them in the market economy (Boserup 1970; Rogers 1980).[2] From this perspective gender bias reflects outdated norms and values that are no longer functional for society. The favored prescription is to invest more in women's human capital. Emphasis is placed on the large gains in overall efficiency that can result from a reduction in sex discrimination. Women's position in industrial countries such as the United States is held up as a model for women in developing countries.

The gender and development approach is less optimistic. It emphasizes the persistent, structural character of inequality between men and women (Benería and Sen 1981; Sen and Grown 1987; Kabeer 1994). Merely incorporating women into the development process will not improve their welfare—the process itself must be modified. But this modification will meet resistance from men because it will entail a redistribution of income along gender lines that may not be fully compensated by gains in overall efficiency. The position of women in industrial countries is not inspiring because they remain disadvantaged, particularly regarding the distribution of the costs of children (Folbre 1994).

Although much has been written on the distinction between these two approaches, their theoretical underpinnings remain largely unexplored. Advocates of the women in development approach tend to employ quantitative methods, particularly human capital models. Advocates of the gender and development approach often rely on descriptive data and historical narrative, with liberal applications of the word "empowerment." Both sides of this debate can be reinterpreted using the concepts of the new institutional economics. Indeed, examined this way, the gender and development literature provides strong support for the institutionalist theory of rent-seeking coalitions.

An Institutionalist Primer

The new institutional economics focuses on the evolution of social institutions, which form the context in which individual decisions are made (North 1981, 1990; Olson 1982; Hodgson 1987). Broadly defined, social institutions are means of social coordination, ranging from organizations such as the firm, the family, and the state to the political rules and social norms that help such organizations function.[3] Their stability, efficiency, and incentive structures influence the process of economic development (Williamson 1995) and the empowerment of social groups designated by gender, nation, race, class, or other dimensions of collective identity (Folbre 1994).

What forces shape the evolution of social institutions? In answering this question most institutional economists stress the dictates of efficiency enforced by the pressures of competition. In the long run the social institutions that provide the most efficient solution to coordination problems prevail. Coase's (1960) concise formulation of this approach provided a basis for later applications to the family (Becker 1981) and the firm (Williamson 1985). In applying this perspective to economic history, North widened its purview to the analysis of social norms (1981, 1990).

The transaction costs perspective maintains that current social institutions may not be perfectly optimal. Some are at risk of being eliminated by heightened competition. Some may be adjusting to changes in relative prices and incomes with an uncomfortable lag because of inertial tendencies. Cultural norms, in particular, cannot be changed overnight. But despite these imperfections and lags, social institutions are evolving toward an efficient, Parieto-optimal equilibrium. This theoretical perspective implicitly underlies much of the women in development literature.

Its basic reasoning runs: a gender wage differential emerges in traditional agrarian economies partly because men have greater physical strength, which is an especially important factor of production (Goldin 1990). Also, the high fertility rates that characterize agrarian economies make women dependent on male support. Social institutions, including social norms, both reflect and enforce male dominance. In the course of economic development, however, technological change increases the importance of mental skills relative to physical strength and encourages fertility decline (Becker 1981; Schultz 1993). This change destabilizes the traditional gender division of labor: male dominance becomes less efficient. But, traditional social norms (as well as mistaken development policy) may impede the adjustment to modern egalitarian norms.

An alternative view, which might be termed the "distributional conflict paradigm," insists on the importance of processes of collective aggrandizement. As Knight (1992, p. 19) puts it, "the ongoing development of social institutions is not best explained as a Pareto-superior response to collective goals or benefits but, rather, as a by-product of conflicts over distributional gains." Social institutions such as the firm or the family may enhance efficiency, but they may also serve the interests of particular groups. Obstacles to social change are not only manifestations of lagged adjustment, they often reflect active resistance on the part of powerful groups, who may be willing to pay a price, in lower efficiency, for continued control over a disproportionate share of output.

Gender-Based Conflict

The best known proponents of the distributional conflict paradigm have shied away from any direct consideration of gender. Olson (1982) describes how distributional coalitions can clog the process of efficient allocation but focuses on interest groups rather than groups that individuals do not choose to join.[4] He never considers the possibility that men and women might be groups contending over the distribution of resources. Neither Buchanan (1980) nor Krueger (1974) describe men as a group that might engage in rent seeking through the state. But there is no reason why this theoretical framework cannot be applied to groups based on gender.

Men and women are not literally interest groups. Most individuals do not choose their gender in the same way that they join a club. But they often identify with others of their same gender, define common interests, and engage in collective action, ranging from participation in explicit political activity to less formal efforts to defend or develop advantageous social norms. A large body of feminist theory, as well as much of the gender and development literature reviewed in this article, illustrates how male collective action has led to the development of social institutions that give men important economic advantages in control over property, income, and labor. It also shows that women have increasingly begun to engage in collective action to contest and modify such institutions (see Folbre 1994).

There is much to be gained, however, by moving beyond purely descriptive accounts to more analytical efforts to test the hypothesis that gender bias reflects the rent-seeking efforts of gender coalitions. More open debate over this issue could help overcome a certain reticence evident in the literature today. Among policymakers, at least, there is a strong tendency to avoid consideration of social conflict, partly out of fear of intensifying it. The women in development approach, with its "everybody gains" emphasis on increasing efficiency, is especially appealing to policymakers and multilateral institutions (Klasen 1993; Kardam 1990).

But policymakers could benefit from a more forthright analysis of the distributional gains and losses that policies impose on distinct social groups. One of the insights of the new institutional economics is that rent-seeking coalitions are often successful at blocking changes that could benefit society as a whole, partly because of the difficulty of devising and enforcing the kinds of side payments that could partially compensate for distributional losses (Libecap 1989). More open consideration of distributional conflict, in other words, may help resolve rather than intensify it.

At the same time, devoting more attention to the new institutional economics could encourage gender and development theorists to move beyond a documentation of inequality to an analysis of its functional implications. Unpleasant though the political implications may seem, hierarchy and inequality may serve economic functions by lowering transaction costs and solving coordination problems. More egalitarian alternatives are unlikely to be successful unless they are at least as efficient. For instance, challenges to traditional male authority must be accompanied by alternative ways of enforcing familial obligations and encouraging commitments to children. The experience of industrial countries suggests that the weakening of patriarchal relations within the family is often accompanied by a weakening of intrafamily income flows and growth in poverty among mothers and children living on their own (Folbre 1994).

Finally, more serious efforts to examine gender-based conflicts could address a serious theoretical weakness in the distributional conflict paradigm—the difficulty of specifying the relationship among different types of social groups and resulting overlaps among different types of rent-seeking activity. There is a clear analogy between forms of collective aggrandizement based on gender and those based on other dimensions of collective identity, such as nation or race or class. Men often gang up on women. Likewise, men and women in strong groups often gang up on men and women in weak groups.

Women's best interests are not always best served by gender solidarity alone. As many scholars and activists from developing countries have emphasized, women identify themselves as members of coalitions based on nation, race, or class that claim their allegiance (Mohanty 1991; Agarwal 1994b). The forms of inequality that women resist and the types of collective action that they engage in depend largely on specific political and historical circumstances. Research on the form, timing, and intensity of gender conflict in different countries could help economists decipher the behavior of distributional coalitions in general.

Collective Action, Gender, and Property Rights

> Please go and ask the sarkar [government] why when it distributes land we don't get a title. Are we not peasants? If my husband throws me out, where is my security?
>
> —*West Bengali woman, cited in Agarwal (1994b)*

Economists emphasize the significant impact that property rights have on incentives to work, invest, and innovate (Libecap 1989). Yet relatively few have systematically examined gender-based differences in rights to land ownership. The gender and development literature offers evidence of such differences, which have strong implications not only for agricultural productivity but also for women's bargaining position within the family and the labor market.

Land Ownership, Family Law, and Colonial Policies

Property rights to land are bound to family law because most claims to property are earned through either inheritance or marriage. Analysis of these rights is complicated considerably by conflicting sets of laws (formal compared with customary, secular compared with religious) and large discrepancies between legal precepts and actual practices. Most of the detailed research on these issues has focused on Sub-Saharan Africa and South Asia, although there is some evidence from Latin America. In general, women have far less access to land than men and, largely as a result, less access to credit and technical extension services (Holt and Ribe 1991; Staudt 1978). Patriarchal rules of land transmission and ownership do not follow a market logic and certainly do not allow women to compete on even ground with men. Although they may have some functional logic, patriarchal rules also enable men to extract monopolistic rents from women—not in the literal sense of charging them money, but in the broader sense of reducing their income per hour worked. Patriarchal rules establish the male head of household as the residual claimant of the household enterprise and provide economic incentives to maximize his share of output and leisure (Alchian and Demsetz 1972). The extent to which these incentives are countervailed by familial altruism is empirically uncertain (this point is made in Becker 1981 and later in this article).

Traditional tribal law in most areas of Sub-Saharan Africa accorded access to land based on relationship to a kinship group. While women enjoyed the right to use land, protected by custom, their formal rights were almost always subordinate to those of men (Martin and Hashi 1992a). Despite enormous diversity among tribes, most women did not have inheritance rights to a father's or a husband's property. This gender bias was intensified and, in a sense, homogenized, by colonial policies that imposed privatization. Land titles were almost always handed out to male heads of household (Martin and Hashi 1992a).

Today, women in Sub-Saharan Africa often do not have formal ownership rights to land, even if they provide the bulk of agricultural labor (Martin and Hashi 1992c; Blackden and Morris-Hughes 1993). The disjuncture between ownership and labor has been heightened by extensive male outmigration. But this problem cannot be explained as a simple legacy of the past; relatively recent policies set by independent African governments have reinforced male property rights. For instance, the Zimbabwe constitution of 1980 did not grant women legal guarantees of joint ownership, inheritance from husbands, or even control over earnings, despite the efforts of women's organizations (Cheater 1981). Zimbabwean women have benefited little from the modest resettlement program, which is based on government purchases of land from white farmers. Only male settlers who are married or widowed and female widows with dependents have been eligible to receive land—women on their own, whether deserted, divorced, or widowed, have been excluded. As a result the economic position of widows and orphans is worse than what it was in traditional rural settings, in which the husband's kin assumed some responsibility for them (Munachonga 1988).

In South Asia women have seldom worked as independent farmers with separate plots or crops. But they often provide agricultural labor, and land ownership is a crucial determinant of their economic welfare. More is known about the history and evolution of gendered land rights in this region than in any other area of the world because of the pioneering work of Agarwal (1994a, 1995). The precolonial period was characterized by considerable regional variation, with some communities in northeastern and southern India and in Sri Lanka practicing matrilineal or bilateral inheritance. Agarwal argues that women had greater bargaining power in the family and greater freedom of movement in these areas, though they seldom enjoyed any of the prerogatives of controlling or managing land (1994a).

As in Africa, colonialism and national integration imposed more uniform standards of inheritance, which weakened women's access to land in many respects. Privatization itself led to a reduction in access to resources such as fodder and fuel, with a concomitant rise in the amount of time and effort women were forced to devote to meeting their households' subsistence needs.

Legal reforms adopted after the demise of formal colonialism furthered women's legal rights to land. In India the Hindu Succession Act of 1956 gave daughters, widows, and mothers of intestate men rights equal to those of sons. In Pakistan the West Pakistan Muslim Personal Law Application Act of 1962 legally entitled Muslim women to inherit agricultural property. But even within these reformed systems, gender bias has been exacerbated by enforcement problems, particularly in regions governed by customary law (Agarwal 1994a). In addition, government-sponsored land reform programs typically distributed land to male heads of households. As a result few women own land and only a very few exercise effective, independent control over it.

The picture for Latin America is remarkably similar: although in many communities women have enjoyed bilateral inheritance longer than in South Asia, they remain far less likely than men to own land. Most reforms implemented after World War II redistributed property that was under oligarchical control to individual men, with little provision for wive's co-ownership and active disregard for single women and those heading their own households (Deere and León 1987). More recent land reforms in Honduras were not so egregiously biased. But although single women were legally eligible to receive redistributed land, stricter conditions were imposed on them than on men (Safilios-Rothschild 1988).

Male Control of Property: An Institutional Explanation

Why is women's lack of access to property a characteristic shared across regions? It reflects men's control over political and legal institutions, which have enforced patriarchal marriage and kinship systems (Martin and Hashi 1992b). In most countries women have only begun to participate in the formal specification of property rights. Social systems based on a male monopoly over property emerged in many different contexts and prevailed, unchallenged, for long periods of time. Why?

Part of the answer may lie in an institutional logic linking relationships between men and women to those between parents and children. In traditional patriarchal regimes land ownership gave fathers considerable leverage over children and allowed them to expect at least some benefits in the form of labor contributions and support in old age (Caldwell 1982). Although this system raised the economic incentives for coercive forms of control over women, it also established an implicit rate of return for women's reproductive labor within the family economy. Men who abused or neglected their children or the mothers of their children lowered their own economic welfare. In the aggregate, male control over property provided an enforcement mechanism that created incentives for paternal care of dependents, with pronatalist, but also profamily effects.[5]

One conspicuous side effect of such an incentive structure is relative neglect of female children, often motivated by institutional arrangements (such as patrilineal property transmission and dowry) that make it easier for families to gain economically from sons than from daughters. But, ironically, the existence of such gender differentials testifies to the larger influence of pecuniary incentives—probably operating through social norms rather than through actual parental calculations—and suggests that the reduction of these incentives through loss of male control over land may contribute to neglect of both sons and daughters. Neglect is especially likely if there is little cultural or technical support for family planning and if the economic costs of children are rising more rapidly than fathers anticipated.

With the increase in individually based employment and declining farm sizes, obligations to care for kin become increasingly dependent on altruism. Men have less to gain from children's labor and from fulfilling responsibilities to mothers and children. Maximizing fertility becomes a less attractive economic strategy, and family commitments become more costly. Also, development typically reduces access to common property rights.[6] Under these circumstances the negative distributional consequences of exclusive male property rights become more salient for women and children, who become dependent on transfers that are increasingly contingent and unreliable. Furthermore, as women shift more of their time away from childcare and household services and into work outside the home, male monopolies over property become increasingly costly to them.

These adverse effects are exacerbated by the economic and demographic trends characteristic of most developing countries: the growth of employment outside agriculture has been relatively slow, and the agricultural labor force is becoming increasingly feminized in South Asia and Latin America (Agarwal 1994a; Deere 1995). Both male outmigration and cultural modernization lead to increased rates of desertion, separation, and divorce. And women become increasingly dependent on land ownership (even if only a small parcel) for economic security. Furthermore, several studies suggest that adult children's remittances to their parents are a positive function of parental asset ownership (Hoddinot 1992; Lucas and Stark 1985). Thus elderly women without land rights may be particularly vulnerable.

By lowering the returns to their labor, the absence of property rights also lowers women's reservation wage in the labor market. As women are becoming increasingly dependent on their individually earned wage, it is hardly surprising that they are beginning to realize that they need rights to family property. Women in many countries are increasingly engaging in forms of collective action designed to enhance such rights. And if they are not successful, their economic position is likely to worsen.

Family Law, Bargaining, and Intrafamily Distribution

Another set of nonmarket institutions has a substantial impact on the welfare of women: the claims of mothers and children on the income of fathers. Such claims, which can be considered both property rights and human rights, are shaped by explicit contracts (defined by law) and implicit contracts (defined by social norms). Historically, these contracts have been defined largely by men and have given men important benefits, which can be thought of as monopoly rents.

The traditional neoclassical theory of marriage holds that both partners benefit from efficiency gains if men specialize in market production and women in childrearing (Becker 1981). Yet no major tradition of family law actually guarantees married women's claims on their husbands' income stream (Glendon 1989). The transfers they receive depend almost entirely on the altruism of family members with access to market earnings. Fathers are expected and exhorted to provide a basic level of subsistence for mothers and children. But if they fail to do so, they seldom receive formal punishment.

Ten years ago the claim that there might be less-than-perfect altruism in the family, leading to significant welfare inequalities there, was considered far-fetched. Since then, however, publication of several (though a still relatively small number of) empirical studies has shifted the burden of proof to those who assume that the family can be treated as an undifferentiated unit (Alderman and others 1995; Dwyer and Bruce 1988; Schultz 1990; Thomas 1990). The traditional neoclassical model of joint utility and perfect altruism in the family has been supplemented, if not supplanted, by a new generation of bargaining power models.

Most important from an institutionalist perspective are models that show how property rights, contractual obligations, and social norms external to the household set the stage for unequal distributional outcomes. McElroy (1990) clearly demonstrates how "extra-environmental parameters" set by social policy influence a woman's fallback position (her income should she leave the household). Lundberg and Pollak (1993) incorporate cultural norms by arguing that the traditional division of labor and income is the fallback position for men and women bargaining over an alternative allocation. Sen (1990) observes that social norms may prevent women from noticing, much less resisting, inequality in the family.

Because men enjoy gains or rents as a result of extra-environmental parameters, they are motivated to act collectively to maintain those most advantageous to them.

At the same time extra-environmental parameters motivate women to act collectively to improve their bargaining position within the household. In particular, women's groups in northwest Europe, the United States, and Latin America have consistently fought for improved specification of maintenance and child support responsibilities (Folbre 1994).

Another legal issue that has received considerable attention is the enforcement of legal rights to physical safety. A recent World Bank study finds that rape, domestic violence, and sexual abuse impose major health costs, even in countries with seemingly strict legal protections (Heise, Pitanguy, and Germain 1994). Women are the primary victims; and when they respond with gender-based collective action, they often meet intense resistance. In 1968, for instance, women's groups in Kenya supported the Marriage Bill, which would have made wife-beating a criminal offense. It was defeated by male parliamentarians on the grounds that wife-beating was a customary practice and the bill threatened to impose foreign values on traditional culture (Gage and Njogu 1994). More recently, women in Latin America have developed women-only police stations, which facilitate reporting of domestic abuse (Heise, Pitanguy, and Germain 1994). Other community factors, such as the availability of public assistance for women, influence the probability that domestic violence will occur (Tauchen, Witte, and Long 1991).

The explicit and implicit contracts that define the rights and responsibilities of family life vary considerably among cultures and regions. In Sub-Saharan Africa many traditions have militated against income pooling, and mothers have traditionally been expected to provide for themselves and their children. This expectation remains in force today. Particularly in polygynous unions, mothers pay a disproportionate share of child maintenance costs (Gage and Njogu 1994). In most southern African countries maintenance laws are full of loopholes (Armstrong 1992). About Ghana, Abu (1983, pp. 161–62) writes, "the social forces constraining a man to look after his wife and children are relatively weak, and there is a considerable voluntary element in the arrangement." The economic consequences may not be negative as long as children are able to contribute to family income or the larger kinship unit is willing to help assume their costs. But as the demand for schooling increases along with school fees, the economic burden on mothers will rise.

Laws and norms governing income pooling within the household are stronger in other regions of the world. But a considerable body of research documents substantial gender inequality. Many empirical studies confirm what might be termed "the good mother" hypothesis: women generally devote a far larger share of their income and earnings to family needs than do men (Benería and Roldán 1987; Blumberg 1989; Chant 1991). Income that is controlled by women is more likely to be spent on children's health and nutrition and less likely to be spent on alcohol and adult goods (Dwyer and Bruce 1988; Hoddinott, Alderman, and Haddad forthcoming).

Unequal distribution of resources to male and female children within the household is also significant. Inequalities vary by region. In South Asia there is considerable evidence of preference for sons (Rosenzweig and Schultz 1982; Sen 1988). In Brazil mothers may spend more on daughters, fathers more on sons (Thomas 1990).

In Sub-Saharan Africa boys and girls are treated fairly equally (Haddad and Reardon 1993), possibly because brideprice rather than dowry customs are in effect.

Supporting Households Headed by Women

An emphasis on intrahousehold allocation is misleading because it deflects attention from the high percentage of households with children but no adult male. In Kenya 24 percent of all households were headed by women in 1980. A rural income distribution survey conducted in Botswana in 1974–75 found that 28 percent of households were headed by women, with no adult male present (Koussoudji and Mueller 1983). In rural India 30–35 percent of all households are headed by women (World Bank 1991). In Ghana female-headed households rose from 22 percent to 29 percent between 1960 and 1987–88 (Lloyd and Gage-Brandon 1993).

Men may leave their households to search for higher-paying jobs and may remit large shares of their wage income. But the experiences of the United States and northwestern Europe suggest that female headship is often associated with the attenuation of income flows from men to women and children. Accurate data on the number of households economically maintained by women alone, which can be generated only through detailed household surveys, are a priority for future research (Folbre 1990).

Female headship does not necessarily increase economic vulnerability, as shown by studies of Brazil (Barros, Fox, and Mendonca 1993) and Jamaica (Louat, Grosh, and van der Gaag 1992). But women who are raising small children without the help of male income are at great risk economically, as are their children. The extensive data available for industrial countries show that these families are highly susceptible to poverty, even in countries that provide them with some public assistance (Folbre 1994). Relatively little attention has been devoted to studies of their welfare in the developing world, although Desai (1991) found that children of single mothers in three Latin American countries (such as those born to women in consensual unions) were more like to be undernourished than those living with both parents.

Family dissolution and out-of-wedlock births are extremely costly to mothers because prevailing family laws offer little protection. Only a few countries in northwestern Europe, most notably France and Sweden, have successfully developed mechanisms for enforcing child support. In the United States less than half of all mothers raising children on their own are awarded child support, and only about half of these (25 percent of the total) receive the full amount they are due. Moreover, the level of payments is low and has declined in recent years (Beller and Graham 1993). In Japan a 1988 study revealed that only about 14 percent of divorced fathers made some kind of payment for their children (Goode 1993).

Little is known about enforcing child support in developing countries because data are not systematically collected. Indeed, data were not collected in the United States until 1980, when women's groups successfully lobbied Congress to require the Census to conduct regular surveys. Women in developing countries have been less successful in raising the issue. In Kenya an affiliation act that would have required men to provide financial support for their children born out of wedlock was repealed in 1969 by an all-male assembly (Morgan 1984). Ghana passed a decree in 1977 establishing family tribunals, but it had no discernible effect (Gage and Njogu 1994). Even in Columbia and Peru, where many conspicuous forms of gender bias in family law were eliminated in the 1970s, mothers and children enjoy only a weak legal claim on fathers' income (Ramirez 1987). Evidence from Argentina suggests that paternal child support responsibilities are poorly enforced (Goode 1993). Brachet-Marquez (1992) explains how and why the Mexican legal system makes it easy for men to avoid financial responsibility. A recent study of children born to adolescent Chilean women finds that 42 percent of the children have received no support from their fathers by the time they are six years old (Buvinic and others 1992). Jamaican law stipulates that children have a right to support from any coresident male, but actual contributions are small and intermittent (Bolles 1986).[7]

The willingness and ability of some fathers to "divorce" their children without penalty makes mothers aware of the risks of abandonment and puts them in a weak bargaining position in the family. After many decades of focusing on mother-child relationships, social scientists are just beginning to explore fathers' roles. Engle and Breaux (1994) ask whether or not there is a "father instinct." Katzman (1992) of the United Nations Economic Commission for Latin America speculates that men are suffering from a loss of self-esteem due to their loss of power within the family.

An alternative explanation follows from the observation that most family law was forged during an era in which children provided at least some economic benefits to fathers, reinforcing cultural norms of paternal responsibility. Although such traditional circumstances did not guarantee fully adequate protection for dependents, they may have served better than more modern arrangements. Economic development raises the costs of having children by increasing their educational requirements and their economic independence. Adjustments in the form of lower fertility rates are lagged and uneven. As a result development often increases the economic stress imposed on families with children.

Sorting the Responsibilities of Mothers and Fathers

Whether due to biology or culture or some combination, mothers seem to have stronger commitments to children than do fathers. Mothers are thus less affected than fathers by the increasing economic incentives to default on the traditional explicit and implicit contracts of parenthood. These incentives are compounded by economic problems, such as unemployment and famine, and may also be exacerbated by mobility. Migration is a male survival strategy that is often synonymous with desertion (Elson 1992).

This analysis does not imply that economic development always leads to family breakdown or to reductions in paternal commitments. Rather, it suggests that development increases the risk of certain kinds of "family failure," which we might think of as analogous to market failure or state failure, and requires institutional adaptation. Indeed, adaptation is already under way in the form of collective efforts to revise and reform family laws and norms. But it is important to note that men as a group have less to gain economically than women and children from reforms that enforce paternal responsibilities. A theory of distributional coalitions leads us to expect that women's groups seeking such reforms will meet considerable resistance from men—behavior that we have observed (Kerr 1993).

Appreciation of the complexities of gender-based conflict also offers an explanation of why women may not always favor cultural modernization—and may endorse fundamentalist forms of resistance to cultural change. Women confront a paradox: the same aspects of the development process that increase their economic independence as individuals (expansion of education and wage employment) increase their economic vulnerability as mothers. The relative size of these two effects is determined by the political context and pattern of economic development. And under certain circumstances women's groups may correctly calculate that they have more to lose from male-dominated modernization than from male-dominated tradition.

Whether this admittedly speculative analysis of the logic of women's collective action is correct or not, the institutional framework determining family rights certainly affects both economic and demographic decisionmaking. Poor stipulation and enforcement of maintenance laws puts the marital partner who specializes in housework or childrearing at a disadvantage. Lack of protection against domestic violence puts physically weaker family members at risk. These failings encourage men to claim a disproportionate share of family income and leisure and lower the economic costs of children to fathers. More equal sharing of these costs would give men a greater financial stake in limiting their own fertility (Armstrong 1992). Finally, failure to enforce child support responsibilities on the part of fathers increases the economic incentives for paternal desertion.

Gender and the Labor Market

Inferior property rights and poorly enforced claims on family members lower women's share of family wealth and income relative to men's. One result is a reduction in women's reservation wages, increasing their willingness to accept low-paying jobs. Yet these institutional factors have been largely ignored by the conventional economic literature on gender wage differentials, which focuses primarily on the individual characteristics of male and female wage earners. This literature also sidesteps the issue of cultural norms, which may generate differences in preference for wage employment between men and women.

Empirical research based on human capital models has made important contributions, clarifying the limits of employer-based discrimination and demonstrating the implications of differences in men's and women's access to education. But human capital models fall far short of providing a complete picture of gender inequality in the labor market. In addition to ignoring the asymmetry of rights and responsibilities that affects the supply of women's labor, these models provide little insight into the demand side of the labor market.

Employer Discrimination

Significant gender-based wage differentials characterize labor markets in every country in the world: women earn, on average, 60–70 percent as much as men (World
Bank 1995). These differences would be more extreme if wage data included
women engaged in unpaid family work and work in the informal sector. Part of the
gender wage differential can be explained by differences in levels of education, often
a result of public policies that have emphasized educating men more than women.
Investments in women's education increase their earnings and their productivity,
generating a big payoff for the economy as a whole (Subbarao and Raney 1993;
King and Hill 1993).

Evidence of discrimination, narrowly defined as lower wages for individuals with
the same education and experience, is mixed. Of the six studies of wage discrimination in Latin America and Africa included in Birdsall and Sabot (1991), only two
provide strong evidence of gender wage discrimination. But most of the twenty-one
studies of Latin America included in Psacharopoulos and Tzannatos (1992) find a
substantial gender gap in wages that cannot be explained by human capital differences. The U.S. experience clearly shows that women's increased access to education does not eliminate the gender wage differential (Goldin 1990). The
discriminatory behavior of both private employers and the state plays an important
role.

Differences in the demand for men's and women's labor may reflect a taste for
discrimination, or a cost-minimizing statistical discrimination, based on the presumption that women are less committed to the labor force than men and should
therefore be limited to low-skilled jobs for which performance does not suffer from
high turnover. Anker and Hein (1985) report that employers often explicitly express
a preference for male workers and think that turnover among women is higher than
it actually is. In any case women are more likely to show high turnover rates if they
are restricted to relatively unskilled, poorly paid jobs.

Policy-Based Discrimination

The demand for women's labor is also limited by policy-based or public discrimination. Many public regulations increase the relative price of women's labor by imposing the cost of maternity benefits or childcare on individual employers, despite the
fact that the International Labor Office's Maternity Protection Convention stipulates that individual employers should not be individually liable for the cost of
maternity benefits (Anker and Hein 1985; Winter 1994). As a result many employers hire fewer women than they otherwise might; some even require women to provide medical certification that they are not pregnant.

In Eastern Europe and the former Soviet Union both state and private enterprises
once provided large subsidies for maternity leave and childcare. These subsidies
have now been reduced substantially. Privatization has created an economic environment in which firms that continue to provide such benefits may not be able to

compete successfully with those that do not. Research on the effects of privatization on female workers has produced mixed results. Women in eastern Germany have had a greater risk of losing their jobs and a lower probability of finding new ones (Bellmann and others 1992; Maier 1993). Women make up a disproportionate number of the registered unemployed in Russia, Poland, and the Czech Republic (Klasen 1993; Levin 1993; Commander, Liberman, and Yemtsov 1993). In Slovakia the gender wage differential declined between 1988 and 1991 (Ham, Svejnar, and Terrell 1995). And in Slovenia men have suffered greater job and wage losses than women, possibly because women are, on average, slightly better educated (Abraham and Vodopivec 1993; Orazem and Vodopivec 1994).

Unfortunately, similar attention has not been devoted to an empirical analysis of differences between mothers and nonmothers in the workplace—women responsible for the care of young children or other dependents are far more likely than other workers to be affected by the loss of public support for family labor. If these women drop out of the labor force in disproportionate numbers because of policy changes, they exacerbate the selectivity bias in measures of women's wages. It is difficult to find any systematic account of actual reductions in childcare, family allowance, and parental leave provisions in recently privatized economics, although many scholars have commented on such reductions (Fong and Paul 1992; Levin 1993). Nor is much known about the de jure or de facto structure of worker's rights, including protections against overt discrimination.

Another topic of serious concern in both industrial and developing economies is the gender bias built into the structure of benefits based on wage employment, such as social security programs. Disproportionately concentrated in part-time, intermittent, and informal employment, women are less likely than men to work in jobs that are covered by benefits. Their claims on family benefits are typically attenuated by desertion or divorce. Married female employees pay the same taxes but receive lower benefits than their male counterparts: in both Latin America and Sub-Saharan Africa survivors' benefits are given to widows of covered male workers, but strict conditions are imposed on survivors' benefits given to widowers of covered female workers (widowers must be dependent invalids in order to qualify). In other words the programs transfer more income to an eligible man with a spouse than to an eligible woman with a spouse. And although the retirement age is often lower for women than for men, benefits are lower as well. Family allowances give male workers an additional stipend if they have a dependent wife, but female workers do not receive extra amounts to help them pay for the cost of childcare (Folbre 1993b).

These types of gender bias in employment benefits violate International Labor Office guidelines, as well as the United Nations' Convention on the Elimination of All Forms of Discrimination Against Women. Many individual countries also have laws against sex discrimination. But although these regulations may affect policies in the public sector (where women enjoy more and better-paid opportunities), they are seldom enforced in the private sector; imported standards are often incompatible with the local legal and political climate. For instance, Latin American legal systems generally disallow class action suits and do not permit judicial verdicts to influence future rulings (Winter 1994). These regulations affect the collection of data and the level of enforcement. In the United States court cases and lawsuits have provided evidence of explicit sexual discrimination that would not otherwise have been revealed (Bergmann 1986).

There has been remarkably little analysis of the impact of public policies on women's wages or employment in developing countries. Future research should attempt to quantify the impact of maternity-related legislation, which varies sufficiently among countries to provide a basis for comparison. The effect of antidiscrimination efforts could also be estimated, following the example set by Beller's (1982) analysis of the impact of equal rights legislation on women's pay in the United States.

In general, export-oriented growth has been associated with increases in women's employment in manufacturing (Joekes 1987). In some countries, such as the Republic of Korea, gender discrimination has been used as a tool for increasing export competitiveness (Seguino 1994). In others, such as Ireland, public policies have explicitly and successfully sought to increase male rather than female employment (Pyle 1990).

Gender-biased employment policies must be analyzed in the same terms as policies prescribing property and family rights—as an outcome of distributional conflict. In this case collective interests based on class as well as gender come into play: workers as a group benefit from protective legislation that helps them to care for their children. In a sense employers owe workers such assistance, because workers are producing the next generation's labor force, often at considerable cost to their own standard of living. But if such assistance reinforces gender inequality, it assigns women a disproportionate share of the costs of parenthood.

It is hardly surprising that policymakers and employers, who are predominantly male, seldom promote gender equality in the labor market beyond measures that have obvious, powerful efficiency effects, such as investing in women's education. What is surprising is that they continue to ignore the limitations of the conventional male model of employment when throughout the world, women are becoming increasingly important labor force participants. Both family leave and family-based benefits could be provided on a gender-neutral basis. A shorter paid workday for both men and women could help individuals combine market work and family responsibilities over the life cycle.

An Institutionalist View of Childcare

It is sometimes suggested that women simply have a greater preference for childcare than do men, and the utility that they gain represents a "compensating differential" for their greater susceptibility to poverty (Fuchs 1988). One could argue, similarly, that differences in preference between genders account for a portion of the gender wage differential. And these differences may be at work, with somewhat reassuring consequences regarding the level of discrimination. But this argument hinges on the conventional neoclassical assumption that tastes and preferences are exogenously given.

An institutionalist approach suggests that individual preferences are partially shaped by social norms, and social norms are in turn strongly influenced by the interests and power of distributional coalitions (Folbre 1994). Thus as women gain collective power, they challenge and modify social norms of femininity that are costly to them. They may also challenge the traditional social construction of masculinity in ways that are threatening to men. "If women no longer want to take care of the kids," men may ask, "who will?" True—if feminine norms of familial altruism are substantially weakened and masculine norms of familial altruism remain unchanged, some countries may run into serious difficulties in taking care of children and other dependents.

These are important issues, not only for relations between men and women, but also for relations between parents and nonparents. Public provision of childcare and assistance to parents would significantly increase overall labor productivity if productivity were defined—as the next section argues it should be—in terms that include the value of nonmarket inputs and outputs.

Household Production and Economic Growth

Contemporary microeconomic theory explicitly recognizes the importance of nonmarket work, largely as a result of the pioneering work of Becker (1981). Many household surveys of developing countries, especially those oriented toward health, document the importance of labor and other inputs into household production. Yet macroeconomic theory ignores the nonmarket sector almost entirely. Despite the criticisms of conventional national income accounting articulated by Eisner (1989) and others, only a few countries in northwestern Europe are systematically imputing the value of nonmarket work.

Some feminist theorists argue that national income accounts are, themselves, based on measures that evolved from accumulated gender bias (Waring 1988; Folbre 1991). Whether there is more resistance to change than might be expected from any challenge to a conventional paradigm is an issue for historians of economic thought. More important from the point of view of economic development are the consequences for assessing social welfare. These are profound, as Blackden and Morris-Hughes (1993, p. i) point out in a recent World Bank analysis of Sub-Saharan Africa:

> The structural presence of women in economic production is largely invisible and overlooked in the prevailing paradigm. This is turn leads to incomplete and partial evaluation of economic outcomes, including adjustment and its effects on the poor, and masks critical interlinkages and complementarities among sectors of economic activity and between the paid and unpaid economies. It also limits assessment of the likely and potential supply response in the economy.

Current estimates suggest that the economic value of household production in most countries amounts to an additional 30–50 percent of gross domestic product (GDP), depending on the method of valuation used (Goldschmidt-Clermont 1982).

Inaccurately Measuring Women's Market Labor

Accounting problems are threefold. First, conventional census and labor force surveys typically mismeasure the number of women working in the market, vitiating both cross-national comparisons and analyses of longitudinal trends. The conventional definition of labor force participation is based on full-time or close to full-time employment for wages or other market income. But women are likely to engage in part-time or periodic market work and still make important contributions to family income. The dichotomous "in or out" definition of a labor force participant fits men's experience better than women's. A better definition would rate both men and women along a spectrum of participation in market activities.

The mismeasurement of women's market activities in the late nineteenth- and early twentieth-century United States has been well documented (Folbre and Abel 1989). This problem is even more serious in developing countries, where both the informal and agricultural sectors absorb a large amount of women's labor (Benería 1981, 1982, 1992). The 1981 Indian census recorded only 14 percent of adult women participating in the market labor force; contemporaneous surveys yielded a much higher estimate of 39 percent (World Bank 1991).

Valuing Nonmarket Labor

A second problem concerns the treatment of labor time devoted to housework and childcare, which is recognized as a crucial input on the microeconomic level but considered macroeconomically unproductive. Human capital theorists do not insist on official imputations of the value of nonmarket inputs into human capital. As Elson (1992, p. 34) puts it, "Macromodels appear to treat human resources as a nonproduced means of production like land." Most economists are reluctant to consider childcare a productive activity. Indeed, a great deal of intellectual attention has been devoted to demarcating a boundary between domestic and nondomestic activities, even though economic theory suggests no distinction between the two (Benería 1992).

Both historical and current studies suggest that if domestic work is included as productive work, the expanded labor force would contain about the same percentage of women as men. Estimates have been provided for the United States between 1800 and 1930 (Folbre and Wagman 1993; Wagman and Folbre forthcoming) and for India (World Bank 1991, p. 14). Collection of more detailed data, accompanied by more concerted efforts to adjust historical statistics, could yield useful comparisons of cross-national differences in the changing composition of women's employment.

Revision of labor force statistics will require further development and institutionalization of time-use surveys. The length and intensity of work—whether in the market or in the home—is an important determinant of economic welfare that is omitted from standard consumption-based models (Floro 1995). Most time-use surveys show that women tend to work much longer hours than men, particularly if they have small children. Hartmann (1981) summarizes several studies reporting this statistic for the United States. Duggan (1993) reports similar results from eastern and western Germany. The United Nations Development Program's *Human Development Report 1995* shows that in thirteen industrial countries women provided, on average, 51 percent of all labor hours, paid and unpaid (UNDP 1995).

Research in developing countries has suggested the same. Brown and Haddad (1994) report longer work days for women in seven countries in Asia and Africa. In Ghana teenage girls work longer weekly hours in both market and domestic work than boys, whether or not they are enrolled in school (Gage and Njogu 1994). A UNDP (1995) analysis of nine developing countries found that women accounted for 53 percent of total labor hours.

Since 1985 the World Bank has carried out several surveys designed to "get inside" the household: the Living Standards Measurement Study and the Social Dimensions of Adjustment series.[8] To date, however, gender analysis of these data has seldom extended beyond education and health (World Bank 1995). The same may be said of many other household survey efforts.

Measuring the Importance of Nonlabor Inputs

A third empirical problem concerns the paucity of efforts to measure the effect of nonlabor inputs, such as public and private investment, on the overall productivity of nonmarket production. For instance, what is the effect of greater provision of public utilities, such as water and gas, on the allocation of women's time devoted to labor? How do improved consumer durables, such as more fuel-efficient cook stoves, affect family welfare? Does the provision of public daycare services increase women's ability to provide other nonmarket services to enhance their families' consumption, as well as their own participation in wage employment? Without empirical analysis of such questions it is impossible to apply the kinds of social cost-benefit criteria that are typically used to evaluate other types of public investment.

Most macroeconomics texts allude to the fact that conventional definitions of GDP overstate the real rate of economic growth because they include additions to net product resulting from women's entrance into wage employment but do not subtract the reduction in household production that normally occurs as a result. But conventional definitions may actually understate the rate of growth in industrial countries because improvements in the productivity of nonmarket work resulting from greater educational attainment and increased public or private capital investment may more than compensate.

Trends in productivity and output in the nonmarket sector, which produces human capital and goods and services that are crucial components of the overall consumption bundle, do not necessarily follow trends in the market sector. Indeed, the two may be inversely related. Many gender and development scholars argue that structural adjustment policies that encourage shifts from production of nontradable to tradable goods have a negative impact on household production and family welfare. Like cutbacks in the provision of social services (health, education, and childcare) they increase demands on women's labor time (Elson 1991; Palmer 1991; Cornia, Jolly, and Stewart 1987).

This result might not be deleterious if women's time were underutilized (the assumption often made by policymakers unaware of actual patterns of time alloca- tion). But many studies reveal unanticipated, adverse effects. Mothers may be forced to withdraw from paid employment or increase their demands on daughters to help with household tasks. Moser (1992) documents such behavior in low-income house- holds in Guayaquil, Ecuador faced with a reduction in community services. Families maintained by women alone are particularly susceptible to such pressures. Tanski (1994, table 2) finds a significant increase in poverty among female-headed house- holds in metropolitan Lima, Peru between 1985 and 1990.

Short-term gains in measurable indicators, such as GDP or budget deficits, may be countervailed by long-run losses in less visible areas of economic output. The resulting macroeconomic distortions have negative consequences for women's income, and welfare effects are exacerbated by the reduction of their bargaining power within the family (Kabeer 1994; Klasen 1993). It is difficult, if not impossi- ble, to quantify these effects, given the lack of systematic survey data. And that is exactly the point: important policy issues cannot be addressed until macroecono- mists concede the importance of monitoring and measuring nonmarket production.

Conclusion

One of the most fascinating aspects of the development process is the way it has destabilized traditional patriarchal relations that once provided men with unques- tioned power over women and children. A combination of technological change, social differentiation, and political struggle has increased individual autonomy, often with positive economic effects. But the shift away from family-based production toward labor markets based on individual wages has had some unanticipated nega- tive effects on the organization of family life. As the costs of children have increased, mothers have borne the brunt of this growing economic burden, which is camou- flaged by conventional measures of economic welfare.

There is a lesson here for policy debates over privatization and reductions in social safety nets. Free markets may provide a good substitute for some previously state-run activities, but they do not provide much support for family life. Childrearing is no longer a remunerative activity, and both individuals and busi- nesses that devote time and money to it will have a hard time competing with those who do not. Yet nonmarket work devoted to raising the next generation makes an enormous contribution to economic welfare, as does education. Children are public goods, and failure to collectively ensure their welfare and invest in their human cap- ital will inevitably hamper economic growth.

Many advocates for women in development emphasize the need for greater equality between men and women. But the process of economic development has taught us that it is easier to gain equal rights for women than to impose equal responsibilities for the care of children and other dependents on men. Some conservatives argue that women have become too powerful; their independence and self-assertion threatens the viability of the family. But it may be that women have simply not become powerful enough to persuade men, and society as a whole, to fairly share the costs of rearing the next generation.

Future trends will depend, in large part, on forms of collective action that will redefine the role of the state, the family, and the firm. And these will depend, in turn, on how well economists, policymakers, and ordinary people understand the gradual but relentless realignment of the relationship between production and reproduction that is central to economic development. This is a process shaped by both conflict and cooperation, in which women will probably exert an increasingly collective influence.

Notes

1. The most recent examples of publications by multilateral institutions include World Bank (1994) and Klasen (1993). In addition, both the World Bank and the office of the United Nations Development Program's *Human Development Report* prepared reports on gender issues for the International Women's Conference in Beijing in September 1995.

2. Boserup's more recent work does not fit neatly into the women in development category. She writes that "men's interest in preserving the traditional ranking order between the sexes should not be underestimated in any analysis of women's position; it should not be overestimated either" (1993, p. 2).

3. A more explicit definition is given by Andrew Schotter: "A regularity in social behavior that is agreed to by all members of society, specifies behavior in specific recurrent situations, and is either self-policed or policed by some external authority" (1981, p.11). This definition, however, virtually precludes the possibility that some groups impose social institutions on others.

4. In what I consider the best chapter of *The Rise and Decline of Nations,* chapter 6, Olson does consider racial and caste groups. But he does not devote much attention to the difference between voluntary and involuntary groups. For a slightly more detailed discussion of this issue, see Folbre (1993a).

5. This argument is distinct from that developed by Becker (1981) in his Rotten Kid Theorem because it emphasizes that the seemingly altruistic behavior of the male head of household is partially motivated by individual self-interest (in Becker's model, pure altruism rules). Note the similarity with Fogel and Engerman's (1974) classic argument regarding the economic effects of slavery in the United States. Despite their political and personal oppression, slaves may have been relatively well-fed and housed because they were such important factors of production. Their standard of living may have fallen immediately after emancipation because of their lack of access to land.

6. For a discussion of how changes in access to common property resources might affect household distribution, see Haddad and Kanbur (1992).

7. While the World Bank Living Standards Measurement Survey of Jamaica collected data on remittances, it did not specifically ascertain which parents were remitting sums for which children (Wyss 1995).

8. Countries surveyed by Living Standards Measurement Studies include Bolivia, Cote d'Ivoire, Ecuador, Ghana, Guyana, Jamaica, the Kyrgyz Republic, Mauritania, Morocco, Nicaragua, Pakistan, Peru, Romania, Russia, South Africa, Tanzania, Venezuela, and Viet Nam. Social Dimensions of Adjustment surveys are available for Burkina Faso, Burundi, Central African Republic, Chad, Cote d'Ivoire, The Gambia, Guinea, Guinea-Bissau, Kenya, Mali, Mauritania, Senegal, and Zambia.

References

Abraham, Katharine, and Milan Vodopivec. 1993. "Slovenia: A Study of Labor Market Transitions." World Bank, Policy Research Division, Transition Economics Division, Washington, D.C.

Abu, K. 1983. "The Separateness of Spouses: Conjugal Resources in an Ashanti Town." In Christine Oppong, ed., *Female and Male in West Africa.* London: Allen and Unwin.

Agarwal, Bina. 1994a. "Gender and Command Over Property: A Critical Gap in Economic Analysis and Policy in South Asia." *World Development* 22(10): 1455–78.

————. 1994b. "Positioning the Western Feminist Agenda: A Comment." *Indian Journal of Gender Studies* 1(2): 249–56.

————. 1995. *A Field of One's Own: Gender and Land Rights in South Asia.* Cambridge: Cambridge University Press.

Alchian, A., and H. Demsetz. 1972. "Production, Information Costs, and Economic Organization." *American Economic Review* 62(December): 777–95.

Alderman, Harold, Pierre-André Chiappori, Lawrence Haddad, John Hoddinott, and Ravi Kanbur. 1995. "Unitary Versus Collective Models of the Household: Is It Time to Shift the Burden of Proof?" *World Bank Research Observer* 10(1): 1–19.

Anker, Richard, and Catherine Hein. 1985. "Why Third World Urban Employers Usually Prefer Men." *International Labour Review* 124(1): 73–90.

————, eds. 1986. *Sex Inequalities in Urban Employment in the Third World.* New York: St. Martin's Press.

Armstrong, Alice. 1992. "Maintenance Payments for Child Support in Southern Africa: Using Law to Promote Family Planning." *Studies in Family Planning* 23(4): 217–28.

Barros, Ricardo, Louise Fox, and Rosane Mendonca. 1993. "Female-Headed Households, Poverty, and the Welfare of Children in Urban Brazil." PC/ICRW Working Paper. The Population Council, New York, and the International Center for Research on Women, Washington, D.C.

Becker, Gary S. 1981. *A Treatise on the Family.* Cambridge, Mass.: Harvard University Press.

Beller, Andrea H. 1982. "The Impact of Equal Opportunity Policy on Sex Differentials in Earnings and Occupations." *American Economic Review* 72(2): 171–75.

Beller, Andrea H., and John Graham. 1993. *Small Change: The Economics of Child Support.* New Haven, Conn.: Yale University Press.

Bellmann, Lutz, Saul Estrin, Hartmut Lehmann, and Jonathan Wadsworth. 1992. "Gross Flows in a Labour Market in Transition: Panel Data Estimates from Eastern Germany." London School of Economics Working Paper 173. London.

Benería, Lourdes. 1981. "Conceptualizing the Labour Force: The Underestimation of Women's Activities." *Journal of Development Studies* 17(3): 10–27.

————. 1982. "Accounting for Women's Work." In Lourdes Benería, ed., *Women and Development: The Sexual Division of Labour in Rural Societies.* New York: Praeger.

————. 1992. "Accounting for Women's Work: Assessing the Progress of Two Decades." *World Development* 20(11): 1547–60.

Benería, Lourdes, and Martha Roldán. 1987. *The Crossroads of Class and Gender.* Chicago: University of Chicago Press.

Benería, Lourdes, and Gita Sen. 1981. "Accumulation, Reproduction, and Women's Role in Economic Development: Boserup Revisited." *Signs* 7(2): 279–98.

Bergmann, Barbara. 1986. *The Economic Emergence of Women.* New York: Basic Books.

Birdsall, Nancy, and Richard Sabot, eds. 1991. *Unfair Advantage: Labor Market Discrimination in Developing Countries.* Washington, D.C.: World Bank.

Blackden, C. Mark, and E. Morris-Hughes. 1993. "Paradigm Postponed: Gender and Economic Adjustment in Sub-Saharan Africa." Technical Note 13. World Bank, Africa Region, Human Resources and Poverty Division, Washington, D.C.

Blumberg, Rae Lesser. 1989. "Making the Case for the Gender Variable: Women and the Wealth and Well-Being of Nations." U.S. Agency for International Development, Office of Women in Development, Washington, D.C.

Bolles, Lynn. 1986. "Economic Crisis and Female-Headed Households in Urban Jamaica." In June Nash and Helen Safa, eds., *Women and Change in Latin America.* South Hadley, Mass.: Bergin and Garvey.

Boserup, Ester. 1970. *Women's Role in Economic Development.* London: Allen and Unwin.

————. 1993. "Obstacles to Advancement of Women During Development." In T. Paul Schultz, ed., *Investment in Women's Human Capital and Economic Development.* New Haven, Conn.: Yale University Press.

Brachet-Marquez, V. 1992. "Absentee Fathers: A Case-Based Study of Family Law and Child Welfare in Mexico." PC/ICRW Working Paper. Population Council, New York, and the International Center for Research on Women, Washington, D.C.

Brown, Lynn R., and Lawrence Haddad. 1994. "Time Allocation Patterns and Time Burdens: A Gendered Analysis of Seven Countries." International Food Policy Research Institute, Washington, D.C.

Bruce, Judith, and Cynthia Lloyd. Forthcoming. *Families in Focus.* New York: The Population Council.

Buchanan, James. 1980. "Profit Seeking and Rent Seeking." In James Buchanan, Robert Tollison, and Gordon Tullock, eds., *Toward a Theory of the Rent-Seeking Society.* College Station, Tex.: Texas A & M University Press.

Buvinic, Mayra, Margaret Lycette, and William Paul McGreevey. 1983. *Women and Poverty in the Third World.* Baltimore, Md.: Johns Hopkins University Press.

Buvinic, Mayra, J.P. Valenzuela, T. Molina, and E. Gonzales. 1992. "The Fortunes of Adolescent Mothers and Their Children: The Transmission of Poverty in Santiago, Chile." *Population and Development Review* 18(2): 269–97.

Caldwell, John. 1982. *The Theory of Fertility Decline.* New York: Academic Press.

Caldwell, John, and Pat Caldwell. 1987. "The Cultural Context of High Fertility in Sub-Saharan Africa." *Population and Development Review* 13(3): 409–38.

Chant, Sylvia. 1991. *Women and Survival in Mexican Cities: Perspectives on Gender, Labour Markets, and Low-Income Households.* New York: Manchester University Press.

Cheater, Angela. 1981. "Women and Their Participation in Commercial Agricultural Production: The Case of Medium-Scale Freehold in Zimbabwe." *Development and Change* 12(3): 349–77.

Coase, Ronald. 1960. "The Problem of Social Cost." *Journal of Law and Economics* 3(1): 529–46.

Commander, Simon, Leonid Liberman, and Rusland Yemtsov. 1993. "Wage and Employment Decisions in the Russian Economy: An Analysis of Developments in 1992." World Bank, Institute for Economic Forecasting, Russian Academy of Sciences, and Moscow State University, Washington, D.C.

Cornia, G. A., R. Jolly, and F. Stewart, eds. 1987. *Adjustment with a Human Face: Protecting the Vulnerable and Promoting Growth.* New York: Oxford University Press.

Deere, Carmen Diana. 1995. "What Difference Does Gender Make? Rethinking Peasant Studies." *Feminist Economics* 1(1): 53–57.

Deere, Carmen Diana, and Magdalena León, eds. 1987. *Rural Women and State Policy: Feminist Perspectives on Latin American Agricultural Development.* Boulder, Colo.: Westview Press.

Desai, Sonalde. 1991. "Children at Risk: The Role of Family Structure in Latin America and West Africa." Working Paper 28. The Population Council, New York.

Duggan, Lynn. 1993. "Production and Reproduction: Family Policy and Gender Inequality in East and West Germany." Unpublished Ph.D. dissertation, University of Massachusetts at Amherst, Department of Economics.

Dwyer, Daisy, and Judith Bruce, eds. 1988. *A Home Divided: Women and Income in the Third World.* Stanford, Calif.: Stanford University Press.

Eisner, Robert. 1989. *The Total Incomes System of Accounts.* Chicago: University of Chicago Press.

Elson, Diane. 1991. *Male Bias in the Development Process.* Manchester, UK: Manchester University Press.

———. 1992. "From Survival Strategies to Transformation Strategies: Women's Needs and Structural Adjustment." In Lourdes Benería and Shelley Feldman, eds., *Unequal Burden: Economic Crises, Persistent Poverty, and Women's Work.* Boulder, Colo.: Westview Press.

Engle, Patrice L., and Cynthia Breaux. 1994. "Is There a Father Instinct? Fathers' Responsibility for Children." PC/ICRW Working Paper. Population Council, New York, and International Center for Research on Women, Washington, D.C.

Floro, Maria. 1995. "Women's Well-Being, Poverty, and Work Intensity." *Feminist Economics* 1(3): 1–25.

Fogel, Robert William, and Stanley L. Engerman. 1974. *Time on the Cross: The Economics of American Negro Slavery.* Boston: Little, Brown, and Company.

Folbre, Nancy. 1990. "Women on Their Own: Global Patterns of Female Headship." In Rita S. Gallin and Ann Ferguson, eds., *Women and International Development Annual Vol. 2.* Boulder, Colo.: Westview.

———. 1991. "The Unproductive Housewife: Her Evolution in Nineteenth Century Economic Thought." *Signs: Journal of Women in Culture and Society* 16(3): 463–84.

————. 1993a. "Guys Don't Do That: Gender Groups and Social Norms." Paper presented at the annual meeting of the American Economic Association, December, Anaheim, California.

————. 1993b. "Women and Social Security in Latin America, the Caribbean, and Sub-Saharan Africa." Working Paper 5. International Labour Office, Equality For Women in Employment: An Interdepartmental Project, Geneva.

————. 1994. *Who Pays for the Kids? Gender and the Structures of Constraint.* New York: Routledge.

Folbre, Nancy, and Marjorie Abel. 1989. "Women's Work and Women's Households: Gender Bias in the U.S. Census." *Social Research* 56(3): 545–70.

Folbre, Nancy, and Barnet Wagman. 1993. "Counting Housework: New Estimates of Real Product in the U.S., 1800–1860." *Journal of Economic History* 53(2): 275–88.

Fong, Monica, and Gillian Paul. 1992. "Women's Employment in Central and Eastern Europe: The Gender Factor." *Transition* 3(6): 1–3.

Fuchs, Victor. 1988. *Women's Quest for Economic Equality.* Cambridge, Mass.: Harvard University Press.

Gage, Anastasia J., and Wamucii Njogu. 1994. *Ghana/Kenya: Gender Inequalities and Demographic Behavior.* New York: The Population Council.

Glendon, Mary Ann. 1989. *The Transformation of Family Law: State, Law, and Family in the United States and Western Europe.* Chicago: University of Chicago Press.

Goldin, Claudia. 1990. *Understanding the Gender Gap.* Oxford: Oxford University Press.

Goldschmidt-Clermont, Luisella. 1982. *Unpaid Work in the Household.* Geneva: International Labour Office.

Goode, William J. 1993. *World Changes in Divorce Patterns.* New Haven, Conn.: Yale University Press.

Haddad, Lawrence, and Ravi Kanbur. 1992. "Intrahousehold Inequality and the Theory of Targeting." *European Economic Review* 36(2/3): 372–78.

Haddad, Lawrence, and Thomas Reardon. 1993. "Gender Bias in the Allocation of Resources Within Households in Burkina Faso: A Disaggregated Outlay Equivalent Analysis." *Journal of Development Studies* 29(2): 260–76.

Ham, John, Jan Svejnar, and Katherine Terrell. 1995. "Czech Republic and Slovakia." In Simon Commander and Fabrizio Coricelli, eds., *Unemployment, Restructuring, and the Labor Market in Eastern Europe and Russia.* Washington, D.C.: World Bank.

Hartmann, Heidi. 1981. "The Family as a Locus of Gender, Class, and Political Struggle." *Signs: Journal of Women in Culture and Society* 6(3): 366–94.

Heise, Lori L., Jacqueline Pitanguy, and Adrienne Germain. 1994. *Violence Against Women: The Hidden Health Burden.* World Bank Discussion Paper 255. Washington, D.C.

Hoddinott, John. 1992. "Rotten Kids or Manipulative Parents: Are Children Old Age Security in Western Kenya?" *Economic Development and Cultural Change* 40(3): 545–65.

Hoddinott, John, Howard Alderman, and Lawrence Haddad. Forthcoming. "Household Models and Intrahousehold Resource Allocation." In John Hoddinott, Lawrence Haddad, and Howard Alderman, eds., *Intrahousehold Resource Allocation in Developing Countries: Methods, Models, and Policy.* Baltimore, Md.: Johns Hopkins University Press.

Hodgson, Geoffry. 1987. *Economics and Institutions: A Manifesto for a Modern Institutional Economics.* Philadelphia: University of Pennsylvania Press.

Holt, Sharon, and Helena Ribe. 1991. *Developing Financial Institutions for the Poor and Reducing Barriers to Access for Women.* World Bank Discussion Paper 118. Washington, D.C.

Joekes, Susan. 1987. *Women in the World Economy.* New York: Oxford University Press.

Kabeer, Naila. 1994. *Reversed Realities: Gender Hierarchies in Development Thought.* London: Verso.

Kardam, N. 1990. "The Adaptability of International Development Agencies: The Response of the World Bank to Women in Development." In K. Staudt, ed., *Women, International Development, and Politics.* Philadelphia, Penn.: Temple University Press.

Katzman, R. 1992. "Why Are Men So Irresponsible?" *CEPAL Review* 46: 79–87.

Kerr, Joanna. 1993. *Ours by Right: Women's Rights as Human Rights.* London: Zed Books.

King, Elizabeth M., and M. Anne Hill. 1993. *Women's Education in Developing Countries: Barriers, Benefits, and Policies.* Baltimore, Md.: Johns Hopkins University Press.

Klasen, Stephen. 1993. "Gender Inequality and Development Strategies: Lessons from the Past and Policy Issues for the Future." Working Paper 41. International Labour Office, World Employment Programme Research, Geneva.

Knight, Jack. 1992. *Institutions and Social Conflict.* Cambridge: Cambridge University Press.

Koussoudji, Sherrie, and Eva Mueller. 1983. "The Economic and Demographic Status of Female-Headed Households." *Economic Development and Cultural Change* 31 (4): 831–59.

Krueger, Anne O. 1974. "The Political Economy of the Rent-Seeking Society." *American Economic Review* 64(3): 291–303.

Levin, Bozena. 1993. "Unemployment Among Polish Women." *Comparative Economic Studies* 35(4): 135–45.

Libecap, Gary. 1989. *Contracting for Property Rights.* New York: Cambridge University Press.

Lloyd, Cynthia B., and Anastasia J. Gage-Brandon. 1993. "Women's Role in Maintaining Households: Family Welfare and Sexual Inequality in Ghana." *Population Studies* 47(1): 115–31.

Louat, Frederic, Margaret Grosh, and Jacques van der Gaag. 1992. "Welfare Implications of Female Headship in Jamaican Households." Paper presented at the intrahousehold resource allocation conference: policy issues and research methods. International Food and Policy Research Institute–World Bank, February 12–14, Washington, D.C.

Lucas, Robert E. B., and Oded Stark. 1985. "Motivations to Remit: Evidence from Botswana." *Journal of Political Economy* 93(5): 901–18.

Lundberg, Shelley, and Robert A. Pollak. 1993. "Separate Spheres Bargaining and the Marriage Market." *Journal of Political Economy* 101(6): 988–1010.

Maier, Friederike. 1993. "The Labour Market for Women and Employment Perspectives in the Aftermath of German Unification." *Cambridge Journal of Economics* 17 (3): 267–80.

Martin, Doris M., and Fatuma Omar Hashi. 1992a. "Gender, the Evolution of Legal Institutions, and Economic Development in Sub–Saharan Africa." Working Paper 3. World Bank, Africa Region, Poverty and Social Policy Division, Technical Department, Washington, D.C.

————. 1992b. "Law as an Institutional Barrier to the Economic Empowerment of Women." Working Paper 2. World Bank, Africa Region, Poverty and Social Policy Division, Technical Department, Washington, D.C.

————. 1992c. "Women in Development: The Legal Issues in Sub-Saharan Africa Today." Working Paper 4. World Bank Africa Region, Poverty and Social Policy Division, Technical Department, Washington, D.C.

McElroy, Marjorie. 1990. "The Empirical Content of Nash-Bargained Household Behavior." *Journal of Human Resources* 25(4): 559–83.

Mohanty, Chandra Talpade. 1991. "Under Western Eyes: Feminist Scholarship and Colonial Discourses." In Chandra Talpade Mohanty, Ann Russo, and Lourdes Torres, eds., *Third World Women and the Politics of Feminism.* Bloomington, Ind.: Indiana University Press.

Morgan, Robin. 1984. *Sisterhood Is Global.* Garden City, N.Y.: Anchor Books.

Moser, Caroline. 1992. "Adjustment from Below: Low-Income Women, Time, and the Triple Burden in Guayaquil, Ecuador." In H. Ashfar and C. Dennis, eds., *Women and Adjustment Policies in the Third World.* New York: St. Martin's Press.

————. 1993. *Gender Planning and Development: Theory, Practice, and Training.* New York: Routledge.

Munachonga, Monica. 1988. "Income Allocation and Marriage Options in Urban Zambia." In Daisy Dwyer and Judith Bruce, eds., *A Home Divided: Women and Income in the Third World.* Stanford, Calif.: Stanford University Press.

North, Douglass. 1981. *Structure and Change in Economic History.* New York: Norton.

————. 1990. *Institutions, Institutional Change, and Economic Performance.* Cambridge: Cambridge University Press.

Olson, Mancur. 1982. *The Rise and Decline of Nations: Economic Growth, Stagflation, and Social Rigidities.* New Haven, Conn.: Yale University Press.

Orazem, Peter, and Milan Vodopivec. 1994. "Winners and Losers in Transition: Returns to Education, Experience, and Gender in Slovenia." Policy Research Working Paper 1342. World Bank, Policy Research Department, Transition Economics Division, Washington, D.C.

Palmer, Ingrid. 1991. *Gender and Population in the Adjustment of African Economics: Planning for Change.* Geneva: International Labor Office.

Psacharopoulos, George, and Zafiris Tzannatos, eds. 1992. *Case Studies on Women's Employment and Pay in Latin America.* Washington, D.C.: World Bank.

Pyle, Jean Larson. 1990. *The State and Women in the Economy: Lessons from Sex Discrimination in the Republic of Ireland.* New York: State University of New York Press.

Ramirez, Carmen O. 1987. *La mujer: Su situación jurídica in veintiseis países americanos.* Cordoba, Argentina: Marcos Lerner.

Rogers, B. 1980. *The Domestication of Women: Discrimination in Developing Societies.* London: Kogan Page.

Rosenzweig, Mark R., and T. Paul Schultz. 1982. "Market Opportunities, Genetic Endowments, and Intrafamily Resource Distribution: Child Survival in Rural India." *American Economic Review* 72(4): 803–15.

Safilios-Rothschild, Constantina. 1988. "The Impact of Agrarian Reform on Men's and Women's Incomes in Rural Honduras." In Daisy Dwyer and Judith Bruce, eds., *A Home Divided: Women and Income in the Third World.* Stanford, Calif.: Stanford University Press.

Schotter, Andrew. 1981. *The Economic Theory of Social Institutions.* Cambridge: Cambridge University Press.

Schultz, T. Paul. 1990. "Testing the Neoclassical Model of Family Labor Supply and Fertility." *Journal of Human Resources* 25(4): 599–634.

———. 1993. "Introduction." In T. Paul Schultz, ed., *Investment in Women's Human Capital and Economic Development.* New Haven, Conn.: Yale UniversityPress.

Seguino, Stephanie. 1994. "Gender Wage Discrimination and Export-Led Growth in South Korea." American University, Department of Economics, Washington, D.C.

Sen, Amartya. 1988. "Family and Food: Sex Bias in Poverty." In T.N. Srinivasan and Pranab Bardhan, eds., *Rural Poverty in South Asia.* New York: Columbia University Press.

———. 1990. "Gender and Cooperative Conflicts." In Irene Tinker, ed., *Persistent Inequalities: Women and World Development.* New York: Oxford University Press.

Sen, Gita, and Caren Grown. 1987. *Development, Crises, and Alternative Visions: Third World Women's Perspectives.* New York: Monthly Review Press.

Staudt, Kathleen. 1978. "Agricultural Productivity Gaps: A Case Study of Male Preference in Government Policy Implementation." *Development and Change* 9(3): 439–57

Subbarao, K., and Laura Raney. 1993. *Social Gains from Female Education: A Cross-National Study.* World Bank Discussion Paper 194. Washington, D.C.

Tanski, Janet. 1994. "The Impact of Crisis, Stabilization, and Structural Adjustment on Women in Lima, Peru." *World Development* 22(11): 1627–42.

Tauchen, Helen V., Ann Dryden Witte, and Sharon K. Long. 1991. "Domestic Violence: A Nonrandom Affair." *International Economic Review* 32(2): 491–511.

Thomas, Duncan. 1990. "Intra-Household Resource Allocation: An Inferential Approach." *Journal of Human Resources* 25(4): 635–64.

UNDP (United Nations Development Programme). 1995. *Human Development Report 1995.* New York: Oxford University Press.

Wagman, Barnet, and Nancy Folbre. Forthcoming. "Household Services and Economic Growth in the United States, 1870–1930." *Feminist Economics.*

Waring, Marilyn. 1988. *If Women Counted: A New Feminist Economics.* New York: Harper and Row.

Williamson, Oliver. 1985. *The Economic Institutions of Capitalism: Firms, Markets, Relational Contracting.* New York: Free Press.

———. 1995. "The Institutions and Governance of Economic Development and Reform." In Michael Bruno and Boris Pleskovic, eds., *Proceedings of the World Bank Annual Conference on Development Economics 1994.* Washington, D.C.: World Bank.

Winter, Carolyn. 1994. "Gender Discrimination in the Labor Market and the Role of the Law: Experiences in Six Latin American Countries." World Bank, Latin America and the Caribbean Technical Department, Washington, D.C.

World Bank. 1991. *Gender and Poverty in India.* Washington, D.C.

————. 1994. *Enhancing Women's Participation in Economic Development.* A World Bank Policy Paper. Washington, D.C.

————. 1995. "Gender and Development: Equity and Efficiency." Poverty and Social Policy Department, Gender Analysis and Policy, Washington, D.C.

Wyss, Brenda. 1995. "Gender and the Economic Support of Jamaican Households: Implications for Children's Living Standards." Unpublished Ph.D. dissertation. University of Massachusetts at Amherst, Department of Economics, Amherst, Mass.

Comment on "Engendering Economics: New Perspectives on Women, Work, and Demographic Change," by Nancy Folbre

Elza Berquó

Nancy Folbre's article competently and courageously addresses crucial issues that map out both our concern for and responsibility toward future generations. It documents the difficult role confronting women all over the globe in bearing the high cost of raising children. There can be no doubt that the burden remains much heavier for women in developing countries, where they cannot count on social, economic, and institutional resources to protect their rights, and where they remain subjected to rigid and restrictive family hierarchies.

A growing awareness of "gender bias" (often cloaked in different terms) in both public and private spheres was the mainspring for the collective action that emerged as the feminist movement of the 1960s. But according to the feminist critique of the 1980s, the strategies that sought to promote women's status were not successful because they did not distinguish between the "condition" and the "position" of women (Young 1988). In other words, by focusing exclusively on building women's human capital—jobs, wages, education, and health—this approach failed to consider the structural factors perpetuating women's oppression and exploitation (Moser 1989).

The concept of empowerment emerged when Development Alternatives with Women for a New Era (DAWN) inaugurated the "empowerment approach" in 1985. Empowerment demanded radical changes in laws, property rights, and any other institution supporting and perpetuating male domination (Batliwala 1994). My question is whether the empowerment approach can be used to confront the gender bias that results from male rent-seeking coalitions.

In societies in which income inequality remains significant and poverty and social exclusion prevail, forms of protest and attempts to challenge the status quo involve all who are oppressed, regardless of gender. Gender bias emerges at a more advanced stage of development, when struggles involving class bias and race bias, among others, emerge. In these situations women may be torn between social or racial group identity and gender identity.

Elza Berquó is president of the National Council of Population and Development in São Paulo, Brazil.
Annual World Bank Conference on Development Economics 1995
©1996 The International Bank for Reconstruction and Development / THE WORLD BANK

A good example of this situation is found in the Afro-Brazilian movement. In Brazil people identifying themselves as black account for almost half the total population. They make up the poorest segments of the population and face social discrimination. When black men commit violent acts against their wives, women usually do not report these incidents to the police. They justify this behavior in two ways. First, they do not wish to fuel the discrimination against blacks, whom the white population holds responsible for the high crime rates in Brazil. Second, they depend on their husbands; financial support will disappear if their husbands are put in jail.

Another relevant issue that is not explicitly considered in Folbre's article concerns the effect that gender bias, which women have been exposed to for most of their lives, has on women's welfare in old age. Demographic and social studies in Latin America and the Caribbean have found that elderly women have lower levels of education and income than elderly men (Pérez and Restrepo 1993). Women are less able to meet their essential needs during this stage of their lives, particularly because the great majority of women over sixty years of age are widowed, single, or separated. Because these women have had less access to education, limited participation in the labor market, and less opportunity to obtain better occupations, they are left without social security benefits and with insufficient pensions.

Despite the transformations that family structures and functions are now undergoing, the domestic setting is still the space shared by men and women in their emotional and sexual relations. Protected by its privacy, the domestic world has remained socially invisible (Jelin and Paz 1992). Even in industrial countries, where gender bias against women has been overcome in different spheres of public life, asymmetrical gender relations still persist within the private space of the family. Since 1965 demographic studies in industrial countries have demonstrated the persistence of systematically reduced fertility rates, the postponement of first children, the decline in legal marriage rates, the growth in divorce and separation rates, and the increase of informal unions. Undoubtedly, these changes reflect women's weighing of the opportunity costs of time, pitting marriage, pregnancy, and raising children against market work. This cost analysis takes into account that little or no cooperation can be expected from their partner or the father of their children in meeting the costs—economic, domestic, and emotional—of raising children. Even where pronatal public incentives exist, they have not been very effective.

It is in this sense that women face a paradox appropriately stressed by Folbre: the same development processes that contribute to increasing their human capital make them more vulnerable as mothers. We might ask the following:

- Is this development inevitable and, therefore, does it play a role in women's struggles in developing countries?
- Could this development represent the last step in a process of change toward symmetrical gender relations in all spheres? If this is the case, will we see significant changes in male identity and behavior during the next millennium, with important repercussions for gender relations?
- Because mechanisms perpetuating gender identities and relations are constructed within the family, involving a complex web of asymmetrical power

relations (Jelin and Paz 1992), will mothers educate their children in ways that contribute to the elimination of these asymmetrical relations?

• Does the growing concern of international organizations and agencies in stimulating research and studies on male identity, attitudes, and behavior work to undermine gender bias, especially within the family?

References

Batliwala, Srilatha. 1994. "The Meaning of Women's Empowerment: New Concepts from Action." In Gita Sen, Adrienne Germain, and Lincoln C. Chen, eds., *Population Policies Reconsidered: Health, Empowerment, and Rights.* Cambridge, Mass.: Harvard University Press.

Jelin, Elizabeth, and G. Paz. 1992. "Familia y genero en America Latina: cuestiones historicas y contemporaneas." Proceedings of the conference on the Peopling of the Americas. Veracruz, Mexico.

Moser, Caroline. 1989. "Gender Planning in the Third World: Meeting Practical and Strategic Needs." *World Development* 17: 1799–1825.

Pérez, E.A., and H. Restrepo. 1993. "Analisis comparative del envejecimiento en Brasil, Colombia, El Salvador, Jamaica, y Venezuela." Technical Working Paper 38. Pan-American Health Organization, Washington, D.C.

Young, Kennety. 1988. *Gender and Development: A Relational Approach.* Oxford: Oxford University Press.

Comment on "Engendering Economics: New Perspectives on Women, Work, and Demographic Change," by Nancy Folbre

Lawrence Haddad

It is always a pleasure to read an article by Nancy Folbre, especially when I am given the opportunity to comment on it in this type of forum. Along with the classic 1982 paper by Rosenzweig and Schultz, Folbre's 1986 paper, "Hearts and Spades: Paradigms of Household Economics" was one of the first to stimulate my interest in the economics of households and gender. The title of that paper refers to psychological tests that involve flashing playing cards of different suits in front of subjects who are then asked to identify the suit they see. The experiment was tried using cards with black hearts instead of red hearts. And the subjects reported that they saw spades, not hearts. Folbre's point was that one sees what one expects to see, and that economists have tended to see the household as a place of harmony, sporting one set of agreed upon preferences. Folbre's current article pushes the debate about gender bias beyond the household and the family and into the more general realm of social institutions.

Much of the article implicitly argues for a model of social institutions (such as the household) in which resource allocation decisions rely not on individual productivities and joint household preferences, but rather on individual preferences, bargaining, and opportunities that may not have been acted upon. Such models show how gender-specific, rent-seeking coalitions can influence gender bias in social institutions and allow us to assess how economic development affects the evolution of gender bias within these institutions. Folbre places her central question—does economic development affect the behavior of gender coalitions and the evolution of gender bias?—in a number of different contexts: asymmetries in property rights to land, access to male income, public policy toward job benefits and pensions, and the measurement of the value of nonmarket labor.

In patriarchal societies women lack formal ownership rights to land despite the fact that they provide the bulk of agricultural labor. Folbre argues that male land ownership gives the father leverage over children in terms of bequests, and children thus have extra incentives to take care of their parents. Incentives for fathers to treat

Lawrence Haddad is director of the Food Consumption and Nutrition Division at the International Food Policy Research Institute.

Annual World Bank Conference on Development Economics 1995

their wives well are also generated in this way. But development affects this story. On the one hand land becomes a less important source of income, and markets for insurance and social security develop. As a result, Folbre argues, the incentives for men to invest in their children and families may erode. On the other hand women's labor productivity becomes less dependent on land ownership, and this may increase women's reservation wage, which may lead to increased investment in women and children.

How changing male-female asymmetries in access to land affect individual welfare is an interesting question, and it will be on our minds as we witness the increasing urbanization of Sub-Saharan Africa and South Asia over the next twenty years. But, unlike Folbre, I would like to emphasize not only the asymmetry in access to land that women will use, but the asymmetries in access to land that they may not use. What is the point of looking at asymmetries in access to land if the land may not be used? The common preference or "unitary" model of social institutions would argue that there is little point. But models that permit differences in individual preferences show that there is much to be gained.

An example that my co-authors and I cite in a recent paper is that of rights to common property (Alderman and others 1995). Suppose that a local government introduces a scheme that reduces the barriers to access to common property resources. How will this policy affect intrahousehold inequality and, in particular, the well-being of those with poorer access (women, for the sake of argument)? Assume that improved access to common property resources increases a woman's ability to earn income outside the household or other social institution but that this income does not exceed that which a woman would receive from joint production within the social institution. Hence a woman's bargaining position within the household or social institution is improved because of her enhanced potential to earn higher income outside the institution, even though she remains engaged in joint production. Her bargaining position—and therefore her claim on resources within the household—is improved even if the common property is not actually used. This policy thus has a long reach: it alters intrahousehold allocation by changing outside options, even if those options are not acted upon. The unitary model is, however, silent on this issue.

Folbre's Challenges

Folbre's article issues a number of challenges to economists and other social scientists, particularly those working in the poverty, natural resources, and human resources fields. First, economists must do better in measuring efficiency losses arising because of underinvestment in women. A review by Quisumbing (1994) finds that there are virtually no convincing quantitative estimates of the efficiency losses due to women's lack of access to complementary farm inputs, although there are many qualitative studies suggesting that these losses are large. A recent paper by Udry and others (forthcoming) begins to fill this gap. Using data from male- and female-controlled plots in Burkina Faso, his analysis implies that the value of household output could be increased by 10 to 15 percent simply by reallocating factors of production across plots.

A second challenge is to narrow the gap between the women in development and the gender and development approaches to development. Recall that Folbre characterizes these two approaches at their extremes—as quantitative approaches that focus on the economic aspects of individual status (women in development) and qualitative approaches that focus on empowerment (gender and development), which are typically eschewed by economists. This issue came up at a panel that Amartya Sen and I were on in November 1994. At that seminar Professor Sen contextualized economists' attempts to shut themselves off from the gender and development approach by quoting from a film starring Peter Sellers, the late English actor and purveyor of wry humor. In the film Sellers is walking an impressive-looking dog, when he bumps into an acquaintance. The acquaintance admires the dog. As he leans down to pet the dog, he says to Sellers, "Does your dog bite?" and Sellers answers, "No." The acquaintance pets the dog, and the dog promptly bites him. The acquaintance, indignant and in pain, says, "I thought you said your dog doesn't bite?" to which Sellers calmly replies, "This isn't my dog."

Now if the biting dog is a women in development approach—one that ignores qualitative information—not all economists would disown it. But some economists who once might have disowned the biting dog are now sending it to obedience school instead. Encouragingly, some progress has already been made from both ends of the women in development–gender and development spectrum. Including Rao's work on fertility decisions and on domestic violence (Rao and Greene 1993; Rao and Bloch 1993) and Schuler and Hashemi's (1994) work on quantifying empowerment from participation in credit collectives, there is a small but growing body of innovative research that attempts to use qualitative and quantitative techniques as complements rather than as substitutes to study collective behavior.

The third challenge is to make progress on the intergenerational resource allocation front, sometimes with a gender focus, sometimes not. Recent work by Quisumbing (1995) illustrates the importance of incorporating the preferences and characteristics of three generations—grandparents, parents, and children—into models that intend to explain investments in children, for example.

Fourth, there is a need for more work on collective action. Folbre admits that her analysis of the logic of women's collective action is speculative. To this challenge we can bring to bear the work of people like Elinor Ostrom. Ostrom and Gardner's (1993) study of the management of common-pool resources in Indonesia, Nepal, and the Philippines shows that interventions designed without an understanding of the mutual dependencies and obligations among the users of the common-pool resource can disrupt these arrangements, resulting in the increased generation of externalities that reciprocity had previously minimized. This line of work is especially challenging because of the back-and-forth nature of the interactions between coalitions. For example, Goetz and SenGupta (1994) point out that credit targeted to women's groups can be appropriated by men. Does the nominal increase in status that women retain as credit recipients translate into an increase in real status? In other words, can women keep the credit or at least demand a quid pro quo in return for granting men access to the credit? Or is women's status lowered in that women spend time obtaining the credit, only to have it taken away against their will, perhaps at the risk of violence?

Fifth, all of these conceptual and analytical challenges generate data collection challenges that may be less glamorous, but that remain our bread and butter when it comes to testing these hypotheses. Folbre comments on the usefulness—and lack thereof—of the World Bank's Living Standards Measurement Study data in understanding what goes on inside the household. First, let me say that these data are not unique in being insufficiently disaggregated to enable meaningful intrahousehold analysis. Second, and perhaps more important, many data sets do collect disaggregated information—often in order to accurately construct a household-level variable such as household income—but frequently the individual data are not used in the analysis. Third, extra data collection need not be costly—an extra question or two in a standard household survey module may be more than justified in terms of the analytic possibilities that are unlocked.

Conclusion

In closing, I return to Folbre's 1986 paper, "Hearts and Spades." I think that this title has a deep meaning. I interpret the paper as arguing that altruism, represented by hearts, is not a convincing explanation for why women tend to spend more time in work, represented by spades—which means shovel in British English and signifies manual labor.

By the same token, the current article might be called "Clubs and Diamonds: Paradigms of Social Institution Economics." Clubs represent the threat of conflict, while diamonds represent the lure of cooperation—both negative and positive bargaining strategies in the context of social institutions. I may yet place a copyright on that title. I am sure that ten years ago no one would have cared if I did. Today, thanks to the work of people like Folbre, the field of intrahousehold resource allocation is becoming more competitive. And, as we all know, when the competition for scarce resources heats up, it is useful to have a bargaining chip or two up one's sleeve.

References

Alderman, Harold, Pierre A. Chiappori, Lawrence Haddad, John Hoddinott, and Ravi Kanbur. 1995. "Unitary Versus Collective Models of the Household: Time to Shift the Burden of Proof?" *World Bank Research Observer* 10 (1): 1–19.

Folbre, Nancy. 1986. "Hearts and Spades: Paradigms of Household Economics." *World Development* 14(2): 245–55.

Goetz, Anne-Marie, and Rita SenGupta. 1994. "Who Takes the Credit? Gender, Power, and Control Over Loan Use in Rural Credit Programmes in Bangladesh." Institute of Development Studies Working Paper. Brighton, U.K.

McElroy, Marjorie. 1992. "The Policy Implications of Family Bargaining and Marriage Markets." Paper presented at the International Food Policy Research Institute–World Bank conference on intrahousehold resource allocation: policy issues and research methods, February 12–14, Washington, D.C.

Ostrom, Elinor, and Roy Gardner. 1993. "Coping with Asymmetries in the Commons: Self-Governing Irrigation Systems Can Work." *Journal of Economic Perspectives* 7(4): 93–112.

Quisumbing, Agnes. 1994. "Gender Differences in Agricultural Productivity: A Survey of Empirical Evidence." Education and Social Policy Division Working Paper 36. World Bank, Poverty and Social Policy Department, Washington, D.C.

———. 1995. "The Extended Family and Intrahousehold Allocation: Inheritance and Investments in Children in the Rural Philippines." Food Consumption and Nutrition Division Discussion Paper 3. International Food Policy Research Institute, Washington, D.C.

Rao, Vijayendra, and Francis Bloch. 1993. "Wife-Beating, Its Causes and Its Implication for Nutrition Allocation in Children: An Economic and Anthropological Case-Study of a Rural South Indian Community." World Bank, Poverty and Human Resources Division, Washington, D.C.

Rao, Vijayendra, and Margaret Greene. 1993. "Marital Instability, Spousal Bargaining, and Their Implication for Fertility in Brazil: An Interdisciplinary Analysis." Working Paper. University of Chicago, Population Research Center.

Rosenzweig, Mark R., and T. Paul Schultz. 1982. "Market Opportunities, Genetic Endowments, and Intrafamily Resource Distribution: Child Survival in Rural India." *American Economic Review* 72(4): 803–15.

Schuler, Sydney Ruth, and S. M. Hashemi. 1994. "Credit Programs, Women's Empowerment, and Contraceptive Use in Rural Bangladesh." *Studies in Family Planning* 25(2): 65–76.

Udry, Chris, Harold Alderman, John Hoddinott, and Lawrence Haddad. Forthcoming. "Gender Differentials in Farm Productivity: Implications for Household Efficiency and Agriculture Policy." *Food Policy.*

Floor Discussion of "Engendering Economics: New Perspectives on Women, Work, and Economic Change," by Nancy Folbre

S alvador Valdés-Prieto (discussant from another session) observed that in Folbre's model women's bargaining power within the family depended on the value of their fallback position, which is a traditional Nash bargaining solution. But research in game theory has shown that this outcome works only if there is an external agent who can take away the gains of joint production if one partner does not agree to the distribution. He wondered if Folbre's conclusions were vulnerable to the objection that if a threat to withdraw from bargaining is not credible, it does not influence outcomes. Lawrence Haddad (discussant) agreed that credible threats were crucial for Nash bargaining models to work, and he likened the situation to the conference itself. If Haddad were in the audience, the chair had ways to shut him up: she could turn off his microphone, for example. When Haddad was onstage, she could not do that. Nash bargaining models were more general than neoclassical unitary models, but not as general as people would like them to be. They impose structure, but the standard neoclassical model imposes even more structure.

Folbre agreed that there was much to be said for the theoretical and analytical possibilities of this new genre of bargaining power models. The problem was that the genre puts too much emphasis on the notion that individuals are constantly assessing the costs and benefits of different actions in the family or household. At one extreme is the notion that families are totally altruistic; this genre carries analysis to the opposite extreme, assuming that individuals are constantly asking if they could possibly extract a little more utility from their partner—in Folbre's view, a violent caricature of the family. The most perceptive treatment of bargaining power was the model developed by Lundberg and Pollak (1993), which suggests that the fallback position in bargaining is simply the social norms governing how much work men and women should do and who should do which tasks.

Most people do not spend a lot of time arguing about these details, Folbre added. The fallback tends to be what everyone else is doing, or what has normally or traditionally been done. This puts the bargaining process in a subtle new light: individu-

This session was chaired by Joanne Salop, chief economist, South Asia Regional Office, at the World Bank.

Annual World Bank Conference on Development Economics 1995
©1996 The International Bank for Reconstruction and Development / THE WORLD BANK

als get resources and decide, "I don't like these traditional norms, I don't like the way things have always been done, I don't want to follow these rules, and guess what? I've got enough resources that I don't have to. I can change. I don't have to conform. I can bargain." Given all the transaction costs of bargaining in the household, one would have be at a fairly high level of frustration and have a fair chance of success in order to be willing to bargain. And what does bargaining achieve? If enough people bargain, social norms change; allocation in every household—not just your own—is affected. A gradual, more long-term, more institutionally mediated process of bargaining develops in which most people are not arguing all the time, but a few people raise a ruckus and get people to question the status quo, and in the process they modify it. This was the process that led Folbre to draw attention to the way social institutions affect social norms and their potential to complement the new approach to comparative statistics and microeconomics.

A participant from the United Nations Development Programme's *Human Development Report* office wondered how much work Folbre had done on harmonizing the different types of law operating in most developing countries, including Africa: common law, traditional laws, customary laws, and religious laws. Under common law women have the right to own property, but when common law conflicts with traditional and customary law (as it often does), traditional and customary law generally prevail, especially in rural areas. Rephrasing the problem, Elza Berquó (discussant) said that having laws was not synonymous with having rights, as Brazil illustrated. Laws that protect women from discrimination are not necessarily obeyed, often because women must be able to afford to hire a lawyer to defend their rights.

A participant from Indonesia observed that women can be found in any market from East Asia to South Asia, sometimes dominating the marketplace. So women there have always had money, which gives them different bargaining power within the household. In many Southeast Asian households, she said, women hold the household pursestrings, although few are land owners. Indonesia is also fairly polygamous, having the highest divorce rate in Southeast Asia. And although women there used to marry young, they are increasingly marrying later now and following a general world pattern: marriage, followed by short intervals of nonmarriage, followed by remarriage. These developments change the rules of the household game. Still, the women's issue is different in Indonesia than in the West: society and government in Indonesia are still dominated by men. So how does Indonesia fit into Folbre's paradigm?

A participant from Zaire wondered where Zaire fit in the paradigm. Zairian women were more interested in having money than in owning land. Women were not victims in Zaire; they were dynamic people and simply needed credit. What solutions did the panelists see for giving such women more access to credit, especially through World Bank policies and projects?

A participant from Bangladesh responded that a recent estimate of credit flows into rural Bangladesh had shown that five nongovernmental organizations that now account for about 65 percent of institutional credit (including banks) offered 80–90 percent of their credit to women. That sort of access to credit—which economists increasingly consider an important variable in terms of command over assets—should change the pattern of relationships in a household. But practically speaking, while access to credit may be differentiated by gender, the family continues to share command over income streams. And the flow of output from women's assets and distributional norms within the household are equally influential no matter who receives the credit. So unless a specific policy intervention is backed up by relevant interventions affecting the household distribution of income and consumption, simply changing command over assets may not fully solve the problem.

Folbre said that she did not feel equipped to answer questions specific to Indonesia or Zaire. Her argument was that the kind of data that is needed to ask important questions or to test hypotheses is not being collected. Census data on households headed by women are not available; there are no time-use or household-budget surveys that help to explain the intrafamily life-cycle distribution between young and old, between men and women, and between parents and nonparents; and national income accounts do not impute the value of nonmarket household production and services. Therefore it impossible to ask how the development of institutional credit affects the allocation of leisure time in a region, or how a certain kind of land reform affects the allocation of resources between parents and children. Without these types of data there is no way to understand what is going on.

Michael Lipton (discussant from another session) asked the panelists whether men and women suffer different types of poverty that require different policies and different types of collective action. There is good reason to believe, for example, that chronic total poverty is greater for women, whose prospects for escaping poverty are dimmer because of educational deprivation and the double day. Moreover, when women move from rural to urban areas, their (age-specific) rate of participation in work seems to fall; this does not happen for men. Is the structure of poverty different for men and women? And what are the policy implications if it is?

It would be interesting to see whether women are overrepresented in chronic poverty, as opposed to transitory poverty, responded Haddad. He had found it difficult to get data on women's representation among the poor, but there were certainly reasons to design different interventions for chronic and transitory poverty. The problem with targeting policies toward chronically poor women is that there are second- and third-round knock-off effects. According to a 1994 paper by Goetz and SenGupta, for example, although women's collectives have been successful in providing credit to women, it turns out that men are getting access to credit through the women. Thus it is not clear whether increased credit allocations represent a real improvement in women's status or whether their status has worsened because men are threatening them with violence if they do not get loans for the men. Haddad suggested that studies be undertaken to see whether intrahousehold rules have changed because of institutions like the Grameen Bank. It was his belief that the rules of the game are endogenous and that it takes a while for them to change.

Joanne Salop (chair) closed by saying that Folbre's presentation was interesting because it built on two observations. First, over time, with development, the returns parents can appropriate from their children decline, so men want to have fewer children. Second, women care more, so if the men want to leave they can, because they know that the women will remain with the kids. Thus pressures for legal change and new institutional arrangements are developing because we have reached the stage where the appropriable value of children has declined.

References

Goetz, Anne-Marie, and Rita SenGupta. 1994. "Who Takes the Credit? Gender, Power, and Control Over Loan Use in Rural Credit Programmes in Bangladesh." Institute of Development Studies Working Paper. Brighton, U.K.

Lundberg, Sheldon, and Robert A. Pollak. 1993. "Separate Spheres Bargaining and the Marriage Market." *Journal of Political Economy* 101(6): 988–1010.

Why Is There Multilateral Lending?

Dani Rodrik

If lending by the World Bank, the International Monetary Fund, and regional development banks has an independent rationale, it rests on the advantages generated by the multilateral nature of these institutions. In principle, there are two such advantages. First, since information on the investment environments in different countries is in many ways a collective good, multilateral agencies are better positioned than private agents or bilateral agencies to internalize the informational externalities that may arise. This information advantage creates a rationale for multilateral institutions, particularly in terms of monitoring government policies in recipient countries. Second, as long as multilateral agencies retain some autonomy from the governments that own them, their interactions with the countries to which they lend are less politicized than are the interactions between governments. This official yet less politicized contact gives multilateral agencies an advantage in the exercise of conditionality, that is, in lending that is conditional on changes in government policies. Neither of these two potential advantages of multilateral agencies has much to do with lending, however, and the empirical analysis finds little evidence that multilateral lending has acted as a catalyst for private capital flows. Still, lending by multilateral institutions may be required to maintain confidence in the quality of their policy monitoring and conditionality.

The World Bank and the International Monetary Fund (IMF) are so prominent on the international economic landscape that it is surprising to discover that there has been little systematic analysis of the question posed in this article's title. As it turns out, the question is a tough one to answer. What is the rationale for multilateral lending in a world of well-developed private capital markets and bilateral aid programs?

Dani Rodrik is professor of economics and international affairs at Columbia University. Some of the ideas in this article originated in an earlier paper written with Michael Gavin, whose contribution the author acknowledges. The author is also grateful to Ishac Diwan, William Easterly, Olga Jones, Nathaniel Leff, and Jeffrey Sachs for useful comments, Sudarshan Gooptu for help with data, Peter Boone for his political variables, and Euysung Kim and Maggie McMillan for research assistance and comments.

Annual World Bank Conference on Development Economics 1995
©1996 The International Bank for Reconstruction and Development / THE WORLD BANK

Until the World Bank and the IMF were created at the Bretton Woods meetings fifty years ago, multilateral lending had taken place only occasionally, and it had never been institutionalized (Gavin and Rodrik 1995). "Permanent, organized, intergovernmental economic cooperation was so revolutionary an idea in 1919 that it was not even considered by the statesmen who drafted the Treaty of Versailles," writes Oliver (1975, p. xiii). "By 1945, however, it was an idea acceptable to most of the people of the world, and its acceptance has become institutionalized through special agencies of the United Nations. . . ." These specialized agencies were founded on the idea that private capital markets could not be relied on to provide the resources needed for postwar reconstruction. One of the perceived lessons of the interwar period was that international capital flows tended to exacerbate— rather than stabilize—global business cycles and that private external financing was often lacking for projects that were otherwise sound and profitable. But since 1945 private capital markets have developed to an extent that the Bretton Woods delegates could not have foreseen.[1] In addition, economists' faith in the capacity of governments—let alone intergovernmental bureaucracies—to make investment decisions superior to those of private capitalists has waned.

Of course, private creditors are not motivated by humanitarian considerations, and the flow of resources to poor countries may be inadequate from a broader perspective. But if such humanitarian—as well as political or strategic—considerations are of concern to donor governments, they can take them into account in their bilateral assistance programs. It is not clear that multilateral institutions actually increase the aggregate flow of humanitarian assistance, since the same donor governments finance concessional flows from multilateral sources. Once again, what additional role do multilateral agencies perform?

If lending by the World Bank, the IMF, and regional development banks has an independent rationale, it rests on the advantages generated by the multilateral nature of these institutions. In principle, there are two such advantages. First, since information on the quality of investment environments in different countries is in many ways a collective good, multilateral agencies are better positioned than private agents or bilateral agencies to internalize the externalities that may arise. This advantage rationalizes multilateral lending in terms of information provision, particularly in terms of monitoring government policies in recipient countries. Second, as long as multilateral agencies retain some degree of autonomy from the governments that own them, their interaction with recipient countries is less politicized than intergovernmental links. This in turn endows multilateral agencies with an advantage in the exercise of conditionality (in lending that is conditional on changes in government policies).

Neither of these two potential advantages of multilateral lending has much to do with lending. In fact, it is possible to envisage multilateral agencies monitoring government policies and exercising conditionality on behalf of bilateral and private lenders without engaging in lending activities. But in the absence of multilateral lending there could be severe incentive problems in the provision of these functions. In particular, private creditors might question the quality of the monitoring and conditionality exercised by multilateral agencies if these agencies did not back up their recommendations with their own resources. Put differently, multilateral agencies could be perceived as having little incentive to produce quality work if they were not risking their own money.

Where concessional lending is concerned, multilateral lending may have a third role that is related to humanitarian considerations. Bilateral flows tend to be heavily influenced by political and military considerations. Thus, while in principle governments could take humanitarian considerations into account in their bilateral lending, in practice such considerations get swamped by others—at least where the major donors (the United States, the European Union, and Japan) are concerned. By delegating authority over some of their lending to multilateral agencies, governments can be seen as committing themselves in advance to levels of humanitarian lending that they might later be unable to deliver on their own, for political reasons.

Whatever the merits of that argument, this article does not address it. The focus here is on the efficiency and economic implications of multilateral lending. It should be noted, however, that humanitarian considerations provide at best a weak justification for multilateral lending, at least as it is now carried out. The reason is that the bulk of such lending takes place at nonconcessional terms: during the early 1990s less than a quarter of gross disbursements from multilateral sources were concessional.

The first part of this article elaborates on the informational and conditionality rationales for multilateral lending and discusses their relevance and plausibility. The second part provides empirical evidence on whether multilateral lending has acted as a catalyst for private flows or been a signal of development potential. While some of the results are mixed, on balance there is little evidence that multilateral lending has been able to catalyze private capital flows.

Multilateral and Other Flows

I begin by surveying some quantitative characteristics of multilateral lending relative to other types of flows. Private, bilateral, and multilateral flows to developing countries since 1970 are shown in figure 1.[2] Several points are noteworthy. First, private resource transfers are highly cyclical. They were large until 1982, then disappeared as developing countries succumbed to the debt crisis (between 1984 and 1989 private net transfers were negative), then rapidly recovered. In 1993 the combined net resource transfer to developing countries from private sources was larger (as a percentage of recipient GNP) than ever. The consequences of the recent Mexican crisis will almost certainly be reflected in a substantial drop in these flows. Such swings are only the latest in a series of boom-bust cycles in international lending that have taken place since at least the beginning of the nineteenth century (Eichengreen 1991).

Second, net transfers from multilateral sources are significant. Together with bilateral flows, multilateral lending has played an important stabilizing role, especially in the 1980s when private flows disappeared. Multilateral lending is small compared with private flows only during certain periods, such as during the late 1970s or 1992–94. And net transfers from multilateral agencies have never turned negative in the aggregate.

Of the ten countries receiving the largest gross flows during 1990–93, China, Mexico, and Indonesia make the list in all three flow categories, and Argentina and Brazil make the list for multilateral and private flows (table 1). Indeed, the three types of flows are closely correlated in terms of recipients (table 2). The cumulative shares of the recipients of the largest flows reflect the greater concentration of private flows in a smaller number of countries: the top ten recipients account for 70 percent of gross private flows to developing countries, but less than 50 percent of multilateral and bilateral flows. Private flows generally have become less concentrated since the 1970s, and the gap in this respect between private and multilateral flows has shrunk considerably since then (table 3). Note also that private flows tend to concentrate on large economies, as reflected by the greater share of the top ten recipients of such flows in the aggregate GNP of developing countries (see table 1).

Rationales for Multilateral Lending

That private capital flows are highly cyclical and geographically concentrated is often read as evidence that private capital markets are inefficient. There are indeed good reasons to believe that private capital markets are subject to bandwagon effects. The magnitude of private flows notwithstanding, this should make us wary of viewing the operation of these markets as optimal. But the possibility of market failures in private capital markets is not a direct rationale for multilateral lending.

Figure 1. *Net Flows to Developing Countries, 1970–93*

Percentage of recipient GNP

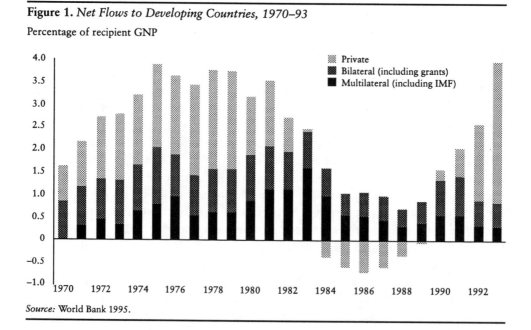

Source: World Bank 1995.

Table 1. *Top Ten Recipients of Gross Capital Flows, 1990–93*
(percent)

Type of flow/country	Share of total	Cumulative share of total	Cumulative share of developing country GNP
Multilateral			
India	10	10	6
Mexico	9	18	13
Argentina	5	23	18
Indonesia	5	28	21
China	4	33	30
Pakistan	3	36	31
Venezuela	3	39	32
The Philippines	3	42	33
Turkey	3	45	36
Brazil	3	47	47
Private			
China	15	15	9
Mexico	12	27	16
Korea	6	33	23
Brazil	6	39	34
Russia	6	45	45
Indonesia	5	51	48
Thailand	5	56	50
Portugal	5	61	52
Argentina	5	65	57
Malaysia	4	70	58
Bilateral			
Russia	10	10	11
Egypt	7	17	12
Indonesia	6	24	15
China	4	28	24
India	4	32	30
Turkey	3	35	33
Mexico	3	38	40
The Philippines	3	40	41
Algeria	2	43	42
Pakistan	2	45	43

Source: Calculated from World Bank 1994.

Table 2. *Correlation Coefficients between Different Types of Flows, 1990–93*

Type of flow	Multilateral	Private	Bilateral
Multilateral	1.00	0.68	0.56
Private		1.00	0.52
Bilateral			1.00

Source: Calculated from World Bank 1994.

Table 3. *Herfindahl Indexes of Concentration of Gross Capital Flows, by Type*

Period	Multilateral	Private	Bilateral
1970–75	0.05	0.10	0.08
1976–81	0.04	0.09	0.04
1982–87	0.04	0.05	0.03
1988–93	0.04	0.06	0.03

Source: Calculated from World Bank 1994.

One must first ask why markets fail, to ensure that the distortions are tackled with the appropriate instruments. Second, one must ask why the same purposes could not be served equally well by bilateral flows as by multilateral flows. As I indicated earlier, I believe that the answers to these questions involve informational and enforceability problems in international finance (Gavin and Rodrik 1995).

Multilateral Aid As Information Gathering and Monitoring

The level of private capital flows to individual developing countries is determined by a number of factors. The availability of high-yielding investment opportunities is obviously a chief consideration. Of equal importance are the government policies that shape the economic environment in which projects are undertaken. This point becomes obvious when private flows take the form of bank loans to public agencies or international bonds issued by them—the repayability of such borrowing depends on sound government policies. But there is an important connection even for foreign direct investment: as entrepreneurs in developing countries have learned, macroeconomic and microeconomic policies impinge significantly on the profitability of specific projects. A project that is profitable under one set of trade and exchange rate policies, for example, can easily go bankrupt under a different set. These kinds of policy risks are one of the chief impediments to capital inflows in economies where the rate of return to capital is otherwise high.[3]

Multilateral lending agencies employ thousands of analysts who closely follow economic developments and policies in developing countries. These analysts prepare detailed country reports, sectoral reports, and cross-country analyses. Their evaluations of policymaking in member countries—as revealed most clearly in the level of multilateral lending to these countries—are an important input to the decisions made in private capital markets.

To get a sense of how important such monitoring and information-gathering activities are and to asses whether private institutions perform them as well, consider the following thought experiment. Suppose that the government of a country that was hitherto closed to the outside world decides to open up its economy and to invite foreign investors. It announces that it is eliminating trade and investment restrictions and that it is committed to fiscal and monetary restraint. To attract foreign investors, the government points out that the country has adequate infrastructure and is rich in natural and human resources. Assume that all of this is true and that the government is indeed committed to reform. How are foreign investors likely to respond?

From the perspective of individual investors information about the availability of profitable projects is, for the most part, a purely private good. For example, a multinational mining firm could retain most of the benefits of a discovery of mineral deposits in this country by contracting with the government for extraction rights. A foreign manufacturing firm that establishes a subsidiary in the country will be, by and large, the sole beneficiary of the market research it undertakes. In general, then, there are sufficient incentives for private investors to collect information where specific projects are concerned.

On the other hand information about the broader investment environment and the quality of government policymaking is a public good: such information benefits all potential investors, regardless of their specific projects. Were such information to become available to any one private investor, it would be socially efficient to share it with other potential investors. But given the public nature of the benefit, individual investors have inadequate incentives to devote resources to information gathering of this kind, and very little incentive to share the information they do gather. One way of overcoming this problem is for the government to invite the World Bank or the IMF to provide the informational public goods. As multilateral institutions, these organizations are not—or should not be—subject to the incentive problems that confront individual investors. These institutions regularly carry out intensive consultations with the government to determine the state of the economy and to catalogue prevailing government policies. From this perspective, then, when these institutions certify the quality of government policies or place their seal of approval on a country, they are effectively providing a collective good to investors at large.[4]

This role clearly exists in other situations as well. Think of a country that has attracted considerable private capital inflows because of its market-oriented policy reforms. Especially if the inflows are liquid and short term, investors will need reassurance that the government's macroeconomic policies are sound and sustainable. The World Bank and the IMF are well positioned to undertake the requisite monitoring, both because they can internalize informational externalities and because they have access to the right kind of government data and analytical talent. Or consider a country that comes under pressure in international capital markets for reasons that its government feels are unjustified by economic fundamentals. This government may benefit from inviting the IMF and the World Bank to monitor its monetary and fiscal policies.[5]

In these examples the role played by multilateral institutions is purely informational. In principle this role could be played without attendant lending. But in practice close monitoring of a government's policies is almost always undertaken in the context of a lending program, even when the government has access to private flows and no demonstrable need to borrow from multilateral sources. The World Bank or IMF seal of approval takes the form of a loan, not a pronouncement. There are two possible explanations for this linkage. First, governments may be less willing to open up their books to outsiders if doing so does not lead directly to financial flows. Although this explanation carries weight in some instances, it is not a strong argument for linking monitoring with lending: if governments themselves do not attach sufficient value to the monitoring role of multilateral agencies, then prima facie this role cannot be that important.

The second argument is more credible. In the absence of direct lending by multilateral agencies, there is very little to ensure that these agencies will exercise their informational function as competently as possible. If their own money is not at stake, they may be more easily influenced by political demands—from their major shareholders or developing countries—in their certification of creditworthiness. By putting their money where their mouth is, they have an incentive for truthful reporting. On the other hand the insistence of multilateral lenders that their claims take precedence over private claims undercuts the signaling value of their exposure.[6] If these lenders really wanted to signal confidence, wouldn't they subordinate their claims? In addition, lending may make multilateral agencies reluctant to acknowledge problems in countries to which they have large exposure.

The private market for the type of information provided by multilateral agencies is not entirely undeveloped. Major bond-rating agencies assess the issues of sovereign creditors, including a number of developing countries. In addition, a number of private services evaluate the creditworthiness or the investment climate of countries around the world. Moreover, none of these agencies combines its informational function with its financial transactions. The breadth and scope of their coverage is limited, however, compared with the work undertaken by the World Bank and the IMF. Still, some investors would prefer the Economist Intelligence Unit's most recent quarterly report to a World Bank document on their first visit to an unfamiliar country.

In addition, even if multilateral lending has a potential role along the lines outlined above, multilateral institutions have not necessarily strived to fill it. The World Bank and regional development banks have traditionally confined their primary role to lending, relegating information provision to second place. Much of the information generated by the World Bank and the IMF in the course of their country work is not even made public. These institutions defend their secrecy by arguing that governments would not otherwise share their data. But such secrecy simply makes it more difficult for multilateral agencies to fulfill the potential of their informational role.

Finally, where multilateral agencies have played an informational role through their lending activities, they have not always been successful. In the recent Mexican crisis, for example, the World Bank and the IMF were arguably at fault for not having clearly and emphatically publicized the danger signals early on.[7] If the unsustainability of Mexico's exchange rate policy—which was evident to many academic observers—had been made evident to money managers in the United States, Mexico would not have been allowed to fall so deep into crisis and some of the spillovers to other countries could possibly have been avoided. On the other hand, by advertising the danger signals the World Bank and the IMF could have precipitated the crisis and ended up being blamed for it. In such instances these institutions have to walk a fine line between withholding criticism of inadequate policies and sounding alarm bells that may lead private investors to overreact. But their long-term credibility and effectiveness require that they play it straight with market participants. Ultimately, then, whether multilateral lending performs a useful monitoring and signaling role is an empirical question.

Multilateral Lending As Conditionality

The second role for multilateral lending—exercising conditionality—subsumes information gathering and monitoring and goes much further. With conditionality, multilateral lending assumes a much more active and intrusive role involving policy advocacy, leverage, and bargaining. Information gathering and monitoring activities also can have some of these elements, but because conditionality is directed specifically at changing government policies—rather than simply reporting and evaluating them—the two roles are conceptually different.

The need for conditionality in international lending arises from the time inconsistency problem inherent in many creditor-debtor relationships. A simple example helps illustrate the issues. Consider a liquidity-constrained government with two possible courses of actions, cutting public consumption or cutting public investment. Foreign lenders can choose either to lend or not to lend.[8] Assume that lenders will be paid back in full only if the government chooses to cut consumption rather than investment. The government prefers cutting investment, but will cut consumption if that is the only way it can borrow. If the government cannot credibly commit itself to cutting consumption, lenders will refuse to lend. The government's inability to commit itself thus leads to a suboptimal situation for all parties.

That conditional lending—lending contingent on certain actions by the government, here a cut in public consumption—has a useful role in such cases is clear. Conditionality can be a commitment tool that allows borrowing governments to make decisions that are desirable ex ante in circumstances where the rational strategies differ ex post.[9] Whether conditionality is effective in practice is unclear. Sovereign entities obviously can and do renege on their commitments. It is also not clear that multilateral institutions are inherently better at exercising conditionality. Despite the vast literature on conditionality (see, for example, Guitian 1982; Mosley 1987; Polak 1991), there has been practically no discussion of why policy conditionality has become an almost exclusively multilateral affair. Could conditionality not be applied as effectively by ad hoc groupings of private or government creditors, or both, depending on the particulars of each case? In fact, until 1945 that was precisely the form that conditionality took, whether through gunboat diplomacy, organized bondholders' committees, or some combination that brought recalcitrant debtors into line. These types of conditionality often were more direct and intrusive than today's model: it was not uncommon, for example, for government tax revenue on imports to be earmarked for foreign debt service.

What has changed is the political acceptability of these old forms of persuasion. And therein lies the main argument favoring multilateral conditionality: in an era of highly prized and zealously guarded national sovereignty, the current form of conditionality is more politically palatable to all parties. This is partly because debtor governments are shareholders of the multilateral institutions. But since power in these institutions is effectively exercised not by developing countries but by industrial countries, the political acceptability of multilateral conditionality derives more from the perception that the World Bank and the IMF operate somewhat autonomously from Western policymakers and in a relatively apolitical manner. Although the United States, in particular, exercises considerable leverage over both institutions, the relationship is still an arm's length one. Consequently, negotiations with borrowing governments can be held to the technical and economic level.

Something along these lines has been implicit in much of the thinking on multilateral conditionality but has rarely been articulated in full. The Pearson report (1969, pp. 213–14) provides an early statement of the idea:

> The aid dialogue involves sensitive questions of performance monitoring and advice and persuasion in matters of policy and planning. By playing a leading role as intermediaries in this ongoing debate between the suppliers and users of aid, international organizations do much to endow development assistance with the character of a truly international effort, reducing any overtones of charity or interventionism which have at times embittered the aid process in the past.

A number of safeguards help ensure that multilateral operations are relatively apolitical. The World Bank and the IMF, as well as many of the regional development banks, are prohibited by their charters from allowing political considerations to influence their lending programs and country policies. The high caliber and professionalism of their staffs is another important factor. In addition, both the World Bank's and the IMF's chief executives have traditionally been rather independent from their respective boards. Finally, since the World Bank's nonconcessional lending is financed by borrowing from international capital markets, it is difficult for it to deviate from market and creditworthiness criteria in its lending decisions. None of this, of course, is to deny that these institutions often act under political constraints or that they get embroiled in controversy in developing countries.[10] Both institutions are frequently viewed by groups on the left as tools of the U.S. government, or of international capital. But the fact that they are none too popular in Western capitals or with the U.S. Congress belies such simplistic characterizations.

Two pieces of evidence support the proposition that multilateral flows are less governed by political considerations than are bilateral flows. The first consists of the regional distribution of official development assistance by type of provider (table 4). The distribution of bilateral aid tends to be heavily biased toward regions of political or strategic interest to the donor government. U.S. aid is concentrated in the Middle East, Japanese aid in East and Southeast Asia, and European Union aid in Sub-Saharan Africa. Multilateral aid flows, on the other hand, are generally free of such regional biases. The regional distribution of multilateral aid is closest to that of the Nordic countries. Since the Nordic countries tend to be the donors most responsive to humanitarian needs and least motivated by strategic considerations, this similarity is meaningful.

The second piece of evidence is more formal. Following the recent work of Boone (1994b), I ran panel regressions on the determinants of net resource transfers from bilateral and multilateral sources (table 5). The panel consists of country data averaged over four five-year subperiods (1970–74, 1975–79, 1980–84, and 1985–89). In each regression the dependent variable is the net resource transfer from bilateral or multilateral sources as a share of recipient GNP. The independent variables are a set of economic indicators, region and period dummies, and three additional dummy variables intended to capture the presence of political motives in bilateral flows.[11] These last three dummy variables, denoted as Friends of the United States, Friends of OPEC, and Friends of France, are taken from Boone (1994b) and are used to identify recipient countries that are politically important to each of these donors. Friends of the United States and Friends of OPEC are countries that receive more than 1 percent of U.S. and OPEC aid budgets, respectively, while Friends of France are members of the French franc zone in Africa. The results confirm that political variables are important for bilateral lending, but not for multilateral lending. Hence the analysis supports the more casual evidence gleaned from the data on the regional distribution of official development assistance.

If multilaterals have an advantage in the exercise of conditionality, this veneer of autonomy and political neutrality is an important part of it. It allows sovereign governments to swallow a bitter pill without appearing to cave in to either another sovereign government or a private entity. Once again, however, the exercise of conditionality does not necessarily require that lending activities go with it. Multilateral institutions could simply negotiate the conditions to be followed by governments and leave lending to private and bilateral creditors. The argument for lending in this context must again rely on incentives: putting their own resources at

Table 4. *Regional Distribution of Official Development Assistance, 1990–91*
(percent)

Lender	Sub-Saharan Africa	South Asia	Other Asia and Oceania	Middle East and North Africa	Latin America and the Caribbean
United States	11.8	6.7	3.6	58.1	19.8
Japan	11.5	15.3	53.2	11.7	8.3
European Union	58.2	7.2	4.9	19.7	10.1
Nordic countries	59.6	15.4	8.0	6.9	10.1
Multilateral institutions	43.6	34.9	11.7	1.1	8.6

Source: OECD, *Development Cooperation,* various issues.

risk helps keep the World Bank and the IMF honest about which policy changes will work and which will not. In addition, the ability of both institutions to lend their own resources bolsters their independence and autonomy from governments and private creditors. That, in turn, helps them maintain their apolitical image.

Table 5. *Determinants of Bilateral and Multilateral Net Transfers*

Variable	Bilateral net transfers		Multilateral net transfers	
	1	2	3	4
Friends of the United States	0.92	0.76	−0.28	−0.12
	(2.78)	(2.41)	(−1.37)	(−0.60)
Friends of OPEC	1.90	1.61	0.75)	0.37
	(4.15)	(4.12)	(2.64	(1.49)
Friends of France	1.09	1.00	−0.03	−0.08
	(3.07)	(2.88)	(−0.13)	(−0.36)
Log of GDP per capita	−2.19	−1.96	−0.84	−0.79
at beginning of subperiod	(−9.36)	(−8.23)	(−5.75)	(−5.27)
Log of population	−0.64	−0.58	−0.22	−0.23
	(−7.74)	(−7.64)	(−4.35)	(−4.98)
Lagged growth of GDP per capita	0.18		−1.15	
	(0.05)		(−0.51)	
Lagged change in terms of trade	−0.65		−0.65	
	(−0.41)		(−0.66)	
Infant mortality		1.68		1.27
		(0.22)		(0.27)
Life expectancy		−0.37		0.25
		(−0.17)		(0.18)
Sub-Saharan Africa	0.06		0.45	
	(0.12)		(1.41)	
Asia	0.60		0.51	
	(1.23)		(1.69)	
Latin America and the Caribbean	0.05		0.72	
	(0.12)		(2.52)	
1975–79	0.78	0.89	1.00	1.00
	(2.51)	(2.94)	(5.12)	(5.29)
1980–84	1.28	1.40	1.64	1.65
	(3.98)	(4.44)	(8.19)	(8.38)
1985–89	1.00	1.25	0.40	0.43
	(2.85)	(3.84)	(1.82)	(2.09)
Constant	23.19	22.34	7.91	6.98
	(10.51)	(2.56)	(5.74)	(1.28)
Number	269	277	269	277
Adjusted R^2	0.58	0.55	0.37	0.35

Note: See text for description of political dummy variables. The dependent variable is the average for each of four five-year subperiods (1970–74, 1975–79, 1980–84, 1985–89) of net transfers from bilateral or multilateral sources as a percentage of recipient GNP. Numbers in parentheses are t-statistics.
Source: Calculated from World ; Bank 1994. Barro and Lee 1994; Boone 1994b.

Why Private Creditors Are Not Very Good at Monitoring and at Exercising Conditionality

As mentioned earlier, since World War II it has become rare for creditor governments to exercise conditionality. The task has been increasingly left to multilateral institutions. The exceptions have occurred when a close security relationship existed between governments, as with the United States in the Republic of Korea during the 1950s and early 1960s, or France in several African cases. Conditionality exercised by private creditors has been rarer still.

There has been one well-publicized case of private conditionality, involving Peru. In 1976, facing a growing balance of payments problem, the Peruvian government allowed a consortium of six U.S. banks to impose conditions on it and to monitor their implementation. In return the banks extended a $240 million loan to the government. The experiment did not last long. Amid all-around discontent, IMF assistance was requested in 1977. I discuss this case here, relying on the account provided by Stallings (1979) and by the financial press at the time, because it illustrates the difficulties private entities face in monitoring government policies and exercising conditionality.

In 1968 the civilian government of Fernando Belaunde Terry was overthrown by General Juan Velasco Alvarado. The military government proceeded to adopt expansionary fiscal and industrial policies. It also alienated the U.S. government by nationalizing Standard Oil's subsidiary (the International Petroleum Company), defending a 200-mile offshore fishing limit, and establishing close relations with socialist countries. As a result the Velasco government was practically cut off from official lending. Peru received almost no loans from the U.S. Agency for International Development or the Export-Import Bank between 1969 and March 1974 and received only one loan from the World Bank between 1968 and late 1973. Private international banks, however, continued to pour vast sums into the country because of its apparent mineral wealth (copper and oil). As one local banker put it, "foreign bankers wanted to give us money before we asked for it. The Italians had lira for a dam. The French had francs for our steel mill" (*Wall Street Journal*, 1 September 1977, p. 1). In 1974 the dispute between Peru and the United States over the nationalization of the Standard Oil subsidiary was resolved, allowing large sums to come in from U.S. sources as well.

Meanwhile, the government's economic mismanagement led in 1975 to another coup within the junta, with General Francisco Morales Bermudez, the prime minister, taking over as president. Some half-hearted adjustment measures were introduced, with little impact. In the words of Stallings (1979, p. 237):

> By early 1976, then, the Peruvian economy faced a serious crunch, owing to a combination of bad luck, bad planning, and the inevitable dilemmas of dependent capitalist development. The bad luck had to do with the failure of the expected oil bonanza, the disappearance of the anchovy schools that had provided a major Peruvian export, and the fall in copper prices. Bad planning reinforced these problems through over-fishing and borrowing money to build a billion-dollar pipeline before the extent of oil reserves was known.

At this point the Peruvian government decided that the obvious next step, an IMF standby loan, was too drastic, and that commercial banks might prove more flexible. Consequently, in March 1976 the Peruvian authorities asked the major U.S. banks for a large balance of payments loan without an IMF agreement in place. The bankers were initially reluctant but eventually accepted (Belliveau 1976). According to Stallings (1979, p. 238), their reasoning was that:

> if the crunch were to come [from an IMF standby arrangement], General Jorge Fernandez Maldonado and the left-wing faction of the government might come out on top and lead Peru back toward a radical nationalist position. . . . One New York banker involved in the negotiation put the point very clearly. He said the "main reason" for the loan was "to perpetuate Morales Bermudez in power," since the banks considered this the best bet for getting their money back.

The U.S. banks then drew up an agreement with the Peruvian government that had three components: an orthodox stabilization program, "though of a milder sort than the IMF would have imposed" (Stallings 1979, p. 239), involving a 44 percent devaluation, price increases, credit controls, and minor budget cuts;[12] more favorable treatment of foreign investment, including the reopening of the jungle and coastline to private oil companies and the promise of an agreement with Marcona on a price to be paid for its nationalized iron mine; and partial withdrawal of the state in favor of local private enterprise. The loan was divided into two equal tranches, with the first released immediately. It was a clear provision of the agreement that the banks would monitor the government's management of the economy to ensure that the conditions on the budget, among others, were met. However, no specific numerical targets were set, unlike in an IMF program (Belliveau 1976). The second tranche would be released only if 75 percent of the lenders (in dollar-weighted terms) were satisfied with Peru's economic progress. In the words of Stallings (1979, p. 239), "not since the 1920s had private banks become so involved in the domestic affairs of a Latin American government."

Problems were evident from the beginning. The package had been put together by Citibank, Bank of America, Chase Manhattan, Manufacturers Hanover, Morgan Guaranty, and Wells Fargo, which collectively formed the steering committee. The committee banks found it difficult to get European and Japanese banks to take part—the European and Japanese shares were not arranged until the first half of 1977, even though the original announcement was made in July 1976.

The stabilization plan turned out to be a failure. Government spending continued to rise in real terms, and by early 1977 inflation was higher than ever (Thorpe 1979). When the Peruvian government approached the banks for additional financing, the banks referred it to the IMF. Stallings (1979) lists several reasons why the banks were not keen on repeating the experience. First, there was strong opposition among the banks to their monitoring role. Opposition from the left had been expected, but the opposition that the steering committee encountered within the banking community came as a surprise. As a representative of Continental Illinois (which along with another U.S. bank, Bankers Trust, refused to join the steering committee) put it:

> For a private bank to police the actions of sovereign governments puts it into a difficult position. International agencies have a more neutral role and are better suited for this. (cited by Stallings 1979, p. 243)

Bankers were worried that their role would be perceived as "Wall Street imperialism" (Shapiro 1976). European bankers were also highly skeptical and complained about politicization. A Citicorp vice chairman concluded, "the reaction to this loan was a signal to me that I want no part in deals with this kind of discipline in the future" (cited by Stallings 1979, p. 243). Banks did not want the publicity and controversy that came with setting macroeconomic conditions and monitoring their implementation.

Bringing in the IMF was seen as a way of allowing the banks to close their ranks and present a "more neutral facade for imposing conditions" (Stallings 1979, p. 249). The banks had finally realized that the IMF would demand tougher conditions than they had and believed that the situation had deteriorated sufficiently to warrant more serious treatment. An IMF mission began working in Lima in March 1977. The IMF's relationship with the Peruvian government also proved to be rocky, but this time the banks were content to watch from the sidelines.

This episode indicates how unworkable private monitoring and conditionality can be—even when the host government prefers it. In this case Peru's military government was unconstrained by public opinion and did not worry about appearances when it opened its books to private bankers.[13] It was the bankers, mindful of their reputation in other countries and their apolitical role in international finance, who found themselves uncomfortable. In the end it was the bankers—and not the Peruvian junta—who more completely internalized the norms of the postwar era.

Empirical Evidence

The efficiency and efficacy of multilateral lending is ultimately an empirical question. But in line with the arguments so far, the empirical issue is not simply whether this lending has been productive, but whether it has played the informational roles that justify the existence of multilateral lending institutions. Here I present some empirical results, necessarily crude, intended to determine whether multilateral lending has acted as a catalyst for private capital flows and whether multilateral lending has been an accurate indicator of future economic growth in borrowing countries.

Is Multilateral Lending a Catalyst for Private Capital Flows?

One way to gauge the success of multilateral lending as a provider of information on the quality of government policies is to ask whether countries that have received substantial inflows from multilateral sources have subsequently received large private capital flows as well. Based on simple monitoring or conditionality, it could be expected that governments whose policies have been "ratified" by significant multilateral lending will have been perceived by private investors as desirable countries with which to do business. Everything else being equal, multilateral flows should act as a catalyst for private flows.

The basic procedure followed here is to test across countries whether net transfers from multilateral sources are a predictor of subsequent net private capital flows, controlling for past private flows. For this purpose the 1970–93 period was divided into four subperiods of six years each, and for each subperiod and country the averages of bilateral, multilateral, and private net transfers (as a share of GNP) were calculated. Six years seems to be a reasonable length of time for discerning regularities in the data, given the inevitable lags in the formation of country reputations. It is a compromise between using shorter subperiods, which could exhibit great volatility in flows, and longer subperiods, which could lead to averaging out a series of years during which net multilateral transfers were highly positive. Six-year intervals also have the advantage of coinciding fairly well with the aggregate cycles in private capital flows: private flows were relatively stable during 1970–75 but increased rapidly during 1976–81, only to collapse during 1982–87. During 1988–93 private flows rapidly increased once again.

The basic regression takes the following form:

$$\text{PRIV}_{i,t} = \alpha + \beta\,\text{PRIV}_{i,t-1} + \gamma\,\text{MULT}_{i,t-1} + \delta\,\text{BILA}_{i,t-1} + \Sigma\,\zeta_t\,D_t + \Sigma\,\eta_J\,D_J + \varepsilon$$

where PRIV, MULT, and BILA stand for private, multilateral, and bilateral net transfers as a percentage of recipient GNP;[14] D_t and D_J are dummy variables for subperiods and country groupings based on income and indebtedness levels; ε is the error term; i is the country index; and t is the subperiod index. I also have generated data that further disaggregate each type of flow (for example, distinguishing between concessional and nonconcessional lending), as well as separate results for each subperiod. The first subperiod (1970–75) is not used in the regression because of a one-period lag in the specification. This regression helps determine whether countries that receive large net transfers from multilateral organizations subsequently experience an increase in private capital flows, controlling for past levels of private and bilateral flows.[15] Since past private flows are explicitly entered in the regression, factors that make countries attractive to foreign investors other than past multilateral lending should be controlled for.

Two sets of results for the basic regression are presented in table 6. One is for the full sample and one is for a restricted sample, with countries receiving net transfers of more than 10 percent of GNP (in any of the subcategories of flows) removed from the relevant subperiods. This restriction essentially eliminates small countries that, during certain time periods, received aid flows amounting to a substantial portion of their GNP. In both cases the coefficient on past multilateral lending is negative but not statistically significant. The coefficient on past private flows is positive but much smaller than unity, reflecting the volatility of private capital flows. Interestingly, the coefficient on past bilateral transfers is positive and significant at the 5 percent level in both regressions. Hence it appears that bilateral transfers—not multilateral transfers—act as a catalyst for private flows.

Further disaggregation of flows to the restricted sample reveals some interesting details (table 7). The catalytic effect of bilateral transfers seems to come from their effect on foreign direct investment and on commercial bank loans. And with respect to multilateral lending, there seems to be a sharp dichotomy between the IMF and other multilateral organizations. Net transfers from multilateral sources other than the IMF have a negative effect on subsequent private flows, significant at the 10 percent level. This effect seems to operate through commercial bank loans. The deterrent effect of (non-IMF) multilateral lending is particularly strong in the two subperiods after 1982. Countries that received large net transfers from the World Bank and regional development banks during 1976–81 and 1982–87 appear to have done worse in terms of private capital flows during the two subsequent subperiods. Regionally, the effect is confined to Sub-Saharan Africa, where the negative coefficient is statistically significant at the 5 percent level (table 8).[16]

Table 6. *Determinants of Private Net Transfers*
(dependent variable, $PRIV_{i,t}$)

Variable	Full sample	Restricted sample[a]
$Private_{i,t-1}$	0.42	0.22
	(7.76)	(4.27)
$Multilateral_{i,t-1}$	–0.14	–0.11
	(–1.10)	(–0.93)
$Bilateral_{i,t-1}$	0.06	0.17
	(2.01)	(3.61)
1982–87	–0.02	–0.02
	(–3.78)	(–5.59)
1988–93	–0.01	–0.01
	(–1.52)	(–3.32)
Severely indebted low-income countries[b]	–0.01	–0.01
	(–2.87)	(–3.74)
Severely indebted middle-income countries[b]	–0.02	–0.01
	(–3.12)	(–2.95)
Moderately indebted middle-income countries[b]	0.00	–0.01
	(0.06)	(–1.79)
Moderately indebted middle-income countries[b]	–0.01	–0.01
	(–2.56)	(–2.34)
Constant	0.02	0.02
	(5.22)	(6.20)
Number	300	261
Adjusted R^2	0.26	0.25

Note: Numbers in parentheses are t-statistics.
a. Excludes countries receiving net transfers of more than 10 percent of GNP in any subcategory of flows.
b. See World Bank 1994 for country categorizations.
Source: Calculated from World Bank 1994.

These are puzzling findings. There seems to be no simple explanation for the empirical regularities revealed by the regressions, namely that bilateral lending acts as a catalyst for private flows while multilateral lending (excluding the IMF) either acts as a deterrent or has no impact. For bilateral lending the results may reflect the perception on the part of private investors that the presence of significant official government flows acts as a political guarantee of better treatment by host governments. For multilateral lending the results certainly run counter to the expectation articulated earlier in this article.

Can these results be attributed to a bias arising from the tendency of multilateral lending to focus on countries that are already "sick"? Suppose, to make the best possible case for multilateral lending, that private capital flows to sick countries would have been even smaller in the absence of multilateral lending. Could our estimated negative coefficient then just reflect the fact that these countries are getting fewer private inflows than healthier countries? There are three reasons to doubt that a bias like this is operating. First, since the regressions include indebtedness dummy variables and lagged private inflows, we have already largely con-

Table 7. *Determinants of Net Private Transfers for Restricted Sample, by Type*

Variable	All private	Foreign direct investment	Portfolio investment	Bonds	Commercial bank loans
Private					
Foreign direct investment$_{t-1}$	0.49	0.40	0.00	0.01	0.09
	(6.16)	(8.52)	(0.71)	(0.42)	(1.36)
Portfolio$_{t-1}$	13.22	12.14	13.13	−12.82)	0.76
	(0.74)	(1.17)	(12.37)	(−2.93)	(0.05)
Bonds$_{t-1}$	0.83	0.13	0.00	0.84	−0.13
	(3.31)	(0.87)	(0.15)	(13.71)	(−0.67)
Commercial bank loans$_{t-1}$	−0.06	−0.05	−0.01	−0.01	0.01
	(−0.77)	(−1.20)	(−2.25)	(−0.36)	(0.18)
Multilateral					
IMF$_{t-1}$	0.09	−0.03	0.01	0.04	0.07
	(0.52)	(−0.29)	(0.96)	(0.88)	(0.53)
Other multilateral$_{t-1}$ (concessional)	−0.20	−0.18	−0.01	0.02	−0.03
	(−1.16)	(−1.77)	(−1.26)	(0.51)	(−0.24)
Other multilateral$_{t-1}$ (nonconcessional)	−0.63	0.19	0.01	−0.02	−0.81
	(−1.67)	(0.88)	(0.37)	(−0.18)	(−2.71)
Bilateral					
Grants$_{t-1}$	0.11	0.08)	−0.00	−0.02	0.06
	(1.78)	(2.14)	(−0.39)	(−1.54)	(1.18)
Other bilateral$_{t-1}$	0.37	0.17	−0.00	−0.00	0.21
	(3.40)	(2.62)	(−0.05)	(−0.16)	(2.42)
Number	261	261	261	261	261
Adjusted R^2	0.32	0.40	0.45	0.43	0.25

Note: Period dummies, country group dummies, and constant term were included in the regressions but are not shown in the table. Restricted sample excludes countries receiving net transfers of more than 10 percent of GNP in any subcategory of flows.

Source: Calculated from World Bank 1994.

trolled for the effects of an economy's health on subsequent private flows. Second, the statistically significant effects come from non-IMF lending. This is important because IMF lending tends to be more heavily correlated with economic crisis than other types of multilateral lending. Hence the bias, if it exists, should have been most evident in IMF lending. Third, even if the bias is operative, so long as multilateral lending has not focused entirely on sick countries, but includes countries that eventually improved—that is, as long as multilateral lending was effective—the coefficients would be biased toward zero, but not toward a negative number.[17]

As a final exercise I checked to see whether multilateral lending has actually followed rather than led private flows (table 9). In this analysis net transfers from multilateral sources are used as the dependent variable. There is some evidence that multilateral lending has played the role of follower. In particular, countries that have received large flows from commercial banks appear to have subsequently received larger net transfers from the IMF. In all likelihood this reflects the fact that most countries that borrowed heavily from commercial banks until 1982 found them-

Table 8. *Determinants of Private Net Transfers for Restricted Sample, by Subperiod and Region*

Variable	1976–81	1982–87	1988–93	Sub-Saharan Africa	Rest of the world (excluding Sub-Saharan Africa)
Private					
Foreign direct investment$_{t-1}$	0.31	0.49	0.81	0.53	0.33
	(2.02)	(3.71)	(4.98)	(5.52)	(2.44)
Portfolio$_{t-1}$		–133.04	24.33		27.04
		(–1.28)	(1.43)		(1.33)
Bonds$_{t-1}$	1.15	–0.85	–0.17	0.97	–0.09
	(3.01)	(–1.11)	(–0.27)	(3.83)	(–0.16)
Commercial bank loans$_{t-1}$	0.11	–0.13	0.04	–0.22	0.05
	(0.49)	(–1.34)	(0.40)	(–2.11)	(0.51)
Multilateral					
IMF$_{t-1}$	–0.72	0.05	–0.24	0.02	0.27
	(–0.59)	(0.24)	(–0.70)	(–0.11)	(0.83)
Other multilateral$_{t-1}$ (concessional)	–0.12	–0.58	–0.14	–0.34	0.02
	(–0.12)	(–1.96)	(–0.63)	(–1.52)	(0.06)
Other multilateral$_{t-1}$ (nonconcessional)	0.71	–1.33	–1.08	–1.29	0.01
	(0.59)	(–1.91)	(–2.45)	(–2.54)	(0.03)
Bilateral					
Grants$_{t-1}$	0.09	0.14	0.06	–0.01	0.19
	(0.64)	(1.48)	(0.60)	(–0.16)	(1.81)
Other bilateral$_{t-1}$	0.19	0.66	0.20	0.42	0.24
	(0.74)	(3.55)	(1.01)	(3.22)	(1.23)
Number	83	88	90	101	160
Adjusted R^2	0.1	0.5	0.4	0.53	0.30

Note: Country group dummies and constant term were included in the regressions but are not shown in the table. Restricted sample excludes countries receiving net transfers of more than 10 percent of GNP in any subcategory of flows.

Source: Calculated from World Bank 1994.

selves in economic trouble subsequently and in need of IMF medicine. It also seems to be the case, however, that non-IMF multilateral lending has followed bilateral transfers. It is less obvious why this is so.

If multilateral lending follows private flows, there is a possibility that multilateral institutions end up bailing out private creditors. Since external resources are fungible, any multilateral lending that helps governments service their private debt is a form of subsidy to private entrepreneurs (the seniority of multilateral aid notwithstanding). For example, Dooley (1994, pp. 5–6) argues that commercial bank lending during the 1970s was conditioned on the expectation of official bailouts if things were to go wrong: "banks were rational in the sense that they realized a bad outcome was possible but also realized that losses generated by bad outcomes could be shifted to their own governments." According to Dooley, that is how the debt crisis eventually worked out. Commercial banks stopped lending in

Table 9. *Determinants of Net Multilateral Transfers for Restricted Sample*
(restricted sample)

Variable	*All multilateral*[a]	*All multilateral*	*All multilateral*	*IMF*	*IMF*	*Other multilateral*
Private$_{t-1}$	0.12	0.00		0.04		−0.04
	(2.28)	(−0.08)		(2.10)		(−1.23)
Foreign direct investment$_{t-1}$			−0.14		−0.02	
			(−2.39)		(−0.57)	
Portfolio$_{t-1}$			1.80		2.23	
			(0.14)		(0.36)	
Bonds$_{t-1}$			−0.22		−0.07	
			(−1.23)		(−0.75)	
Commercial bank loans$_{t-1}$			0.12		0.09	
			(2.27)		(3.43)	
Multilateral$_{t-1}$	0.40	0.36		−0.08		0.43
	(3.22)	(4.28)		(−1.94)		(6.23)
IMF$_{t-1}$			0.08		−0.10	
			(0.66)		(−1.80)	
Other multilateral$_{t-1}$			0.64		−0.05	
			(5.55)		(−0.94)	
Bilateral$_{t-1}$	0.16	0.11		−0.00		0.10
	(5.45)	(3.20)		(−0.19)		(3.74)
Grants$_{t-1}$			0.11		0.01	
			(2.50)		(0.29)	
Other bilateral$_{t-1}$			−0.03		−0.01	
			(−0.32)		(−0.28)	
Number	300	261	261	261	261	261
Adjusted R^2	0.34	0.36	0.41	0.19	0.20	0.43

Note: Period dummies, country group dummies, and constant term were included in the regressions but are not shown in the table. Resricted sample excludes countries receiving net transfers of more than 10 percent of GNP in any subcategory of flows.

a. Full sample.

Source: Calculated from World Bank 1994.

the 1980s and multilateral creditors stepped in, with the consequence that interest payments to banks came at least in part from multilateral loans.[18] If this story of anticipated (and realized) bailouts is correct, multilateral lending should follow (and not lead) private lending. At least with respect to the IMF, this indeed seems to be the picture.

Is Multilateral Lending an Accurate Indicator of Country Growth?

The second hypothesis I explore is whether multilateral institutions, because of their close monitoring of government policies, have an informational advantage in determining which countries have superior growth prospects. From this perspective countries that receive considerable lending from multilateral institutions are presumably the ones whose government policies these institutions have judged to be most deserving of support. Note that the association, if any, between multilateral lending and subsequent growth is not expected to arise from the direct economic effects of lending.[19] Rather, it is the role of multilateral lending as a possible signal of future growth that is the focus here.

The setup for this empirical analysis is similar to the one used earlier. The basic regression takes the following form:

$$\text{GROWTH}_{i,t} = \alpha + \beta\,\text{PRIV}_{i,t-1} + \gamma\,\text{MULT}_{i,t-1} + \delta\,\text{BILA}_{i,t-1} + \sum \eta_k\,X^k_{i,t-1} + \sum \zeta_t\,D_t + \varepsilon$$

where X^k stands for a number of economic variables that are commonly included in growth regressions, D_t is a dummy variable for subperiods, i is the country index, and t is the subperiod index. All the economic variables except for the data on net transfers (which are the same as those used earlier) are taken from the Barro and Lee (1994) data set on a panel of countries. Since the Barro and Lee data set uses different subperiods, the subperiods have been changed to 1970–75, 1975–80, 1980–85, and 1985–90 (table 10).

The estimated coefficient on lagged multilateral lending is uniformly negative and becomes statistically significant in some versions of the regression. The coefficient on bilateral transfers, on the other hand, is positive and borderline significant in one of the regressions. This exercise is repeated in another set of regressions that disaggregates further each category of flows and adds dummy variables for country groups by level of indebtedness (table 11). These results are more favorable to multilateral flows. In particular, the coefficient on net lending by the World Bank is consistently positive, and significant at the 5 percent level in one case.

One way to read this evidence is to conclude the multilateral lending has tended to go, on average, to heavily indebted countries with poor future growth potential. But once the level of indebtedness is controlled for, some of that lending (the World Bank's) appears to have focused on highly indebted countries that subsequently did better than others. This can be seen as evidence favoring the proposition that mul-

Table 10. *Determinants of Growth*
(dependent variable, GROWTH$_{i,t}$)

Variable	Full sample		Restricted sample[a]	
	1	*2*	*3*	*4*
Pivate net transfers$_{i,t-1}$	0.02	−0.02	0.11	0.06
	(0.22)	(−0.24)	(1.07)	(0.63)
Multilateral net transfers$_{i,t-1}$	−0.09	−0.18	−0.47	−0.57
	(−0.39)	(−0.82)	(−1.76)	(−2.13)
Bilateral net transfers$_{i,t-1}$	0.11	0.08	0.17	0.22
	(1.51)	(1.14)	(1.40)	(1.78)
Number	178	178	161	161
Adjusted R^2	0.30	0.30	0.36	0.34

Note: Each regression includes the following additional variables: initial per capita GDP at the beginning of the subperiod, average years of secondary schooling in the population over 25 years old at the beginning of subperiod (male and female are entered separately), initial life expectancy, investment share in GDP (lagged in regressions 1 and 3 and contemporaneous in regressions 2 and 4), lagged government consumption expenditure net of defense and education as a share of GDP, subperiod dummies, and a constant term. See Barro and Lee (1994) for more detail on these variables.

a. Excludes countries receiving net transfers of more than 10 percent of GNP in any subcategory of flows.

Source: Calculated from World Bank 1994; Barro and Lee 1994; Boone 1994b.

Table 11. *Determinants of Growth, with Disaggregated Flows and Country Group Dummy Variables*

Variable	Full sample		Restricted sample[a]	
	1	*2*	*3*	*4*
IMF$_{i,t-1}$	−0.05	−0.11	0.17	0.06
	(−0.09)	(−0.21)	(0.30)	(0.10)
Other multilateral$_{i,t-1}$ (concessional)				
IDA	0.52	0.49	−0.49	−0.64
	(0.74)	(0.69)	(−0.65)	(−0.83)
Other	−0.20	−0.39	−1.10	−1.03
	(−0.38)	(−0.74)	(−1.61)	(-1.45)
Other multilateral$_{i,t-1}$ (nonconcessional)				
IBRD	0.99	0.32	1.96	1.20
	(1.45)	(0.49)	(1.94)	(1.17)
Other	−0.77	−0.40	−0.14	−0.26
	(−0.67)	(−0.33)	(−0.10)	(−0.19)
Number	178	178	161	161
Adjusted R^2	0.38	0.34	0.44	0.39

Note: Same as table 10, but includes dummies for severely indebted low-income countries, severely indebted middle-income countries, moderately indebted low-income countries, and moderately indebted middle-income countries. Parameter estimates shown only for multilateral flows.

a. Excludes countries receiving net transfers of more than 10 percent of GNP in any subcategory of flows.

Source: Calculated from World Bank 1994; Barro and Lee 1994; Boone 1994b.

tilateral lenders have been able to act on better information than is generally available to private markets regarding countries' growth potential.

Conclusion

Multilateral lending since 1945 has been a historically unique experiment. The role played by multilateral institutions—or the role that they ought to play—has always been controversial, with no consensus in sight. As early as 1943 the *New York Times* ran an editorial (cited in Oliver 1975, pp. 160–61) expressing skepticism about the need for the World Bank, then under discussion by the U.S. and U.K. governments, in strikingly contemporary terms:

> If a loan seems really sound—so sound that private investors would voluntarily risk their own money in it—why should it not be left to such investors? People are far more likely to be careful in lending their own money than in lending other people's money. It is no reply to say that many bad private foreign loans were made after [World War I]; the record of repayment is at least incomparably better for these than for Government loans, most of which should probably have been gifts! The defaults on private loans, moreover, did not cause any international bitterness remotely approaching that caused by default on the Government loans.
>
> Under the proposed plan for a World Bank American taxpayers would make foreign loans to Governments whether or not these taxpayers individually considered the loans to be sound. If the creditor Governments had no control over the internal economic and fiscal policies of the debtor Governments to which they made loans, they might be pouring their taxpayers' money down a bottomless pit. If, on the other hand, the creditor Governments did insist on control over the internal policies of the debtor Governments, there would be more sources of international friction and bitterness.
>
> The chief economic need of the postwar world is not new governmental super-machinery. It is the return by individual governments to policies under which a restoration of international confidence and international lending will be possible.

Private flows have indeed increased tremendously since 1945, undermining the belief that multilateral lending is needed to make up for inadequate international capital.[20] In any case the specific advantages of multilateral machinery over bilateral aid programs were never quite clear.

I have argued that the rationale for multilateral lending lies in certain informational functions that if carried out successfully improve the workings of international capital markets. Monitoring helps direct private investors to countries where the policy environment is sound; exercising conditionality helps ensure that governments are not tempted to change the rules of the game against foreign investors once investments have been made. Multilateral institutions may also have an advantage in concessional lending for humanitarian or other noneconomic reasons insofar as political considerations generally figure less prominently in the decisionmaking machinery of these institutions.

One can think of additional rationales for multilateral lending in terms of coordinating official flows from multiple sources, taking advantage of economies of scale and scope, and acting as a lender of last resort. Where large-scale flows to individual countries have taken place (or been contemplated), as in Russia or Mexico, multilateral institutions have played a significant role. But ad hoc groupings of official creditors can also play the coordinating role in such instances, as they have done successfully before, for example, the OECD Consortium for Turkey and the Inter-Governmental Group on Indonesia.

Jeffrey Sachs, who has made a forceful case for the importance of external support in stabilizing high-inflation economies, recently discussed a number of such cases: the Bank of England loan to the Reichsbank in 1923, the Marshall Plan in Europe, the U.S. bridge loan to Mexico in 1988, the U.S. loan to Israel in 1985, the Polish stabilization fund provided by the G-7 countries, and Britain and Sweden's return of prewar gold to Estonia in 1992 (Sachs 1995). But these successful cases all involved lending (or support) from bilateral sources. A multilateral machinery can nonetheless be useful as a coordinating device, particularly for small countries lacking powerful patrons. The success with which this coordinating role can be played, however, still depends on the ability of multilateral agencies to perform the basic functions discussed in this article: providing information and monitoring and exercising conditionality.

From this perspective, multilateral lending has no independent economic rationale. It is needed only insofar as policy monitoring and conditionality cannot be performed adequately unless backed by credits from multilateral sources. In other words, lending plays a subsidiary role to the informational functions.

The results of the empirical analysis of whether multilateral lending has played the informational functions I have ascribed to it are quite mixed. There is no evidence that multilateral lending has acted as a catalyst for private flows. At the same time there is some evidence that World Bank lending has focused on countries with brighter economic futures (once levels of indebtedness are accounted for). These empirical results should be treated with caution, however. Alternative specifications may well result in different findings, and in any case cross-country comparisons of this type need to be supported by case studies.

It is perhaps not too surprising that the empirical results—preliminary as they are—are not more favorable to multilateral lending. The World Bank and other multilateral agencies view their role primarily as one of lending. Their informational activities have taken a back seat to their lending activities, rather than the other way around. Consequently, the empirical analysis evaluates multilateral institutions from a perspective that is not entirely consonant with their own self-image. A reexamination of this self-image, so as to place information, monitoring, and conditionality at the top of these institutions' agendas, would have important implications for what they do and how they do it. These implications are wide-ranging. I mention here just a few of the more obvious ones.

First, multilateral agencies need to develop mechanisms for the routine dissemination of information to the investment community and the general public. This could include detailed economic data as well as staff reports and evaluations of government policies. Second, they need to seriously reconsider the rules of secrecy and confidentiality that govern their operations and interactions with client governments. Secrecy only diminishes the value of any information that is eventually made public. Third, analytical country work, much of which takes place in the research divisions of these agencies, has to be tightly integrated with operational and lending work. Fourth, lending needs to make a clear distinction between good and bad performers—or good and bad policy environments—and to concentrate on the good performers. If multilateral institutions cannot make this distinction sharply enough, their ability to play a signaling or catalytic role is severely compromised. Finally, these institutions need to create new incentive mechanisms for rewarding and promoting staff. In particular, the importance of lending activities has to be downgraded relative to monitoring and informational activities.

This is a tall order. But looking at the role of multilateral agencies in these terms has the advantage that it creates an explicit, well-articulated rationale for these agencies, in an era where their total lending is small compared with both the needs of their clients and the magnitude of private capital flows that are already available.

Notes

1. As Bulow, Rogoff, and Bevilaqua (1992, p. 221) put it, "Generally speaking, the extensive evolution of private capital markets over the past twenty years makes the missing market rationale for IFI [international financial institution] lending considerably more dubious than in the years immediately following Bretton Woods."

2. Unless otherwise specified, private flows are foreign direct investment, portfolio equity flows, bond issues, commercial bank lending, and other private lending. Bilateral flows are loans, credits, and grants from governments (excluding technical cooperation grants). Multilateral flows are loans and credits from the IMF, the World Bank, regional development banks, and other intergovernmental agencies. Net transfers are disbursements minus repayments and interest charges. For foreign direct investment and portfolio equity flows, data on profits or earnings accruing to the foreign investor—analogous to the interest on bank loans or bonds—are unavailable. The source for flow data is the World Bank's 1995 *World Debt Tables;* the reader is referred to this source for more information on each of these categories.

3. Reviewing the literature on international capital mobility, for example, Feldstein (1994, pp. 683–84) points to the "importance of two aspects of the risk of international investing: political and currency risk. Although there may be little political risk associated with portfolio investment within the OECD countries, there are more substantial risks when investments are made in the emerging markets. Even within the OECD there is always the risk of some kind of capital controls or convertibility restrictions. These risks, which are not reflected in the covariance matrices that analysts use to calculate risk-return trade-offs of internationally diversified portfolios, tend to make portfolio investors more reluctant to invest abroad.

The risks of changes in government policies are even more important for direct foreign investments than for portfolio investments since direct investments are much more difficult to reverse. Even OECD governments can change tax rules, government procurement rules, and other regulations in ways that are particularly disadvantageous to foreign investors."

4. This assumes, of course, that the assessment is well done. If it is not, collective "bads" result.

5. The example is more than hypothetical—it is the strategy followed by Argentina in the wake of the recent Mexican crisis: "The International Monetary Fund is to lend Argentina $420 million . . . and mon-

itor its fiscal accounts every quarter as part of a campaign to restore credibility to the country's economy." (*Financial Times*, 6 March 1995, p. 6).

6. Whether multilateral claims are senior in practice is another matter. Bulow, Rogoff, and Bevilaqua (1992) argue that they are not.

7. Karin Lissakers, the U.S. executive director of the IMF, admitted that "the whole surveillance process [in Mexico] did not work the way it should have. . . . We were too tolerant." (*New York Times*, 19 March 1995, p. E3).

8. The argument is laid out in more detail in Diwan and Rodrik (1992).

9. One reason is that governments often find it politically expedient to cave in to economic interests once the money is borrowed. In the words of *The Economist* (11 March 1995, p. 18), "The [International Monetary] Fund enables the people pursuing sensible policies to defend them against lobbyists and populists by saying, 'We cannot give you more money because that would put the IMF loan at risk.'"

10. As Polak (1991, pp. 30–31) puts it: "Clear cases of political decisionmaking occur [in the IMF] when decisions on access or potential access are not supported by a staff judgement on the adequacy of a country's program. The deviation may be in either direction. Some countries may be barred from access for political reasons even if they have technically adequate programs. Some other countries may be granted access for political reasons . . .

The list of countries denied access on political grounds is very short, and each case would be difficult to document. It seems to me beyond question, however, that, from the mid-1980s, South Africa was unable to use the Fund as long as it maintained apartheid and that China would have been unable to draw during the first year after Tiananmen Square. An arrangement with Vietnam that would have been technically possible has likewise been blocked by political considerations. . . ."

11. These regressions differ from those in Boone (1994b) in two ways: I use net transfers on all flows, rather than gross official development assistance flows, as my dependent variable, and I distinguish between bilateral and multilateral sources.

12. Thorpe (1979, p. 122), however, claims that the program "was generally assessed afterwards as having been almost as stringent as the Fund's would have been."

13. Still, the authorities were reluctant to acknowledge that the banks were imposing conditionality (*Institutional Investor*, October 1976).

14. Multilateral flows are those from the IMF, the World Bank, and regional development banks. Bilateral flows include grants.

15. While net transfers are a better measure than gross flows in this context, there is a problem with their use. Since repayments on past multilateral loans enter negatively in this measure, they make it difficult to distinguish cases where multilaterals make a big commitment. For example, suppose that the World Bank makes a large loan to two countries. If one country has no past loans coming due and the other does, it will appear as if the Bank has made a bigger commitment to the first country. One way to eliminate this problem is to use an event-study methodology, rather than rely on net multilateral transfers.

16. Here it is worth distinguishing between project- and policy-based lending. Policy-based lending is presumably more closely linked with conditionality, but both types of lending can be expected to play an informational and possibly catalytic role. However, the World Bank (1995) does not provide data on this breakdown.

17. To see this point, suppose the sample contains three groups of countries: healthy countries, sick countries that are following the right policies, and sick countries that are following the wrong policies. Subsequent private capital flows would be highest in the healthy countries, next highest in the sick countries with the right policies, and lowest in the sick countries with the wrong policies. Assume that the regressions do not control for these country groups, and that multilateral lending focuses on sick countries with the right policies. The level of multilateral inflows would now be correlated with the country status of this middle group. Since countries in this group still receive larger flows than sick countries with the wrong policies, the bias is downward, but not necessarily toward a negative number.

18. See Bulow, Rogoff, and Bevilaqua (1992) for evidence supporting the view that multilateral debt is not senior to private debt; any debt that goes into problem countries is shared with existing private creditors.

19. See Boone (1994a) for a sobering analysis of the effects of aid on growth.

20. According to Oliver (1975, p. 239), John J. McCloy, the World Bank's second president, believed that the Bank "would go out of business in due course because the long-term capital needed for development would eventually be provided directly by private investors."

References

Barro, Robert J., and Jong-Wha Lee. 1994. "Data Set for a Panel of 138 Countries." National Bureau of Economic Research, Cambridge, Mass.

Belliveau, Nancy. 1976. "What the Peru Experiment Means." *Institutional Investor* (October): 31–35.

Boone, Peter. 1994a. "The Impact of Foreign Aid on Savings and Growth." London School of Economics, London.

———. 1994b. "Politics and the Effectiveness of Foreign Aid." London School of Economics, London.

Bulow, Jeremy, Kenneth Rogoff, and Afonso S. Bevilaqua. 1992. "Official Creditor Seniority and Burden-Sharing in the Former Soviet Bloc." *Brookings Papers on Economic Activity* 1. Washington, D.C.: The Brookings Institution.

Diwan, Ishac, and Dani Rodrik. 1992. *External Debt, Adjustment, and Burden Sharing: A Unified Framework.* Princeton Studies in International Finance 73. Princeton University, Princeton, N.J.

Dooley, Michael P. 1994. "A Retrospective on the Debt Crisis." NBER Working Paper 4963. National Bureau of Economic Research, Cambridge, Mass.

Eichengreen, Barry. 1991. "Trends and Cycles in Foreign Lending." In Horst Siebert, ed., *Capital Flows in the World Economy.* Tubingen, Germany: J.C.B. Mohr (Paul Siebeck).

Feldstein, Martin. 1994. "Tax Policy and International Capital Flows." *Weltwirtschaftliches Archiv* 130(4): 675–97.

Gavin, Michael, and Dani Rodrik. 1995. "The World Bank in Historical Perspective." *American Economic Review, Papers and Proceedings* (May): 329–34.

Guitian, Manuel. 1982. "Economic Management and International Monetary Fund Conditionality." In Tony Killick, ed., *Adjustment and Financing in the Developing World.* Washington, D.C.: International Monetary Fund.

Mosley, Paul. 1987. *Conditionality as Bargaining Process: Structural Adjustment Lending, 1980–86.* Princeton Essays in International Finance 168. Princeton University, Princeton, N.J.

Oliver, Robert W. 1975. *International Economic Cooperation and the World Bank.* London: Macmillan.

Pearson, Lester B. 1969. *Partners in Development: Report of the Commission on International Development.* New York: Praeger.

Polak, Jacques J. 1991. *The Changing Nature of IMF Conditionality.* Princeton Essays in International Finance 184. Princeton University, Princeton, N.J.

Sachs, Jeffrey. 1995. "Russia's Struggle with Stabilization: Conceptual Issues and Evidence." In Michael Bruno and Boris Pleskovic, eds., *Proceedings of the World Bank Annual Conference on Development Economics 1994.* Washington, D.C.: World Bank.

Shapiro, Harvey D. 1976. "Monitoring: Are the Banks Biting Off More Than They Can Chew?" *Institutional Investor* (October): 26–28.

Stallings, Barbara. 1979. "Peru and the U.S. Banks: Privatization of Financial Relations." In Richard R. Fagen, ed., *Capitalism and the State in U.S-Latin American Relations.* Stanford, Calif.: Stanford University Press.

Thorpe, Rosemary. 1979. "The Stabilization Crisis in Peru 1975–78. In Rosemary Thorpe and Laurence Whitehead, eds., *Inflation and Stabilization in Latin America.* London: Macmillan.

World Bank. 1994. *World Debt Tables 1994–95: External Finance for Developing Countries.* Washington, D.C.

Comment on "Why Is There Multilateral Lending?" by Dani Rodrik

Guillermo A. Calvo

Dani Rodrik's article highlights two central roles for multilateral financial institutions: information dissemination and conditionality. Both roles, he contends, could be fulfilled even in the absence of multilateral lending. Multilateral lending is judged not to be essential in itself, but rather as a device for keeping multilateral institutions honest. One of the article's main implications is that if multilateral agencies' dissemination and conditionality efforts were more successful, their programs would generate more loans from the private sector.

The empirical part of the article examines the relationship between multilateral loans and both private sector loans and growth. Rodrik's results do not bode well for the multilaterals: as their loans increase, private sector loans and growth decline or do not rise significantly.

My comments focus on central conceptual issues, paying only casual attention to the empirical estimates. I argue that the multilaterals' key advantage over the private sector or bilateral agencies is their ability to impose effective and credible punishment in the case of default and that under some circumstances such an advantage is enhanced by multilateral lending.

Punishment Technology

Multilateral institutions share structural similarities with police departments: they represent a large number of people (countries), even potential criminals (loan defaulters); they operate according to established rules; they obtain information to prevent crimes and prosecute criminals; and they are overseen by political institutions (boards of directors) that occasionally change the rules.

These characteristics are important to the functioning of multilaterals because the rules are agreed to by countries before lending takes place, helping to legitimize them; punishment is less likely to be seen as a vendetta; and if punishment is called for, the loan defaulter will find it difficult to obtain loans from other

Guillermo A. Calvo is distinguished university professor and director of the Center for International Economics at the University of Maryland at College Park.

Annual World Bank Conference on Development Economics 1995

countries. In this respect information gathering is essential to prevent unfair indictments and to facilitate contingent punishments, that is, punishments contingent on past and future behavior (much like the parole system in criminal justice). For example, a country's contingent punishment could be made less severe if default were the result of external shocks rather than deliberate action, or if it were followed by tough and credible fiscal adjustment rather than by vague policy commitments.

These functions could be performed by multilateral nonfinancial institutions, such as the Hague Tribunal. After all, ministries of justice are not banks and they often participate in bankruptcy proceedings. Why do we need multilateral financial institutions or, more specifically, multilateral lending?

In my view multilateral lending is most useful in two circumstances: when loans require dealing directly with governments, as in the case of loans for the provision of public goods, and when a borrowing country defaults, and new loans are needed to ensure smooth adjustment.

In the first example multilaterals clearly are in a better position to negotiate—and, if necessary, punish—sovereign borrowers. The second example also might involve the government directly, but multilateral lending may have a role to play even if that is not the case. This is because contingent lending—especially during a crisis—is a complex creature requiring exhaustive macroeconomic information. The defaulting country may have been dealing with a wide variety of banks and financial institutions, none of which had gathered the information required for *timely* contingent lending (in part because gathering exhaustive economic data is an expensive and time-consuming process). Still, these considerations do not necessarily rule out separating multilaterals from the lending process and leaving lending to the private sector. However, private lenders are unlikely to relinquish all the monitoring to multilaterals (because, as Rodrik points out, multilaterals are not free from moral hazard difficulties). This creates a situation in which multilaterals and the private sector are likely to duplicate monitoring, unduly increasing costs relative to loans that are mostly granted and monitored by multilaterals.

Multilateral Functions

I now turn to the specific roles highlighted by Rodrik, namely, information dissemination and conditionality.

Rodrik examines the role multilaterals play in information gathering and dissemination and concludes that—because of their views on the confidentiality and sensitivity of data—they are falling short in these areas. I agree. To the reasons Rodrik lists I would add that multilaterals are subject to strong diplomatic and political pressures that result in long delays, if not outright censorship, in the release of critical information.

I have previously argued, however, that information gathering, as distinct from dissemination, is essential if the multilaterals are to establish a fair and efficient punishment system (especially as it involves contingent punishment). Thus I favor information gathering by multilaterals even if the results are not fully released to the public.

Rodrik places relatively more weight on conditionality—even in the absence of multilateral lending—as a device for ameliorating time-inconsistency problems. Conditionality schemes should thus reflect the underlying time-inconsistency problems. These problems are a function of many factors, ranging from the type of available institutions to the type of goods in which the country has a comparative advantage. Thus it is unlikely that uniform conditionality schemes will be optimal. Unfortunately, uniformity of treatment across countries is a guiding principle in these institutions and thus may prevent the implementation of optimal conditionality schemes.

Furthermore, if time inconsistency is a relevant consideration within a specific country, outside institutions will need a lot of "muscle" in order to make a difference. Multilaterals have an advantage in this regard because of the punishment technology discussed earlier. The effectiveness of this technology would be strengthened if most loans to such countries were channeled through multilaterals. Therefore, if uniformity-of-treatment constraints are not very serious, time-inconsistency considerations provide another rationale for multilateral lending, not just the monitoring as suggested by Rodrik.

Conclusion

There are still compelling reasons for multilateral lending. Multilateral institutions have a punishment technology that makes them especially well suited for dealing directly with sovereign entities. This technology makes multilateral lending especially appropriate for public goods projects and emergency funding. In addition, the case for multilateral lending is reinforced if time-inconsistency problems are deemed critical.

Private sector lending is highly desirable, but making it a central objective of multilateral institutions may jeopardize their role as honest brokers. For example, the private sector may come to see multilaterals as public relations offices for their member countries.

The empirical association between multilateral lending and private sector loans is ambiguous. For example, if multilateral lending is directed toward public goods, a positive association is to be expected. By contrast, multilateral lending that has an important emergency component may discourage private lending. The nature of multilateral lending is more complex than the data in Rodrik's analysis suggests. Thus I consider the article's empirical results to be an interesting but not particularly relevant evaluation of multilateral lending.

Comment on "Why Is There Multilateral Lending?" by Dani Rodrik

Stijn Claessens

ani Rodrik's article is a timely one, coming at a time when the role of the Bretton Woods institutions is being discussed in various forums commemorating their fiftieth anniversaries. Prompting much of this review and reevaluation of their roles has been the increase in private capital flows over the past few years and the recent crises in some developing countries. Rodrik's article provides some new thinking about what these roles could be and some preliminary empirical analysis of their past performance. In the first part of the article Rodrik establishes the conceptual case for multilateral institutions and lending. He excludes from his analysis multilateral lending for humanitarian reasons and focuses on lending on commercial terms, similar to that offered by private lenders and investors. Although I agree with much of what he says about multilateral institutions, I would add some clarification to the roles he identifies as important for these institutions.

Monitoring and Information Dissemination

The multilateral institutions' preferential access to information, together with the professional staffs they have to analyze and disseminate it, allows them to signal to private lenders and investors the economic and policy stance of a country. This signaling must be linked with multilateral lending to be credible, however, because otherwise a moral hazard problem could arise. The International Monetary Fund (IMF) and the World Bank recognize the need for this combination of signaling and lending, as reflected, for example, in recent discussions within the IMF on the nature of shadow programs, precautionary agreements, and enhanced surveillance. Three problems arise, however: lending exposes the multilaterals to risks, disengagement is difficult, and there is no established mechanism for conveying a negative signal about countries in which the multilaterals are not engaged.

The preferred creditor (seniority) status of the multilaterals is one way of protecting their claims, but this status lowers the value of their signaling. The IMF and

Stijn Claessens is senior financial economist in the Finance and Private Sector Development Division of the Europe–Central Asia and Middle East–North Africa Technical Department at the World Bank. The author thanks Ishac Diwan and Aslï Demirgüç-Kunt for sharing their thoughts on this comment.

Annual World Bank Conference on Development Economics 1995

the Bank could resolve this conundrum by providing a mix of their own loans and administered aid. If the pool of aid available to the multilaterals were limited but dispersed according to the same principles as their loans, then such aid could serve as a signal about a country, if only relative to other countries.

The disengagement problem can arise because the multilaterals may not want to precipitate a situation in which their own loans are at risk or their reputations are tarnished by reversing an earlier positive signal. As Managing Director Michel Camdessus of the IMF admits, Fund officials tend "to give the benefit of the doubt to member governments pursuing shaky policies" (*Washington Post,* 19 April 1995, p. F1). This concern could be partly allayed through the aid mechanism mentioned above. Once a signal is given through the aid mechanism, the multilateral owes no further commitment and need not pursue a game of wait and see, unwilling to reverse an earlier, positive signal.

Disengagement can also arise from regulatory capture. Clients end up influencing the regulator or monitor, so that the monitor is no longer objective in its actions and decisions. As the managing director of the IMF admits, "there is a need for more frankness or harshness when [IMF members] don't want to see something" (*Financial Times,* 25 April 1995, p. 6). Clear rules and limited discretion on the part of Bank and IMF staff and management, possibly backed up by independent internal evaluation units, are the answer. But the multilateral nature of the Bank and the IMF makes even this move difficult. As the managing director of the IMF put it, "I have nowhere in my charter the role of providing early warning signals for the markets. . . . We are dealing with sovereign countries here, and they sit on our governing board" (*Washington Post,* 19 April 1995, p. F1). How to solve this conundrum? The answer may be that the multilaterals should just collect information, do their analysis, disseminate it regularly, and let private parties draw the (obvious) conclusions, as Rodrik advocates. I have much sympathy for this suggestion, and the decision by the IMF to require countries to regularly publish statistics on important macroeconomic variables already goes in this direction.

A third problem, related to the second, arises when private creditors continue to lend to a country with poor policies despite the information and analysis disseminated by the multilaterals. Particularly when the multilaterals are not making loans to that country, private creditors may ignore the (perhaps) subtle warning signals from the multilaterals (when the multilaterals are involved, withholding a loan is a fairly clear signal). Should the multilaterals be more proactive and denounce the private lending? Such an approach would likely clash with the multilateral nature of these institutions. Yet the excessive private lending that led to the debt crisis of 1982 suggests that private markets are not always able to read the writing on the wall. Here, no obvious solutions exist.

Conditionality

The second idea in Rodrik's article (and in Sachs 1989; Claessens and Diwan 1990; and Diwan and Rodrik 1992, among others) is that the multilaterals can commit governments to certain policies, presumably policies they would have found difficult to agree to ex ante without the lending or monitoring support of the multilaterals. By attributing this power to the multilaterals, Rodrik defines another possible role for them. While I agree that the multilaterals have some power of conditionality, Rodrik treats conditionality as though it were some kind of technology possessed only by the multilaterals, without providing enough explanation for its existence or origins. Yes, multilaterals can monitor, and to some extent conditionality is nothing but monitoring (in the case of Russia, for example, the IMF releases monthly tranches based on performance). But conditionality is really about giving the government a valid excuse to say no to some domestic constituencies ex post. If multilateral lending is to have the power not only to induce the government to agree ex ante to certain policies, but also to say no to some groups ex post, there must be a payoff for some constituency that the government was not able to provide on its own.

This analysis means that the positive case for conditionality relies on a political economy argument (domestic or external). But economists have often ignored that argument, and so the implications for the design of conditionality are not well understood (see Haggard, Lafay, and Morrison 1995). In practice, the positive case for conditionality may therefore not be as compelling as Rodrik claims. Given the progress some countries have made without multilateral conditionality, it may well be that dissemination of ideas (through research and operational interactions with countries) works much better than conditionality tied to lending to achieve policy reform. In any case Rodrik's discussion should be seen as laying out a research agenda, rather than a definite answer, on what determines conditionality and how it can be used to deal with the time-consistency problems governments face.

Coordination

Rodrik does not discuss coordination in any detail. He does discuss the herd behavior found in some financial markets—large capital inflows or outflows for reasons that are not justified by economic fundamentals. In part this behavior may result because the rules of the game in international lending are ill-defined, involving as it does the sovereignty of nations. An approach advocated recently by Jeffrey Sachs (and discussed at the IMF's 1995 Interim Meetings) calls for the equivalent of an international bankruptcy court, possibly administered by the IMF. But short of that approach no solution other than increased integration of developing countries with the world economy appears feasible. Herd behavior can also arise because markets lack information or analysis about a country. Here Rodrik rightly points out that the multilaterals may perform a useful function through their monitoring and conditionality.

But there can also be a pure coordination or free-rider problem in international financial markets. Take the recent situation in Mexico. The crisis, spawned by a lack of information and analysis, in some ways resembled a run on a bank and ultimately required the coordinating role of multilaterals, backed by significant lending. Or take Mexico in 1982, when commercial banks were interested only in recalling their loans. The coordination required to achieve at least the second-best solution—continuing to lend and rolling over their loans—may not always emerge from markets or bilateral lenders. Here the multilaterals could, by their charters, be the coordinators. The IMF already plays this role in balance of payments crises—as it did in Mexico, where it is the monitor as well as the provider of a large share of the financing package. The World Bank plays this role to some extent in coordinating aid, a role made more useful given the often diverse objectives of donors. Arguably, these roles could be strengthened, benefiting from the multilateral nature of these institutions, which makes coordinating more acceptable to all parties. Of course, moral hazard problems arise if there are designated lenders of last resort, and this would have to be guarded against.

Empirical Evidence

I have the most trouble with Rodrik's two empirical claims. First, that multilateral lending other than that by the IMF does not catalyze private flows (while bilateral flows do). Indeed, Rodrik asserts that non-IMF multilateral flows may follow private flows, raising the possibility that multilaterals bail out private creditors. Second, that economic growth is positively associated with multilateral nonconcessional lending, but not with multilateral concessional flows. Note that Rodrik does not test the growth effect of multilateral lending itself. Rather, he tests whether multilateral lending is a signal of future growth, consistent with his argument that lending for projects with high rates of return is not a sufficient justification for multilateral lending (or multilateral institutions), because private creditors could do this lending.[1]

On the first point: several papers have found that IMF lending does not induce private flows (see Killick 1995). This could be expected—IMF lending often signals that a country is experiencing balance of payments difficulties (in fact, the IMF's charter stipulates a "need" criteria, making IMF support a more negative signal). Depending on how long the crisis lasts and how much improvement IMF lending and monitoring effects, the coefficient on IMF net transfers could easily be negative.

Rodrik does not find, however, a significant negative effect of IMF lending, but the coefficients for other multilateral lending (concessional and nonconcessional) are significantly negative, especially during the mid-1980s. I find this puzzling. One of Rodrik's explanations is that multilaterals bailed out private creditors.[2] I offer a different explanation. During the late 1970s and early 1980s the multilaterals may have refrained from lending to countries receiving large private (and bilateral) flows because they considered their policy environments too weak or because they were not willing to compete with private flows. Then, after the debt crisis developed in 1982 and private net transfers became sharply negative, the multilaterals may have found that their policy-based lending at the margin had a high payoff in terms of changing policies in these countries. Multilaterals basically came in to revive the patient, while private creditors withdrew. Ex post, this shows up in the regressions as a bailout of private creditors for some period of time. But eventually, as the patient recovered, private flows reemerged. This result would show up in Rodrik's regressions if a longer time period were used.[3]

In general, the effect of the debt crisis and the access of countries to private flows may contribute much to Rodrik's results. Many countries, such as those in Sub-Saharan Africa, never had access to private flows because of their limited credit-worthiness, but they have received multilateral loans. Since there are many countries in Africa, the regression results may rely too heavily on African data. Arguably, Africa is a special case—one would not expect much lending by the private sector, even if the multilateral lending effort had its desired development impact. The opposite case involves countries that relied very little on multilateral lending for all periods because they had ample access to private flows. These two types of situations may imply that on a cross-sectional basis, private flows are likely to be negatively correlated with multilateral flows. The fact that the regressions use a mixture of time-series and cross-sectional data may influence the results. In any case it would be useful to run the regressions with and without Sub-Saharan Africa and with and without countries that received very little in the way of multilateral flows.

In general, I found these regression results puzzling, particularly the result that bilateral lending would induce larger transfers from private creditors. I cannot think of many cases in which bilateral flows could have had this catalytic effect. Perhaps Indonesia, the Republic of Korea, Taiwan (China), and Turkey could fall in this category for some periods. But otherwise—especially given the wide variety of objectives bilateral donors pursue—the only explanation is that bilateral donors give the wrong signal to private creditors, perhaps lulling them into a false sense of security.[4]

My apprehension about the regressions was heightened by Rodrik's assertion that foreign direct investment (FDI) depends on nonconcessional bilateral flows. Causality tests show that for many countries FDI is not related to any other capital flow (Fry and others 1995). The boom in FDI in the late 1980s was a result of many factors—overall improvements in developing countries, factors in industrial countries—and is unlikely to have been triggered by bilateral flows. In general, FDI investors do not need much signaling, perhaps not even by multilaterals but definitely not by creditors with such diverse objectives as bilateral donors.

I believe that it would be much more meaningful to study the catalytic role of multilateral lending by using detailed country cases and either longer subperiods or greater concentration on the more recent period. For example, there is enough evidence to suggest that the turnaround in private flows to Latin America in the late 1980s and early 1990s was induced at least in part by the policies supported by the multilaterals during the mid-1980s. South and East Asia's ability to attract private flows also suggests a positive effect of past multilateral involvement.

Rodrik's article finds that nonconcessional (World Bank) flows are significantly and positively associated with higher growth. Thus while World Bank involvement may not catalyze private flows, it does have a positive impact on country performance. Rodrik also reports that multilateral concessional flows have a negative relationship with growth, albeit not significant. The latter result is to be expected because concessional aid flows are positively associated with poor performance since they are, in part, motivated by desires to alleviate poverty.[5] In other words, concessional flows may go to countries that perform worse, not better. This is particularly true for bilateral support, which is often grounded in political and commercial considerations. Rodrik's regressions confirm this finding—coefficients for bilateral concessional flows are more negative than those for Bank concessional flows.

These regressions make clear that the impact of multilateral lending should be measured not by subsequent private flows alone, but also by its developmental impact, including growth, poverty reduction, and increased domestic confidence (as reflected in investment, for example). At the same time I would not put too much faith in such regressions. Easterly and others (1993) have shown that there is little persistence in growth over time, raising serious doubts about the results of regressions that use short (five-year) subperiods.

Notes

1. Admittedly, private lenders may not be willing to take certain long-term policy and political risks. This "market failure" in long-term private lending to developing countries is, however, closely related to the potential conditionality role of the multilaterals. Applying multilateral conditionality would presumably reduce the risk.

2. This is also suggested by the positive coefficients for private flows when trying to explain multilateral flows. Other explanations, which Rodrik did not put forward, are that the multilaterals have a superior lending technology that crowds out private lending or that the other multilaterals bail out the IMF.

3. Rodrik studies actual net transfers—disbursements minus repayments for principal and interest. Actual disbursements lag commitments, with the time lag longer for multilateral flows (on average, about four years) than for private flows. This difference could bias the results. Any intended signaling value of commitments for new lending will not appear in the net transfer data until four years later. Since Rodrik uses five-year intervals, the regression results may simply reflect this lag.

4. This is more likely because bilateral flows are often intended (explicitly or implicitly) to spur private flows from the same donor country to the same developing country.

5. Boone (1994) and others have shown that, even when correcting for the link between aid and income levels and growth, the effect of aid on growth is often negative.

References

Boone, Peter. 1994. "The Impact of Foreign Aid on Savings and Growth." London School of Economics, London.

Claessens, Stijn, and Ishac Diwan. 1990. "Investment Incentives: New Money, Debt Relief, and the Critical Role of Conditionality in the Debt Crisis." *World Bank Economic Review* 4: 21–42.

Diwan, Ishac, and Dani Rodrik. 1992. *External Debt, Adjustment, and Burden Sharing: A Unified Framework.* Princeton Studies in International Finance 73. Princeton University, Princeton, N.J.

Easterly, William, Michael Kremer, Lant Pritchett, and Lawrence H. Summers. 1993. "Good Policy or Good Luck? Country Growth Performance and Temporary Shocks." *Journal of Monetary Economics* 32: 459–83.

Fry, Maxwell J., Stijn Claessens, Peter Burridge, and Marie-Christine Blanchet. 1995. "Foreign Direct Investment, Other Capital Flows, and Current Account Deficits: What Causes What?" Policy Research Working Paper 1527. World Bank, International Economics Department, International Finance Division, Washington, D.C.

Haggard, Stephen, Jean-Dominique Lafay, and Christian Morrison. 1995. *The Political Feasibility of Adjustment in Developing Countries.* Paris: OECD Development Center.

Killick, Tony, 1995. "A Principal-Agent Analysis on Conditionality—A Reader's Digest." Overseas Development Institute, London.

Sachs, Jeffrey, 1990. "Conditionality, Debt Relief, and the Developing Countries' Debt Crisis." In Jeffrey Sachs, ed., *Developing Country Debt and Economic Performance: The International Financial System,* vol.1. Chicago, Ill.: University of Chicago Press.

Floor Discussion of "Why Is There Multilateral Lending?" by Dani Rodrik

A participant said that in addition to multilateral organizations that operated worldwide, there were many regional multilateral lending organizations, including the Inter-American Development Bank and the Asian Development Bank. Could these regional organizations be rationalized in the same way as Rodrik had rationalized international organizations? Rodrik replied that one might find a rationale for regional development banks in a focus on information about externalities that were local rather than public.

Willem Buiter (discussant from another section) asked Rodrik how he visualized multilateral conditionality with private lending, as he seemed to suggest was possible. Conditionality is of an "or else" nature, and the kind of conditionality Rodrik proposed would be toothless unless multilaterals were given seats on the boards of private lending institutions so that they could cut off or hold back loans. What could multilaterals threaten if they did not control the resource transfers going to these countries?

Rephrasing the question—what sanctions could the World Bank and the International Monetary Fund (IMF) apply if they were not lending their own money?—Rodrik replied that yes, that was a problem. But in practice the Bank and the IMF are not usually the primary lenders anyway. Rather, they turn on the metaphorical green light that unleashes private flows. Rodrik envisaged a scenario in which the IMF and the World Bank essentially give a country their seal of approval, indicating that it had introduced the right policies. Under stabilization and structural adjustment programs the role that the two institutions play is to unleash private flows, facilitate the restructuring of private debt, and so on.

A participant from the Delegation of the European Commission repeated Stanley Fischer's (Roundtable participant) observation that recent IMF standby loans to Russia and Ukraine had received relatively little attention. Most of the noise was occasioned by the IMF's lending money to Russia when so little progress had been made in resolving the conflict in Chechenya. Some observers, she noted, lauded this political neutrality. Others deplored it.

This session was chaired by Jean-François Rischard, vice president, Finance and Private Sector Development, at the World Bank.

Annual World Bank Conference on Development Economics 1995
©1996 The International Bank for Reconstruction and Development / THE WORLD BANK

A participant from the World Bank felt that Rodrik's regressions might be biased because of three problems in defining the variable "net transfers." First, private net transfers had been nonmarginal, discrete, and discontinous while those for multilateral net transfers had been smooth. During the 1980s private net transfers were actually negative. Second, the composition and maturity structures were different for private net transfers and concessional and nonconcessional multilateral loans. Private loans were all commercial, and their interest rate structure was totally different. So two different sets of variables were being captured for commercial and multilateral loans. And there was no way to compare maturity structures of forty years (International Development Association), fifteen to twenty years (International Bank for Reconstruction and Development), and five years (commercial loans). Third, the net transfers did not include remittances, dividends, and profits from foreign direct investment, so some variables could be missing. Jean-François Rischard (chair) agreed.

The foreign direct investment issue was serious, Rodrik agreed. He had been unable to use the net transfer concept for foreign direct investment, as he had for the multinational categories. He was not sure of the direction of the bias and was unwilling to say that it was necessarily biased in any direction except for making the coefficient biased downward toward zero because of the error in measurement. He was aware that private and multilateral flows were different in terms of concessionality and maturity structure, and he had tried to distinguish between concessional and nonconcessional multilateral lending in order to show how nonconcessional multilateral lending affected future private lending and private growth. On the whole, Rodrik agreed with his discussants. He stressed that the growth regressions were not intended to examine whether multilateral lending improves future growth but to examine whether it signals future growth, a different question altogether.

Was there, as Stijn Claessens (discussant) had suggested, a third role for multilaterals: to solve the coordination problem or to act as a lender of last resort? Yes, Rodrik thought that role existed, but if you examine the roles closely, they really boil down to two: information and conditionality. It was not lending that was critical; it was the ability to say which countries were deserving, where the problem was liquidity and where it was solvency, and what kinds of policies were needed to resolve a crisis. And those were the roles that multilaterals could play best. Claessens had also been skeptical about the effectiveness of conditionality. Rodrik did not disagree with the points he made; he agreed that there were serious problems. But if everybody agreed that conditionality must be at the core of the role these institutions perform, the question should really be how to make it more effective.

Rodrik liked Guillermo Calvo's (discussant) analogy of multilaterals and police departments. Calvo had filled in a big gap in the discussion, which Claessens also touched on: that Rodrik had talked about conditionality without examining the kinds of credible commitment or punishment technology available to make conditionality effective. Rodrik had simply presumed that conditionality would be effectively exercised. His main problem with seeing multilaterals as police officer was that we have had two centuries of capital flows but multilaterals have developed only over the past fifty years. At different periods the global economy has been extremely open in terms of capital flows and has managed without multilateral institutions. What has been so special about the past fifty years? The point that he had hoped to make was that the political environment had changed, and the role of police officer could no longer be played by private creditors or even by individual governments. Multilateral institutions, because they have some degree of autonomy from governments, could exercise a relatively apolitical conditionality. For that reason they had a useful role to play. That, he thought, distinguished the postwar period from the two preceding centuries.

Rischard wrapped up the session by saying that at least four Bank vice presidents had concluded that multilateral institutions were complex creatures whose roles would evolve over time. Their lending role would probably continue, but over time they would probably become development services institutions rather than development lending institutions—disseminating best practices, coordinating efforts, and, as Claessens had suggested, serving as a trustee for certain programs.

Incentives, Rules of the Game, and Development

Elinor Ostrom

This article presents some paradoxical empirical findings from a recent study of irrigation systems in Nepal and describes earlier efforts to improve the physical infrastructure of irrigation systems there. Incentives facing officials of government irrigation systems, staff at donor agencies, and farmers working within self-organized irrigation systems are examined to explain these empirical findings. A game-theoretical analysis of institutional choice on self-organized systems illustrates the variety of factors that affect the adoption of any particular rule configuration. External assistance does not always improve performance, but one externally funded intervention—described here—has been evaluated as highly successful. These findings have some practical policy implications.

In this article I analyze the incentives and rules of the game governing the finance, design, construction, operation, and maintenance of irrigation infrastructures, a topic of concern in the development field. The World Bank's *World Development Report 1994* was devoted entirely to the issue of infrastructure for development. The authors of that report concluded that infrastructure investment *"can deliver major benefits in economic growth, poverty alleviation, and environmental sustainability— but only when it provides services that respond to effective demand and does so efficiently"* (World Bank 1994, p. 2, italicized in original). They argue that major investments in infrastructure projects made in developing countries are yielding neither the quantity nor the quality of outcomes demanded. They conclude that the *"causes of past poor performance, and the source of improved performance, lie in the incentives facing providers"* (World Bank 1994, p. 2, italicized in original).

Elinor Ostrom is codirector of the Workshop in Political Theory and Policy Analysis, and Arthur F. Bentley Chair at Indiana University. The research on which major portions of this article is based was supported by the Ford Foundation and the Decentralization: Finance and Management Project, sponsored by the U.S. Agency for International Development. The author is deeply appreciative of this essential support. The author thanks Thráinn Eggertsson and Wai Fung Lam for thoughtful comments and Patty Dalecki for her careful editing.

Annual World Bank Conference on Development Economics 1995
©1996 The International Bank for Reconstruction and Development / THE WORLD BANK

Their conclusions are similar to those reached by the U.S. Agency for International Development (USAID) project, Decentralization: Finance and Management, which examined why so many rural infrastructure projects have been unsustainable. The conclusion reached there was that the underlying cause of unsustainable projects was the "perverse incentives facing participants in the design, finance, construction, operation, maintenance, and use of facilities" (E. Ostrom, Schroeder, and Wynne 1993, p. 8). Among the recommended types of institutional solutions to the problems was giving *"users and other stakeholders a strong voice and real responsibility"* (World Bank 1994, p. 2, italicized in original).

The Empirical Puzzle

A recent study of irrigation systems in Nepal found strong relationships between the physical attributes of irrigation systems and the ways those systems are governed and three dependent variables: maintenance of the physical system, equity of water delivery, and agricultural productivity (Lam 1994; Benjamin and others 1994). A series of multivariant analyses (controlling for terrain, size of system, variance in farmer income, and other variables) found irrigation systems that have been improved by the construction of permanent headworks to be in worse repair, to deliver substantially less water to the tail end than to the head end of the systems, and to have lower agricultural productivity than the temporary, stone-trees-and-mud headworks constructed by farmers (Lam 1994). The same analyses found that irrigation systems governed by the farmers themselves and those in which some sections of the canals are lined with stone or concrete are in better repair, deliver more water to the tail end of the system, and have higher agricultural productivity than unlined systems and those governed by the Nepal Department of Irrigation. An earlier study found greater equity of water delivery in traditional, farmer-managed systems than in more modern, agency-managed systems (E. Ostrom and Gardner 1993).

How is it possible that "primitive" irrigation systems improved only through partial lining significantly outperform systems that have been improved by the construction of modern, permanent, concrete and steel headworks (funded largely by donors and constructed by professional engineering firms)? Controlling for the effect of these two types of physical improvements and other relevant variables, why are farmer-governed irrigation systems able to achieve better and more equitable outcomes than those managed by national agencies?

Many factors contribute to these counterintuitive results. Most of them relate to the different incentives faced by key participants in the finance, design, construction, operation, and maintenance of farmer-governed and agency-run systems. On farmer-governed irrigation systems, farmers craft their own rules, which frequently offset the perverse incentives they face in their particular physical and cultural setting. These rules may be almost invisible to outsiders, especially when they are well accepted by participants who do not even see them as noteworthy.[1]

In project planning most effort focuses on how improving physical capital, such as creating permanent headworks, affects various aspects of the technical operation of a system. How these variables affect the incentives of participants is rarely explored. Unless the changes in physical infrastructure are undertaken with an awareness that they will affect the incentives of participants—sometimes perversely—projects that are intended to do good may actually cause harm.

Past Efforts to Improve the Physical Capital of Irrigation Systems in Nepal

Most efforts by donors and by the national government to improve the operations of the thousands of farmer-governed irrigation systems in Nepal have focused on the physical capital aspect of irrigation systems and ignored the institutional aspects. To illustrate how these interventions have frequently operated in Nepal, I will draw on a study by Rita Hilton (1990, 1992), who analyzed the process of "improving" the Chiregad Irrigation System in the Dang District of Nepal.[2]

The construction of the Chiregad system began in 1983 as part of a joint project of the USAID-funded Rapti Integrated Rural Development Project and the Nepal Department of Irrigation. Completed in 1987, the new system was constructed in an area already served by five irrigation systems built, governed, and managed by the farmers who owned the land served by the systems. The Nepal Department of Irrigation engineers, who designed the project, failed to consult the farmers in the area and never recognized the existence of the systems.

The official system included new permanent headworks and lined main and branch canals. The field channels in the system, however, were left untouched. Several serious design and construction flaws marred the project. Design engineers failed to consider the loose, sand-like soil in the region. As a consequence, the new deep-cut canals have frequently been blocked with mud and have been difficult to operate and maintain. Slides along canal alignments and poor drainage have caused serious problems at many locations of the system.

After construction, a water-users committee was formally established by the Irrigation Department as a mechanism for facilitating farmer participation in irrigation management. The committee was established in a manner similar to that seen in many other agency-constructed systems in Asia: irrigation officials summoned farmers to a meeting and informed them that a water-users committee had been established. The officials simply appointed the pradhan pancha (chairman) of the local panchayat as secretary of the water-users committee; the secretary appointed other members of the committee. As a result the pradhan pancha—who owned no land in Chiregad's service area—was given a crucial role on the formal committee, whereas the water managers of the five farmer irrigation systems serving the area were not even included on the committee.

The water-users committee was designed to serve the entire new system. There was to be no formal organization at branch or field channel levels. Such an institutional arrangement is highly questionable in a system with a number of branch canals along which communities with distinct interests are located. On most farmer-governed irrigation systems of any size, farmers belong to branch-level associations, with their own rules and governance arrangements, as well as to an overall association. Some farmer-organized systems have as many as five levels of organization (Yoder 1994). The water-users committee rarely met and took on few activities. Hilton (1990) found that none of the committee members could provide her with information about the characteristics of the system or how it operated.

The committee was created and recognized by the Irrigation Department without any effort to understand how the existing farmer associations had been organized. Each of these associations was related to a village and coordinated the water distribution and canal maintenance efforts of farmers in that village. The rules for water distribution and for resource mobilization for maintenance for each village differed. Farmers seem to have designed rules that suited the local situation. Moreover, these organizations were strong enough to continue operating for a time even after the water-users committee was established. Because these traditional organizations were not recognized by the Irrigation Department, however, their legitimacy and authority were undermined, and they no longer play important roles.

The five farmer systems used to be able to provide adequate water to farmers located in all five villages. After the Chiregad system was constructed, only farmers in three of the five villages consistently received water from the new system. In one village water delivery is unreliable during the monsoon season, when the canals are often damaged by floods. Another village faces problems of excess water because of poor drainage. So the result of this effort to improve agricultural productivity through investment in physical capital is that a smaller service area is being served, water delivery is unreliable, the newly established water-users committee is nonfunctional, and five farmer organizations that used to keep their systems operating well have been severely weakened. Not only is the physical capital of dubious value, but institutional capital has been substantially reduced as a result of the project. Similar effects have been documented on other government-constructed systems (Laitos and others 1986; Pradhan, Valera, and Durga 1993).

Chiregad is not the most extreme case in Nepal of lack of awareness of the institutional and physical capital already created by farmers. A more extreme case is the initial East Rapti Irrigation Project, funded through credit assistance from the Asian Development Bank. The plan was to build a major diversion weir across the Rapti River to provide irrigation for a vast area in the Chitwan District of Nepal. The project plan projected benefits based on productivity differences between irrigated and unirrigated land. Although more than eighty-five farmer-managed systems were already providing irrigation services to most of the land in the project area (Shukla and others 1993), all of the land in the project area was considered to be unirrigated. That project planners could overlook the irrigation activities of eighty-five farmer-governed systems when designing a large loan and constructing a major system illustrates the blindness of those financing and designing major irrigation investment projects.

Fortunately, members of the Irrigation Management Systems Study Group (IMSSG) at the Institute of Agriculture and Animal Science in Chitwan had already conducted research in the area and had documented the relative efficiency of existing farmer-managed systems. They brought these systems to the attention of the donor community, which successfully challenged the appropriateness of the original plan. As a result the project, which was to have been initiated in 1987, has been significantly downsized. Its current objectives are to rehabilitate the existing farmer-managed irrigation system in the project area, to invest in efforts to check stream bank erosion, to construct better farm-to-market roads, and to install shallow tubewells where appropriate (IMSSG 1993). The destruction of prior institutional and physical capital was averted because local researchers had invested time and energy studying the farmer-governed irrigation systems in the area and could provide excellent documentation.

Other large irrigation projects have also been misconceived. A reduction in the amount of irrigated land following the construction of "improved" systems is not unusual; nor is the weakening—and even destruction—of preexisting farmer organizations (Curtis 1991). Something is wrong when efforts to improve agricultural productivity by investing in physical infrastructure have the opposite result.

One reason for the difference in performance between self-organized and government-organized irrigation systems is the difference in incentive structures facing officials, farmers, and donor agencies. Incentives are the positive and negative outcomes (such as financial rewards and penalties) that actors expect to result from actions taken within a set of working rules, given a particular physical and social setting. Incentives are influenced by rules that affect how individuals are recruited, monitored, and rewarded and by the internal values of individuals and the cultural values shared by members of a community. Thus incentives are the result of the interactions among many different forms of institutional arrangements within a particular sociophysical setting.

Incentives Facing Officials of Government Irrigation Systems

Most professional staff on government systems in Nepal are employed within a civil service system with only two levels, gazetted and nongazetted. Gazetted employees are higher-level civil servants whose appointments, promotions, and transfers are published in the *Nepal Gazette*. Nongazetted employees are lower-level civil service or clerical staff. Staff employed to perform manual labor do not have civil service status. In the Irrigation Department almost all gazetted officials have a degree in engineering, and it is this group that is responsible for managing irrigation systems. Promotion is based largely on seniority, evaluation by superiors, and qualifications. Only four grades exist at both the gazetted and nongazetted level. Because of this narrow range of grades, promotion is slow, with the average employee remaining in the same position for ten to fifteen years.

Several features of the civil service system affect the behavior patterns of irrigation officials (Lam 1994). First, results of civil service examinations and formal qualifications are the two main criteria for recruitment and promotion. Neither criterion reflects the ability of an official to work with farmers or to solve the day-to-day problems of an irrigation system. From the perspective of the officials, their jobs and status are related to their profession rather than to how well they serve the farmers.

Second, promotion is rendered ineffective as a motivational tool by the length of time it takes. Outstanding performance might pay off for an official only after many years. For officials whose discount rates are high, short-term comfort may be preferable to long-term career advancement through hard work. Moreover, if civil servants observe that appropriate rewards do not follow from a good evaluation, they are not likely to treat evaluations seriously.

Third, seniority has effectively become the most important criterion for promotion, suggesting that there is little incentive for officials to actively try to solve farmers' problems. Individual initiative and creativity are discouraged, and irrigation officials who do not commit serious mistakes or offend their superiors will eventually be promoted. The situation becomes even more perverse when local politics affect the assignment of civil servants. Faced with an incentive structure in which pleasing politicians rather than working hard pays off, irrigation officials are strongly tempted to assist politicians in their rent-seeking activities.

Fourth, corruption pervades the day-to-day operations of many government offices. The most serious corruption in the use of public funds comes from large government contracts. Politicians try to bring government contracts to their districts to gain both political support and "commissions." Contractors share a percentage of their commissions with government field representatives, who take their cut and then pass the rest up the bureaucratic hierarchy to the higher-level officials who arranged the commissions in the first place. A contractor describing the system concluded that "in Nepal, only corruption is on an organized basis!" (Benjamin 1989, p. 259). Given the low salaries of civil servants, forgoing the income associated with such "accepted" practices is extremely difficult.

Fifth, engineers pursue higher education at least partly in order to enjoy the status associated with the engineering profession.[3] Being assigned to a division responsible for construction of modern irrigation systems is a source of professional pride for engineers. A much lower status is attached to being assigned to a division responsible for operations and maintenance; such divisions generally lack financial support as well. Moreover, field assignments provide Irrigation Department officials with fewer opportunities for personal income enhancement than assignment to construction jobs.

Sixth, civil servants in Nepal usually prefer to live in urban areas, where better health care and education are available for their children. Assignments in remote areas are considered highly undesirable unless they are related to an active construction phase of a project. Officials assigned as resident engineers on completed projects tend to spend as much time as possible with their families (who usually live in Kathmandu) and lobby for a transfer to headquarters.

In the absence of almost any intrinsic or extrinsic rewards to government officials for keeping an irrigation system in good condition or for encouraging improved agricultural productivity, it is not surprising that most irrigation systems constructed by the government and maintained by engineers assigned to operations and maintenance divisions do not perform as well as farmer-governed systems in similar terrains.

Incentives Facing Staff at Donor Agencies

The activities of donor agencies during the past half-century have affected the incentives of all participants in infrastructure investment in developing countries. In some cases the interaction of incentives has increased rent seeking and corruption (Repetto 1986). This has resulted, in part, from donor requirements to deal directly with national governments. National politicians seek loans and grants that will help them achieve their "objective functions," which may differ substantially from those of the purported beneficiaries. Staff at donor agencies often face incentives that encourage them to fund large projects. The fact that next year's flow of funds depends on rapidly spending this year's budget contributes to the bias favoring large projects (Nelson 1968; Tendler 1975). Projects requiring large expenditures for major capital goods are more likely to be funded than labor-intensive projects using locally manufactured equipment. And as donor organizations such as USAID have reduced the size of their staffs, workloads have increased, making it more difficult to evaluate proposed projects carefully. Fear of external criticism about corrupt practices and lack of control also leads donor agencies to favor funding projects that appear to give project monitors greater control. This usually means funding a few large projects rather than many small ones.

Bilateral donors like USAID face the perplexing problem of creating enduring constituencies within their own countries while seeking appropriate ways to spend foreign aid without disturbing their supporters. The USAID requirement to buy equipment made in the United States, for example, encourages the approval of projects using heavy construction equipment rather than those requiring waivers to allow the use of smaller, foreign-made implements, which are often more effective in developing countries (Tendler 1975).

Montague Yudelman, director of the World Bank's Agricultural and Rural Development Program from 1974 to 1984, provided a perceptive view of the problems facing World Bank staff during that decade (Yudelman 1985, 1989). Reporting on a survey of twelve irrigation projects that "together cost almost twice their expected cost of $800 million and provided water enough to irrigate only two-thirds as much acreage as projected," Yudelman concludes that "weak institutions—whether national, regional, or autonomous—can greatly undermine the performance of irrigation systems" (1985, p. 16).

The difficulty of obtaining accurate information about local conditions, whether on physical variables or local institutions, is another reason for poorly designed systems. National officials have an incentive to provide data that are likely to improve the chances of receiving aid funds. A sure way to increase the projected benefit stream—and a device employed frequently by those who attempt to justify an investment in a new irrigation system—is to estimate generously the area to be served (and thus the benefits that are expected to accrue).

Professional barriers increase the difficulty of obtaining accurate information from farmers, and attempts to include beneficiaries in planning, operating, and maintaining a project have not been entirely successful. What happened on the

Chiregad system—established farmer associations were ignored and a formal water-users committee was arbitrarily created—provides some insights on why farmers do not eagerly participate in systems in which they are asked to participate only when their labor is needed.

Incentives Facing Farmers Working within Self-Organized Systems

On externally designed and constructed systems, someone other than the farmers designs the physical system and service areas, determines the water allocations, and handles maintenance. On self-organized systems farmers make these decisions themselves, selecting the specific projects they think are worthy of investment as well as determining how best to carry out these projects—given the opportunities and constraints they face. Officials of self-organized irrigation systems are usually farmers themselves, and hired staff continue in their positions only as long as their work is satisfactory to the farmers who hire them. Moreover, officials are often paid in grain at the end of the season, and thus have a direct and personal interest in the success of the system. Thus the incentives for those who operate farmer-run systems are often related to overall productivity. Collective-action problems are overcome by the type of rules that are crafted by the farmers themselves (E. Ostrom 1992; Tang 1992; Lam 1994).

The way farmers bargain over rules illustrates how rules affect outcomes. When they bargain successfully, they solve collective-action problems that many analysts, including Yudelman (1985), presume cannot be solved by those involved. The analysis that follows illustrates how a collective-action problem can be analyzed when the question of institutional change is the primary focus. It also illustrates the delicate relationship that exists between the constraints and the opportunities afforded by the physical infrastructure itself.

Underlying Assumptions

For farmers to consider organizing themselves into even a loose association for constructing an irrigation system, they need to have secure enough land tenure to believe that they can reap long-term benefits from their investment.[4] They need to have established a sufficient sense of community that they engage in a full array of face-to-face relationships where a reputation for keeping promises is an important asset. Reaching a high level of common understanding about the structure of incentives they face, the types of individuals with whom they interact, and alternative ways of structuring their relationships is a prerequisite for organizing associations to undertake major, long-term collective action (Aumann 1976).[5] Knowing that individuals share a commitment to keep the promises made to a group—so long as others keep their promises—affects individual expectations about future behavior. The people involved also need to switch levels of action from those of a day-to-day operational situation to those of a rule-making situation (E. Ostrom 1990).

If this set of beliefs—the assessment made by each farmer about the beliefs that others share and the likely strategies that others will adopt—is not shattered by experience, the set of farmers would be able to construct a system and operate it for a long time. If the precommitment that they make by signaling their agreement is followed by behavior consistent with that precommitment, each farmer becomes more certain that others will follow the agreement and will sanction nonconformers (Elster 1979; Schelling 1960). It is then in each farmer's interest to conform to the agreed rules most of the time.[6] In other words an agreement is successful not simply because it creates joint benefits but also because those who contribute to its continuance expect net benefits for themselves and their families that are greater than those expected from the alternatives available to them.

Nothing is automatic about such a process.[7] What is crucial is that the farmers believe that their individual long-term benefits will exceed their long-term costs, that they find a set of rules on which they can agree, and that they adopt strategies that do not constantly challenge the delicate balance of mutual expectations that must be maintained to keep the system going over the long run. Some farmers may end up much better off than others. But even the less advantaged must believe that they are better off by participating, or they will not participate voluntarily. Individual incentives depend on farmers' expectations, the viability of the rules they have established, their consequent beliefs concerning overall net benefits, and the distribution of benefits and costs.

Symmetric Incentives

Let us first assume that ten farmers own equal-size plots of land on an alluvial plain. One of the farmers, who has a reputation for designing prudent and well-conceived community works, has proposed a plan to divert a mountain stream to the area in which he lives. If allocated carefully, the source could provide water for three crops for all ten farmers. The plan involves constructing a short main canal and two branch canals, each serving five families (figure 1). The farmers can obtain a low-interest loan to purchase materials, and they have the skills needed to construct the canals themselves. A diversion works at the source sends water into a relatively short and uncomplicated canal, which is then divided into an X branch and a Y branch, each serving five plots of equal size.

To get this project started, the farmers need to agree on the rules for allocating the expected annual benefits from the project and its associated costs. Farmers will not voluntarily contribute funds or hard work to construct an irrigation system unless they believe that their own discounted flow of future expected net benefits is larger than their share of the costs of construction. For purposes of analysis we treat all farmers on each of the two branches as if they formed two single team players facing each other in a two-player bargaining game. (In other words we ignore within-team differences.) If they fail to reach agreement on the set of rules they will use, the farmers will continue to produce only rainfed crops. The yield from rainfed agriculture thus constitutes the "breakdown" value for each player—that is,

Figure 1. *A Simple Symmetric Irrigation System*

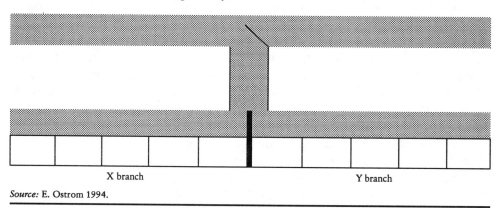

X branch   Y branch

Source: E. Ostrom 1994.

what each farmer can expect to receive if no agreement is reached on constructing a new system.

In this situation two rules are being considered. Both players—branch X and branch Y—must agree to either rule I or rule J, or they will not construct the system (Knight 1992). If they do not agree, they continue with their current rainfed agriculture and obtain the status quo yield (SQ_X, SQ_Y) from growing one crop a year. In the symmetric situation the status quo yield is equal for both branches. If both players agree on one of the rules, they will receive some combination of the total annual expected benefits (B) and costs (C), expressed in crop units, associated with providing this system.[8]

Let us first assume that total annual expected benefits exceed (or equal) total annual expected costs as well as the status quo yield for each branch:

(1) $(B - C) \geq SQ_X + SQ_Y$

Each branch would prefer a situation in which it obtained all the benefits and incurred none of the costs. The other branch would never agree to such a distribution, however, and without agreement no one will contribute to the construction of the systems. Rules used to allocate benefits and costs affect the proportion of benefits and costs that each side obtains. The proportion of the expected annual benefits received by branch X will be e^I if rule I is agreed on and e^J if rule J is agreed on. Similarly, the proportion of expected annual benefits received by branch Y is given by g^I or g^J, depending on the rule selected:

(2) $1 \geq e^I, e^J, g^I, g^J \geq 0$

or

(3) $e^I + g^I = 1$ and $e^J + g^J = 1.$

The coefficients f^I and h^I and f^J and h^J are the proportion of costs assigned to the two branches under the two rules:

(4) $1 \geq f^I, f^J, h^I, h^J \geq 0$

and

(5) $f^I + h^I = 1$ and $f^J + h^J = 1$.

Now assume that all farmers are risk neutral (oriented neither toward taking risks nor toward avoiding them) and have equal and low discount rates, which are omitted from the analysis because their inclusion would not change the result (figure 2).

Rules for Allocating Benefits

Let us first focus on the authority rules that the farmers could use for allocating water. We assume temporarily that the cost of construction and maintenance is divided equally and that the two parties consider two rules:

    Rule 1: All water from the main canal is allocated to branch Y one week and to branch X the next week.

    Rule 2: A permanent dividing weir is constructed so that each branch automatically receives half the flow of the main canal whenever there is water in the main branch.

    The structure of the game described by these two rules (or any similar rule of equal division) is presented in figure 3. Since we are assuming for now that the yield associated with the difference between the benefits and the costs of the irrigation system is greater than the status quo yield for both branches (equation 1), the two parties face a benign coordination situation. There are two pure-strategy equilibria in this game: both sides choose rule 1 or both choose rule 2.[9] Both sides obtain the same payoff in these equilibria, but they must coordinate their actions

Figure 2. *General Structure of Bargaining Game over Rules*

		Y branch	
		Rule I	Rule J
X branch	Rule I	$(e^I B - f^I C), (g^I B - h^I C)$	SQ_X, SQ_Y
	Rule J	SQ_X, SQ_Y	$(e^J B - f^J C), (g^J B - h^J C)$

Source: E. Ostrom 1994.

to achieve one or the other of these equilibria and avoid the less desirable, non-equilibrium outcomes. Since communication is possible, it can be used to solve this coordination problem. If the sides come to agreement, the rule that is finally chosen depends on situation-specific variables.

Rules for Allocating Costs

Now let us focus on a type of rule related to how the farmers allocate responsibilities for providing labor during construction and for maintaining the system once it is built. The proposed rules are not necessarily symmetric in their effect. If, for example, there were one adult son in each family on branch X and no adult sons among the families on branch Y, someone on branch Y might well propose the following rule:

> Rule 3: Each family sends all its adult males to work on the irrigation system on every day designated as a work day.

Because all families own identical plots, this cost allocation is proportionate to the aggregate benefit accruing to each family. Someone in branch X might, however, propose this alternate rule:

> Rule 4: Each family sends one adult male to work on the irrigation system on every day designated as a work day.

Assuming that either rule 1 or rule 2 has already been agreed on, these proposals would result in a bargaining game such as that shown in figure 4.

Assuming that the increased yield exceeds the costs that would be imposed on branch X under rule 3 ($.5B - .67C > SQ_X$), both branches would be better off agreeing to either rule than they would be if no system were in place. Rule 3 assigns a higher proportion of net benefits to branch Y, whereas rule 4 assigns the same benefits to both branches. Branch Y could argue that the irrigation system was providing benefits for all households and that all adult males should therefore pitch in. Branch X could argue that it should not have to contribute twice the amount of labor as branch Y simply because it has more adult males. There are

---

Figure 3. *Payoff Matrix Associated with Rules 1 and 2*

		Y branch	
		Rule 1	Rule 2
X branch	Rule 1	$(.5B - .5C), (.5B - .5C)$	SQ_X, SQ_Y
	Rule 2	SQ_X, SQ_Y	$(.5B - .5C), (.5B - .5C)$

Source: E. Ostrom 1994.

two pure-strategy equilibria to this game: both choose rule 3 or both choose rule 4. Since the results are asymmetric, however, the relative bargaining strength of the participants determines which rule is chosen. For branch Y to get its way, it would have to precommit itself convincingly to the assertion that adoption of rule 3 was an essential precondition for obtaining its agreement to the plan for the irrigation system.

Alternatively, branch Y could recognize the importance of establishing a good continuing relationship and the potential difficulties of getting branch X to continue to honor an agreement it might subsequently come to view as having been forced on it. Even though branch Y really thinks it inappropriate for one-third of the adult males to sit at home while the other two-thirds do all the work, it might recognize that one adult male per household is considered a fair rule in this setting and not hold out for an agreement that it deems more equitable.

Other rules are also likely to be proposed. Branch X could, for example, propose the following:

> Rule 5: All water from the main canal is allocated to a branch in proportion to the amount of labor that the branch provides for construction and annual maintenance.[10]

The existence of rule 5 would alter branch Y's absolute preference for rule 3 over rule 4. Now, whether branch Y prefers rule 3 or rule 4 depends on whether it is combined with rule 5 or rule 1 (ignoring rule 2, which has as an identical outcome function). If the expected benefits of building the system were 100 and the expected costs were 60, the results of different configurations of rules would be as follows:

Rules	*Branch X*	*Branch Y*
Rules 1 and 3	$.50B - .67C = 10$	$.50B - .33C = 30$
Rules 1 and 4	$.50B - .50C = 20$	$.50B - .50C = 20$
Rules 5 and 3	$.67B - .67B = 27$	$.33B - .33C = 13$
Rules 5 and 4	$.50B - .50C = 20$	$.50B - .50C = 20$

Figure 4. *Payoff Matrix Associated with Rules 3 and 4*

		Y branch	
		Rule 3	Rule 4
X branch	Rule 3	$(.5B - .67C), (.5B - .33C)$	SQ_x, SQ_Y
	Rule 4	SQ_x, SQ_Y	$(.5B - .5C), (.5B - .5C)$

Source: E. Ostrom 1994.

Once rule 5 is introduced, branch Y no longer finds rule 3 essential to its interests. Combined with rule 5, rule 3 leaves branch Y with the worst, rather than the best, payoff.

The process of negotiating over rules in a field setting is hardly a determinant process, which proceeds universally through a predetermined series of steps. Although it is useful to model the process as a succession of choices between two rules, the effect of each rule depends on the other rules that have already been agreed on or are to be discussed in the future. The overall effect of one rule may change radically depending on the other rules in the set. In most constitutional processes initial agreements to specific rules are tentative. Eventually, the participants must agree to the entire configuration of rules embodied in some form of agreement.

Asymmetric Incentives

Many variables create potential asymmetries between the players in a choice-of-rules game. In the analysis above we addressed the possibility that the amount of labor available per household could vary between the players. Now let us introduce a substantial asymmetry. Instead of a canal that divides into two small branches, let us assume that the canal enters from one side (figure 5). Under this type of system the first five plots receive water before the last five plots. Water is sufficient to provide an ample supply for the head-end farmers but not for the tail-end farmers. Farmers at the head end of a system are able to capture water and may not fully recognize the costs others bear as a result of their actions. In addition, farmers located at the head end of a system receive proportionately less of the benefits produced by maintaining canals in good working order than do farmers located at the tail. These asymmetries are the source of considerable conflict in many irrigation systems and are sometimes substantial enough to make it impossible for farmers to work together.

In a bargaining situation over the rules, farmers at the head end of a system would prefer a set of rules that allows them to take water first and to take as much as they need. Farmers at the tail end of a system would oppose such a rule because it would leave them with much less water. Farmers at the tail end of a system would prefer a set of rules that would let them take water first and take as much as they need. Both rules are used in the field.

To the extent that head-end farmers depend on the resources that tail-end farmers mobilize to keep a main canal in good working order, the initial bargaining advantage of the head-end farmers is reduced. In other words the greater the amount of resources needed to maintain the system, the greater the bargaining power of farmers at the tail end relative to farmers at the head end.

Several physical factors affect the level of resources needed to keep a system operating. Let us assume that the water source serving the system is a perennial spring and that very little work is needed at the headworks to keep the system operating. We can then posit three kinds of systems depending on the length of the main canal:

Figure 5. *Three Irrigation Systems with Increasing Costs of Maintenance*

5a. $B = 100$, $C' = 25$

5b. $B = 100$, $C'' = 50$

5c. $B = 100$, $C''' = 75$

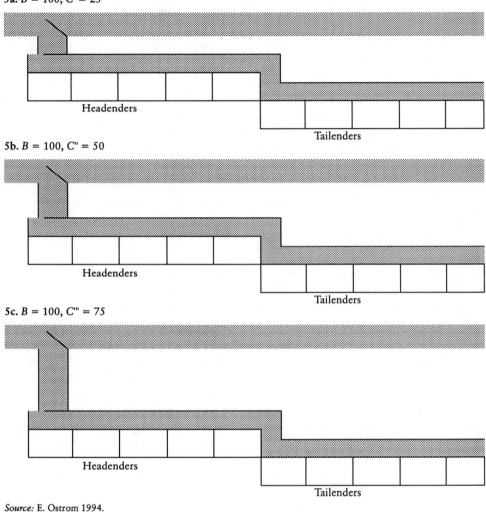

Source: E. Ostrom 1994.

one with no distance between the water source and the headenders, as in figure 5a; one with a short distance between them, as in figure 5b; and one with a long distance between them, as in figure 5c. The costs of maintaining these three systems will be lowest for a 5a-type of system (C'), higher for a 5b-type of system (C''), and highest for a 5c-type of system (C''').

The bargaining advantage of headenders in systems similar to those illustrated in figure 5a is much stronger than in systems such as those illustrated in figure 5b or 5c. To grasp this point, consider the following numerical example. We continue to assume that regardless of the length of the canal, the expected benefit of the water made available is 100 units and that the labor costs of maintaining the systems are 25 units for 5a, 50 units for 5b, and 75 units for 5c. In all three systems, then, the expected annual benefits of the water obtained are greater than the expected annual labor costs.

Let us further assume that two rules were being considered in such a situation:

Rule 6: Head-end farmers are authorized to take as much water as they can put to beneficial use before water is made available to tail-end farmers, and all farmers voluntarily contribute labor to maintain the system (prior-rights rule for headenders).

Rule 7: Half the water is allocated to the head end and half to the tail end, and the labor needed to maintain the system is based on the proportion of water assigned to each set of farmers (equal-split rule).

If rule 6 were agreed on, let us assume the headenders would take 65 units of water per year. All labor would be contributed by the headenders. If rule 7 were agreed on, the headenders would obtain only 50 units of water per year, but they would have to put in only half the labor each year. Both headenders and tailenders would receive zero units of value in the event of a breakdown (figure 6).

In systems in which the cost of labor input is the lowest ($C' = 25$), there are two equilibria: both parties choose rule 6 or both choose rule 7. The headenders would prefer rule 6 and the tailenders would prefer rule 7. The headenders would try to make a credible assertion that they will agree to rule 6 and no other rule and refuse to engage in further bargaining with the tailenders. Although tailenders prefer rule 7, rule 6 does not leave them as disadvantaged as appears to be the case if only the rule's effect on allocating water is examined. Tailenders would not contribute to maintenance of the headworks and would expect an annual return of 40 units (65 units minus 25 units). The tailenders receive only 35 units rather than the 37.5 units ($100/2 - 25/2$) they could receive under an equal split. But since the tailenders do not contribute at all to maintenance, they might even be accused of free riding in such a situation. They could counter such an accusation by pointing to their willingness to work if and only if they obtain an equal share of the water.

The same two pure-strategy equilibria are present in a second situation with labor costs of 50 units. In this case the preferences of the players are reversed. Now the headenders prefer rule 7 whereas the tailenders prefer rule 6, and the bargaining power of the tailenders has improved markedly. The tailenders can credibly assert that the extra water is not worth the labor contribution. Some headenders might end up agreeing to rule 6. Under rule 6 the tailenders gain considerable advantage from their free riding on the work of the headenders, with headenders reaping an annual return of 15 units ($65 - 50$) and tailenders an annual return of 35 units ($35 - 0$)—an example of the "weak" exploiting the "strong" (see Olson 1965).

In systems in which the need for labor inputs is the highest ($C''' = 75$), headenders cannot afford to agree to a rule that allocates prior rights to them. Under rule 6 headenders face a net loss ($65 - 75 = -10$). Consequently, rule 7 is the only equilibrium for a choice-of-rules game involving only rules 6 and 7 in a high-cost environment. To obtain the labor input from the tailenders, the headenders would be

Figure 6. *The Choice of Rules Games for the Irrigation Systems with Increasing Costs of Maintenance*

6a.

		Head end	
		Rule 6	Rule 7
Tail end	Rule 6	35, 40*	0, 0
	Rule 7	0, 0	37.5, 37.5*

6b.

		Head end	
		Rule 6	Rule 7
Tail end	Rule 6	35, 15*	0, 0
	Rule 7	0, 0	25, 25*

6c.

		Head end	
		Rule 6	Rule 7
Tail end	Rule 6	35, −10	0, 0
	Rule 7	0, 0	12.5, 12.5*

* Game equilibria.
Source: E. Ostrom 1994.

willing to guarantee that the tail end receives half the water. Thus the payoff to both parties under the high-cost condition would be 12.5 units.

Why External Assistance Does Not Always Improve Performance

Now the differential impact of permanent headworks and partial lining on agricultural productivity in Nepal can be explained. Constructing permanent headworks dramatically reduces labor contributions (Lam 1994). The headworks may fail to cope with the change in river beds caused by torrential monsoon rains in a mountainous terrain. Farmers near the headworks can reap the primary benefits of such an investment and ignore the consequences for others. Partial lining of canals—sometimes by farmers using local stone and sometimes by contractors as part of aid efforts—benefits mainly farmers located downstream from the lining. Partial lining reduces water loss in the lined portions and also reduces the amount of labor required to keep a system in minimal repair—although not by as much as construction that averts the need to repair diversion works after major rains.[11]

The "equalizer" in many farmer-organized systems is the substantial need for the contributions of resources each year by the tailenders to keep the system well maintained. This need may stem from such physical factors as the yearly reconstruction of the headworks and the clearing and cleaning out of a long canal. In farmer-organized systems in which substantial resources are needed on a regular basis for maintenance, we observe rules that assign water in about the same proportion as resources are contributed (more water allocated to the tail), and higher productivity (Lam 1994; McKean 1992). Sweat equity can generate more equitable outcomes as well as higher levels of outcomes.

The analysis allows us to understand why many effective farmer-organized systems collapse soon after the systems have been modernized using funds provided by donors or central governments. Project evaluations usually consider any reduction in the labor needed to maintain a system as a project benefit. Thus investments in modern engineering works are economically justified because of the presumed increase in agricultural productivity and the reduction in annual maintenance costs. The possibility that greatly reducing the need for resources to maintain a system would substantially alter the bargaining power of headenders relative to tailenders is not usually considered.

Let us assume that an external donor plans to invest in a system with a physical structure and benefit-cost ratio similar to that shown in figure 5c. Before the investment total benefits minus maintenance costs are equal to 25 units. The donor assumes that it is possible to raise benefits to 200 units by teaching farmers new agricultural techniques and by lowering the maintenance cost to 25 units through a one-time investment whose annualized value to the donor is also 25 units. Thus the benefit-cost analysis leads the donor to make the investment because an annual benefit of 150 units (200 − 25 − 25) is substantially above the 25 net annual units achieved prior to the planned improvement. The payoff matrix implicit in the benefit-cost analysis is illustrated in figure 7a, where the only outcome projected is an equal distribution of a higher agricultural yield. The donor assumes that farmers will somehow work out a scheme to share benefits as shown.

What frequently happens in practice, however, is illustrated in figure 7b. Instead of increasing benefits to 200 units, the system stays at 100 units, with the head-end farmers earning 90 units and making no investment in maintenance. Neither the headenders nor the tailenders are required to pay the annualized cost of the donor's investment. The tail-end farmers do not invest in maintenance and receive only 10 units of water. Rule 6 is not agreed on but is rather imposed on the tailenders by the headenders, who simply take the water. Might becomes right.

In such systems the headenders can afford to forfeit the contribution to maintenance of the tailenders because the concrete structures will operate for a few years
without any maintenance. Of course, eventually the productivity of the system will
fall. If the farmers were expected to pay back the costs of the investment in physical capital (or to pay taxes to keep the system well maintained), tail-end farmers
would again find themselves in a better bargaining position relative to headenders.
A very disruptive aspect of many external assistance projects is that they appear to
farmers as if they are free. Without any need for resources from tailenders, headenders can ignore the tailenders' interests and take a larger share of the benefits.

This type of external "help" substantially reduces the short-term need to mobilize
labor (or other resources) to maintain a system each year. The calculations in the
design plans, however, do not always correspond to actual maintenance needs.
Without a realistic requirement to pay back capital investments, host government officials and the more influential farmers are motivated primarily to invest in rent-seeking activities and may overestimate previous annual costs in order to obtain external
aid (Repetto 1986). Such help can also change the pattern of relationships among
farmers within a system, reducing the recognition of mutual dependencies and patterns of reciprocity between headenders and tailenders that have long sustained the
system. By denying the tailenders an opportunity to invest in the improvement of
infrastructure, external assistance may also deny those who are most disadvantaged an
opportunity to assert and defend rights to the flow of benefits (Ambler 1990, 1991).

Figure 7. *Planned and Actual Results of Some Types of Donor Assistance*

7a.

		Head end	
		Rule 6	Rule 7
Tail end	Rule 6	[not in plan]	[not in plan]
	Rule 7	[not in plan]	75, 75

7b.

		Head end	
		Rule 6	Rule 7
Tail end	Rule 6	10, 90	[not feasible]
	Rule 7	[not feasible]	[not feasible]

Source: E. Ostrom 1994.

A Successful Intervention

An example of a successful effort to intervene in and improve the operation of farmer-governed systems is a project funded by the Ford Foundation and designed by the Water and Energy Commission/Secretariat, Nepal, and the International Irrigation Management Institute in Nepal (WECS/IIMI). For this project the capabilities and limits of 119 farmer-organized irrigation systems in the Sindhu Palchok District of Nepal were first assessed. Nineteen irrigation systems that had potential for expanding the irrigated area and were at least minimally organized were identified. To obtain external aid under this program, farmers had to agree on and implement several conditions:[12]

- Forming a water-users organization (if none existed), identifying current and future water users, and devising a water allocation plan acceptable to all identified water users.
- Preparing an initial plan for improvements to and future operations and management of the system.
- Determining the needs for required but unpaid labor and setting the rates for paid labor (within guidelines set by the project). Money saved by lower labor rates could be used to invest in additional improvements.
- Appointing a management committee to assist the field engineer in conducting the site investigation, design work, and day-to-day implementation activities.
- Keeping records of their expenditures and of decisions made at meetings, and making the records available to anyone who asked to see them.

The project hired engineers who would listen to farmers and stressed the design of improvements that the farmers could operate and maintain themselves and that would make a substantial difference in the operation of the system. Farmers were shown the design, suggested improvements, and approved the final designs. Considerable effort was devoted to learning from the farmers how these systems operated and to blending the knowledge of the design engineers with that of the farmers. Once agreement was reached on how each improvement would be designed, the farmers ranked the improvements as first-, second-, and third-level priorities according to their perceived importance. Farmers were told that funds definitely would be provided for the first-priority improvement. If the farmers contributed sufficient labor during the construction phase, the project would try to make the funds go as far as possible to cover second- and third-priority improvements. (In fact, many of the systems were able to construct all of the desired improvements because of the resources that the farmers contributed.) Most of the improvements chosen by farmers related to realignment of canals, lining of canals in some portions, and construction of aqueducts to carry water across ravines.

Among the more ingenious aspects of this project was the farmer-to-farmer training program in institutional design. Farmer representatives were taken from the irrigation systems in the project area to irrigation systems in other districts with similar terrain where farmers had designed particularly effective governance structures. The farmer representatives attended an annual meeting of one of these systems and participated in a special session during which they could ask local farmers about the patterns of association that had evolved on the successful systems. They also toured the entire length of the system in order to understand why the farmers there had used different kinds of weirs and how the weirs were related to water rights. The program enabled farmers who had developed successful institutions in one setting to impart that knowledge to farmers from similar settings.

Agricultural productivity increased substantially in most of the systems, and project costs were modest (WECS/IIMI 1990). In a separate evaluation of this project Lam and Shivakoti (1992) showed that not only was there a significant increase in agricultural yield, but that the project generally enhanced the productive capabilities of the systems as well through a shift into crops that returned more profit to the farmer.

A second set of results shows the difference in the institutions and incentives created by the farmers themselves. A survey was conducted one year later to see what governance and management differences could be observed (Yoder 1991). In all nineteen systems farmers indicated a stronger sense of ownership. Leadership had changed in eleven of the systems but was clearly defined in all nineteen systems at the time of the survey. Nine of the systems reported changes in the rules they had developed for operations and maintenance. Formal meetings with recorded minutes have continued after project completion, and in all systems cooperative efforts to maintain the canal during the monsoon have increased (Yoder 1991). The variety of rules adopted, ways of handling maintenance responsibilities, and ways of monitoring conformance indicate that farmers have not just copied something that an official has shown them but have struggled to develop their own workable systems. The farmers have also had to learn how to enforce their own rules.

Policy Significance

The analysis so far has demonstrated that in one sector of one country the incentives of government officials—as affected by the incentives within and policies of donor agencies—do not generate infrastructure investment processes with a high probability of achieving high, equitable, long-term, positive rates of return. The empirical results generated by these incentive systems lead to lower performance in the systems that have had the highest level of capital investment. The game-theoretic analysis presented shows that farmers who can undertake institutional choice—and not simply strategic choice within a given set of rules—may be able to craft a set of rules that generates long-term, positive rates of return. Success has been documented in the case described earlier, where external aid was provided to self-organized systems that gave farmers in Nepal considerable decisionmaking authority over project design and implementation. Farmers also benefited from the knowledge of other farmers who had developed highly productive and efficient systems in an area with similar terrain.

Are there any lessons that can be derived from these findings that go beyond an analysis of investment in irrigation infrastructure in a single country? Obviously, empirical research conducted in one country cannot be generalized to others. The incentive systems of government agencies, for example, vary substantially, even within Asia. The empirical findings from a statistical analysis of more than one hundred irrigation systems and from detailed case studies in Nepal are, however, consistent with reports on the effects of centralized infrastructure investment in irrigation systems and watershed management in other parts of Asia.[13] When very large sums of loan and grant funds are channeled through processes that enhance the power (and wealth) of politicians who successfully engage in rent-seeking activities, project plans cannot be expected to accurately reflect conditions on the ground. When engineers assigned to operations and maintenance hold low-status positions, are underpaid, and are not dependent on the farmers of a system for budgetary support or career advancement, large government-managed systems cannot be expected to perform very well. The results in Taiwan (China) and the Republic of Korea are quite different from those in Nepal and elsewhere largely because the incentive systems of operations and maintenance divisions reward engineers for drawing on local knowledge and working directly with farmers (Levine 1980; Wade 1982; Lam 1996).

The incentives facing farmers, villagers, and officials are more important in determining performance than is the engineering of physical systems. When farmers select—and reward—their own officials to govern and manage an irrigation system that the farmers own and operate, the incentives faced by the officials are closely aligned to the incentives of farmers on the system, while the performance of the system is linked to that of the officials. On many centralized, national government systems, no such linkage exists. Where the revenue received by an irrigation agency is not linked to taxes levied on the value of crop yield or the amount of water taken, the agency's budget is not even loosely linked to system performance. Where fees are imposed in name only, and do not represent an important source of revenue to the units operating and maintaining systems, and where hiring, retention, and promotion of employees are in no way connected with the performance of a public facility, nothing offsets the dependency of the community on insulated officials.

The evidence that farmers can overcome local collective-action problems when they have sufficient autonomy (either because of the formal legal system or because they live in such remote areas that no one cares what they do) is also consistent with a substantial literature on the capacity of resource users to govern inshore fisheries, mountain commons, grazing areas, and forest resources in all parts of the world.[14] Creating local organizations and selecting people from the community as leaders who are rewarded for their performance can help surmount the substantial difficulties of sustaining long-term collective action.

Instead of presuming that local users face an impossible collective-action problem, policy planners should assume that it is possible, albeit difficult, for collective-action problems to be overcome. The greater the potential joint benefit and the more supportive the political system, the higher is the probability that collective action will be undertaken. The effect of asymmetries among participants depends on the particular types of asymmetries that exist (Keohane and Ostrom 1995).

Donor agencies need to direct their efforts toward enhancing the productive capabilities of a larger proportion of the local community rather than simply trying to replace primitive infrastructures with modern, technically sophisticated ones. Providing substantial funds that serve only to bolster political careers and that build little at the ground level represents a poor investment from a donor's perspective. It makes more sense to invest modest levels of donor funds in local projects in which the recipients are willing to invest some of their own resources than it does to invest in projects in which the recipients are only patrons of a client and are looking for handouts in return for political support. In settings in which users are willing to invest some of their own resources, an infusion of external monetary capital and the construction of physical capital to complement the institutional capital on the ground may generate much higher returns. If the level of external funding becomes very large without being strongly tied to a responsibility for repayment over time, local efforts at participation may be directed more at rent seeking than at productive investment activities.

Entrepreneurship is not limited to the private sector. When there is an enabling environment that enhances their capacities to organize, mobilize resources, and invest in public facilities, local public entrepreneurs can develop a wide variety of efficiency-enhancing solutions to local collective-action problems. Providing fair and low-cost conflict resolution mechanisms, methods of achieving public accountability, and good information about the conditions of natural and constructed resource systems may be a more important task for national governments than attempting to plan and build local infrastructure throughout a country. In some cases donors can encourage national governments to reduce legislated restrictions on the abilities of individuals to form local associations, assess themselves to establish a common treasury, and undertake a wide variety of joint local projects of benefit to the association. Encouraging such groups to form associations of associations enhances their abilities to learn from each other, exchange reliable information about what works and what does not work, and monitor the accountability of their own members.

Investing in the third strategy recommended in *World Development Report 1994*—giving *"users and other stakeholders a strong voice and real responsibility"* (World Bank 1994, p. 2, italicized in original)—may enhance the economic benefits of investments in small and medium-size irrigation infrastructure projects in the future. Investing in short-term projects to enhance citizen participation has frequently failed in the past, however (Sengupta 1991; Uphoff 1986). A "voice and real responsibility" for stakeholders does not come simply from creating short-term projects that involve outsiders "organizing the farmers" in sweeping tours of the countryside. Participating in solving collective-action problems is a costly and time-consuming process. Developing methods that enhance the capabilities of those who take on local entrepreneurial responsibilities is an investment that needs to be carried out over a long time. Changing the incentives of national government officials so that their work enhances rather than replaces the efforts of local officials and citizens is a challenging and difficult task. Reducing the level of corruption involved in externally funded projects is an essential but daunting task (Klitgaard 1988, 1991).

Our analytical models need to illuminate the incentives of participants whose decisions are affected by various sets of factors simultaneously (Hayami and Otsuka 1993). We have misunderstood the rich network of mutual duties and benefits that common-property institutions have generated in much of Africa. Recommendations to destroy these institutions have been based on the assumption that the capacity to transfer ownership is the most important right in the bundle of rights potentially involved in the ownership of any resource (Schlager and Ostrom 1992). Recent studies of the evolution of indigenous land-right systems in Africa have challenged our analytical assumptions substantially (Migot-Adholla and others 1991; Berry 1993). Investments in new institutions, as well as new infrastructure, need to be based on knowledge that takes into account the multiple incentives that are generated by institutions as they interact with social norms and the physical world in any particular setting.

Notes

1. Robert Yoder (1994) warns those interested in helping farmers that they must probe deeply and in nonthreatening ways to get adequate information on the rules used to allocate water and maintenance duties. "Intimidated by the higher status of officials, they may fail to communicate the details of the rules and procedures they use to operate and maintain their system" (p. 39).

2. In addition to Hilton's work, the information about the Chiregad system used in this analysis comes from Shrestha (1988) and from a visit to the site during the spring of 1989 by the author.

3. A source of faulty irrigation designs is often the unwillingness of engineers in Nepal and in many other countries to talk with the farmers about the physical characteristics of a system the farmers know well (P. Pradhan 1989a,b; Uphoff 1986). Educated engineers presume that uneducated farmers do not know enough about hydrology and engineering to warrant consulting them in this process. Consequently, they do not learn from farmers many of the local details about soil conditions, water velocity, and shifting watercourses that are important to make improved engineering works operate better than the "primitive" systems they replace. Nor have irrigation engineers paid much attention to the distribution of water rights that existed prior to the construction of new systems (Coward 1980).

4. This and following subsections draw extensively on E. Ostrom (1994).

5. The assumptions about common knowledge are strong assumptions. If participants had asymmetric and incomplete information, the results described in this section would frequently be different.

6. It is almost impossible for farmers to follow allocation rules in all instances. Given the stakes involved, the temptation to shirk or steal can be very great in some circumstances. Even in systems that have survived for centuries, evidence shows that some shirking and stealing take place (Weissing and Ostrom 1991, 1993).

7. Even though it is possible to discover the structure of these situations and classify them according to the rules that may be adopted as is done in the next section, most of these games have multiple equilibria. Which of the many equilibria are selected depends on many factors—including the shared beliefs and conceptions held by the participants—that are localized in time and space.

8. Alternatively, they could be expressed in labor units, as in the more general game-theoretic analysis presented in E. Ostrom and Gardner (1993). In either case, it is the basic production function between labor input and crop yields that enables one to use a single metric when denoting both benefits and costs. In a fully monetized economy one would simply denote benefits and costs as a monetary unit.

9. Only pure-strategy equilibria are considered. A mixed strategy does not make sense when the alternative is a rule. One can model rule-breaking behavior using mixed strategies (Weissing and Ostrom 1991, 1993).

10. This is a proportional distribution rule and would be considered an example of a "fair rule" according to many criteria, such as the one proposed by Selten (1978).

11. Only 2 days per household per year are devoted to maintenance on systems with permanent headworks, whereas about 5.33 days per household per year are devoted on systems with partial lining (but

without permanent headworks) and 8.5 days per household per year on systems without lining or permanent headworks (Lam 1994, p. 222; p = .02).

12. My thanks to Robert Yoder for reviewing an earlier draft of these conditions and supplying me with a carefully revised list of conditions.

13. Bottrall (1981); Bromley (1982); Carruthers (1981); Chambers (1988); Corey (1986); Coward (1979); Easter (1985); Korten and Siy (1988); Plusquellec and Wickham (1985); Reidinger (1974); Sampath and Young (1990); Singh (1983); Wade (1985, 1988); White and Runge (1994); and Wunsch and Olowu (1995). Meinzen-Dick and others (1994) summarize an extensive body of literature from Asia, Africa, and the Americas that is highly consistent with the findings in this article.

14. Berkes (1989); Blomquist (1992); Bromley (1991); Bromley and others (1992); Dasgupta and Mäler (1992); Eggertsson (1990); Feeny and others (1990); Fortmann and Bruce (1988); Libecap (1989); Martin (1989/1992); McCay and Acheson (1987); Netting (1993); E. Ostrom, Gardner, and Walker (1994); V. Ostrom, Feeny, and Picht (1993); Pinkerton (1989); Sengupta (1991); Tang (1992); Thomson (1992); and Wade (1988).

References

Ambler, John. 1990. "The Influence of Farmer Water Rights on the Design of Water-Proportioning Devices." In Robert Yoder and Juanita Thurston, eds., *Design Issues in Farmer-Managed Irrigation Systems.* Colombo, Sri Lanka: International Irrigation Management Institute.

———. 1991. "Bounding the System: Precursors to Measuring Performance in Networks of Farmer-Managed Irrigation Systems." Paper presented at the International Workshop on Performance Measurement of Farmer Managed Irrigation Systems, November 12–15, Mendoza, Argentina.

Aumann, Robert J. 1976. "Agreeing to Disagree." *Annals of Statistics* 4(6): 1236–39.

Benjamin, Paul. 1989. "Local Organization for Development in Nepal." Ph.D. dissertation, University of North Carolina, Chapel Hill.

Benjamin, Paul, Wai Fung Lam, Elinor Ostrom, and Ganesh Shivakoti. 1994. *Institutions, Incentives, and Irrigation in Nepal.* Burlington, Vt.: Associates in Rural Development.

Berkes, Fikret, ed. 1989. *Common Property Resources: Ecology and Community-Based Sustainable Development.* London: Belhaven Press.

Berry, Sara. 1993. *No Condition Is Permanent: The Social Dynamics of Agrarian Change in Sub-Saharan Africa.* Madison: University of Wisconsin Press.

Blomquist, William. 1992. *Dividing the Waters: Governing Groundwater in Southern California.* San Francisco, Calif.: ICS Press.

Bottrall, Anthony. 1981. *Comparative Study of the Management and Organization of Irrigation Projects.* Staff Working Paper 458. Washington, D.C.: World Bank.

Bromley, Daniel W. 1982. *Improving Irrigated Agriculture: Institutional Reform and the Small Farmer.* Staff Working Paper 531. Washington, D.C.: World Bank.

———. 1991. *Environment and Economy: Property Rights and Public Policy.* Oxford: Basil Blackwell.

Bromley, Daniel W., David Feeny, Margaret McKean, Pauline Peters, Jere Gilles, Ronald Oakerson, C. Ford Runge, and James Thomson, eds. 1992. *Making the Commons Work: Theory, Practice, and Policy.* San Francisco, Calif.: ICS Press.

Carruthers, Ian. 1981. "Neglect of O&M in Irrigation, the Need for New Sources and Forms of Support." *Water Supply and Management* 5: 53–65.

Chambers, Robert. 1988. *Managing Canal Irrigation: Practical Analysis from South Asia.* New York: Cambridge University Press.

Corey, A. T. 1986. "Control of Water Within Farm Turnouts in Sri Lanka." In *Proceedings of a Workshop on Water Management in Sri Lanka.* Documentation Series 10. Colombo, Sri Lanka: Agrarian Research and Training Institute.

Coward, E. Walter, Jr. 1979. "Principles of Social Organization in an Indigenous Irrigation System." *Human Organization* 38(1): 28–36.

———, ed. 1980. *Irrigation and Agricultural Development in Asia: Perspectives from the Social Sciences.* Ithaca, N.Y.: Cornell University Press.

Curtis, Donald. 1991. *Beyond Government: Organizations for Common Benefit.* London: Macmillan.

Dasgupta, Partha, and Karl Göran Mäler. 1992. *The Economics of Transnational Commons.* Oxford: Clarendon Press.

Easter, K. William. 1985. *Recurring Costs of Irrigation in Asia: Operation and Maintenance.* Ithaca, N.Y.: Cornell University Water Management Synthesis Project.

Eggertsson, Thráinn. 1990. *Economic Behavior and Institutions.* New York: Cambridge University Press.

Elster, Jon. 1979. *Ulysses and the Sirens: Studies in Rationality and Irrationality.* Cambridge: Cambridge University Press.

Feeny, David, Fikret Berkes, Bonnie J. McCay, and James M. Acheson. 1990. "The Tragedy of the Commons: Twenty-Two Years Later." *Human Ecology* 18(1): 1–19.

Fortmann, Louise, and John W. Bruce, eds. 1988. *Whose Trees? Proprietary Dimensions of Forestry.* Boulder, Colo.: Westview Press.

Hayami, Yujiro, and Keijero Otsuka. 1993. *The Economics of Contract Choice: An Agrarian Perspective.* Oxford: Clarendon Press.

Hilton, Rita. 1990. *Cost Recovery and Local Resource Mobilization: An Examination of Incentives in Irrigation Systems in Nepal.* Burlington, Vt.: Associates in Rural Development.

———. 1992. "Institutional Incentives for Resource Mobilization: An Analysis of Irrigation Schemes in Nepal." *Journal of Theoretical Politics* 4(3): 283–308.

IMSSG (Irrigation Management Systems Study Group). 1993. "Implementation of Process Documentation in ERIP." IMSSG, Institute of Agriculture and Animal Science, Rampur, Nepal.

Keohane, Robert O., and Elinor Ostrom, eds. 1995. *Local Commons and Global Interdependence: Heterogeneity and Cooperation in Two Domains.* London: Sage.

Klitgaard, Robert. 1988. *Controlling Corruption.* Berkeley: University of California Press.

———. 1991. *Adjusting to Reality: Beyond "State versus Market" in Economic Development.* San Francisco, Calif.: ICS Press.

Knight, Jack. 1992. *Institutions and Social Conflict.* New York: Cambridge University Press.

Korten, Frances F., and Robert Y. Siy, Jr. 1988. *Transforming a Bureaucracy: The Experience of the Philippine National Irrigation Administration.* West Hartford, Conn.: Kumarian Press.

Laitos, Robby, and others. 1986. "Rapid Appraisal of Nepal Irrigation Systems." Water Management Synthesis Report 43. Fort Collins: Colorado State University.

Lam, Wai Fung. 1994. "Institutions, Engineering Infrastructure, and Performance in the Governance and Management of Irrigation Systems: The Case of Nepal." Ph.D. dissertation, Indiana University.

———. 1996. "Institutional Design of Public Agencies and Coproduction: A Study of Irrigation Associations in Taiwan." *World Development* forthcoming (June).

Lam, Wai Fung, and Ganesh Shivakoti. 1992. "A Before and After Analysis of the Effect of Farmer-to-Farmer Training as an Intervention Strategy." Technical Report. Indiana University, Workshop in Political Theory and Policy Analysis, Bloomington.

Levine, Gilbert. 1980."The Relationship of Design, Operation, and Management." In E. Walter Coward, Jr., ed., *Irrigation and Agricultural Development in Asia: Perspectives from the Social Sciences.* Ithaca, N.Y.: Cornell University Press.

Libecap, Gary D. 1989. *Contracting for Property Rights.* New York: Cambridge University Press.

Martin, Fenton. 1989/1992. *Common-Pool Resources and Collective Action: A Bibliography,* vols. 1 and 2. Bloomington: Indiana University, Workshop in Political Theory and Policy Analysis.

McCay, Bonnie J., and James M. Acheson. 1987. *The Question of the Commons: The Culture and Ecology of Communal Resources.* Tucson: University of Arizona Press.

McKean, Margaret A. 1992. "Success on the Commons: A Comparative Examination of Institutions for Common Property Resource Management." *Journal of Theoretical Politics* 4(3): 247–82.

Meinzen-Dick, Ruth, and others. 1994. "Sustainable Water User Associations: Lessons from a Literature Review." World Bank, Agriculture and Natural Resources Department, Washington, D.C.

Migot-Adholla, Shem, and others. 1991. "Indigenous Land Rights Systems in Sub-Saharan Africa: A Constraint on Productivity?" *World Bank Economic Review* 5(1): 155–75.

Nelson, John M. 1968. *Aid Influence and Foreign Policy.* New York: Macmillan.

Netting, Robert. 1993. *Smallholders, Householders: Farm Families and the Ecology of Intensive, Sustainable Agriculture.* Stanford, Calif.: Stanford University Press.

Olson, Mancur. 1965. *The Logic of Collective Action: Public Goods and the Theory of Groups.* Cambridge, Mass.: Harvard University Press.

Ostrom, Elinor. 1990. *Governing the Commons: The Evolution of Institutions for Collective Action.* New York: Cambridge University Press.

———. 1992. *Crafting Institutions for Self-Governing Irrigation Systems.* San Francisco: ICS Press.

———. 1994. "Constituting Social Capital and Collective Action." *Journal of Theoretical Politics* 6(4): 527–62.

Ostrom, Elinor, and Roy Gardner. 1993. "Coping with Asymmetries in the Commons: Self-Governing Irrigation Systems Can Work." *Journal of Economic Perspectives* 7(4) (Fall): 93–112.

Ostrom, Elinor, Roy Gardner, and James Walker. 1994. *Rules, Games, and Common-Pool Resources.* Ann Arbor: University of Michigan Press.

Ostrom, Elinor, Larry Schroeder, and Susan Wynne. 1993. *Institutional Incentives and Sustainable Development: Infrastructure Policies in Perspective.* Boulder, Colo.: Westview Press.

Ostrom, Vincent, David Feeny, and Hartmut Picht, eds. 1993. *Rethinking Institutional Analysis and Development: Issues, Alternatives, and Choices.* 2d ed. San Francisco, Calif.: ICS Press.

Pinkerton, Evelyn, ed. 1989. *Co-operative Management of Local Fisheries: New Directions for Improved Management and Community Development.* Vancouver: University of British Columbia Press.

Plusquellec, Herve L., and Thomas H. Wickham. 1985. *Irrigation Design and Management: Experience in Thailand and Its General Applicability.* Technical Paper 40. Washington, D.C.: World Bank.

Pradhan, Prachanda. 1989a. *Increasing Agricultural Production in Nepal: Role of Low-Cost Irrigation Development Through Farmer Participation.* Kathmandu, Nepal: International Irrigation Management Institute.

———. 1989b. *Patterns of Irrigation Organization in Nepal: A Comparative Study of 21 Farmer-Managed Irrigation Systems.* Colombo, Sri Lanka: International Irrigation Management Institute.

Pradhan, Ujjwal, Alfredo Valera, and K. C. Durga. 1993. "Towards Participatory Management: The Case of an Irrigation System in the Plains of Nepal." In *Advancements in IIMI's Research 1992: A Selection of Papers Presented at the Internal Program Review.* Colombo, Sri Lanka: International Irrigation Management Institute.

Reidinger, Richard B. 1974. "Institutional Rationing of Canal Water in Northern India: Conflict between Traditional Patterns and Modern Needs." *Economic Development and Cultural Change* 23(1) : 79–104.

Repetto, Robert. 1986. "Skimming the Water: Rent-Seeking and the Performance of Public Irrigation Systems." Research Report 41. World Resources Institute, Washington, D.C.

Sampath, Rajan K., and Robert A. Young. 1990. "Introduction: Social, Economic, and Institutional Aspects of Irrigation Management." In Rajan K. Sampath and Robert A. Young, eds., *Social, Economic, and Institutional Issues in Third World Irrigation Management.* Boulder, Colo.: Westview Press.

Schelling, Thomas C. 1960. *The Strategy of Conflict.* Oxford: Oxford University Press.

Schlager, Edella, and Elinor Ostrom. 1992. "Property-Rights Regimes and Natural Resources: A Conceptual Analysis." *Land Economics* 68(3): 249–62.

Selten, Reinhard. 1978. "The Equity Principle in Economic Behavior." In H. W. Gottinger and W. Leinfellner, eds., *Decision Theory and Social Ethics.* Dordrecht, Netherlands: D. Reidel.

Sengupta, Nirmal. 1991. *Managing Common Property: Irrigation in India and the Philippines.* New Delhi: Sage.

Shrestha, S. P. 1988. "Helping a Farmers Organization: An Experience with Chiregad Irrigation Project." Kathmandu, Nepal: International Irrigation Management Institute.

Shukla, A. K., and others. 1993. *Irrigation Resource Inventory of East Chitwan.* Rampur, Nepal: Irrigation Management Systems Study Group, Institute of Agriculture and Animal Science.

Singh, K. K. 1983. "Farmers Organization and Warabandi in the Sriramasagar (Pochampad) Project." In K.K. Singh, ed., *Utilization of Canal Waters: A Multidisciplinary Perspective on Irrigation.* New Delhi: Central Board for Irrigation and Power.

Tang, Shui Yan. 1992. *Institutions and Collective Action: Self-Governance in Irrigation.* San Francisco, Calif.: ICS Press.

Tendler, Judith. 1975. *Inside Foreign Aid.* Baltimore, Md.: Johns Hopkins University Press.

Thomson, James T. 1992. *A Framework for Analyzing Institutional Incentives in Community Forestry.* Rome: United Nations Food and Agricultural Organization.

Uphoff, Norman T. 1986. *Improving International Irrigation Management with Farmer Participation: Getting the Process Right.* Boulder, Colo.: Westview Press.

Wade, Robert. 1982. *Irrigation and Agricultural Politics in South Korea.* Boulder, Colo.: Westview Press.

———. 1985. "The Market for Public Office: Why the Indian State is Not Better at Development." *World Development* 13(4): 467–97.

———. 1988. *Village Republics: Economic Conditions for Collective Action in South India.* New York: Cambridge University Press.

WECS/IIMI (Water and Energy Commission/Secretariat, Nepal, and International Irrigation Management Institute, Nepal). 1990. *Assistance to Farmer-Managed Irrigation Systems.* Colombo, Sri Lanka: IIMI.

Weissing, Franz J., and Elinor Ostrom. 1991. "Irrigation Institutions and the Games Irrigators Play: Rule Enforcement without Guards." In Reinhard Selten, ed., *Game Equilibrium Models II: Methods, Morals, and Markets.* Berlin: Springer-Verlag.

———. 1993. "Irrigation Institutions and the Games Irrigators Play: Rule Enforcement on Government- and Farmer-Managed Systems." In Fritz W. Scharpf, ed., *Games in Hierarchies and Networks: Analytical and Empirical Approaches to the Study of Governance Institutions.* Boulder, Colo.: Westview Press.

White, T. Anderson, and C. Ford Runge. 1994. "Common Property and Collective Action: Lessons from Cooperative Watershed Management in Haiti." *Economic Development and Cultural Change* 43(1): 1–43.

World Bank. 1994. *World Development Report 1994: Infrastructure for Development.* New York: Oxford University Press.

Wunsch, James S., and Dele Olowu, eds. 1995. *The Failure of the Centralized State: Institutions and Self-Governance in Africa,* 2d ed. San Francisco, Calif.: ICS Press.

Yoder, Robert D. 1991. "Peer Training as a Way to Motivate Institutional Change in Farmer-Managed Irrigation Systems." In *Proceedings of the Workshop on Democracy and Governance.* Burlington, Vt.: Associates in Rural Development.

———. 1994. *Locally Managed Irrigation Systems.* Colombo, Sri Lanka: International Irrigation Management Institute.

Yudelman, Montague. 1985. "The World Bank and Agricultural Development—An Insider's View." WRI Paper 1. World Resources Institute, Washington, D.C.

———. 1989. "Sustainable and Equitable Development in Irrigated Environments." In H. Jeffrey Leonard, ed., *Environment and the Poor: Development Strategies for a Common Agenda.* Oxford: Transaction Books.

Comment on "Incentives, Rules of the Game, and Development," by Elinor Ostrom

Robert Klitgaard

Let us begin by considering a remarkable fact, or tendency: the World Bank, and many others involved in international aid, confess that most efforts at institutional development have not succeeded.[1] Any admission of failure should make us prick up our ears. Immediately we wonder about the complicated and contestable terms "institution" and "institutional development." We may wonder about the evidence, given difficulties of measurement and many intervening variables. We may mischievously ask why donors might now find it in their interest to confess to so many institutional disappointments in their client countries.[2] (Or for that matter, why some practitioners and scholars focus on "institutions" and others find the concept an intellectual cop-out.)

But let us on this occasion accept the stylized fact purveyed in recent reports that aid for institutional development has tended to disappoint. *Why* all the failures? Elinor Ostrom's work, here and elsewhere (especially Ostrom, Schroeder, and Wynne 1993), correctly emphasizes that the disappointments can be partially understood as a failure (not just by donors) to address incentive and information problems in the institutions involved with aid efforts. This failure can itself be "explained" as a rational if lamentable response by government officials and aid providers to the incentives and information they possess. "Solutions" should therefore be sought in better incentives and information in both the countries the World Bank assists and within the World Bank itself. This in turn may require refashioning the donor–recipient relationship.

Sick Institutions

Development strategies are shifting from policy reform to institutional reform. As we learn that economic policy reforms are not enough for economic success, that multiparty democracy is not enough for political success, that better laws are not enough for better justice, we focus on the institutions through which economic, political, and legal activities are carried out and mediated.

Robert Klitgaard is professor of economics at the University of Natal in Durban, South Africa.

Annual World Bank Conference on Development Economics 1995

If the past fifteen years were notable for macroeconomic and macropolitical reforms, I believe that the next fifteen years will be the era of *institutional adjustment:*

- In the private sector, not just the declaration of "competitive markets," but the improvement of market institutions, especially with respect to the poor.
- In public administration, not just (or even) less government and fewer employees, but systems of information and incentives that encourage productivity, decentralization, and participation and discourage rent seeking and abuse.
- In democratic policies, not just multiparty elections, but legislative reform and strengthening, limits on campaign financing, and improvements in local governments.
- In legal systems, not just better laws and constitutions, but systematic initiatives to improve the honesty and capacity of police, prosecutors, and judges.

These topics are obviously sensitive and context specific, and there is less agreement internationally about the nature of the reforms to be pursued than there is on, say, the move to multiparty democracy. But the dynamics of reform in this area will not, I believe, require that all countries agree to the same agenda—or even that all participate. The problem will be less one of persuading sovereign governments to "do something" about institutional development than of advising them on how to do it. The new wave of democratically elected governments in the developing world is recognizing that neither free markets nor multiparty democracies will succeed if the institutions of the private and public sectors are riddled with institutional failure. And as a few countries make progress, others will follow.

But what exactly are these "institutional failures" to which "institutional development" is the purported answer? Let us focus on public sector institutions.[3] We may usefully distinguish *inefficient institutions,* which do not fulfill their purported aims of service delivery, fair judgment, and efficient allocation, from *sick institutions,* a phenomenon prevalent in though not confined to Africa, the formerly communist countries, and some parts of Asia and Latin America and the Caribbean. It is provocative to speak of sick institutions—and indelicate to indicate their geographical concentration. I make this distinction not to be sensational but simply because I find it amazing that more people outside the countries affected—more people, for example, at the World Bank—do not seem to put sick institutions front and center.

Sick institutions are those in which a substantial number of employees do not come to work or do other work (or nothing at all) while there; where corruption and favoritism are not isolated instances but the corrosive norm; where pay scales in real terms have collapsed so that low- and middle-level employees cannot feed and house their families on their official pay; and where employees therefore seek other forms of compensation, including travel, study allowances, nonwage benefits (which have exploded in many countries), as well as illicit payments for doing (or not doing) their public duties.

Sick institutions do not function. (I leave aside here a second category of sick institutions, those that function effectively but serve ends that are sick—for example, an apartheid state, a military apparatus, a secret police, and perhaps in the view of some readers some transnational economic institutions.) Public service becomes a source of public embarrassment or indignation. In many countries both multiparty democracy and free market reforms, such as they are, are threatened not just by inefficiency in government, but also by institutions that have grown sick.

Why are there sick institutions? Incentives in many countries have collapsed. Real wages in the public sector have fallen 30–40 percent in Latin America since the early 1980s and even more in Africa and the formerly communist countries (Naim 1995; Nelson and others 1994; Klitgaard 1989). Moreover, good performance goes relatively unrewarded and bad performance relatively unpunished. Information and evaluation are scarce and expensive, which inhibits internal and external controls. Information-processing skills are weak at both the individual and institutional levels as a result, for example, of low levels of education and the scarcity of computers, as well as the lack of specialists such as accountants, auditors, statisticians, and so forth. Political monopolies dominate, sometimes coupled with violence and intimidation. Countervailing institutions are weak, in part because of information and incentive problems but also because of hostile actions by the state. Some governments face soft budget constraints, meaning that foreign aid will fill a good part of any deficiency resulting from inefficiency or corruption.

Note that sick institutions can be analyzed in economic terms, without immediately invoking other factors that may be important, such as political leadership or social and cultural features. Economics also provides insights into possible solutions, which must be tailored to local political, social, and cultural realities.

Institutional Adjustment

Yet economics has not been the metaphor through which international aid has usually conceptualized "institutional development." I believe that in the decade ahead we will rethink institutional development in economic terms, based on information, incentives, and organizational structure. The principles of institutional adjustment will include:

- Enhancing information and evaluation, and putting these functions in the hands of clients, legislators, and those with official oversight (regulators, auditors, judges, and so forth).
- Improving incentives and linking them to information about the attainment of agreed-on objectives.
- Promoting competition and countervailing forces—including the institutions of civil society, the media, the legislature, the courts, and political parties—and procedures that allow these different interests and voices to make a difference in policy and management.
- Attacking systematic corruption (Klitgaard 1988, forthcoming).
- Hardening the budget constraint. One possibility is to reduce foreign assistance. Another is to make aid contingent on progress in institutional adjustment.

This approach contrasts with previous approaches to institutional development based on *more:* more training, more resources, more buildings, more coordination, more central planning, more technical assistance. The argument is that *without institutional adjustment,* "more" will not heal sick institutions.

There are interesting similarities and differences between institutional adjustment and structural adjustment. In the case of structural adjustment, we worried about "getting prices right" for private sector agents; here we worry about "getting incentives right" for public sector agents. There we tried to create open and transparent markets; here we try to create open and transparent governments. There we worried about property rights and privatization in order to decentralize economic decisionmaking efficiently; here we worry about empowering stakeholders and optimally decentralizing public services. There we worried about economic competition; here we worry about administrative and political competition, including the involvement and empowerment of indigenous institutions.

There are, however, important differences that affect the process of designing adjustment strategies in the two domains. I will exaggerate to make a point. Devising a structural adjustment program centers on a few crucial decisions at the top, such as devaluating the currency, freeing prices, lowering tariffs, removing quantitative restrictions, deregulating, and cutting spending. A few people can make and dictate these decisions in a relatively short time. In Turkey, for example, fewer than ten technocrats under Turgut Özal knew the content of reforms before they were announced (Krueger 1993). If the political leadership wants it done, it is done. (Aside to readers who are political leaders: I did say I was exaggerating.)

In contrast, institutional adjustment requires extensive tailoring to specific circumstances, and it requires ownership not only by top leaders but by the rank-and-file officials who will implement the institutional reforms. Thus in most cases institutional adjustment requires extensive consultation, participation, and joint learning. Process is crucial.

This difference implies, among other things, a greater emphasis on experimentation. The word "experiment" may carry unwanted connotations, but it captures an important element of successful institutional adjustment. A lesson from many past efforts at administrative reform is that attempts to craft once-and-for-all, systemwide changes fail. For one thing, the very complexity and finality of such reforms offer too many chances for vested interests to resist. Experiments that are limited in time and scope, in which the vested interests can help design the ways to measure success, give reforms a chance.

Correcting Donors' Incentive Problems

But progress with institutional adjustment *over there* may have to begin with institutional adjustment *right here.* Consider, for example, three incentive problems.

First, technical assistance personnel are usually not paid for training successors or developing capacity, but for completing a certain technical job (or simply for being on site for a contractually specified length of time).

Second, staff members of donor institutions often lack appropriate incentives. They operate through projects, which inhibits their ability to tackle such cross-cutting institutional issues as information and incentives (for a World Bank example, see Paul 1990, p. 45). Their compensation and promotion depend not on the eventual success of "their" projects, but on shorter-run measures of "craft" quality and even of amounts moved through the donor bureaucracy.

Third, lending agencies do not optimally share the risks that their conditional aid entails. In principle, the amount repaid should depend in part on how good their advice turns out to have been, assuming the recipient follows it. Currently, the risks are borne disproportionately by recipients.

These incentive problems have been noted before, and there is no illusion that they will be easy to remedy. But institutional adjustment is needed in donor agencies as well, and this, too, will require an experimental attitude, participation of staff and clients in experimental efforts, and an openness to learn with other donors and with recipients.

The Donor-Recipient Relationship as an Institution

Would the aid relationship itself benefit from institutional adjustment? Here the economic metaphor, though useful, seems especially incomplete. If it is true that aid resembles a transaction involving risk sharing and appropriate incentives, it is also true that aid is a relationship or partnership. Thomas Bucaille (1990) has usefully noted that aid is, or should be, a pedagogical relationship in the best sense of that dangerous word. To understand and improve our individually and mutually inappropriate incentives requires joint learning, which may suggest new processes for together analyzing and experimenting with our incentive structures.

An even more provocative analogy might be suggested by the metaphor of sick institutions: the aid relationship as a therapeutic one, correctly understood, correctly reconsidered. The therapist brings, or should bring, specialized theory and comparative experience; the patient brings unique knowledge of problems that, though unique, may be illuminated by theory and experience elsewhere. Aided by the therapeutic relationship, the patient ultimately is responsible for conceptualizing and realizing curative measures.

At the end of *Childhood and Society* Erik Erikson (1963) concludes that the therapist has to become a partner and transcend certain historical roles. As we consider ways to improve aid and institutional development, do Erikson's words also resonate for the aid giver, the foreign adviser, the expatriate activist?

> In a more enlightened world and under much more complicated historical conditions the analyst must face once more the whole problem of *judicious partnership* which expresses the spirit of analytic work more creatively than does *apathetic tolerance or autocratic guidance*. The various identities which at first lent themselves to a fusion with the new identity of the analyst—identities based on talmudic argument, on messianic zeal, on punitive

orthodoxy, on faddist sensationalism, on professional and social ambition—
all these identities and their cultural origins must now become part of the
analyst's analysis, so that he may be able to discard archaic rituals of control and learn to identify with the lasting value of his job of enlightenment.
Only thus can he set free in himself and in his patient that remnant of *judi-
cious indignation* without which a cure is but a straw in the changeable wind
of history. (Erikson 1963, p. 424; emphasis added)

Notes

1. A recent report by the World Bank's Operations Evaluation Department estimates that more than
half the Bank's projects have unsatisfactory results in terms of institutional development (World Bank
1994; see also Paul 1990 and Schacter 1995).

2. Some critics argue that donors are emphasizing failures of governance in recipient countries in part
to excuse the failures of the donors' invalid policy prescriptions, such as structural adjustment programs.
Others might argue that institutional failures are a smoke screen to hide shortcomings in human capital,
that "with people like these" even exemplary institutions would underperform.

3. As I and others have emphasized elsewhere, many private sector institutions also need "adjustment"
to overcome incentive and information problems that render them inefficient and often biased against
the poor and disadvantaged groups (Klitgaard 1991, 1995).

References

Bucaille, Thomas. 1990. "Métamorphoses du problème africain: l'économie africaine et la coopération
français depuis 1945." *Etudes* 373(1–2): 1–15.

Erikson, Erik H. 1963. *Childhood and Society*, 2nd ed. New York: W.W. Norton.

Klitgaard, Robert. 1988. *Controlling Corruption*. Berkeley and Los Angeles: University of California
Press.

———. 1989. "Incentive Myopia." *World Development* 17(4): 447–59.

———. 1991. *Adjusting to Reality: Beyond "State versus Market" in Economic Development*. San
Francisco, Calif.: ICS Press.

———. 1995. *Institutional Adjustment and Adjusting to Institutions*. World Bank Discussion Paper 303.
Washington, D.C.: World Bank.

———. Forthcoming. "National and International Strategies for Fighting Corruption." Paper presented
at the Symposium on Corruption and Good Governance, Organization for Economic Cooperation and
Development, Paris.

Krueger, Anne O. 1993. *Political Economy of Policy Reform in Developing Countries*. Cambridge, Mass.:
MIT Press.

Naim, Moisés. 1995. *Latin America's Journey to the Market: From Macroeconomic Shocks to Institutional
Therapy*. Occasional Paper 62. San Francisco, Calif.: ICS Press and International Center for Economic
Growth.

Nelson, Joan, and others 1994. *Intricate Links: Democratization and Market Reforms in Latin America
and Eastern Europe*. New Brunswick, N.J.: Transaction Books for the Overseas Development Council.

Ostrom, Elinor, Larry Schroeder, and Susan Wynne. 1993. *Institutional Incentives and Sustainable
Development: Infrastructure Policies in Perspective*. Boulder, Colo.: Westview Press.

Paul, Samuel. 1990. "Institutional Development in World Bank Projects: A Cross-Sectoral Review." Policy
Research Working Paper 392. World Bank, Country Economics Department, Washington, D.C.

Schacter, Mark. 1995. "Recent Experience with Institutional Development Lending in the Western Africa
Department." World Bank, Western Africa Department, Country Operations Division, Washington, D.C.

World Bank. 1994. *Evaluation Results for 1992*. A World Bank Operations Evaluation Study.
Washington, D.C.: World Bank.

Comment on "Incentives, Rules of the Game, and Development," by Elinor Ostrom

Margaret Levi

Some of the presentations for this conference, including Elinor Ostrom's, take me back in time—until I remember the times in which we are living. The emphasis on decentralization and participatory planning is reminiscent of the 1960s and early 1970s. It is also, at least for my taste, dangerously close to current popular prescriptions for giving central government authority over to lower-level jurisdictions. Ostrom tends to steer clear of most of the shoals that lie in wait for those who propose either prescription thoughtlessly. She does not claim that village communities always and everywhere devise solutions to common pool resource problems. Nor does she reject altogether a role for central governments.

Even so, I think that in her emphasis on the efficiency gains accruing from the support and development of local institutional solutions to common pool resource problems Ostrom pays insufficient attention to two important political considerations. First, what are the effects, if any, of her proposed strategy on the distribution of local political resources? Second, what are the means for changing the incentives for central government providers so that they are more likely to produce socially efficient outcomes? I suspect that if push comes to shove, Ostrom would fit into the anarcho-communitarian tradition Bardhan describes (this volume).

In speaking to what Ostrom offers us as well as what she does not, I draw examples from experiments in alleviating poverty in industrial as well as developing countries. Antipoverty projects in Australia, the United States, and other OECD countries represent large expenditures of resources from governments and donors. By considering cases from countries that have longstanding democratic governments and electoral politics alongside those that do not, it is easier to clarify the role of political structures. I also consider examples from the history of development in what is now considered the industrial world.

My argument, like Ostrom's, fits with the new economic institutionalism. Her emphasis is on efficiency gains that arise when farmers negotiate their own rules (endogenous rule design). I emphasize how vested interests, political power, and

Margaret Levi is professor of political science at the University of Washington.

Annual World Bank Conference on Development Economics 1995

national government institutions can undermine the possibility of local institutional solutions. In emphasizing these factors, I seem to be in good company with several others at this conference. However, I do not wish to leave the matter there. Claiming a role for political economy or recognizing the importance of effective government does not inform us about the process by which effective government comes into being.

Efficiency Gains

Ostrom's brief was to speak on how the structure of incentives and rules of the game may influence effectiveness. She does this admirably and imaginatively, at least for specific physical and infrastructure projects, such as irrigation dams. She clarifies how reliance on local groups and their institutions not only solves information problems but also contributes to better design and better maintenance of the project. Although donors and central governments remain essential for providing the funds to subsidize such projects, local solutions are the key to almost every other aspect of the effectiveness of such projects. The big payoff for Ostrom, however, comes in getting the incentives and the rules right, which not every donor or local group can do. Her combination of empirical research and game theoretical analysis considerably enhances our understanding of the conditions under which it is possible to devise rules of the game that promote effectiveness.

There is one additional efficiency gain that her analysis implies but does not amplify. Local organizations may have a comparative advantage not only in designing solutions but also in determining which kinds of projects represent the best use of development resources. An example comes to mind of a program in Australia in the 1970s. The Department of Urban and Regional Planning decided to give money to communities that came up with plans for improving their neighborhoods. One working-class community in a flat, run-down suburb of Sydney proposed the construction of a hill in a local park. The agency staff found the idea outrageous, but the department head insisted that they fund the project, which, after all, had been designed by the community according to the specified rules of participation. The subsequent construction of the hill led to other park improvements, beautification of the surrounding homes, cooperation with other communities to clean up the polluting river that ran through the area, and ultimately to a higher quality of life. The hill was not something a central government or a large donor was likely to conceive of as a means to enhance development. However, by paying attention to the expressed needs of the residents, the planning agency effected changes that went well beyond its relatively small initial investment.

The Distribution of Political Resources

Local participation in the determination of funded projects does not figure centrally into Ostrom's analysis. Even more important, given her focus, is the neglect of the effect of donations and subsidies on intercommunity and intracommunity distributions of power. Certainly, control over fiscal resources enhances the bargaining clout of the farmers on whom the development projects depend. It encourages farmers to organize for collective action, which may be translatable to other spheres, and makes central government actors, who require the farmers' cooperation, more willing to make concessions.

Ostrom demonstrates that some communities are more likely than others to devise institutional solutions and are therefore also more likely to profit from the largesse of donors. Demonstration projects and the education of members of other communities go some way to equalizing the benefits, but it may be too little too late for some communities. This can have long-run consequences on the distribution of both political influence and economic well-being. Where central government will not or cannot act to equalize the distribution of political and economic resources, the disparities are likely to increase. To the extent that the resources are being put to efficient social uses, this is not necessarily a bad thing for development. However, to the extent that the poorer communities lag because they lack money or influence rather than the capacity to create effective local organizations and institutions, the distributional effects can be disastrous.

Moreover, funding worthy, workable solutions does not necessarily improve the distribution of power within communities. The War on Poverty in the United States gave us countless examples of struggles between neighborhood-based community organizations and local governments over funds provided by the federal government and private foundations. In the end it was those who were already relatively powerful politically who received funding. The economic benefits they reaped, moreover, allowed them to strengthen their relative political clout. If funds for irrigation projects are allocated to the community leadership, no incentives are put in place to break up the existing distributional coalitions of rich and poor, dominant ethnic and minority ethnic, male and female. In a different context, Smith and Lipsky (1993) argue that privatization of social services undermines universalistic rules and opportunities and remind us of the important role central government can play in enforcing rules of the game that undermine discrimination and level the playing field. Central governments can and must provide national standards.

These last arguments deal more with equity than with efficiency losses. However, political inequality and frustration, particularly if coupled with economic disadvantage, may even reduce efficiency in the long run. First, as Folbre (this volume) reminds us, distributional coalitions do not automatically disappear; threatened groups may form new distributional coalitions. The effect of the ensuing conflict may be to undermine institutional efficiency. Second, those who have a history of suffering discrimination have good reason not to trust local leadership, government, and other bureaucratic agencies. Given that those who have an inclination to trust are likely to do better in economic and political exchanges, not only does the gap increase over time but the willingness of those on the bottom to attempt change is reduced (Hardin 1993). Third, the consequences of social distrust or, worse, a perception of leadership and government betrayal can induce noncooperation and even sabotage that eventually undermine the existing institutional arrangements (Scott

1985; Levi 1990). The end result is the reduction of incentives to comply, participate, or consent.

Changing the Structure of Incentives on Government

One of the principal findings from the critiques of pluralist versions of democratic theory is that not everyone gets heard politically. In the absence of responsive government, even those who are active and have organized may not have an effective voice. This raises the central question: What makes for responsive government?

Ostrom notes the incompatibility between the incentives facing bureaucrats and those facing both donors and the local communities that must maintain projects. She says less about central government policymakers. Effective government depends, however, not only on a rationalized and relatively honest bureaucracy but also on political leadership with enough coercive power to enforce property rights and sufficient constraints so that power cannot become rapacious or indifferent. Both government leaders and bureaucrats must be able to credibly commit to serving the public good.

Ostrom seems to suggest that the best way to deal with the bureaucrats is to ignore them to the extent possible, to make end runs around them. However, for development to succeed over time, it is important to consider how to alter the incentives facing bureaucrats so that their long-term interests are tied to promoting productive outcomes and not just to avoiding short-term trouble.

Corruption is one problem that faces bureaucracies. Another is the bureaucratic conservatism that results from seniority systems. Rewards for good performance and punishment for poor performance and dishonesty are crucial in establishing an effective bureaucracy. An emphasis on merit would alter bureaucratic incentives. These are difficult but not impossible rule changes. Equally important in changing the incentives of bureaucrats is creating positive returns from an investment through reputation. Professionalism is one means to achieve this; paying bureaucrats well and creating a system in which bureaucratic careers lead to important positions in the private sector are others.

The importance of bureaucratic reform and its salutary effects on bureaucrats, other government actors, and local residents deserves and receives considerable emphasis (Levi and Sherman forthcoming; Rose-Ackerman 1978 and this volume; Klitgaard 1988 and this volume). However, bureaucratic reform is not easy to achieve and is seldom internally generated. Evans (1992) claims that reform will result from embedding both the bureaucracy and government in society. Wade (1993) argues for the importance of embedding bureaucrats in the local community they are meant to serve. Geddes (1994) argues that reform involves insulating the bureaucracy from political pressures. The first two approaches leave the bureaucracy open to capture, the last to unaccountability. Certain institutional arrangements, particularly democratic rules, are the answers that beg the question. First, a rationalized bureaucracy is one of the steps in the process toward democracy (Levi 1988). Second, one cannot legislate democracy; it has to have strong support among the population, within the government, and within the military.

To transform moribund or corrupt bureaucracy requires committed political leadership, and here lies the rub. What are the incentives for leaders to provide governance that is energetic in its pursuit of long-term development and other social goods? What motivates powerful actors in a society to commit to democratic institutions or to sustain them? As Przeworski (1991) argues, the very definition of a democracy is the existence of losers who accept their losses without attempting to overthrow government or ignore election results (as in Algeria or Myanmar). This requires confidence that there will be another round, that the losers will win some as well as lose some, and that the losses they suffer, although possibly large, will be contained. How is such confidence to be achieved?

One key, I believe, is the creation of demands and constraints on government that emanate from civil society. Ostrom offers us a starting point. A community with the capacity to organize itself for institutional design and maintenance of irrigation systems or some other collective good has the potential capacity to organize politically. According to Putnam (1993) a high level of participation in any kind of horizontal, associational life enhances political involvement and demands on government. He argues that soccer clubs, choral societies, and bird watching groups are at the heart of an active, democratic polity as much as if not more than are more overtly political organizations. When the associational life Putnam describes or the institutional solutions Ostrom defines do not arise spontaneously, donors can provide resources to spark them into life. Donors can take the form of large corporate organizations, such as governments or the World Bank, but they can also be churches and political parties and labor unions that send organizers to local communities. A few political entrepreneurs can make a big difference in the emergence of collective action, as many revolutions, trade union histories, and the U.S. War on Poverty demonstrate so well.

Associational life may enhance the likelihood of demands for effective programs and may create constraints on predatory rulers (Levi 1988), but it provides only one of a set of incentives on government actors. Equally important in the development of relatively effective states is the reliance of central government actors on internal funds. In order to extract sufficient money from the polity, rulers need to convince taxpayers that they are getting something in return and to promote economic growth that increases their long-run return. They must inspire what I label quasi-voluntary compliance (Levi 1988) and, eventually, the more positive act of contingent consent (Levi 1990; Levi forthcoming). Government actors can reduce their transaction costs of enforcement by encouraging citizens to comply willingly. To do this, government leaders must provide assurances that they will keep their policy promises and that they will see to it that everyone pays his or her share.

We have considerable collective knowledge about the conditions that lead to such credible commitments. Critical is a relatively long time horizon. Low discount rates will not emerge where there is civil war or a tinpot dictator. Long time horizons may emerge in relatively stable political systems where there is a payoff to the ruling elites from long-term investments both in the countryside and in long-distance trade.

The combination of participation, returns from investments, and government actors who find it in their interest to create contingent consent are necessary conditions for the creation of effective governance. Only then will the state be able to forcefully and legitimately provide the necessary national institutional backdrop to local institutions and community.

Even with all of this in place—and we know how difficult it is to get all of this in place—development is not the immediate outcome. Democracy and capitalism took hundreds of years to evolve in France, the United Kingdom, and other industrial countries, even after the critical technical breakthroughs had been made. Contemporary developing countries will also need time to develop endogenous social norms, local institutions, and national institutions that support each other, support development, and support democracy. This is a hard fact to remember in our impatient world, a world full of poverty and destructive conflicts. Recognizing the importance of time is not, however, a recipe for inaction or indifference. Rather, it is a call for continuing to keep our sleeves rolled up while we help lay the foundations for a higher standard of living and for the establishment of the democratic institutions, both local and national, that are essential for creating and maintaining redistribution with growth.

References

Evans, Peter. 1992. "The State as Problem and Solution: Predation, Embedded Autonomy, and Structural Change." In Stephan Haggard and Robert R. Kaufman, eds., *The Politics of Economic Adjustment*. Princeton, N.J.: Princeton University Press.

Geddes, Barbara. 1994. *The Politician's Dilemma*. Berkeley: University of California Press.

Hardin, Russell. 1993. "The Street-Level Epistemology of Trust." *Politics & Society* 21(4): 505–29.

Klitgaard, Robert. 1988. *Controlling Corruption*. Berkeley: University of California Press.

Levi, Margaret. 1988. *Of Rule and Revenue*. Berkeley: University of California Press.

————. 1990. "A Logic of Institutional Change." In Karen Cook and Margaret Levi, eds., *The Limits of Rationality*. Chicago: University of Chicago Press.

————. Forthcoming. *The Contingencies of Consent*.

Levi, Margaret, and Richard Sherman. Forthcoming. "Rational Compliance with Rationalized Bureaucracy." In Christopher Clague, ed., *Institutions and Economic Development*. Ann Arbor: University of Michigan Press.

Przeworski, Adam. 1991. *Democracy and the Market*. New York: Cambridge University Press.

Putnam, Robert. 1993. *Making Democracy Work: Civic Traditions in Modern Italy*. Princeton, N.J.: Princeton University Press.

Rose-Ackerman, Susan. 1978. *Corruption*. New York: Academic Press.

Scott, James. 1985. *Weapons of the Weak*. New Haven, Conn.: Yale University Press.

Smith, Stephen R., and Michael Lipsky. 1993. *Non-Profits for Hire: The Welfare State in the Age of Contracting*. Cambridge, Mass.: Harvard University Press.

Wade, Robert. 1993. "Institutions and Bureaucracies: A Comparative Study of Korea and India." Paper presented at Stanford University and World Bank Conference on the East Asian Miracle, Stanford, California.

Floor Discussion of "Incentives, Rules of the Game, and Development," by Elinor Ostrom

A specialist on governance and development from Bangladesh felt that Ostrom had stopped short on the conclusions that naturally emerge from her analysis. In particular, did Ostrom identify notions of community as an independent variable in explaining different performance levels in irrigation systems? As Robert Putnam's work has shown, community involvement plays a significant role in building and maintaining strong institutions. Development that is obsessed with individualism and markets subverts the notion of community, the participant said, and donors and consultants that assume they are dealing with individuals rather than communities undermine a central premise of successful development.

Another important conclusion that emerges from Ostrom's presentation, the participant continued, involves the notion of participation. Participation is not just a matter of different choruses singing together. It is also a sense of sharing in the process and benefits of development, a goal that is achieved by having more equitable access to the assets from which development flows. Locally managed institutions succeed because there is a capacity for egalitarian distribution and a history of people working together to get the best returns on investment. Rent seeking is not just a function of imperfect markets; it is also a function of imperfect distribution of power, which often derives from imperfect access to productive capacities and economic opportunities. Reform designs that fail to incorporate participation may be missing out on a central element in reform.

Ostrom agreed that community was important but said that many naive notions of community (that it is a good thing) fail to address the tough situations that arise when trying to build it. She had been involved in studies of diverse fisheries, forests, and irrigation systems around the world and has never found a robust institution that survived for long without monitoring. It is important to draw on the social capital of community and mutual trust. Institution building that enhances a sense of community rather than tears it down must be a part of the process. This, however, is a challenging task and not one accomplished by simply dealing with communities

This session was chaired by Robert Piccioto, director-general, Operations Evaluation, at the World Bank.

Annual World Bank Conference on Development Economics 1995
©1996 The International Bank for Reconstruction and Development / THE WORLD BANK

rather than individuals. Ostrom realized that her approach was rather reductionist but believes that it is important to dig below terms like *community* and *participation* to understand how these processes are sustained over time—because they are not self-sustaining. They require individuals who understand systems and how to keep them going.

The participant from Bangladesh concluded that what is really needed is a bureaucracy that is captured by and accountable to a community that is both creating assets and deriving benefits from it. Who had designed the irrigation systems for the U.S. Agency for International Development, and what happened to the expatriate consultants involved? Were they in jail or were they designing irrigation systems somewhere else? Ostrom responded that she wished she could report that the builder of Chiregad had been discovered. Ironically, it might even be the case that he had moved on to Bangladesh.

A participant who had researched agriculture in Indonesia said that in reviewing the literature to analyze the role of women in Indonesian agriculture she had found few studies that even looked at people, let alone women. She pleaded for Ostrom to include women in her analysis. Ostrom responded that questions about distribution within a household were complex and worthy of research but were not the focus of this research, which is why it was gender neutral.

The participant from Indonesia also observed that in Ostrom's model all landowners were farmers and all farmers were landowners. Her own work in Indonesia suggested that labor is often provided by landless laborers and that the community to which they contribute is really the community of the rich. Ostrom responded that farmer-governed irrigation systems in Nepal had a high proportion of landowners who owned very small pieces of land. And while there are landless workers in many irrigation systems, many systems have institutional arrangements to share risk among those who participate in the maintenance of the system.

Is Growth in Developing Countries Beneficial to Industrial Countries?

Richard N. Cooper

Growth in developing countries, particularly that induced through trade liberalization, will benefit industrial countries as well. Incomes will rise in industrial countries. Though there will be some dislocation, it will be small relative to the numerous other disturbances that constantly assail modern economies, and the cost of dealing with it can be relatively low if the required adjustments are phased in over time. Increased competition may spur innovation, and some currently developing countries will become economic innovators. Terms of trade are unlikely to change significantly over time and, except for possible increases in oil prices, any change is likely to modestly favor industrial countries. Investment in emerging markets will permit higher returns and, judiciously managed, reduce overall investment risk through diversification. Growth is likely to increase rather than reduce emigration from developing countries for a number of years, but if history is a guide, successful countries will become destinations rather than origins of migrants. Environmental degradation will worsen along some dimensions, while diminishing along others. Finally, the growth of some poor countries will, on past evidence, lead initially to some political instability, but eventually to an improvement in civil and political liberties.

In the past four decades per capita output has grown in an ever-increasing number of countries, raising material well-being to levels unimaginable even a few generations earlier. But this change has transformed modes of living and social relations in ways that have created new challenges and stresses. In particular, many countries once labeled "less developed" according to United Nations terminology have grown rapidly and have urbanized extensively. They are no longer poor by historical standards, although they are still much poorer than the richest countries. This relatively recent process includes not only the countries now on everyone's mind—the four Asian tigers and their follow-ons in Southeast Asia. In the early 1950s Italy, Japan, Spain, and many other countries that are now well-to-do were poor. Some countries

Richard Cooper is Maurits C. Boas Professor of International Economics at Harvard University. This article was written in parallel with, and benefited from, the draft of World Bank (1995).

Annual World Bank Conference on Development Economics 1995
©1996 The International Bank for Reconstruction and Development / THE WORLD BANK

that were initially left behind have been surging forward in the past decade, most notably China and India, which together contain 38 percent of the world's population. Others, especially countries in Sub-Saharan Africa, have grown little, if at all, and some have even regressed in material well-being. Formerly communist countries are in a unique situation, fundamentally transforming their economic and political systems and suffering the disruptions and dislocations of that transformation.

In general, countries with initially low levels of per capita income have grown more rapidly than rich countries. On average Asian countries experienced a nearly fourfold increase in per capita income since 1950, compared with a threefold increase in OECD countries (Maddison 1989, p. 19). But initially middle-income Latin American countries did less well on average, and poor African countries fared even worse. Mankiw, Romer, and Weil (1992) suggest a strong tendency toward convergence— that is, countries that were relatively poor in 1960 grew relatively rapidly—if rates of investment in physical and human capital are controlled for. But the rate of convergence is slow, and some poor countries have lagged badly in investment. As a result there has been a divergence in per capita income over the past three decades.

Curiously, the historically rapid growth of developing countries is seen as a threat by some people in Europe and North America and has even been implicated in the high unemployment currently prevailing in Europe. Industrial countries fear not being able to compete, as capital and technology (here, a generic term meaning practical knowledge) move to developing countries and combine with relatively cheap labor. Examples of relocation of specific economic activities can be found. But generalization to an overall loss of employment and output contains a serious fallacy— it neglects that higher labor productivity in poor countries generates higher incomes which generate higher expenditures. In other words, increases in exports generate increases in imports.

Can growth in developing countries harm industrial countries? If so, how? In addressing this question, I focus on growth generated by trade liberalization and look first at linkages through trade, flows of capital, and technology and the impact of trade on factor incomes. Environmental implications are addressed briefly, and political changes within developing countries are examined briefly for possible implications for industrial countries. This analysis finds that growth in developing countries is beneficial to industrial countries in several ways, and although the effects of growth are not likely to be large, they will probably exceed the few negative effects that can be identified.

Growth and Trade

I consider economic growth to mean increases in an economy's total output or output per capita. Growth over a long period implies an increase in the capacity of a country to produce. But over short intervals output can increase by using existing capacity more intensively. Growth is not the same as economic development, which involves the evolution of public and private institutions and conventions that are conducive to continued growth and to sustaining the high standard of living achieved. But historically, growth has been highly correlated with development; the major exceptions have been booms in exports of raw materials that temporarily increased output and incomes.

Growth can be achieved by using more factors of production—conventionally labor, capital, and agricultural land—or by increasing total factor productivity. Productivity in turn can be increased through several channels: improving the quality of factor inputs (for example, educating the labor force); increasing the intensity with which factor inputs are applied (reducing slack employment or underutilization of machinery); reducing waste of intermediate products (improving the efficiency of energy use); and, more generally, discovering and installing better ways of converting inputs into outputs—a process that is ultimately limited only by the basic laws of physics and by human ingenuity.

What Does Theory Tell Us?

The relationship between international trade and economic growth is as complicated as the process of growth itself. The impact of growth in developing countries on trade with industrial countries depends on the sources of growth in developing countries. Growth can either foster or inhibit trade (Hicks 1953; Johnson 1958, chapter 3). Growth due to factor accumulation will be biased against trade if the factor that is scarce relative to its abundance in the rest of the world grows relative to the other factors of production (for example, in developing countries capital accumulation is likely to be biased against trade, all other things being equal). Growth arising from increases in productivity will be biased against trade if the productivity increases are focused either in the import-competing industries or in all sectors using the relatively scarce factor of production. Growth will also be biased against trade if consumers have a strong preference for exported goods, so that as incomes rise, the relative consumption of the export goods rises. Growth will be biased in favor of foreign trade if the opposite conditions prevail, if economies of scale are significant, or if consumers value product variety in their consumption.

To examine the direction of bias for different sources of growth, assume that two countries are trading. One is richly endowed with capital and the other with labor. Both countries produce manufactured goods and agricultural products. The capital-rich country exports manufactured goods in exchange for agricultural goods from the labor-rich country. The income elasticity of demand for manufactures is assumed to be greater than one and that for agricultural products less than one. Technical change can occur in the manufacturing sector only, in either country, or it can occur at equal rates in manufacturing and agriculture. A growing labor force presses on fixed amounts of land. If diminishing returns are relatively weak, workers can be readily absorbed into the agricultural sector; if they are strong, most of the additional workers must go into manufacturing.

What is the impact of technical change, capital accumulation, and labor force growth in each of the countries on international trade at constant prices (that is, before allowing for the price adjustments that may be required to restore equilibrium and assuming that the sources of growth are autonomous)? The impact arising from changes in production and in consumption are combined—income growth at constant prices in either country will, by assumption, result in a more-than-proportionate increase in demand for manufactured goods. Of the ten cases identified in table 1, two will increase trade between the two countries, five will reduce trade, and three could have either effect, depending on the relative strength of an antitrade bias in consumption and a protrade bias in production.

Of the two cases that result in greater trade, one involves neutral technical change in the labor-rich country, in which rising incomes will be spent on manufactures (the imported good), and the other involves labor force growth in the capital-rich country under conditions of strong diminishing returns in agriculture, in which production of manufactures (the exported good) will increase more rapidly than demand for manufactures; in addition, the growing population will require more food imports.

Consider an extreme example of growth biased against trade. If trade between two regions is generated entirely by different endowments of factors of production, as in the Heckscher-Ohlin model, then relative capital accumulation in the region initially less-endowed with capital will result in a gradual diminution of trade. And when the relative factor endowments of the two regions become identical, trade will cease. In this case the region that did not experience factor accumulation will be worse off than it was initially—the gains from trade that it enjoyed will disappear as its terms of trade deteriorate to the relative prices that prevailed under autarky. Of course, if the other region continues to accumulate capital beyond this point some gains from trade will reemerge, and the static country will find itself exporting the products it formerly imported. This admittedly extreme example assumes that the countries use the same technology and have similar tastes and that economies of scale are absent or minor. But it illustrates the theoretical possibility that growth may diminish rather than increase trade and that a country may be made worse off if its trading partner grows.

Another extreme case arises if growth in a region is strongly biased toward its export sector, yet world demand for the export product is highly inelastic. Under these circumstances growth can reduce welfare because the growing country loses more

Table 1. *Sources of Growth and Impact on Trade*

Source of growth	Capital-rich country	Labor-rich country
Technical change		
Manufacturing only	+/−	−
Equal in both sectors	−	+
Capital accumulation	−	+/−
Labor force growth		
Mild diminishing returns	−	+/−
Strong diminishing returns	+	−

Note: A + indicates an increase in trade, a − a decrease.
Source: Adapted from Johnson 1958 (p. 82).

through the worsening of its terms of trade than it gains through growth. Output rises, but real income falls (Bhagwati and Srinivasan 1983). Of course, the worsening in the terms of trade for the exporting region represents a gain for the importing region. In effect, all the benefits of the growth, and then some, have been passed on to the importing region through lower prices, which raise real incomes there.

What Have We Observed?

We have not observed a decline in foreign trade as the world economy has grown in recent decades; on the contrary, in real terms foreign trade has grown more rapidly than output in every year since 1950, except for 1982. Over 1980–92 world merchandise exports grew (in volume) by 3.9 percent a year, compared with 2.5 percent growth in world output, meaning that trade grew about 55 percent faster than output (calculated from GATT 1993, p. 2).

In most cases exports grew more rapidly than GDP during both 1965–80 and 1980–90 for all countries as a whole and for country groups defined by income level (table 2). The exceptions include China and India during 1965–80, a period in which both countries were striving for self-sufficiency; middle-income countries during 1965–80, when many of these countries were pursuing import-substitution policies; and other low-income countries during 1980–90, particularly those in Sub-Saharan Africa, whose exports declined during the 1980s. Still, the general tendency for international trade to grow more rapidly than national output is unmistakable.

This tendency can be seen even more sharply in instances of rapid, sustained growth, such as in Italy, Japan, and the Republic of Korea, three countries that began poor and grew rapidly for more than twenty-five years (table 3). In these three countries foreign trade—both imports and exports—grew much more rapidly than GDP, and export volume grew more than import volume. The differential growth rates reflect two factors. First, the terms of trade moved against all three countries, due partly to increases in world oil prices in the 1970s. The gap between growth in exports and growth in imports is lower in dollar terms than it is in constant prices.

Table 2. *Annual Growth in GDP and Exports, 1965–80 and 1980–90*
(percent)

Country group	1965–80		1980–90	
	GDP	Exports	GDP	Exports
China and India	4.9	4.1	7.6	9.8
Other low-income[a]	4.8	5.8	3.9	1.5
Middle-income	6.3	3.9	2.5	3.8
High-income[b]	3.7	7.3	3.1	4.3
World	4.0	6.6	3.2	4.3

Note: Calculations were made in constant prices.
a. Annual per capital income of less than $610 in 1990.
b. Annual per capita income of more than $7,700 in 1990.
Source: World Bank 1992 (tables 2 and 14).

Second, all three countries, especially Korea, had substantial current account deficits at the beginning of the twenty-five-year period, reflecting their status as poor, capital-importing countries. Although Italy and Korea also had current account deficits at the end of the period, the deficits were proportionately much smaller, and Japan had become a substantial net exporter of capital.

How can we explain these observations? First, we should recognize, as the taxonomy of table 1 does not, that technical change is not independent of trade. Trade forces contact between economies, and contact enables the transmission of ideas. Moreover, trade in capital goods transmits technology directly, embodied in the goods themselves. But this transfer does not further trade—insofar as differences in technology are a source of mutually beneficial trade, diffusion of that technology would reduce, not increase, the incentive to trade.

Trade also is thought to depend on differences in factor endowments, with industrial countries specializing in capital-intensive goods and developing countries exporting resource-intensive or labor-intensive goods. Over the past twenty-five years the capital-labor ratio has probably grown more rapidly in industrial countries taken together than in developing countries, in part because of higher investment ratios and slower growth of the labor force. The capital-labor ratio in the seven major industrial countries (the G-7: the United States, Japan, Germany, France, United Kingdom, Italy, Canada) increased by about 50 percent during 1980–92 (calculated from OECD 1994d, tables 14 and 15). Although comparable data are not available for developing countries, the corresponding growth rate was certainly less than 50 percent. Therefore trade based on factor endowments should have increased. But a paradox arises. The capital-labor ratio probably rose by more than 50 percent in the newly industrialized countries, mainly in East Asia, yet their share of world trade increased sharply over this period. Where the capital-labor ratio probably grew much less than 50 percent—in Africa, Latin America, and South Asia—the share of world trade declined, contrary to expectations based on factor endowments.

How Do We Explain Recent Trade Patterns?

It is possible that technical change has been biased in favor of trade and that change has occurred more rapidly in labor-abundant countries (one of the possi-

Table 3. *Annual Growth in GDP and Trade in Three Rapidly Growing Countries*
(percent)

Indicator	Italy 1951–76	Japan 1956–81	Republic of Korea 1966–91
Real GDP	5.0	7.6	9.0
Export volume	11.0	12.8	16.0
Import volume	9.6	9.6	14.0

Note: The quarter-century of most rapid transformation was chosen for each country.
Source: Calculated from IMF, various years; and Maddison 1989.

bilities noted in table 1). Or it could be that economies of scale are more important than the direct evidence from industrial plants suggests (Weiss 1976), as
assumed but not shown in some of the modern trade literature (for example,
Helpman and Krugman 1985). Also, preferences could be such that an increasing
share of rising incomes is spent on import goods, perhaps reflecting a desire for
greater variety and overcoming the tendency to spend more on (largely nontraded)
services. Unfortunately, we do not have strong enough evidence to weigh these
possibilities.

But we do know one source of increased trade: the substantial reduction in trade
barriers. Barriers have fallen as a result of technological improvements in the transportation sector, especially the advent of large bulk carriers, super-tankers, and inexpensive air freight, and as a result of the lowering of legal barriers to trade,
especially tariffs and quantitative restrictions. Since 1947 import tariffs on industrial
goods have been reduced by more than 90 percent in a series of multilateral trade
negotiations (calculated from CEA 1995, p. 205), culminating in the 40 percent
reduction agreed in 1994 in the Uruguay Round. Industrial countries have largely
eliminated the quantitative restrictions that prevailed during the 1950s, except on
some agricultural and textile products. This liberalization permitted rapid growth in
trade, which may in turn have stimulated economic growth.

Lower trade barriers and improved air transport have particularly encouraged
"production slicing"—the international farming out of different parts of a step-wise
production process, mainly to take advantage of lower labor costs. Not only does
production slicing create more trade in intermediate products, but because trade is
recorded as the gross value of the merchandise moving across national boundaries,
production slicing will raise the ratio of recorded trade to total output, which is
measured in terms of value added.

As this brief discussion suggests, the impact of growth in developing countries on
industrial countries depends on the source of growth, as well as on the economic
linkages between the two groups of countries. To measure the full impact, we would
need to build a complete and detailed model of developing countries, which differ
greatly from one another, that could interact with a fairly detailed model of industrial countries (also referred to as OECD countries). That task is far beyond the
scope of this article. The work that has been done on the interactions between these
two groups of countries has been exploratory and, for our purposes, is far too primitive. Typically, developing countries are modeled as one or two blocs, exporting
primary products and importing manufactured goods. There are no interactions
within the blocs, and the blocs are endogenous reactors to events (such as policy
changes) in OECD countries. Moreover, this work generally focuses on relatively
short-run changes in demand rather than on long-run changes in the capacity to
produce (see, for example, Currie and Vines 1988; McKibbin and Sachs 1991;
Henderson and McKibbin 1993; Allen and Vines 1993). In the following discussion
I focus on growth in developing countries that is generated by their response to
trade liberalization in industrial countries and to trade and capital liberalization in
their own economies.

Trade Liberalization As a Source of Growth

Trade liberalization can increase the capacity of a country to produce through several channels. In general, it will permit more efficient specialization of production, with or without economies of scale. It will increase competition, thus helping to break up domestic monopolies. Competition may also stimulate greater innovation. Greater incomes will generate savings, which may be used to increase productive capacity. Liberalization may stimulate additional foreign investment and make existing foreign investment more efficient. Finally, liberalization undertaken by a country's trading partners may improve its terms of trade, raising real incomes relative to output and thus giving savings a further fillip (of course any worsening of the terms of trade will cut in the other direction).

Estimation of the Gains from Trade

Many economists have estimated the gains from trade in recent years in connection with the anticipated conclusion of the Uruguay Round of the General Agreement on Tariffs and Trade (GATT) and in connection with the North American Free Trade Agreement (NAFTA), including Canada, Mexico, and the United States. These estimates are strongly dependent on assumptions about the extent of trade liberalization and assumptions about the structure of national economies and their responses to trade liberalization (see Deardorff 1994 for a summary and discussion of estimates on the trade, income, and employment effects of the Uruguay Round).

To illustrate, consider the set of estimates prepared by the GATT Secretariat (table 4). The authors had to make several decisions about economic structure and response to the Uruguay Round and developed three different estimates (Francois, McDonald, and Nordström 1994). The first estimate assumes perfect competition in all sectors and constant returns to scale, and it yields global gains of $65 billion in 1990 (assuming that the Uruguay Round results are fully phased in). These gains are due to improved efficiency from the reallocation of resources among sectors in different countries. The second estimate allows for some increasing returns to scale and monopolistic competition in manufacturing sectors. Trade liberalization in this

Table 4. *Economic Gains in 1990 from the Uruguay Round*
(billions of 1990 dollars)

Version	World	OECD[a]	Other[b]
Constant returns to scale, perfect competition	65	63.6	1.4
Increasing returns to scale, monopolistic competition	181	141.2	39.8
Dynamic[c]	291	223.5	67.5

a. OECD countries are divided into six categories.
b. Other countries are divided into only three categories: China, Taiwan (China), and others.
c. Includes higher output through greater investment and is therefore not strictly comparable to the first two rows.
Source: Francois, McDonald, and Nordström 1994 (table 11a).

case enables improved efficiency through scale economies and improved competition, increasing the estimated global gains to $181 billion. The third estimate assumes that the higher income arising from trade liberalization will increase the rate of global savings and investment, and reports a further increase in output due to this additional investment. Gains in output are augmented to $291 billion, or about 1.3 percent of gross world product in 1990. Note that while the income gains in the first and second estimates reflect increased efficiency for a given amount of inputs, the third version adds the increased output that would result from augmenting the capital stock. Thus the figures are not strictly comparable. These estimates are somewhat higher than others, but they capture the flavor of most estimates.

In terms of the distribution of gains, non-OECD countries gain very little under the first estimate—pure competition without economies of scale. But in the second and third estimates 23 percent of the gains accrue to non-OECD countries, corresponding roughly to their share in gross world product at market prices—1.2 percent of their 1990 GDP. The GATT model also suggests that world merchandise exports under the third estimate will increase by about 23 percent after the tariff reductions are fully phased in and agricultural and textile apparel quotas are phased out. Not surprisingly, the largest expected increases in exports are in clothing (192 percent) and textiles (72 percent), but substantial increases are also expected in transport equipment (30 percent) and steel (25 percent). Developing countries other than China and Taiwan (China) will raise their exports by 37 percent, according to the third estimate (compared with 14 percent under competition and constant returns to scale), and account for 51 percent of the total increase in exports (Francois, McDonald, and Nordström 1994).

One shortcoming of the GATT model is that it does not permit us to quantify the contribution that increased trade with developing countries makes to the estimated gains in income—a weakness shared by most other estimates. Most of the increased trade is among industrial countries or regions, and most of the gains come from this increased trade. Indeed, the structure of the estimation allows for no increases in trade or income arising from increases in trade among developing countries, which accounted for 9 percent of world exports in 1992, because (apart from China) they are lumped together.

A rough guide would suggest that economic gains are shared in proportion to increases in imports, and thus most of the gains will accrue to OECD countries. This presumption must be modified to the extent that reductions in protection will be greater in developing countries, which initially have higher levels of protection, and gains are related to (the square of) the reduction in protection. As suggested above, the estimated gains in the GATT study are about the same relative to GDP for industrial and developing countries. Because developing countries account for about half of the growth in exports attributable to the Uruguay Round and receive almost a quarter of the gains in income, it is reasonable to attribute at least 20 percent of the growth in industrial country income to increased trade with developing countries.

It is worth noting that across regions the increase in income attributable to the Uruguay Round is positively but not perfectly correlated with the increase in exports attributable to the Uruguay Round (ρ = .60 across nine regions). The reason is that exports draw resources away from other economic activities. Exports by themselves do not increase income in the GATT model; production increases because of the more efficient use of resources that unimpeded trade permits. Thus as noted above, gains in income are more closely associated with increases in imports. In short, the presumption of deficient demand, in which exports are assumed to increase income and imports to detract from production, is not made here even though it figures (usually implicitly) heavily in political debates over trade policy.

It should also be noted that although the third version of the GATT study attempts to capture the gains from more efficient production, economies of scale, and increased investment associated with increased domestic savings, it does not capture the gains that might flow from increased competition, increased innovation, increased foreign investment, or reduced uncertainty associated with a clearer set of rules and provisions for settling disputes. Nor does it address increased trade in services or possible changes in the terms of trade. These factors together may be more important than the estimated gains from merchandise trade.

Estimates of the gains from NAFTA, while only regional, address directly the gains that some industrial countries will derive from greater trade with a developing country. Hufbauer and Schott (1992, 1993) estimate that a fully implemented free trade area will increase U.S. imports from Mexico by $7.7 billion and increase U.S. exports to Mexico by $16.5 billion, representing a 41 percent increase in two-way trade. Capital repatriation and increased foreign investment will finance Mexico's enlarged current account deficit. The static increase in income associated directly with increased trade is $1.9 billion, of which only $193 million will accrue to the United States (Hufbauer and Schott 1993, pp. 23–4). Hufbauer and Schott judge that "enhanced competition and larger markets might benefit the Mexican economy by as much as $12.5 billion annually" (p. 24). They acknowledge that dynamic gains might also accrue to the United States, but give no quantitative estimate. Thus we are left with the conclusion that although the gains from NAFTA are substantial, most accrue to Mexico, the small, highly protected trading partner. Because most Mexican exports already enter the United States at low duties, the scope for efficiency gains from free trade with Mexico is limited. But the increase in net exports from the United States under NAFTA, due largely to increased investment in Mexico, is expected to increase U.S. employment by 171,000, representing the creation of 316,000 new jobs and the elimination of 145,000 existing jobs. However, these employment calculations are made sector by sector, and they neglect macroeconomic considerations. If employment is slack, then new jobs may be created. But if the U.S. economy is already fully employed, there will be no net job creation. Any jobs created will lead to job destruction elsewhere in the economy, brought about if necessary by a deliberate tightening of monetary policy to combat inflationary pressures.

Hufbauer and Schott (1994) have also undertaken the more ambitious task of estimating the gains that might result from a free trade area encompassing the entire western hemisphere—in effect, the addition of the Caribbean and the rest of Latin America to NAFTA. Using a method that is reasoned but not wholly persuasive, Hufbauer and Schott suggest that if a notional western hemisphere free trade area (WHFTA) had been inaugurated in 1990, real GDP in Latin America (other than Mexico) would be $273 billion (18 percent) higher by 2002, exports in constant 1990 prices would be 42 percent higher, and imports would be 51 percent higher. It is assumed that some income-enhancing reforms in Latin America continue to be adopted, even without WHFTA. These estimates include some powerful dynamic effects, which augment the static increases in trade by about one-fifth. In particular, Hufbauer and Schott implicitly assume that output in Latin America has been constrained by limited demand for exports rather than by a shortage of capital, human skills, or other factors. WHFTA will augment export demand and foreign exchange earnings and thus permit a substantial increase in Latin American output.

As noted, U.S. exports (in constant prices) to Latin America are estimated to grow by 51 percent by 2002, compared with their estimated value without WHFTA, and U.S. imports from Latin America are estimated to grow by 42 percent (Hufbauer and Schott 1994, p. 60). These increases are substantial, even relative to total U.S. trade. The authors make no attempt to translate these increases in trade into gains in U.S. income and output. But using the reasoning they applied to NAFTA estimates, the increase in U.S. income would be about $700 million (2.5 percent of increased imports of $28 billion, in 1990 prices), or about 0.01 percent of U.S. GDP in 2002. This estimate makes no allowance for any of the dynamic effects discussed above. Net job creation is estimated at 60,800 (before allowing for macroeconomic adjustments), largely because U.S. exports grow more rapidly than U.S. imports—a result of increased net foreign investment in Latin America. Foreign investment contributes to higher growth in Latin America, but not to higher income in the United States.

Innovation

One channel through which growth in developing countries could affect well-being in industrial countries is trade- or growth-induced innovation. Greater innovation and more rapid technical change in industrial countries could result from increased scale in production or a response to competitive pressure. After a long period of absorbing and imitating foreign technology, Japan became an important innovator in consumer and capital goods in the 1980s. Other countries will presumably follow a similar course, after sufficient development. Such innovations benefit the world economy in general, including industrial countries, except in those rare cases when they severely worsen a country's terms of trade.

There is some anecdotal support showing that import competition stimulates innovation within industrial countries, arising from increased competitive pressure on particular industries. For example, Wood (1994) assumes that import competition is important in reducing demand for low-skilled labor in industrial countries. But there is no systematic evidence. As Baldwin (1994, p. 44) sums up, "neither existing endogenous growth models nor what empirical evidence is available on the subject seem to support this conclusion [that increased import competition has induced the productivity increases we observe]." This conclusion is not entirely surprising. The relationship between trade and innovation is complex, and in theory trade can either increase or reduce the rate of innovation, depending on how trade affects incentives and demand for factors that are used intensively in innovation, such as research and development (for a theoretical exploration of these issues, see Grossman and Helpman 1991, especially chapter 9).

Terms of Trade Effect

Another channel through which growth in developing countries could affect well-being in industrial countries is changes in the terms of trade. The entrance of more producers into traditional manufacturing industries will put downward pressure on the prices of goods such as clothing, textiles, steel, and toys. Industrial countries will gain or lose depending on whether they are net exporters or net importers of such products. But as a group, industrial countries will benefit. In addition, higher rates of investment and rapid capital accumulation in developing countries will put upward pressure on the prices of capital goods, resulting in gains to net exporters and losses to net importers of these products. Again on balance, industrial countries will gain from this development. But the impact is likely to be small.

Broad categories of the international commodity terms of trade have not shown substantial trend movements over time (Spraos 1980), although particular products have done so. Oil prices rose drastically during the 1970s, peaked in 1981, then receded during the 1980s, remaining relatively higher than their level prior to 1973. Probably the most dramatic decline in commodity terms of trade has been that experienced by electronic computers. Computational capacity that cost more than $9 million (in 1995 prices) in the early 1970s could be purchased for less than $3,000 in 1995 (a 99.7 percent drop).

Most of the studies of the impact of the Uruguay Round or of NAFTA do not address the question of likely changes in the terms of trade, implicitly assuming that balanced growth of imports and exports will leave the terms of trade unchanged. One exception is Goldin, Knudsen, and van der Mensbrugghe (1993), who emphasize the impact of trade liberalization on agricultural products. They find that such liberalization, followed by the resulting shifts in demand and supply, would significantly increase world prices for wheat, sugar, beef, and dairy products and significantly reduce world prices for rice, coffee, and cocoa.

These changes would tend to benefit industrial countries as a whole and to help some developing countries while hurting others, depending on the commodity composition of their trade. For instance, Indonesia, Sub-Saharan African countries, and the countries around the Persian Gulf would lose modestly from full liberalization of agricultural trade. But full liberalization is a distant possibility. The Uruguay Round made only a modest nod in that direction. Agricultural employment declines as countries grow because productivity growth outstrips the demand for food, but countries tend to protect the farm sector from too-rapid change. This pattern has been seen in the United States, Europe, and Japan, and more recently in Korea.

Terms of trade effects might be substantial in the area of energy, particularly petroleum. Rapid growth in developing countries will increase the demand for energy of all kinds. Coal can be mined in many places without a great increase in cost. But the domestic supply of oil will not keep pace with the demand for oil, putting upward pressure on world prices. The extent of the price rise depends on the investment strategy of Saudi Arabia and several other Persian Gulf countries. The world supply of oil could be greatly increased at roughly constant cost. But will it be increased? And will the world want to further increase its already heavy dependence on the Persian Gulf supply?

If the answer to either question is no, the world price of oil will rise. One well-known forecaster suggests that world demand for petroleum will rise by 8 million barrels a day between 1993 and 2000, whereas non-OPEC supply will rise by only 1 million barrels a day, leaving 7 million barrels a day to be supplied by OPEC, mainly from the Persian Gulf (DRI/McGraw Hill 1994, p. 29). The price rise, in turn, will stimulate additional supply in other parts of the world and will induce substitution away from oil, as seen during the 1980s. But in the medium run these results will only lessen, not reverse, a worsening in the terms of trade for oil importers and an improvement for oil exporters, among both industrial and developing countries. On balance, however, a rise in the world price of oil would generate a transfer of real income from industrial to developing countries and thus would represent (from the viewpoint of consumers in industrial countries) a negative effect of more rapid growth in developing countries.

The International Energy Agency's (IEA) projections of world oil demand and supply to 2010 assume that OECD countries will grow by 2.4 percent a year and that developing countries will grow by 5.1 percent a year over 1990–2010 (table 5). Eastern European countries and the successor states to the Soviet Union are assumed to grow by 1.4 percent a year over this period. World oil prices are expected to increase to $30 a barrel (in 1993 dollars) by 2010 (representing an increase of 1 percent a year from the temporary high of 1990). Under these circumstances world demand for petroleum will increase by 25.8 million barrels a day from the level demanded in 1990, of which only 0.1 million barrels a day will come from countries outside the Middle East and Venezuela.

If developing countries grow faster, at 6.4 percent a year, an additional 5.1 million barrels a day would be added to world demand by 2010, with all of the difference having to come from Venezuela and the Middle East (see the last column in table 5). Absent the necessary investments, the price of oil would rise by more than the amount assumed. Some additional oil could come from the former Soviet Union, since costs there are thought to be low enough to make additional investment profitable at the assumed prices. But technical, legal, tax, and political (affecting transport) considerations have so far conspired to prevent new investment in oil extraction in that part of the world and show no signs of resolution (IEA 1994).

Growth and Economic Dislocation

Growth means change, change means dislocation, and dislocation means discomfort or worse. Some firms will close. Some workers will have to change jobs or retire, even if the economy is growing. For example, over the past two decades the United States has experienced dramatic changes in the pattern of employment. Between 1970 and 1990 total employment rose by 50 percent. But during the same period agricultural employment fell by 36 percent and manufacturing employment remained virtually unchanged. Within manufacturing, employment in textiles and apparel declined by 23 percent and employment in the primary metals industries declined by 39 percent.

The same forces that increase trade also alter the commodity composition of trade. Changes in the pattern of production in developing countries will differ from changes in the pattern of consumption, and some dislocation and pressure on commodity and factor prices will arise in their trading partners as a result. Much concern has been expressed in recent years about what impact increased trade with and investment in developing countries will have on employment, especially low-wage employment, in industrial countries (for example, Wood 1994, chapter 6; Allais 1994; Goldsmith 1995).

It is important to note that dislocation occurs continually in growing economies, apart from the influence of foreign trade. Technological change is constantly "destroying" jobs, as are changes in the pattern of demand, such as the decline in the defense industries in the NATO and ex-Warsaw Pact countries after the Cold War. Job destruction arising from changes in the pattern of foreign trade must be set in this broader context. And, at least for the United States, such changes result in much less dislocation than do technological change and changes in the composition of demand. During 1985–90, for instance, 8.9 million U.S. workers were displaced from and not recalled to their jobs because of plant or firm closure or layoffs, of

Table 5. *Future World Oil Demand and Supply, 1990–2010*
(millions of barrels a day)

Demand/supply	1990	2000	2010	High growth 2010
Demand[a]	67.0	77.5	92.8	97.6
Supply[b]				
OECD	15.9	15.3	13.8	13.8
Eastern Europe and former Soviet Union	11.8	8.6	10.6	10.6
Middle East and Venezuela	20.0	31.1	45.4	50.5
Rest of world	17.9	20.8	21.1	21.1

a. Including rise in stocks.
b. Excluding gains from processing.
Source: IEA 1993 (pp. 27, 32).

which 735,000, or 8 percent, were in import-sensitive sectors (Podgursky 1992, tables 1 and 2). The nearly 9 million workers displaced represented more than 8 percent of total U.S. nonfarm employment in 1990. Total employment rose by 12 million during this period, and total unemployment fell by 2 million, so on balance the displaced workers found new jobs. But they endured a period of dislocation.

Some idea of the relative importance of foreign trade in job displacement can be garnered by comparing the Hufbauer and Schott (1994, tables B4, B5) estimates of the impact on U.S. trade and employment arising from the creation of WHFTA. They find that by 2002, the establishment of WHFTA (in 1990) would have created 544,000 new U.S. jobs in export industries, nearly offset by the loss of 483,000 jobs in import-competing industries. The job losses would be spread widely among industries, although the greatest effect would be felt in certain apparel and agricultural sectors. The total, however, would represent less than 2.5 percent of total U.S. job displacements expected during the 1990s.

Problems of adjustment will be mitigated to some extent because much of the growth in international trade in manufactures between industrial and developing countries has taken place within the same industrial sector. Since 1970 the share of intraindustry trade between the G-7 countries and non-OECD countries has more than doubled in all of the G-7 countries except Canada (table 6).

Growth will continually change trade composition over time, making it important for all countries to maintain a buoyant macroeconomic environment (adjustment is much easier during a period of growth than during stagnation) and to encourage flexibility in labor (and capital) markets, so labor can move smoothly between jobs. Promoting flexibility in labor markets entails a host of issues, including retraining, low barriers to hiring, and a flexible housing market if physical relocation is required.

Relative changes in factor prices ease adjustment. Lower wages for displaced workers facilitates their rehiring. Wage adjustment seems to work better in the United States than in Western Europe. But it has given rise to a concern about a

Table 6. *Intraindustry Trade As a Share of Total Trade in Manufactured Goods between G-7 countries and Non-OECD Countries, 1970, 1980, 1991*
(percentage of total trade in manufactures)

Country	1970	1980	1991
Canada	13	20	23
France	16	26	42
Germany	19	27	38
Italy	18	28	44
Japan	11	15	28
United Kingdom	24	36	53
United States	23	31	48

Note: Trade at the three-digit standard industrial trade classification (SITC) level.
Source: OECD 1994a (p. 41).

growing disparity in wages between the upper-middle class and the working poor. Wage dispersion has certainly increased in the United States during the past two decades, with the well-to-do having become much better off and the poorest people having suffered a decline in real earnings.

How much of this increased dispersion can be explained by foreign trade, particularly by increased imports of manufactured goods from low-wage countries? Several researchers have approached this question (see, for example, Lawrence and Slaughter 1993; Sachs and Shatz 1994; Cooper 1994 and the references cited there). The labor and trade economists participating in a 1994 symposium held by the Federal Reserve Bank of New York (FRBNY) reached a consensus that about 10 percent of the relative reduction in wages of low-skilled workers in the United States could be attributed to foreign trade. The remainder was attributable to technological change (60 percent) and other factors (30 percent), such as immigration and changes in wage-setting practices (FRBNY 1995, p. 34). Cooper (1994) also derived an estimate of 10 percent.

The relatively small effect is primarily the result of the small number of unskilled workers released from the manufacturing sectors because of import competition relative to both the size and the growth of employment of unskilled workers in other sectors of the U.S. economy, notably the retail sector. Cooper (1994) also found that import competition from low-wage developing countries was not a significant factor underlying the growth of unemployment in the major European countries during the past decade, except possibly France, but that it could account for some of the modest increases in wage dispersion seen in several European countries.[1]

Again the Hufbauer-Schott (1994, table B6) calculations for a notional WHFTA are of interest. A rough calculation of the impact of WHFTA on the median weekly wage in the United States shows little difference between the 1990 average weekly wage in the U.S. industries that export to Latin America ($442) and those that import from Latin America ($435). Hufbauer and Schott inexplicably assume that the composition of U.S. exports to Latin America will remain unchanged under WHFTA. But they find that U.S. imports of low-wage products will increase more than average, reducing the (1990) wage associated with imports in 2002 to $410 a week with WHFTA, compared with $419 a week without WHFTA (but with continuing economic reforms in Latin America). Thus increased imports from Latin America do put downward pressure on wages, although the incremental contribution from WHFTA is small (2 percent of the initial wage). This effect arises solely from a change in trade composition; it does not represent the market response to WHFTA and is consistent with (the unlikely possibility of) wages remaining static in all sectors.

Increased foreign trade will put downward pressure on the prices of factors that are used intensively in domestic production experiencing greater import competition and upward pressure on the prices of factors that are used intensively in export industries. With respect to increased trade between OECD countries and developing countries, these pressures are likely to mean downward pressure on the wages of low-skilled workers and upward pressure on the wages of high-skilled workers in OECD countries. The effects are likely to be small but modestly helpful to growth insofar as workers are induced to upgrade their education and skills.

A similar argument could be made for capital: insofar as OECD exports are relatively capital intensive, increased trade with developing countries will tend to raise the return to capital. But the evidence on the capital intensity of exports, at least for the United States, is ambiguous—it is not clear that U.S. exports are more capital intensive than import-competing goods (Baldwin 1971 and Maskus 1985).

The growth effects of investment in developing countries by industrial country investors seeking higher expected returns are likely to be more significant. Greater investment in developing countries will also tend to pull upward the return to capital in OECD countries, possibly encouraging savings there but also discouraging domestic investment, which will have to achieve a higher rate of return to attract investors. The suppression of domestic investment will deter growth in industrial countries. Again, the magnitude of this influence is small and is likely to remain small for several years, even in the presence of new investment opportunities. For instance, even if the entire Mexican current account deficit (that is, net capital inflows) of 8 percent of GDP in 1994 had been financed from the United States, that amount would have represented only 0.3 percent of U.S. GDP and 2 percent of U.S. gross domestic investment.[2]

Growth-Induced Movements in Factors of Production

Growing countries offer good investment opportunities for mature economies, providing both higher yields and opportunities to diversify risk. There are three broad forms of foreign investment: "fixed" interest loans, portfolio equity investments, and direct investment. Loans can be privately negotiated (such as bank loans) or publicly issued (such as bonds). They can be made from one public authority to another (such as official foreign assistance loans or World Bank loans), from public authority to private parties, from private parties to public borrowers (such as the bank consortium loans of the 1970s and early 1980s), or from private lenders to private borrowers.

In mid-1994 the claims of commercial banks in eighteen industrial countries on all developing countries totaled $492 billion, of which $127 billion was on public sector borrowers, $175 billion was on banking institutions, and the remainder was on other private borrowers (BIS 1995, p. 2). In addition, nearly $100 billion in bonds and notes of developing countries were estimated to be held abroad at the end of 1993 (calculated from Goldstein and Folkerts-Landau 1994, p. 126). The yields on these loans were several hundred basis points higher than the yields on loans to or bonds of industrial countries (UNCTAD 1994, p. 35), even after allowing for any exchange risk (although most of the loans were denominated in currencies of industrial countries). For example, only $85 billion of the $492 in bank claims was denominated in local currencies, and that was largely offset by bank liabilities in local currencies.

Another possible form of investment in developing countries is purchases of local company shares. Such investment was negligible before the 1980s but became substantial in the early 1990s as investment in "emerging markets" came into vogue. The creation of numerous mutual funds specializing in these securities promoted

---

investment in emerging markets because the funds were able to mediate between the relatively unsophisticated investor and nascent and still volatile equity markets in developing countries. In addition, privatization of state-owned enterprises encouraged some developing countries, such as Argentina and Mexico, to seek fresh equity capital from OECD countries. New international equity issues by developing countries grew from $1.3 billion in 1990 to $11.9 billion in 1993. Also, as much as $40 billion in equities was purchased abroad in secondary markets in 1993, up from $14 billion in 1992 and virtually nothing in 1989 (Goldstein and Folkerts-Landau 1994, p. 84). Although data are not yet readily available, such purchases probably declined sharply and may have become net sales in late 1994 and early 1995, following the financial community's temporary disillusionment with Mexico. By the end of 1994 OECD countries' total holdings of equity securities on developing countries amounted to about $125 billion.

Investing in equity in seven Asian markets during the 1980s would have roughly doubled the yield earned from investing in companies listed on the New York Stock Exchange (NYSE), from an annual average of 12.5 percent to about 25 percent (calculated from Rhee 1992, p. 80). In addition to raising yields, investments in emerging markets can reduce portfolio risk since the returns in these markets are less than perfectly correlated with equity returns in industrial countries (and with each other). Individually, emerging markets in Asia are substantially more volatile than the NYSE, but because of the low correlation with the NYSE some investment in these markets could reduce overall market risk and increase total return (table 7).

A schedule of rate of return and risk of a portfolio made up of equity investments in OECD countries (in proportion to market capitalization) and equity investments in twenty-five emerging markets (as reported by the International Finance Corporation) is derived for 1989–93 (figure 1). The share of emerging markets in

Table 7. *Risk and Return on Equities in Asian Markets*

Country	Market capitalization, end-1989 (billions of dollars)	Annual return, 1980–89 (dollars)	Volatility,[a] 1980–89	Correlation with New York Stock Exchange[b]	Beta[c]
Japan	4,260	26.4	.058	.27	.32
Taiwan (China)	236	37.0	.117	.25	.61
Korea, Republic of	140	20.4	.064	.13	.17
Hong Kong	78	7.3	.110	.38	.87
Malaysia	40	1.3	.097	.51	.97
Singapore	36	7.1	.071	.51	.75
Thailand	26	16.6	.064	.36	.48
Philippines	12	−13.5	.104	.12	.26
United States (NYSE)	3,030	12.5	.048	1.00	1.00

a. Standard deviation of monthly changes, in dollars.
b. Monthly averages.
c. A deviation from unity indicates a lack of co-movement with the New York Stock Exchange.
Source: Rhee 1992.

total investment can vary from 0 to 100 percent. Increasing that share from 0 to 22 percent over 1989–93 would have roughly doubled the rate of return, from 7.5 to 15 percent, and reduced overall portfolio risk. Raising the share of emerging markets in total investment above 22 percent would have increased yields further, but only at the expense of increasing portfolio risk. Most investment portfolios in OECD countries held much less than 22 percent in emerging markets, thus offering a "free lunch" of higher returns and lower risk until that share was reached.

Fischer and Reisen (1994, p. 23) argue that OECD pension funds and other long-term investors should greatly increase the share of their investments in emerging markets from the 0.2 percent share estimated for 1992. As the populations of OECD countries age, financing public pension payments on a pay-as-you-go basis, as do most European countries, the U.S. social security system, and Japan, will be increasingly burdensome to the working population. Even if pension funds are funded, earnings on domestic investments paid to pensioners will, other things being equal, reduce the incomes of the working population.

If, however, funded pension funds are invested in rapidly growing economies, they can simultaneously stimulate growth in capital-short countries and increase returns to mature economies. In the long run the returns to equity investments, mediated through corporate profits and dividend payments, are likely to be positively correlated with overall economic growth. Investments in higher-growth economies will both stimulate growth abroad and bring about higher returns. At the same time, however, such investment on a large scale could reduce growth in domestic output in the investing countries, even while increasing growth in national income, because of reduced investment at home.

Figure 1. *Efficient Frontiers: Share of Emerging Markets (IFC Composite Index) in Total Investment Portfolio, 1989–93*

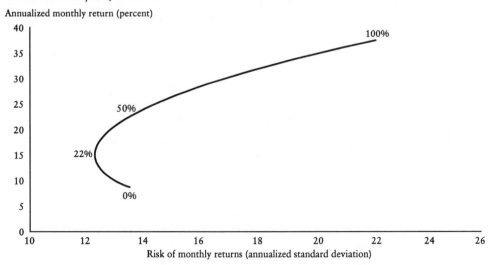

Annualized monthly return (percent)

Risk of monthly returns (annualized standard deviation)

Source: Fischer and Reisen 1994.

The third form of foreign investment in developing countries is direct investment, that is, equity investment that involves management control. Direct investment has been the most controversial form of investment historically, but developing countries are becoming increasingly more confident about their ability to deal with foreign firms on at least equal terms. They are thus more receptive to the advantages foreign direct investment can bring in technical or managerial know-how and in overseas market development. Outstanding direct investments from the ten largest OECD countries in developing countries exceeded $365 billion at the end of 1992, and new foreign direct investment reached $38 billion during 1992 (calculated from OECD 1994b).

The main advantage of foreign direct investment to the home countries is enhanced return to capital, and the secondary advantage is diversification of market risk. Overall U.S. direct investment abroad earned 14.8 percent on historic cost in 1992, compared with an average return of around 12 percent in the United States. The return was 17.6 percent on investment in Latin America, 25 percent in Asia (excluding Australia and Japan), and more than 30 percent in Africa and the Middle East (calculated from *Survey of Current Business,* June 1994). Comprehensive data are not available on returns to all foreign direct investment in developing countries from OECD countries.

Migration

A discussion of international factor movements would not be complete without an examination of the relation between economic growth and migration. Many think that economic growth in developing countries will reduce emigration. And it might in the long run. But the relationship is not simple. Economic growth is associated with increased internal migration from rural to urban areas. Once people are dislodged from traditional lifestyles, they may set their sights beyond the nearest urban conglomeration and emigrate. Emigration is especially likely if relatives or others from the same village have already moved abroad. Moreover, people earning higher income have more options for movement. So, initially, growth in poor countries is likely to be associated with increased emigration.[3] On the other hand a more promising long-term economic future at home will attract home successful emigrants who left earlier. Taiwan (China), for instance, has experienced a substantial reflow of former expatriates in recent years, especially from the United States. And both Italy and Japan, important sources of net emigration in the 1950s, had by the early 1990s become destinations of immigrants from poorer countries.

Stabilization of World Aggregate Demand

Trade with developing countries can help to reduce fluctuations in aggregate demand and output in industrial countries. At several points in the past two decades, notably 1974–75, 1981–82, and the early 1990s, demand has been insufficient to fully employ the productive capacity of the major industrial countries, resulting in increased unemployment and reduced corporate profits. Despite the effects of substantial built-in stabilizers (working through income taxes and extensive unemployment compensation) and despite the occasional active use of fiscal and monetary policy to stabilize the growth of output along its medium-term trend, industrial countries have not successfully eliminated the business cycle. These fluctuations continue to be troublesome, aggravating unemployment and increasing public debt.

Exports to developing countries have helped to mitigate the size of economic fluctuations in OECD countries. The absence of perfect correlation between the patterns of economic activity in developing countries and in OECD countries helps to mitigate fluctuations in both parts of the world. Comparing the GDP gap in the G-7 (which together accounted for about 85 percent of OECD GDP in 1990) over the past two decades with the deviation in exports (in constant prices) from OECD countries to developing countries around their two-decade trend growth of 3.1 percent a year shows that export deviations tended to be positive in years of GDP shortfalls from capacity in the G-7 nations (figure 2). The low correlation between the two series, −0.16, suggests that exports to developing countries played a stabilizing role, although their impact was not great quantitatively, amounting in the early 1990s to about 0.3 percent of GDP in OECD countries.

Unquestionably, the global recessions of 1974–75 and 1981–82 would have been much deeper if developing countries had not maintained their growth in demand during these periods. Oil-exporting countries could buy more with their large oil revenues, but oil-importing developing countries had to borrow abroad to sustain their imports, thus laying the basis for the debt crisis of the 1980s. Nonetheless, their borrowing helped stabilize global demand during downturns in industrial

Figure 2. *Relationship between G-7 GDP Gap and Deviation from Trend of Real OECD Exports to Developing Countries*

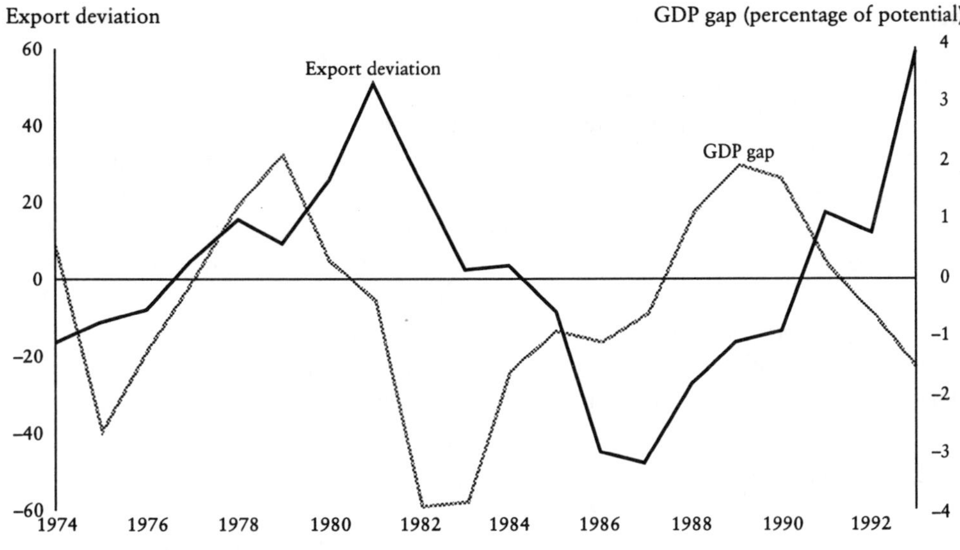

Source: Fischer and Reisen 1994.

countries. Again, during the prolonged slump of the early 1990s, with recession in the United States, the United Kingdom, and Canada followed by recession in Japan and continental Europe, exports to developing countries helped to prevent aggregate demand from falling more than it did.

As developing countries grow relative to OECD countries, their contribution to economic stabilization in OECD countries will become even greater, unless economic activity becomes more synchronized in the two regions, or until developing countries become so large that their collective activity dominates that of today's OECD countries.

Growth and the Environment

A rapidly growing literature is examining the relationship between growth and the environment (see World Bank 1992 and Beghin, Roland-Holst, and van der Mensbrugghe 1994 for useful compilations of recent work). Not surprisingly, there are few definitive relationships, but some tentative generalizations can be made.

Economic growth, associated with increased use of commercial energy, generally increases greenhouse gas emissions. In particular, both China and India have substantial indigenous reserves of coal that if used at increasing rates would substantially increase emissions of carbon dioxide and possibly exacerbate global warming. Also, greater worldwide production and consumption generate greater amounts of solid waste.

By the same token, however, rising incomes increase demand for environmental improvements. This effect is manifest even at low levels of income with respect to sanitation and clean water for human use, which show steady improvement as incomes rise. Air and water pollution (suspended particulate and sulfur compounds in the air, oxygen demand and heavy metals in the water) tend to rise when income increases from low levels, but peak and then decline after per capita income reaches $3,000 to $6,000 (Grossman and Krueger 1993). Toxic waste and lead in the air show a similar inverted U pattern as income rises (Hettig, Lucas, and Wheeler 1992; Selden and Song 1994; Wheeler, Hettig, and Mani 1995). Increasing per capita income tends to move tastes gradually away from pollution-intensive production of goods (especially primary metals) toward services. Finally, enforcement of environmental regulation seems to increase steadily with higher per capita income (Wheeler, Hettig, and Mani 1995).

Even from this brief review it is clear that higher rates of growth in developing countries are likely to lead to environmental improvement in some respects and worsening in others. The net effect is likely to depend on the initial level of per capita income, with a general worsening of environmental variables at low levels of income followed by an improvement at higher levels of income.

Economic Growth and Political Evolution

Growth in per capita income enlarges economic possibilities, reduces despair, and creates hope for the future. Over time it leads to pressures for democratic pluralism as people cease to be preoccupied with where their next meal is coming from. And as they become better educated, they want a voice in the political decisions that affect their lives. Growth tends to be associated with political evolution toward democracy, particularly after per capita incomes rise above $1,000 (in 1990 dollars; see Huntington 1991, Helliwell 1994, and Diamond 1992).

The process, however, is typically not smooth or linear. Economic growth gives authoritarian leaders greater resources with which to suppress domestic dissent and threaten their neighbors. If the dislocation that comes from growth is not well managed, internal unrest, turmoil, even revolution or civil war may ensue (Huntington 1968). Greater national wealth may also foster greater international ambitions, leading to more intense regional conflict.

For years political scientists have associated political instability with high or growing income inequality, although recently some questions have been raised about the methodologies employed (see Lichbach 1989 and the references cited there). Insofar as economic development from low levels of income widens income disparities during the early phases of development, political unrest and instability may follow.

Recent research suggests that civil and political liberties are related to per capita income in a complex way. They first rise as annual per capita income increases from very low levels to about $2,500 (1985 dollars), fall as per capita income rises to $3,000, and then rise again before leveling off at per capita incomes of about $5,000 (Lipset, Seong, and Torres 1993). This relationship is tested on cross-country data, but it is thought also to apply over time within a particular country.

Today's industrial countries have a strong interest in both the process and the outcome. Democratic countries are much less likely to threaten their neighbors than authoritarian countries. Thus national security is enhanced by an evolution toward democracy. But industrial countries also have an interest in creating an international environment for conflict resolution, both internal and external, to ensure as much as possible that the political evolution is relatively smooth.

Conclusion

It may be useful to pull together the largely qualitative judgments that have been made about the influence on industrial countries of higher growth in developing countries, brought about largely by global trade liberalization. First, trade liberalization itself will raise incomes in the rich countries, both directly and indirectly, through increased saving and investment. Greater competition may induce greater innovation, although it is difficult to find direct evidence in support of this effect. Over time, some developing countries will become sources of innovation, to the benefit of (almost) all, but that effect is likely to be distant.

Changing patterns of trade resulting from growth will create dislocations in industrial countries. But if the past is any guide, these dislocations will be small relative to those caused by technological change and changes in the pattern of domestic (especially government) demand. And they can be absorbed easily if economies are buoyant and if labor and capital markets are functioning well.

There is not much expectation of a movement in the terms of trade, although on balance any such movement is more likely to favor industrial countries than not— assuming sufficient investment occurs in the Middle East to supply the consequent increases in demand for oil. Absent an increase in supply the terms of trade could turn notably against all importers of oil, industrial and developing countries alike.

Increased growth in developing countries and improved capital markets enlarge profitable investment opportunities for savers in industrial countries; it would be reasonable to expect that developing countries will achieve rates of return in the near future that exceed those in industrial countries by at least 3 percentage points. Given the current levels of net claims on developing countries of about $1 trillion, a 3 percentage point difference would result in (at least) $30 billion a year, a small amount relative to total income in industrial countries. As investment increases, returns may fall, but not rapidly as long as developing countries continue to grow rapidly.

Investment in developing countries not only raises income in industrial countries, it also stabilizes incomes, since fluctuations in growth and earnings in the two sets of countries are not perfectly correlated. Thus higher average returns can be garnered at lower aggregate risk, for a well-diversified investment portfolio.

An analogous argument applies to earned income and investment income: fluctuations in output in developing countries do not closely mimic those in OECD countries, and therefore, through trade, they help to stabilize output and employment in OECD countries. Although the effect is small at present, it will grow as developing countries gain in relative economic importance, provided the fluctuations in output do not become more closely correlated over time.

The main point to note about environmental degradation is that it is largely local (or occasionally regional) in character, and thus is not likely to affect industrial countries directly. Growth from low levels of income is likely to increase pollution. But higher levels of income lead to a reduction in demand for pollution-intensive goods and, more important, to growing demand for environmental improvement. Thus growth in middle-income countries is likely to lead to reductions in pollution.

A similar inverted U pattern can be discerned with respect to political instability when countries are at low levels of per capita income: growth involves change, and change involves stress, particularly in traditional processes of collective decisionmaking and dispute settlement. In many cases these periods of stress are managed relatively smoothly, but in some countries they erupt into political violence that affects not only the residents of that country, but also their neighbors and the international community.

Notes

1. Wood (1994) judges the impact to be greater than that found by most other researchers. But his methodology is critically flawed in that it imputes to industrial countries the labor input coefficients recorded for poor countries (adjusted for relative differences in factor prices) but allows for only limited substitution away from consumption products imported from developing countries, despite the enormously high prices they would command if produced in industrial countries. He argues that modern technology in manufacturing is now available to developing countries. But his labor coefficients are drawn from the average recent production structures, not from newly available best practice, which would pre-

sumably show lower labor inputs. Even so, Wood's primary finding is that imports from developing countries cumulatively reduced the demand for unskilled labor in the OECD countries by only 5 percent; his larger estimate is reached by quadrupling this number on the grounds that it does not allow adequately for service transactions or for trade-induced, labor-saving innovation (pp. 10–11, chapter 4).

Using a simple two-sector industrial country-developing country analytical framework with plausible coefficients, Krugman (1995) suggests that total imports of manufactured goods from developing countries under free trade would raise unemployment in industrial countries by only 1.4 percentage points, under the extreme assumption of downwardly rigid wages in industrial countries.

2. Bosworth (1993, p. 86) estimates that a 1 percentage point rise in the real interest rate will reduce the rate of change of the business capital stock in the OECD countries by only 0.09 percentage point—a negligible amount.

3. With respect to Mexico Martin (1993) suggests that NAFTA will stimulate accelerated migration out of agriculture that will, for a while, lead to increased emigration to the United States. But eventually migration will decline as urban and rural prosperity in Mexico become more attractive. See also Meissner's summary of an OECD conference on migration and development, that emphasizes the migration paradox, whereby emigration increases for the first ten to fifteen years as development occurs (OECD 1994c, p. 299–301). Based on the experience of Latin America and Southeast Asia, Richards (1994, p. 159) concludes "the more frequent relationship between freer trade and migration flows is a complementary one, not one in which trade and migration are substitutes."

References

Allais, Maurice. 1994. "La concurrence des pay à bas salaires." *Le Figaro* 20 (December): 2.

Allen, Chris, and David Vines. 1993. "Macroeconomic Interactions between North and South." Paper presented at Centre for European Policy Research Conference, April, Oxford, United Kingdom.

Baldwin, Robert E. 1971. "Determinants of the Commodity Structure of U.S. Trade." *American Economic Review* 61 (March): 126–46.

———. 1994. "The Effect of Trade and Foreign Direct Investment on Employment and Relative Wages." *OECD Economic Studies* 23 (Winter): 7–54.

Beghin, John, David Roland-Holst, and Dominique van der Mensbrugghe. 1994. "A Survey of the Trade and Environment Nexus: Global Dimensions." *OECD Economic Studies* 23 (winter): 167–92.

Bhagwati, Jagdish, and T.N. Srinivasan. 1983. *Lectures in the Theory of International Trade.* Cambridge, Mass: MIT Press.

BIS (Bank for International Settlements). 1995. *The Maturity, Sectoral, and Nationality Distribution of International Bank Lending, First Half 1994.* Basle.

Bosworth, Barry P. 1993. *Saving and Investment in a Global Economy.* Washington, D.C.: The Brookings Institution.

CEA (Council of Economic Advisers). 1995. *Economic Report of the President.* Washington, D.C.: U.S. Government Printing Office.

Collins, Susan M., and Barry P. Bosworth, eds. 1994. *The New GATT: Implications for the United States.* Washington, D.C.: The Brookings Institution.

Cooper, Richard N. 1994. "Foreign Trade, Wages, and Unemployment." Harvard University Economic Research Paper 1701. Cambridge, Mass.

Currie, David, and David Vines, eds. 1988. *Macroeconomic Interactions between North and South.* Cambridge: Cambridge University Press.

Deardorff, Alan V. 1994. "Economic Effects of Quota and Tariff Reductions." In Susan M. Collins and Barry P. Bosworth, eds., *The New GATT: Implications for the United States.* Washington, D.C.: The Brookings Institution.

Diamond, Larry. 1992. "Economic Development and Democracy Reconsidered." *American Behavioral Scientist* 35 (March/June): 450–99.

DRI/McGraw-Hill. 1994. *Review of the U.S. Economy: Ten-Year Projections.* Lexington, Mass.

Fischer, Bernhard, and Helmut Reisen. 1994. *Pension Fund Investment From Ageing to Emerging Markets.* OECD Development Center Policy Brief 9. Paris: OECD.

Francois, Joseph F., Bradley McDonald, and Håkan Nordström. 1994. *The Uruguay Round: A Global General Equilibrium Assessment.* Geneva: GATT.

FRBNY (Federal Reserve Bank of New York). 1995. "Colloquium on U.S. Wage Trends." *Economic Policy Review.* New York.

GATT (General Agreement on Tariffs and Trade). 1993. *International Trade: Statistics, 1993.* Geneva.

———. 1994. "The Results of the Uruguay Round of Multilateral Trade Negotiations." Geneva.

Goldin, Ian, and Dominique van der Mensbrugghe. 1995. "The Uruguay Round: An Assessment of Economywide and Agricultural Reforms." World Bank, International Economics Department, International Trade Division, Washington, D.C.

Goldin, Ian, Odin Knudsen, and Dominique van der Mensbrugghe. 1993. *Trade Liberalisation: Global Economic Implications.* Paris: OECD.

Goldsmith, Sir James. 1995. "Global Free Trade: Recipe for a Lumpenplanet." *New Perspectives Quarterly* 12 (Winter): 39–41.

Goldstein, Morris and David Folkerts-Landau. 1994. *International Capital Markets: Developments, Prospects, and Policy Issues.* Washington, D.C.: International Monetary Fund.

Grossman, Gene M., and Elhanan Helpman. 1991. *Innovation and Growth in the Global Economy.* Cambridge, Mass.: MIT Press.

Grossman, Gene M., and A.B. Krueger. 1993. "Environmental Impacts of a North American Free Trade Area." In P. Garber, ed., *The U.S.-Mexico Trade Agreement.* Cambridge, Mass.: MIT Press.

Helliwell, John. 1994. "Empirical Linkages between Democracy and Economic Growth." *British Journal of Political Science* 24: 225–48.

Helpman, Elhanan, and Paul Krugman. 1985. *Market Structure and Foreign Trade: Increasing Returns, Imperfect Competition, and the International Economy.* Cambridge, Mass.: MIT Press.

Henderson, Dale W., and Warwick J. McKibbin. 1993. "An Assessment of Some Basic Monetary Policy Regime Pairs: Analytical and Simulation Results from Simple Multiregion Macroeconomic Models." In Ralph C. Bryant, Peter Hooper, and Catherine L. Mann, eds. *Evaluating Policy Regimes.* Washington, D.C.: The Brookings Institution.

Hettig, H., R.E.B. Lucas, and D. Wheeler. 1992. "The Toxic Intensity of Industrial Production: Global Patterns, Trends, and Trade Policy." *American Economic Review* 82 (May): 478–81.

Hicks, J.R. 1953. "An Inaugural Lecture." *Oxford Economic Papers* 2 (June): 117–35.

Hufbauer, Gary Clyde, and Jeffrey J. Schott. 1992. *North American Free Trade: Issues and Recommendations.* Washington, D.C.: Institute for International Economics.

———. 1993. *NAFTA: An Assessment.* Washington, D.C.: Institute for International Economics.

———. 1994. *Western Hemisphere Economic Integration.* Washington, D.C.: Institute for International Economics.

Huntington, Samuel P. 1968. *Political Order in Changing Societies.* New Haven, Conn.: Yale University Press.

———. 1991. *The Third Wave: Democratization in the Late Twentieth Century.* Norman, Okla.: University of Oklahoma Press.

IEA (International Energy Agency). 1993. *World Energy Outlook.* Paris: OECD.

———. 1994. *Russian Energy Prices, Taxes, and Costs, 1993.* Paris: OECD.

IMF (International Monetary Fund). Various years. *International Financial Statistics.* Washington, D.C.

Johnson, Harry G. 1958. *International Trade and Economic Growth.* London: Allen and Unwin.

Krugman, Paul. 1995. "Growing World Trade: Causes and Consequences." *Brookings Papers on Economic Activity 1.* Washington, D.C.: The Brookings Institution.

Lawrence, Robert Z., and Matthew Slaughter. 1993. "International Trade and American Wages in the 1980s: Giant Sucking Sound or Small Hiccup?" *Brookings Papers on Economic Activity 2.* Washington, D.C.: The Brookings Institution.

Lichbach, Mark Irving. 1989. "An Evaluation of 'Does Economic Inequality Breed Political Conflict?' Studies." *World Politics* 41 (July): 431–70.

Lipset, Seymour Martin, Kyoung-Ryung Seong, and John Charles Torres. 1993. "A Comparative Analysis of the Social Requisites of Democracy." *International Social Science Journal* 136: 155–75.

Maddison, Angus. 1989. *The World Economy in the 20th Century.* Paris: OECD.

Mankiw, Gregory, David Romer, and David Weil. 1992. "A Contribution to the Empirics of Economic Growth." *Quarterly Journal of Economics* 152 (May): 407–37.

Martin, Philip L. 1993. *Trade and Migration: NAFTA and Agriculture.* Washington, D.C.: Institute for International Economics.

Maskus, Keith E. 1985. "A Test of the Heckscher-Ohlin-Vanek Theorem: The Leontief Commonplace." *Journal of International Economics* 19 (November): 210–12.

McKibbin, Warwick J., and Jeffrey D. Sachs. 1991. *Global Linkages: Macroeconomic Interdependence and Cooperation in the World Economy.* Washington, D.C.: The Brookings Institution.

OECD (Organization for Economic Cooperation and Development). 1994a. *Economic Outlook.* Paris.

———. 1994b. *International Direct Investment Statistics Yearbook 1994.* Paris.

———. 1994c. *Migration and Development.* Paris.

———. 1994d. *National Accounts, 1980–1992.* Paris.

Podgursky, Michael. 1992. "The Industrial Structure of Job Displacement, 1979–1989." *Monthly Labor Review* 115 (September).

Reisen, Helmut. 1994. "On the Wealth of Nations and Retirees." In *Finance and the International Economy 8.* London: Oxford University Press for American Express.

Rhee, S. Ghon. 1992. *Securities Markets and Systemic Risks in Dynamic Asian Economies.* Paris: OECD.

Richards, Anne. 1994. "Trade Liberalization and Migration Flows: Some Evidence from Developing Countries." In OECD, *Migration and Development.* Paris: OECD.

Sachs, Jeffrey D., and Howard J. Shatz. 1994. "Trade and Jobs in U.S. Manufacturing." *Brookings Papers on Economic Activity* 1. Washington, D.C.: The Brookings Institution.

Selden, Thomas M., and Daging Song. 1994. "Environmental Quality and Development: Is There a Kuznets Curve for Air Pollution Emissions?" *Journal of Environmental Economics and Management* 27 (September): 147–62.

Spraos, John. 1980. "Statistical Debate on the Net Barter Terms of Trade." *Economic Journal* 96 (March): 107–28.

UNCTAD (United Nations Conference on Trade and Development). 1994. *Trade and Development Report, 1994.* Geneva.

Weiss, Leonard W. 1976. "Optimal Plant Size and the Extent of Suboptimal Capacity." In Robert T. Masson and P. David Qualls, eds., *Essays in Industrial Organization.* Cambridge, Mass: Ballinger.

Wheeler, David, Hemamala Hettig, and Muthukumara Mani. 1995. "Pollution Intensity and Economic Development: Confronting the 'Pollution Havens' Problem." World Bank, Policy Research Department, Environment, Infrastructure, and Agriculture Division, Washington, D.C.

Wood, Adrian.1994. *North-South Trade, Employment, and Inequality: Changing Fortunes in a Skill-Driven World.* Oxford, U.K.: Clarendon.

World Bank. 1992. *World Development Report 1992: Development and the Environment.* New York: Oxford University Press.

———. 1995. *Global Economic Prospects and the Developing Countries 1995.* Washington, D.C.

Comment on "Is Growth in Industrial Countries Beneficial to Industrial Countries?" by Richard N. Cooper

Willem H. Buiter

Almost inevitably, Richard Cooper paints with a brush that is both broad and nonspecific. Ideally, we would like to be able to make unconditional, quantitative predictions about the effect on economic performance and economic well-being in industrial countries of policies and events that promote growth in developing countries and of changes in the policy regimes governing trade, financial, and other interactions between the two groups of countries. But the best we are able to make are conditional, qualitative conjectures.

I disagree outright with a few of Cooper's points. There are also some differences in perspective and emphasis between us. I will focus on four key propositions:

- Increased economic integration between developing and industrial countries is potentially beneficial to industrial countries. Given a benevolent and competent government, industrial countries could adopt policies that would ensure that they benefit from increased economic integration with developing countries.
- The ball is in the court of the industrial countries. Depending on the policy actions taken by industrial countries, the effects of increased integration with developing countries can be anything from helpful to harmful.
- There are bound to be losers. Gains and losses in industrial countries from increased integration with developing countries are likely to be unequally distributed, with the most injured being those groups that are economically weak and vulnerable to begin with (such as unskilled and semiskilled workers in traditional manufacturing industries like apparel, textiles, and footwear).
- The capacity of industrial countries to provide flexibility in their markets and security for their workers and citizens will determine whether there are net benefits or losses from increased integration. A well-designed welfare state

Willem H. Buiter is professor of international macroeconomics at the University of Cambridge. This comment benefited from work completed for the International Economics Department of the World Bank, which resulted in Buiter (1994), written for World Bank (1995). The author thanks those who contributed to chapter 4 of World Bank (1995), especially Swati R. Ghosh, for many helpful comments and suggestions on Buiter (1994).

Annual World Bank Conference on Development Economics 1995

will reduce the costs of change for individuals, including the costs incurred as a result of the economic emancipation of developing countries. Because the welfare state can cushion these changes, it reduces industrial and political resistance to change and pressure for protection, and therefore enhances productivity and security.

Increased Trade Integration

Several points should always be made when international trade policy is being discussed. First, trade is not a zero-sum game. Gains from trade may result from differences in tastes, differences in endowments, static scale economies, dynamic increasing returns, and love of variety in the presence of fixed costs of adding variety. Second, a general equilibrium perspective is essential to any discussion of the consequences of trade policy changes. Cooper discharges his duty to the profession when he stresses the importance of tracing the disposition of the income increases generated by higher labor productivity in developing countries: higher production implies higher income, which implies higher expenditure; increases in exports generate increases in imports.

Therefore, the presumption must be that increased trade integration is beneficial. For increased trade integration to be harmful, one of three conditions must be satisfied. First, there is at least one preexisting domestic distortion (such as a factor market distortion) that cannot be remedied or offset with the available policy instruments. Second, the policy itself is distortionary—it turns potential gains into actual losses. Third, the government is restricted in its ability to compensate losers. Note that it is actual compensation that matters, not potential compensation. The ability to compensate is of no interest unless it is actually exercised.

Cooper handles the first two presumptions well. But his discussion of the distribution of gains and losses in industrial countries is inadequate. This issue is central to understanding the political economy of resistance to change. The neglect of distributional issues may be an unfortunate by-product of much of international trade theory, which treats nations as representative agents. Nations don't consume; individuals or households do. Nations don't produce; farms, firms, and enterprises do. Convergence between (among) nations can occur together with divergence within nations.

I have a minor quibble with the title of Cooper's article. Questions about the effect of trade on growth or growth on trade are virtually guaranteed to be ill-posed because both trade and growth are endogenous. For a small, open economy growth in the rest of the world can be taken as exogenous with respect to that country's own growth and trade performance. But when we are considering growth in the developing world and economic performance in the industrial world, the questions and counterfactuals must be formulated more carefully.

A meaningful counterfactual, addressed for example in World Bank (1995, chapter 4) and Buiter (1994), concerns the consequences of the Uruguay Round on trade, output, and material well-being for the world and for specific regions. But it is very hard to come up with numbers that can be taken seriously. Estimates of the static gains from the Uruguay Round differ greatly depending on whether constant returns and perfect competition are assumed or static increasing returns and imperfect competition. They also double in magnitude at regular intervals, without explanation. Attempts to allow for medium-term and long-term dynamic effects through capital accumulation require that we decide what constitutes an appropriate empirical growth model. Applications of the new endogenous growth theory to these issues are preliminary at best (Baldwin 1989; Buiter 1994, which uses Baldwin's methodology; World Bank 1995, chapter 4). One reason is that the theoretical models (such as Rivera-Batiz and Romer 1991a,b or Grossman and Helpman 1992 and Baldwin 1992) are not yet applicable to empirical testing. Almost without exception, they incorporate unrealistic assumptions about unbounded static increasing returns to scale. Some of the testable implications of these assumptions are so obviously counterfactual that it is hard to attach much confidence to any estimates of gains from trade integration based on these models. Some of the key dynamic effects, operating through Schumpeterian mechanisms such as induced innovation and reductions in X-inefficiency, are uncertain in magnitude and in sign (Horn, Land, and Lundgren 1995). World Bank (1995, chapter 4) bravely treads on new ground, discussing intelligently the merits of the few recent attempts at quantification.

Cooper points out, citing work by Hufbauer and Schott (1994), Lawrence and Slaughter (1993), Sachs and Shatz (1994), and Cooper (1994), that the effects of increased trade integration with developing countries have been small thus far—certainly much smaller than the consequences of technological change, immigration, and other domestic developments in industrial countries. The only scholarly contribution (Wood 1994) to reach the opposite conclusion is unconvincing in its methodology. But although the effect of developing country growth on the industrial world has been minor thus far, it will not remain so if recent growth differentials are maintained.

A focus on nations is appropriate to this discussion for two reasons. First, an important factor of production, labor (and the human capital embodied in it), tends to be much less mobile across than within national boundaries. Second, economic policy tends to be made mainly at the national level (an obvious exception is the European Union). But international economic integration creates winners and losers that are not all covered by a common redistribution or compensation framework. This is one reason why dislocations associated with changes in the international trade regime tend to be very sensitive politically. Another reason is undoubtedly xenophobia.

A country's entire economic policy arsenal determines how it responds to challenges like those posed by increased economic integration between developing and industrial countries—whether there are aggregate gains and how these gains are distributed. In what follows I take as given those policy actions aimed directly at influencing the nature and scope of interaction with developing countries—policies affecting trade, international financial flows, factor mobility, migration, intellectual property rights, and so on. I will focus on domestic policy actions in the industrial world, especially those aspects of policy that have the greatest effect on the flexibility of the resource allocation mechanism and on individual or household security.

Flexibility has two dimensions. The first concerns the ability of relative prices (real wages, interest rates, rental rates) to move freely in response to shifts in demand and supply. The second concerns the cost of moving factors of production among alternative uses (between industries, occupations, regions, or countries). Of the industrial countries, the United Kingdom and the United States exhibit the greatest degree of relative price flexibility, as reflected, for example, in the behavior of average real wages and earnings differentials. Regarding the ability to move resources from declining to expanding sectors, there is no clear evidence that Japan or the allegedly more sclerotic regions of Western Europe have been less effective than the United States over the past fifty years. Massive changes in the structure of production and employment have occurred in every industrial country since 1945.

Flexibility is directly affected by policies such as minimum wage legislation, legislation defining union rights, the compulsory imposition of industrywide collective bargaining agreements, and employment protection legislation. The duration, generosity, and conditionality of unemployment benefits and active labor market policies (such as retraining) also play a role, as do housing market policies that affect the cost of moving. Adjustment assistance policies are ostensibly designed to help workers move out of declining industries, although many do not condition assistance on such movement.

By security I mean the ability to insure, individually or collectively, against adverse shocks to material standards of living. Flexibility and security are not independent of each other, nor are they necessarily in conflict (see, for example, Blank 1994). In the Arrow-Debreu paradigm maximum insurance and maximum flexibility go hand in hand. Producers face no uncertainty. Consumers suffer only the unavoidable consequences of nondiversifiable aggregate risk. But in practice moral hazard and adverse selection severely limit the extent to which individuals can insure privately against major income risks, such as poor health, unemployment, or reductions in the market value of skills.

In Western Europe more emphasis is traditionally placed on the collective provision and financing of security than in the United States. Although the collective financing of income security can raise nonwage labor costs or reduce enterprise profitability in other ways, an intelligently designed social safety net can be a source of flexibility. With such a safety net defensive reactions against the threat of foreign competition, including lobbying for trade protection, employment protection, and other measures favoring the status quo, are less likely to occur and be effective.

A good welfare state pursues its distributional objectives efficiently. Using the tax-transfer mechanism, it insures risks that cannot be insured privately in an efficient or equitable manner (unemployment insurance, health insurance) and thus reduces the private costs of change and the political resistance to change. A bad welfare state pursues policies that are merely a cover for incumbent protection, a fig leaf for rent seeking. Most employment protection legislation falls into this category, as do policies that reduce labor force participation in order to keep measured unemployment down.

The indiscriminate dismantling of the welfare state in the pursuit of flexibility—an activity that is high on the political agenda in many industrial countries—has potentially adverse distributional consequences and may reduce efficiency by increasing resistance to change.

Increased Capital Market Integration

As pointed out by Feldstein and Horioka (1980), there has been very little net international lending among industrial countries. Current account imbalances tend to be small. This is true country-by-country and for industrial countries relative to developing countries. Domestic capital formation tends to be financed by domestic saving. Although this pattern is not evidence of imperfect capital mobility, it needs to be explained.

One interpretation of the (relative) quantitative insignificance of international resource transfers maintains that it is the international manifestation of the quantitative unimportance of financial intermediation in general. This view holds that within industrial countries the lion's share of corporate investment is financed out of retained earnings. Stock markets appear to be insignificant as sources of funds (the primary-issue markets) or as instruments of corporate governance (the secondary markets), even in the Anglo-American corner of the industrial world. The same holds for many of the transition economies. Poland, for instance, is experiencing growth without financial intermediation. In several transition economies the net resource transfer (or primary balance) between the banking sector and the nonbank enterprise sector is toward the banks.

Does this mean that the importance of financial intermediation, including international financial intermediation, has been overestimated?[1] Or is the quality of the resources transferred through intermediation so much higher than that of internally generated resources that intermediation matters despite being quantitatively insignificant? In other words, is there a huge nonlinearity (or nonconvexity) that makes the social returns to the last dollar of investment enabled by access to foreign funds so much higher than the returns to all inframarginal investment? And are the quantitative patterns of the past likely to change as developing countries continue to grow and expand their share of global economic activity?

A number of salient facts arise in moving from net flows and stocks to gross flows and stocks. First, there are more gross flows now than there were until just recently. Second, there are still very little—the home bias in portfolio allocation remains strong. Third, risk-adjusted rates of return are thought to be higher in many of the emerging markets than in the industrial markets (Harvey 1994a,b; World Bank 1995). There is also considerable scope for diversifying risk, given the negative covariances between returns in industrial markets and returns in emerging markets.

This is good news for savers in industrial countries: by reallocating funds from their markets to emerging markets, they can achieve a superior combination of risk and return. The news is less good for the owners of claims on income streams derived from immobile industrial country productive assets. (This issue is discussed at greater length below.)

One of the beneficial global effects of the 1994–95 Mexican crisis is that it burst the euphoria bubble that made reasoned discussion of risk and return in emerging markets so difficult. A good case can be made that until very recently the risk of investing in emerging markets was systematically underestimated. The main risk (one unlikely to be captured in variance-covariance estimates based on return data covering only a few recent years) is the risk of major policy reversals or political instability. There tend to be huge swings in the perception of this risk. And these swings are only tangentially related to fundamentals; contagious waves of optimism and pessimism affect even the specialists operating in these markets.

The portfolio experiment that Cooper reviews is either partial equilibrium in nature or assumes that the joint distribution of returns in the developing world is independent of the amount of wealth allocated to these activities and of the scale of the productive activities that generate these returns. Because the partial equilibrium assumption is clearly unacceptable given the magnitude of the capital reallocation under consideration, the numbers make sense only if returns to scale are constant in the internationally movable inputs (capital). This heroic assumption is also made by Obstfeld (1994). It leads to overestimates of the gains from asset market integration and portfolio reallocation.

In evaluating the gains from financial market integration, it is important to distinguish between the degree of international mobility of financial capital (ownership claims to future income streams) and the degree of mobility of physical productive inputs (physical capital, human capital, raw labor, and so on). Obstfeld (1994) obtains very generous estimates of the gains from international financial integration because he assumes that, following financial market integration, both financial and physical capital (the only productive input in his model) can be reallocated costlessly and instantaneously between sectors and between nations. If the assumption of frictionless international financial markets is hard to swallow, "flying capital" is an extremely poor description of the ease with which the means of production move across national boundaries.

Even if returns to internationally mobile factors are constant in the long run, there are bound to be short-run costs of adjustment. If such factor reallocation costs are increasing and strictly convex, increased financial market integration will be associated with capital gains or losses (which may be large) for the owners of these quasi-fixed factors.

Some productive inputs are completely immobile internationally, including most labor inputs, land, and some physical capital assets. The rent paid to immobile factors in industrial countries (such as unskilled labor) will fall if the stock of complementary mobile factors falls, even absent adjustment costs. Unless the owners of these immobile inputs are insured against adverse developments in product or asset markets or are de facto insured because they own a well-diversified portfolio of financial assets, they can be severely affected by trade integration. The last time I checked, Lloyds was not offering Uruguay Round insurance. Few workers own the world portfolio. Their only de facto insurance is the country's safety net. And that safety net is being whittled away steadily. As a result individual income insecurity is growing.

The magnitude of the capital losses suffered by owners of internationally immobile factors of production will be less if there are alternative profitable domestic uses for the affected inputs. The true losers are the owners of specific factors, those inputs that are immobile both domestically and internationally and used in industries that will shrink as a result of the newly emerging dynamic comparative advantage.

Migration and the Environment

Given the "demographic deficit" that has emerged in virtually all industrial countries, there is little doubt that most of them will try to encourage (or at least tolerate) selective immigration by young workers from developing countries. Selective immigration will be economically beneficial to industrial countries because it will enhance—for several decades at least—the viability of the (probably much reduced) pay-as-you-go component of social security retirement schemes. Adding this benefit to the higher returns offered to savers, at least the older generations in industrial countries should favor increased trade and financial integration with developing countries.

Finally, Cooper's article is too sanguine about the transitional increase in global atmospheric and water pollution that will inevitably accompany successful growth in developing countries. Between thirty and sixty years of massively increased greenhouse emissions may be transitory but will seem like a long time to those suffering through it.

Note

1. Because foreign direct investment tends to be bundled with the transfer of technical knowledge, managerial skills, and other efficiency-enhancing knowledge, it plays a unique role in the financial interaction between industrial and developing countries. I therefore exclude foreign direct investment from my conjecture about the general unimportance of international financial intermediation.

References

Baldwin, Richard. 1989. "On the Growth Effects of 1992." *European Economy* (October).

Blank, Rebecca M., ed. 1994. *Social Protection Versus Economic Flexibility: Is There a Trade-Off?* Chicago, Ill.: University of Chicago Press.

Buiter, Willem H. 1994. "Economic Integration, Scale Effects, Market Structure, and Growth." World Bank, International Economics Department, Washington D.C.

Cooper, Richard N. 1994. "Foreign Trade, Wages, and Unemployment." Economic Research Paper 1701. Harvard University, Department of Economics, Cambridge, Mass.

Feldstein, M. and C. Horioka. 1980. "Domestic Saving and International Capital Flows." *Economic Journal* 90: 314–29.

Grossman, Gene M., and Elhanan Helpman. 1992. *Innovation and Growth in the Global Economy.* Cambridge, Mass.: MIT Press.

Willem H. Buiter 283

Harvey, Campbell R. 1994a. "Conditional Asset Allocation in Emerging Markets." NBER Working Paper 4623. National Bureau of Economic Research, Cambridge, Mass.

———. 1994b. "Predictable Risk and Returns in Emerging Markets." NBER Working Paper 4621. National Bureau of Economic Research, Cambridge, Mass.

Horn, H, H. Land, and S. Lundgren. 1995. "Managerial Effort Incentives, X-inefficiency, and International Trade." *European Economic Review* 39(1): 117–38.

Hufbauer, Gary C., and Jeffrey J. Schott. 1994. *Western Hemisphere Economic Integration.* Washington D.C.: Institute for International Economics.

Lawrence, Robert Z., and Matthew Slaughter. 1993. "International Trade and American Wages in the 1980s: Giant Sucking Sound or Small Hiccup?" *Brookings Papers on Economic Activity* 2. Washington, D.C.: The Brookings Institution.

Obstfeld, Maurice. 1994. "Risk Taking, Global Diversification, and Growth." *American Economic Review* 84: 1310–29.

Rivera-Batiz, Luis A., and Paul M. Romer. 1991a. "Economic Integration and Endogenous Growth." *Quarterly Journal of Economics* 106 (2): 531–56.

———. 1991b. "International Trade with Endogenous Technological Change." *European Economic Review* 35: 971–1001.

Sachs, Jeffrey D., and Howard J. Shatz. 1994. "Trade and Jobs in U.S. Manufacturing." *Brookings Papers on Economic Activity* 1. Washington, D.C.: The Brookings Institution.

Wood, Adrian. 1994. *North-South Trade, Employment, and Inequality: Changing Fortunes in a Skill-Driven World.* Oxford: Clarendon.

World Bank. 1995. *Global Economic Prospects and the Developing Countries 1995.* Washington, D.C.

Comment on "Is Growth in Developing Countries Beneficial to Industrial Countries?" by Richard N. Cooper

Matthew J. Slaughter

Richard Cooper has written a fine piece on a potentially cumbersome topic. For the most part he manages to focus on key issues in developing his thesis that growth in developing countries will, on balance, moderately benefit industrial countries.

Cooper's Analysis

To make the topic manageable, Cooper analyzes seven links between industrial and developing countries. I comment on each in turn.

Trade with Industrial Countries

Cooper makes the basic point that the effect of growth on the terms of trade and the volume of trade depends, among other things, on the source of growth. This ambiguity was first pointed out by Hicks (1953) and Johnson (1958) and has been reiterated more recently by, for example, Krugman (1994) and Leamer (1995).

In theory, then, growth in developing countries has an ambiguous effect through trade on industrial country welfare. In reality, however, trade-stunting growth seems not to have occurred. Since 1950 growth in world trade has exceeded growth in world output in every year except 1982. In addition, trade growth has exceeded output growth for many countries and groups of countries over different periods. This evidence of trade expansion is inconsistent with the occurrence of welfare-reducing growth in developing countries. Cooper argues that trade liberalization was probably the main cause of this trade expansion.

His analysis is correct, but one caveat is worth mentioning. Although trade liberalization has driven a lot of this virtuous trade-growth cycle, successful trade liberalization tends to work itself out of a job—eventually, tariffs and nontariff barriers disappear, leaving no need for liberalization. Thus as trade liberalization continues,

Matthew J. Slaughter is assistant professor of economics at Dartmouth College and faculty research fellow at the National Bureau of Economic Research.

Annual World Bank Conference on Development Economics 1995

other forms of "bad" growth that reduce trade might become more important. But predicting unobserved future growth is even harder than explaining observed past growth, a process that Robert Solow has likened to a "blaze of amateur psychology."

Trade Liberalization and Growth in Both Regions

The relationship between trade and growth cuts both ways: greater trade can increase growth by specializing production, stimulating competition, triggering product innovation, boosting savings and thus investment through higher income, inducing new foreign direct investment and making existing foreign direct investment more efficient, and improving a country's terms of trade.

Cooper surveys recent estimates of the gains to growth from the Uruguay Round and the North American Free Trade Agreement (NAFTA). One common finding is that the size of the estimated gains is sensitive to the model used. Not surprisingly, models that build in strong scale economies and savings multipliers predict larger gains. Nevertheless, all studies show positive gains accruing to both industrial and developing countries. Another common finding is that the more protected the country is initially, the larger are its gains from liberalization. Cooper then looks at possible trends in terms of trade between regions. He points out that energy prices, especially oil, will likely rise as developing country growth boosts demand for energy. Because most of the world's oil comes from developing countries, rising energy demand will hurt industrial countries by lowering their terms of trade (with developing countries). Overall, then, trade liberalization will probably have an ambiguous effect on the industrial world.

Trade liberalization can also increase industrial country growth by shifting demand patterns in developing countries toward industrial country products. As Linder (1961) and others have pointed out, as countries grow their pattern of demand usually shifts from primary products (such as food) toward capital equipment, branded consumer goods, and services (such as power plants, videocassette recorders, and management consulting). Because the industrial world has a comparative advantage in many of these manufactures and services, it will benefit from a surge in demand. Back-of-the-envelope calculations suggest that this surge could be huge. According to Woodall (1994) the OECD has forecast that if China, India, and Indonesia grow 6 percent a year, by 2010 approximately 700 million people will have an average annual income equal to that in Spain today. That number equals the current population of the United States, the European Union, and Japan combined.

Economic Dislocation in Industrial Countries

Cooper points out that growth induces "dislocation" as resources reallocate across industries. Even if developing country growth benefits industrial countries overall, the process of adjustment needed to realize these benefits will result in temporary dislocation. This dislocation is costly. But Cooper correctly points out that dislocation costs are much higher in the cases of aggregate demand shocks and technology shocks.

Cooper also points out that dislocation triggered by developing country growth can harm some industrial country factors of production, even if industrial countries benefit overall. For example, the consensus among economists is that a small percentage (about 10 percent) of the rise in U.S. wage inequality in the 1980s was attributable to international trade. But in the future trade between industrial and developing countries may further pressure unskilled wages in industrial countries. To minimize the reallocation costs, governments should maintain buoyant macroeconomic policies and flexible factor markets.

International Factor Mobility

Growth in developing countries will probably induce some industrial country capital to flow in their direction because many developing country investments will offer higher expected rates of return. Moreover, because the rates of return in industrial countries and developing countries are not perfectly correlated, industrial country investors that diversify into developing country assets may reduce their overall portfolio risk. Thus investment opportunities arising from growth in developing countries could generate a "free lunch" for industrial country investors that delivers both higher expected rates of return and lower expected portfolio variance. Increases in all kinds of capital flows—loans, portfolio equity, and foreign direct investment—are likely.

Developing country growth will probably also affect migration patterns, but in less straightforward ways. As growth triggers rural-to-urban migration within developing countries, some people may choose to emigrate. But the data show that once countries reach a certain level of development, emigrants return home.

Cooper is correct in supposing that allowing capital to flow to developing countries will very likely yield a free lunch. But he ignores the possible impact of these capital flows on labor. In theory, capital mobility can harm industrial country labor: a smaller capital stock implies lower labor productivity and thus lower real wages.

In practice, however, the size of these capital flows has resulted in little damage—although the damage may become worse, especially in light of the large infrastructure needs of countries like China. Krugman (1994) points out that in 1993, the peak year for emerging-market investment, $100 billion flowed from industrial countries to developing countries. But total industrial country investment that year was $3.5 trillion—only 3 percent of investment was diverted from industrial country use. Krugman calculates that since 1990 total industrial country investment in developing countries has reduced the industrial countries' capital stock by only 0.5 percent relative to what it would have been had no investment moved to developing countries. Similarly, Slaughter (1995) finds that in the 1980s U.S. multinationals did not outsource massive numbers of unskilled jobs to foreign affiliates and thus did not contribute to rising U.S. wage inequality. In estimating the pattern of factor demands for these multinationals, I find that parent and affiliate unskilled labor are not strong price substitutes: multinationals do not slash demand for parent labor in the United States when affiliate wages fall in foreign countries. At best, these factors are weak price substitutes and are very likely price complements.

World Aggregate Demand

Because business cycles in both regions are not perfectly correlated, developing countries help stabilize aggregate demand and short-run output in industrial countries. Thus, as long as growth in developing countries does not synchronize cycles in the two regions, it should increase their role as automatic stabilizer for the developing countries.

The Environment

Most countries have displayed a U-shaped relationship between output and pollution. As output rises from low levels, so does pollution. But at moderate levels of income demand for a cleaner environment grows and triggers a decline in overall pollution. The net effect on the environment will thus depend on the path of developing country growth. Here it is important to remember that at low levels of income developing countries might rationally choose to tolerate greater pollution as the cost for higher output. Aside from their concern about externalities from pollution, people in industrial countries should remember this point if they observe different environmental standards in developing countries.

Political Evolution

Political evolution and output also display a U-shaped relationship. Growth at all levels of output usually increases demand for democratic liberties. At low levels of income, however, this demand may be overridden by a repressive government or political turmoil. Insofar as democracies are less likely to threaten other democracies, developing country growth should ultimately benefit industrial countries by enhancing political security.

The Industrial Country Politics of Developing Country Growth

Cooper's prediction that developing country growth will, on balance, benefit industrial countries seems to be the most likely outcome. Others have arrived at this conclusion, including Krugman (1994), Slaughter (1994), and Woodall (1994). Typically, we expect that growth will have beneficial effects overall, and it is valuable to be periodically reminded of this. Still, it is possible, though unlikely, that this expectation will prove wrong. Many scenarios in which developing country growth harms the industrial world can be envisioned. As growth proceeds, articles such as Cooper's will identify where to look (for example, at commodity and factor prices) to judge what this impact may be.

Despite its strengths, Cooper's article does have one major shortcoming: it stops too soon. The section on political evolution ignores such developments in industrial countries. This is a big omission. Industrial country politics will have a big impact on developing country growth, and I am much less confident than Cooper that developing country growth will be politically acceptable in industrial countries. I want to discuss three issues involving the dialectic between industrial country politics and developing country growth.

Defining "Beneficial"

What criteria should industrial countries use to evaluate the impact of developing country growth? Cooper measures benefits almost entirely in terms of economic growth: industrial countries benefit from developing country growth only if their income and output grow as a result. But this definition is too narrow. Cooper correctly points out that development, properly defined, encompasses a host of political and philosophic issues reaching beyond GDP. The same breadth should apply to defining benefit. Do people in industrial countries measure the benefit of developing country growth solely in terms of its impact on their own growth?

As an empirical matter, the answer seems to be no. Many people in industrial countries give time and money to charities and organizations that foster developing country growth. Most government officials, however, do not carry such private beliefs into the public arena. We are much more likely to hear a politician ridiculing foreign aid as "money thrown down a rat hole" than discussing whether slower industrial country growth is an acceptable tradeoff in return for faster developing country growth.

As a normative matter, the answer is open to debate. One can develop consistent ethical arguments on why people in industrial countries should consider developing country growth beneficial even if it means slower industrial country growth. These arguments extend beyond Pareto efficiency. Suppose that 100 million people in India could free themselves from poverty at the cost of one textile worker in Georgia losing a job, thus reducing output in the United States by $50,000. This change is not a Pareto improvement, but would it still be beneficial to industrial countries? The example is rigged, but it makes the point that industrial country growth is not the sole criterion for evaluating developing country growth. In fact, industrial country growth may be neither necessary nor sufficient. Defining the other criteria is beyond the scope of this comment. But Cooper raises one possible noneconomic benefit: political stability. If growth in developing countries fosters their political stability and thus reduces the chance of war, it may compensate for slower industrial country growth.

But governments in industrial countries are not thinking along these lines. For example, consider the way the Clinton administration lobbied for ratification of NAFTA. Its bottom line was growth: NAFTA will stimulate Mexican import growth, Mexican import growth will stimulate U.S. export growth, U.S. export growth will stimulate U.S. job growth. Most economists considered this reasoning to be dubious at best. The administration did not argue that NAFTA could deliver big political benefits as well—a vote of confidence for recent Mexican economic reforms that conferred a good deal of credibility to the Mexican government. Emphasizing reasonable political benefits might have reduced the need to emphasize questionable economic benefits.

Weighing Economic and Political Efforts

Not thinking seriously about the benefits of developing country growth contributes to a second potential problem in industrial countries. Those in industrial countries who fear that they will be or have been hurt by developing country growth will be able to implement policies to counteract this growth, even if their economic size is small. There are at least four reasons for this.

First, developing country growth will not benefit everyone in industrial countries at all times: certain industries or factors of production will be hurt. For example, Cooper predicts that there will be pressure on the wages of unskilled labor in industrial countries. Many others (including Slaughter 1994; Wood 1994; and Woodall 1994) have raised this possibility. Similarly, whole industries may well disappear from industrial countries—apparel and textiles, for example.

Second, those who are hurt by developing country growth will almost certainly be more concentrated and motivated than those who benefit from it. Again, the lessons of trade theory apply here. A primary benefit of freer trade is higher real incomes for everyone resulting from lower prices on imported goods. In the aggregate these gains can be very large, but they are also very diffuse. In contrast, those hurt by freer trade are very concentrated: every unskilled worker whose real wage declines, both capital and labor in an industry facing severe import competition from abroad. Who will have a stronger opinion about freer trade? In most cases the concentrated groups who are hurt will be much more motivated than the general consumer who is enjoying slightly cheaper products.

Neither of these issues is new. But their importance might rise when combined with two other points. Governments do not have a clear idea of how to evaluate the benefits of developing country growth, so those who protest such growth will be able to sway the political debate considerably. In addition, many industrial countries have constituencies that believe that developing country growth is harmful. For example, Ross Perot, who won 19 percent of the popular vote in the 1992 U.S. presidential election, is adamantly against free trade with developing nations and predicts that NAFTA will push U.S. wages down to Mexican levels. Support for this view nearly prevented congressional ratification of NAFTA, and it still exists today. The cover of *Business Week* on March 13, 1995, reads "America's New Populism: Angry Citizens are Rebelling against Big Government, Stagnant Incomes, Moral Decay, and the Global Economy." In France the National Front, whose leader Jean-Marie Le Pen won 15 percent of the vote in the recent presidential primary, proposed expelling 3 million immigrants to "create" three million jobs for French citizens. What drives these beliefs? Largely, the fallacy that a causal link exists between economic problems in industrial countries and economic growth in developing countries. The argument runs: since 1973 trade flows with developing counties have expanded while real wages in the United States have stagnated—surely the first must have helped cause the second. Not necessarily. Many studies have found that trade has not contributed to sluggish real wage growth. Linking troubles in industrial countries to concurrent success in developing countries is understandable but dangerous. And it may become more of a problem as developing country growth becomes more visible and industrial country troubles, like slow productivity growth, continue.

Taken together, these four considerations make a vociferous "anti–developing country growth" political lobby in industrial countries seem very possible. The bad policies they might compel include trade barriers against developing countries and restrictions on foreign direct investment. Some countries are already implementing these policies. For example, the European Union maintains high tariffs on imports of food and steel from Eastern Europe. In the extreme stringent policies could significantly slow or even eliminate growth for both developing and industrial nations.

What Can Economists Do to Support Growth?

The above discussion speculates on one outcome that all countries should try to avoid. I offer it because the sooner issues relating to growth in developing countries are discussed, the sooner sound policy will emerge supporting that growth and establishing the institutions needed to ease adjustment.

Economists can contribute to this discussion in at least two ways. First, more can participate in it. Some economists, especially academic economists, seem reluctant to contribute to policy discussions. But if they do not contribute, the quality of debate can suffer. For all discussions of policy, input from professionals helps. And this is especially pertinent to economics issues, because unlike doctors, lawyers, and many other professionals, economists do not regulate their own supply. Anyone can call herself or himself an economist, regardless of whether she or he understands the difference between absolute advantage and comparative advantage.

In addition, economists can help design policies to minimize the costs that developing country growth imposes on industrial counties. Economists have a comparative advantage in identifying how and where the government can intervene to correct market failures in the least distortive way. For example, if developing country growth dislocates large numbers of unskilled workers in industrial countries, effective retraining and support will be needed. Even giving basic advice like "income subsidies distort less than minimum wages" will help.

References

Hicks, J. R. 1953. "An Inaugural Lecture." *Oxford Economic Papers* 2 (June): 117–35.

Johnson, Harry G. 1958. *International Trade and Economic Growth*. London: Allen and Unwin.

Krugman, Paul. 1994. "Does Third World Growth Hurt First World Prosperity?" *Harvard Business Review* (July/August): 113–21.

Leamer, Edward E. 1995. "A Trade Economist's View of U.S. Wages and 'Globalization.'" Paper prepared for a conference on trade and U.S. jobs, February 2–3, The Brookings Institution, Washington, D.C.

Linder, S. B. 1961. *An Essay on Trade and Transformation*. New York: John Wiley and Sons.

Slaughter, Matthew J. 1994. "The Impact of Internationalisation on U.S. Income Distribution." In Richard O'Brien, ed., *Finance and the International Economy 8: The Amex Bank Review Prize Essays*. Oxford: Oxford University Press.

————. 1995. "Multinational Corporations, Outsourcing, and American Wage Divergence." NBER Working Paper 5253. National Bureau of Economic Research, Cambridge, Mass.

Wood, Adrian. 1994. *North-South Trade, Employment, and Inequality.* Oxford: Clarendon.

Woodall, Pam. 1994. "War of the Worlds: A Survey of the Global Economy." *The Economist,* October 1.

Floor Discussion of "Is Growth in Developing Countries Beneficial to Industrial Countries?" by Richard N. Cooper

A participant from the Library of Congress asked the panelists whether the increasing trade between developing and industrial countries might hinder growth in developing countries. As he saw it, if growth and trade are related, and if international trade has historically gone from industrial to developing countries but recently has expanded slightly among developing countries, then trade among developing countries would be of greater benefit to them than trade with industrial countries. Developing countries could avoid expensive imports from industrial countries when appropriate technology from middle-income countries serves local needs just as well—and at lower cost.

Cooper agreed that as development progressed there would be more trade among developing countries, but he also believes that developing countries will capture an increasing share of trade with industrial countries. In other words, increased trade among developing countries would not compete with increased trade between industrial and developing countries. In particular cases you would see a substitution of Korean goods for Japanese goods, for example, but the Japanese will continue to produce high-quality goods that are different from the goods they were producing fifteen years ago. Cooper predicted that the absolute amount of trade between developing and industrial countries would increase even while trade among developing countries increased as a share of the world total. Would this affect the competitiveness of certain industries in industrial countries? Certainly. As Willem Buiter (discussant) had said, this is a general equilibrium system. As product X gets displaced in market A by another developing country, product Y will become attractive. People should get over the idea that a country is just like a firm, only larger. A country is not a firm. Individual firms will continue to feel competitive pressure from all sources, including but not limited to developing countries. That is not the same thing as saying that entire countries will find themselves under such pressure.

A participant from the Palestinian Economic Development Fund asked whether the links between trade and growth are the same in developing countries as in indus-

This session was chaired by Mieko Nishimizu, director, Risk Management and Financial Policy Department, at the World Bank.

Annual World Bank Conference on Development Economics 1995
©1996 The International Bank for Reconstruction and Development / THE WORLD BANK

trial countries. They are not, responded Matthew Slaughter (discussant). One important difference is that developing countries usually benefit from importing technology that was developed in industrial countries, so in trade between developing countries and industrial countries developing countries stand to gain more than industrial countries. When a country imports technology and know-how, it expands the frontier of production possibilities. It is also important to remember, Slaughter added, that not all goods produced in developing countries are competing with industrial country producers. When industrial countries import goods from developing countries that the industrial countries do not produce, everyone gains; when developing countries produce goods that compete with those produced by industrial countries, the results are more ambiguous.

The participant from Palestine also wondered how the new international order would affect development and the growth of international trade in developing countries. For the most part, Cooper responded, he was a supporter of the current international order, not a critic. The international order that had been established between 1944 and 1947, and that led to the creation of the World Bank, had been largely permissive in promoting development. It had tried to ensure that the international economy created opportunities, leaving it to each country to take advantage of those opportunities. And the countries that had taken advantage of opportunities had done extraordinarily well. In that sense the old international order has been quite successful, so we should be cautious about changing it. Still, Cooper added, a lot of blemishes could be fixed. Eliminating the Multifiber Arrangement, for example, was probably a good idea.

A participant from the World Bank's International Economics Department observed that the discussion had highlighted one of the dilemmas of reverse linkages—namely, that the costs of adjustment are focused (and more amenable to analysis) on the benefits side. At first the traditional benefits appear to be small, but some potentially more important benefits are harder to measure. There is growing evidence, for example, that competition is pushing out the frontier of production in some industries and is breaking up production processes—for example, in footwear and in the assembly of printed circuit boards. Without more research in this area, one should not assume that the benefits will necessarily be small. Just because the benefits cannot be easily quantified does not mean that they do not exist.

Cooper agreed with the spirit of the comment, that it is important to keep in mind things that we consider important that have not been quantified. But, he continued, we also should not assume that because something is identifiable but unquantifiable its impact is powerful. The honest answer is that we do not know. It is an open empirical question. As an economist he considers competition important in keeping economies in good order. But it is useful to recall that the innovation that is now revolutionizing our lives and those of the next generation—the semiconductor—came out of a monopoly. One could ask, as Schumpeter did decades ago, whether such an innovation would have been produced under competitive conditions. Again, there is no way of knowing.

Fiscal Federalism and Decentralization: A Review of Some Efficiency and Macroeconomic Aspects

Vito Tanzi

Decentralization of fiscal activities has become popular in recent years. This approach to intergovernmental finance can improve the allocation of public spending by making it more consistent with the wishes of citizens, and it can provide political glue for countries with regional ethnic diversity. The case for decentralization is a strong one, but it is based on various implicit and explicit assumptions. This article examines such issues as the taxing ability of local governments, tax sharing arrangements, the performance of national and subnational bureaucracies, and the quality of public expenditure management systems in order to identify conditions and institutions that can significantly reduce the benefits of decentralization. The relationship between decentralization and stabilization is also explored—in several cases decentralization has made it harder for countries to eliminate their structural fiscal deficits.

U ntil recently issues of fiscal federalism and decentralization received fairly little attention from economists and other students of economic and political developments. Interest in these issues was confined mainly to specialists. Public finance courses typically allocated no more than one lesson to the topic—and at times not even that. In his monumental treatise on public finance, Richard Musgrave dedicated five pages to "multilevel finance" (Musgrave 1959, pp. 179–83).

The topic began to attract more attention in the 1980s, and by the 1990s the topic had become hot. Furthermore, professional interest in the subject crossed the U.S. border. Several countries established national commissions to study decentralization or the possibility of creating some form of fiscal federalism. Others made decentralization or fiscal federalism the centerpiece of their political campaigns.

Vito Tanzi is director of the Fiscal Affairs Department at the International Monetary Fund. The author is grateful for comments from Ehtisham Ahmad, Jon Craig, Jack Diamond, Ved Gandhi, Neven Mates, John Norregaard, Gerd Schwartz, Anwar Shah, Parthasarathi Shome, and P. Bernd Spahn.

Annual World Bank Conference on Development Economics 1995
©1996 The International Bank for Reconstruction and Development / THE WORLD BANK

Why the Recent Trend to Decentralize?

Many factors account for this change, and some merit brief discussion. Developments in the European Union were one of these factors. The process of creating a central entity that will transcend the European member states in some important economic functions opened up the question of how much economic power to transfer to the European Union. The issues in this debate are similar to those in discussions of the pros and cons of fiscal federalism and fiscal decentralization. Who would be responsible for income redistribution and for stabilization? And which resource allocation functions should be performed by the European Union, and which by the member states? The European debate has forced many European economists (and not just those who specialize in public finance) to look at the fiscal institutions of countries with strong subnational governments and at the literature to see what could be learned that could be relevant to the European question (CEPR 1993).

Another factor was the growing disenchantment with the role of the public sector. The explosive growth of the public sector in many industrial countries during the postwar period, which was associated with the expansion of the central government's role in income maintenance, income redistribution, and stabilization, has recently led to strong reactions. At the political level the 1980s and 1990s have seen a swing toward more conservative attitudes, especially suspicion of powerful central governments. The view that greater reliance should be placed on the market has been accompanied by the parallel view that less power should remain in the hands of the central government. Some influential economists have questioned the effectiveness of government action in stabilizing the economy and improving the distribution of income, thus reducing poverty and unemployment. This challenge has reduced the legitimacy of the central government's action and created a presumption in favor of reducing the size of the public sector while giving more power to both the market and local jurisdictions. Many countries are considering a devolution of some functions to local jurisdictions. In terms of resource allocation various arguments have been advanced to support the view that privatization and decentralization would lead to greater efficiency and a leaner public sector.

Developments in specific countries, such as Canada, China, and some of the new states of the former Soviet Union, have forced a reassessment of multilevel finance. In Canada developments were driven largely by political considerations, with some provinces demanding more independence. In China they were driven by the need to reestablish some control over national public revenue. In the states that emerged from the breakup of the Soviet Union there was a need to create from scratch fiscal arrangements that gave significant responsibilities to subnational governments, especially in Russia, with its regions of widely diverse cultural, ethnic, and economic composition. The interest in fiscal federalism in these countries was the logical outcome of discussions about what political organization these countries should have after the breakup of centralized policymaking. Other countries, such as Ethiopia, have been driven toward decentralization (or regionalization) by ethnic diversity and by the belief that decentralization would help hold the country together.

During the 1980s another group of countries, including Argentina, Brazil, India, and Nigeria, experienced macroeconomic problems that required major adjustments in their fiscal account, through revenue increases or expenditure cuts. These countries were often constrained in their policy choices by constitutional or legal arrangements among governments at different levels. As structural and macroeconomic problems worsened and the need for adjustment grew, so did the attention directed at the legal constraints that limited the central government's scope for policy action. Although not as significant as the factors mentioned above, the World Bank's research and lending policies, which have emphasized the benefits of decentralization, may also have contributed to the present trend. Whatever the causes, the debate on decentralization raises serious questions about its potential impact, merits, and dangers. Whether decentralization is appropriate often depends on many country-specific factors. Still, some general issues are relevant to all countries.

Decentralization and Economic Efficiency

Before discussing the relationship between decentralization and economic efficiency, it is useful to distinguish between *fiscal* and *administrative* decentralization. Fiscal decentralization exists when subnational governments have the power, given to them by the constitution or by particular laws, to raise (some) taxes and carry out spending activities within clearly established legal criteria. Examples of fiscal decentralization include the fiscal federations in Argentina, Australia, Brazil, Canada, India, Germany, Nigeria, Switzerland, and the United States. Administrative decentralization exists when most taxes are raised centrally, but funds are allocated to decentralized entities that carry out their spending activities as agents of the central government and according to the guidelines or controls imposed by the central government. An example of administrative decentralization is provided by Italy, where in 1992 local entities raised about 8 percent of the total net revenue of the general government but spent about 37 percent of total net expenditure. The issues discussed in this article involve both kinds of decentralization but are more concerned with fiscal decentralization.

The main economic justification for decentralization rests largely on allocative or efficiency grounds. There can also be a political argument for decentralization if a country's population is not homogeneous and if ethnic, racial, cultural, linguistic, or other relevant characteristics are regionally distributed (as they are in Russia and Ethiopia). Decentralization may be needed to induce various regions to remain part of a federation. According to this argument, decentralization would be more desirable in, say, Russia than in Japan. By the same token the goal of national unity often has pushed nondemocratic governments toward the forced elimination of regional differences. In democratic societies the economic and political arguments for decentralization tend to converge, since it is argued that decentralization strengthens democracy. Most people are more inclined to engage in local political activities because local policies have a more direct impact on their daily life.

298 Fiscal Federalism and Decentralization: A Review of Some Efficiency and Macroeconomic Aspects

The normative, economic argument for decentralization can be based on both an ex ante and an ex post case (Cremer, Estache, and Seabright 1994). The ex ante theoretical case was best made by Wallace Oates in his classic 1972 book, *Fiscal Federalism*. The ex post case is essentially the one outlined by Tiebout (1956).

The Ex Ante Argument

Oates's case is based on the realization that not all public goods have similar spatial characteristics. Some, such as defense, benefit the entire country. Others, such as regional transportation systems or forestry services, benefit regions. Still others, such as street lighting or cleaning, benefit only municipalities or particular districts. Furthermore, different areas have different preferences for public goods. Thus the supply of public goods must be fitted to the different requirements of different groups. A centralized government might ignore these spatial characteristics and this diversity of preferences, or it might not be well informed about them and thus might supply a uniform package to all citizens. A one-size-fits-all approach does not deliver a basket of public goods that is optimal for all citizens. When "the jurisdiction that determines the level of provision of each public good includes precisely the set of individuals who consume the good" there is "perfect correspondence" in the provision of public goods (Oates 1972, p.34).

In this ideal, normative model, if the spatial characteristics of the public goods differed, at the limit, one might wish to have as many jurisdictions as public goods. Thus, in theory, one would need a highly decentralized public sector with many subnational jurisdictions of varying sizes. In this ideal, theoretical world, "each level of government, possessing complete knowledge of the tastes of its constituents and seeking to maximize their welfare, would provide the Pareto-efficient level of output . . . and would finance this through benefit pricing" (Oates 1972, pp. 34–35). Oates's normative policy conclusion is that "for a public good—the consumption of which is defined over geographical subsets of the total population, and for which the costs of providing each level of output of the good in each jurisdiction are the same for the central or the respective local government—it will always be more efficient (or at least as efficient) for local governments to provide the Pareto-efficient levels of output for their respective jurisdictions than for the central government to provide *any* specified and uniform level of output across all jurisdictions" (Oates 1972, p. 35, italics in original).

The basic message of Oates's decentralization policy is that centralization is costly if it leads the government to provide a bundle of public goods different from the preferences of the citizens of particular regions, provinces, or municipalities. If these preferences vary geographically, a uniform package chosen by a national government is likely to force some localities to consume more or less than they would prefer to consume. As Cremer, Estache, and Seabright (1994, p. 5) put it, "each type of good should be provided by a level of government . . . enjoying a comparative advantage in accounting for the diversity of preferences in its choice of service delivery."

This interpretation assumes that subnational governments already exist, so the relevant question becomes: Which of the existing government levels should be responsible for particular forms of spending? The problem would be much more difficult in trying to determine the degree of decentralization desirable in a world where the spatial characteristics of public goods vary among different public goods and over time and where the preferences of various regions may also change. One could argue that not only should there be many decentralized spending units, but that their geographical boundaries and number would have to change over time to reflect the technological developments that change the spatial characteristics of public goods.

Oates's basic argument can be applied to stabilization policy or even to redistributive policy if the preferences of populations living in different regions are not similar. For example, if the European Union were to force Italy and Germany to pursue a similar stabilization policy objective for inflation and unemployment, when in fact Italians might prefer lower unemployment while Germans might prefer lower inflation, some welfare loss would result. Or, if Italians preferred higher assistance for invalids while Germans preferred higher assistance for orphans, a common redistributive package might also imply a loss of welfare relative to the option in which each country chooses its desired package. In both cases there is the assumption that the national government would or could choose just one package and that local jurisdictions would base their choices on citizen preferences.

The Ex Post Argument

In addition to Oates's theoretical argument, which is based largely on the spatial characteristics of public goods, decentralization can be defended on the basis of other, more practical considerations. Some observers have argued that a decentralized system can become a surrogate for competition, bringing to the public sector some of the allocative benefits that a competitive market brings to the private sector (Israel 1992). There are many angles to this argument, one of them Tiebout's. The final outcome will approach that of an efficient market to the extent that decentralization can help identify different population groups' preferences for public goods, local governments supply these goods, these groups can be made to pay a price (tax) based on the benefit they receive from the public goods, and individuals vote with their feet, by moving to the jurisdiction that best reflects their preferences. At the margin the benefit from consuming the public good or service will be equal to the cost in terms of benefit taxes—in other words, approaching a Pareto optimal solution.

Another potentially important advantage of decentralization is that it allows experimentation in the provision of the output. When the provision of a public service (say, education) is the responsibility of local jurisdictions and when these jurisdictions are free to provide the service in any way they see appropriate, some jurisdictions will discover better ways of providing the service, and other jurisdictions will emulate the successful ones. The more jurisdictions there are, the more simultaneous experiments will take place. When the service is imposed by a national monopoly, which adopts a uniform approach to providing the service, there will be little or no experimentation, and thus dated methods may continue to be used even when there are better alternatives. This outcome is often noted by the supporters of decentralization, who point to the outmoded curriculums in countries with centralized educational systems.

Still another argument in favor of decentralization emphasizes that individuals who are responsible for the results of their actions, and who thus have ownership rights over the outcome, are likely to have stronger incentives to perform better. Therefore, when local officials are directly responsible for providing a public service, and are praised for success and blamed for failure, they will have a greater interest in succeeding. In such cases the community may develop a sense of pride in successful service delivery. Additionally, when the cost of providing a service is borne by the local jurisdiction, the service is more likely to be provided cost-efficiently—to the point where marginal benefits equal marginal costs. This view, that accountability brings responsibility, motivates much of the support for the decentralization of various functions (Shaw and Qureshi 1994). Finally, at a time when large public sectors are considered wasteful and inefficient, some literature has argued that decentralization is desirable because it is likely to be associated with a smaller public sector and a more efficient economy (Brennan and Buchanan 1980; Ehdaie 1994).

Challenges to Decentralization

These powerful arguments help explain why decentralization has become so popular in recent years. Some writers, however, have advanced counterarguments that challenge some of the above conclusions or, at least, outline conditions in which decentralization could be a less attractive policy. The point of this discussion is to identify situations in which decentralization might not lead to the expected results unless important changes are made in the existing conditions.

Many countries have decentralized fiscal structures. Decentralization has worked well in some industrial countries (Austria, Germany, the Scandinavian countries, Switzerland, and the United States) and in Indonesia and perhaps Malaysia among the developing countries, and less well in others (Argentina and Brazil).

While the theoretical case for decentralization is relatively straightforward, the practical case may be less so (Prud'homme 1994; Bird 1994; Oates 1994). As Oates (1994, p. 1) puts it, "fiscal decentralization has much to offer, but it is a complicated enterprise" (see Boadway, Roberts, and Shah 1994 for a discussion of the pros and cons of decentralization).

Insufficient information. As discussed earlier, part of the case for decentralization rests on the spatial characteristics of public goods—some benefit only certain areas of a country. As a result the central government may tend to underproduce or overproduce them because it does not have the necessary information on local preferences, or it may not have the right incentives to act on the available information.

The argument related to lack of information has been challenged on the grounds that central governments can and do assign government officials to local offices and that these officials may be capable of determining local preferences. The central governments of unitary countries often have representatives (for example, the *préfets* in France and Italy or the *intendentes* in Chile) who closely follow local developments and assess local needs. These agents are often highly trained and might even have an incentive to exaggerate the local demand for some public services in order to increase their own power or importance. Therefore, the main question is whether the information these individuals send back to the center is any more or less correct or biased than that available to local policymakers.

Whether local governments are more or less likely than the central government to respond to local preferences depends, of course, on the strength of various incentives and on how political decisions are made. A national government interested in local votes may have a strong interest in meeting local needs. A local government that is not democratic may have little interest in meeting these needs. It should not be automatically assumed that subnational governments are made up of democratically elected officials who necessarily have the public (though local) interest in mind. Where they do, decentralization has a greater chance of succeeding. The basic presumption behind the arguments made by proponents of decentralization is that local democracies are in place and do work. When they do not, the case for decentralization becomes weaker.

Corruption. Prud'homme (1994) and Oates (1994) also mention corruption. Oates does not conclude whether corruption is likely to be greater at the local or central level. Prud'homme believes that corruption is a greater problem at the local level and mentions France and Italy to support his view. This issue cannot be settled by empirical evidence, so we must rely on impressions. In my view corruption may be more common at the local level than at the national level, especially in developing countries (Tanzi 1994). The reason is that corruption is often stimulated by contiguity, that is, by the fact that officials and citizens live and work close to one another in local communities. They have often known each other all their lives and may even come from the same families. Contiguity brings personalism to relationships, and personalism is the enemy of arm's length relationships. When this occurs the public interest often takes a back seat, and decisions are made that favor particular individuals or groups. It should be emphasized that governance issues are problems at all levels of government in many countries; the local bureaucracy is certainly more honest than the national bureaucracy in some countries.

The quality of local bureaucracies. Prud'homme (1994, p. 9) discusses another factor that may reduce the benefits of decentralization: the quality of local bureaucracies relative to national bureaucracies. As he puts it, "Decentralization not only transfers power from central to local government, but also from central to local bureaucracies." And "central government bureaucracies are likely to attract more qualified people . . . because they offer better careers . . . more possibilities of promotion [and better salaries]." Prud'homme's conclusion is strengthened by the argument of Murphy, Shleifer, and Vishny (1991) that talented individuals tend to choose fields that offer better opportunities for advancement over the longer run. To the extent that national bureaucracies offer better opportunities to able individuals than do local bureaucracies, they may attract more qualified and more able individuals. But where qualified individuals are abundant, as is often the case in industrial countries, subnational governments may have staff as qualified as do national governments.[1] On the other hand, where educational standards are low and there is a smaller pool of potentially efficient employees, Prud'homme's point carries more weight. This scarcity of local talent may impede decentralization efforts in, say, Ethiopia and other African countries.

Within countries there are often wide differences across regions in the quality of the personnel of local administrations. In Italy, for example, there is a huge difference in the quality of the local public administrations between, say, Emilia-Romagna, where the quality is very good (perhaps even better than at the national level), and some southern regions, where it is poor (Putnam 1993). In Argentina there is a huge difference between Buenos Aires and some of the other provinces, and in Colombia between Bogota or Medellin and some other provinces. These differences are partly explained by differences in available resources, but cultural factors also play a role.

Another practical issue is that in most countries the composition of local jurisdictions is based on past political, rather than economic, considerations (apart from exceptional circumstances in which multilevel arrangements can be created from scratch and can thus be influenced by knowledge about the spatial characteristics of important public goods). Thus the sizes of states, provinces, regions, and metropolitan areas are fixed and largely the result of historical accidents. These are the subnational governments to which decentralization allocates fiscal responsibilities. The chance that the spatial characteristics of the public goods or services whose responsibility is assigned to the subnational jurisdictions will match the areas covered by these jurisdictions—and so achieve the "perfect correspondence" described by Oates—seems slim indeed. The smaller is the degree of correspondence, the smaller are the potential economic advantages of decentralization.

Technological change and increased mobility. Two other aspects are important in today's world. First, the characteristics of public goods and services are subject to rapid change. Technological and economic developments ensure that new needs for public sector intervention arise continuously. For example, in the past there was a need to protect a city's population from outside attacks and to provide it with information about the time of day. Walls were built around cities and clocks were placed on bell towers to satisfy these needs. The public goods provided by these public services are no longer needed. On the other hand, the need to protect citizens from crime and pollution has become more important.

Second, changing technology, combined with greater mobility on the part of citizens, implies that the spatial characteristics of public goods are also likely to change. For example, when mobility is limited, many of the benefits associated with public education are internalized by the jurisdiction that provides the service. But when mobility is high, extrajurisdictional externalities become important. The jurisdiction that finances education may not reap its benefits if those who are educated in its public schools move to another jurisdiction. Similar considerations apply to spending for health and many other services. On the other hand, this spillover problem can be partly solved through a reciprocity rule, especially if services can be standardized across regions. In such cases the existence of the spillover does not reduce the advantage of providing the service locally. But standardization eliminates one of the basic reasons for decentralization.

These two aspects imply that, to be optimal, decentralization arrangements should be flexible over time. Either the geographical areas covered by local jurisdictions—and thus the number of these jurisdictions—should change over time, or the characteristics of public goods should be continuously reexamined in order to reallocate some of them across the existing jurisdictions. There is no simple mechanism that allows this process to take place. Once a federal structure is determined, local politicians and officials fiercely oppose major changes to borders and tasks. Consequently, fiscal federalism is at times characterized by a mismatch between the spatial characteristics of public goods and the responsible jurisdictions.

Public expenditure management systems. It was mentioned earlier that a strong argument in favor of decentralization is that it allows subnational jurisdictions to experiment with new ways of providing public services. Such experimentation can lead to progress for some jurisdictions and to imitation by others through demonstration effects. Of course, if the quality of local bureaucracies is not as good as that of the national bureaucracy, and if the public interest is not the guiding principle of local officials, independence and experimentation by local jurisdictions may not achieve the desired results.

By definition, decentralization implies that subnational governments or entities take over functions from the national government and thus come to manage larger financial resources than would be the case under a centralized government. Both the flow of revenues necessary to finance these functions and the flow of expenditures to carry them out increase—at times, significantly. Are subnational jurisdictions capable of handling these flows? Public expenditure management systems are not very good in many countries. They are particularly deficient in developing countries (especially in Africa) and transition economies.

In their broadest functions, good public expenditure management systems must include budget offices that are capable of forecasting expected revenue and anticipated spending. They must include budgetary classifications that allow the controlling authorities to determine whether money is actually going to the budgeted items and functions. They must include accounting systems that allow for the monitoring and control of cash flows and that provide, in a timely fashion, information on the status of expenditures and revenues. They must also provide controls over other commitments, even when these commitments do not contribute to additional cash spending in the current fiscal year. The skills required to perform these tasks are scarce in most countries; they are especially scarce in developing countries and transition economies, especially at the local level.

The decentralization of responsibilities to subnational jurisdictions that have not yet developed adequate public expenditure management structures is likely to run into difficulties.[2] Technical assistance missions often have found poor public expenditure management systems and thus a lack of local financial accounting and accountability, especially in developing countries. The most basic statistical information is not often available, even on money spent. There is no information on commitments. When information on cash spending is available, it is often impossible to determine the items or functions for which the money has been spent.

The lack of arm's length relationships between local government officials and local suppliers or banks leads to the creation of "hidden" debt—that is, debt that has not yet shown up in the statistical information available. When, for political reasons, local budgets are soft over the long run, financial difficulties and misallocation of resources are likely to result. Thus the potential benefits of decentralization may be reduced or even disappear if the minimum public expenditure management infrastructure is not in place. Brazil (after the 1988 Constitution decentralized spending decisions) and Italy (after the 1979 reform decentralized some spending decisions) are examples of this problem. Advocates of decentralization would be well advised to pay close attention to this problem.

Decentralization and Stabilization

The relation between decentralization and stabilization has not received the attention it deserves, especially in developing countries. This section identifies some characteristics of decentralization that may have an impact on stabilization.

Assume that subnational governments with clear expenditure responsibilities have been established and that they have been given the exclusive use of a relatively robust tax base from which they can finance some or most of their expenditures. Also assume that the subnational governments can share other tax bases with the national government. The national government provides the subnational governments with relevant information on taxpayers or other technical assistance so that, within limits, they can profitably exploit these shared tax bases. The subnational governments are run by competent officials who are democratically elected or appointed and are thus responsive to the preferences of the taxpayers. Finally, assume that constitutional or legal limitations require that the subnational governments balance their budgets annually.

This description conforms fairly closely to the U.S. situation, which much of the literature on fiscal federalism and stabilization has dealt with or been influenced by. In this literature the responsibility for fiscal policy has been assumed to rest with the central (federal) government (Musgrave 1959; Oates 1972; Commission of the European Communities 1993).

In this context subnational governments cannot take an active part in trying to stabilize the economy. In fact, because they have to balance their budgets annually, they must raise taxes or cut spending during a recession and cut taxes or raise spending during a boom (Bayoumi 1992; de Callatay and Ribe 1994). The question is whether subnational governments should play a more positive, active role in countercyclical fiscal policy.

Suppose that in large countries, such as Canada and the United States, business cycles are not strongly correlated across regions, perhaps because some regional economies depend on the price of particular commodities (say, oil in Texas) that can move independently of the country's general economic conditions, or because different regions trade with different partners that experience unsynchronized cycles. Suppose also that, as argued earlier, different regions have different preferences for macroeconomic variables (some prefer less inflation, others prefer less unemployment). Some economists have argued that under these circumstances a role can be assigned to subnational governments in the pursuit of stabilization policy (Gramlich 1987). The government of the region undergoing the recession may try to stimulate the local economy even though the multiplier effect associated with its efforts may be low.

I have summarized the discussion on stabilization in order to show that it is very much U.S. (or, perhaps, Canadian or European Union) specific and to argue that the issues that are relevant to developing countries are often different from those connected with Keynesian countercyclical policy. In developing countries and in an increasing number of industrial countries, the basic macroeconomic need is not to counter cycles, but to bring about a fiscal adjustment that reduces chronic fiscal imbalances. The issue then is the relationship between decentralization and structural, rather than cyclical, fiscal deficits. Does decentralization contribute to structural macroeconomic problems? Does it make it more difficult to adjust fiscal accounts once a structural deficit has developed?

The experience of many countries suggests that under the circumstances often found in developing countries subnational governments are likely to contribute—sometimes significantly—to the aggravation of macroeconomic problems. Or they make it difficult to correct problems. In several cases local governments have spent more than they have raised in revenue, thus increasing their debt and occasionally forcing the central government to come to their rescue.[3] In other cases the relationship between subnational governments and the central government has constrained the central government's ability to maneuver. At times this outcome is the consequence of arrangements that have shifted spending responsibilities to subnational governments without providing them with adequate resources. At other times political forces push subnational governments toward higher spending or lower taxes.[4] In still other cases poor public expenditure management systems make it difficult to control spending. Weak incentives and lack of information also have played key roles.

When decentralization is based on a clear and comprehensive contract between central and subnational governments that spells out the subnational government's obligations, assigns them sufficient resources to fulfill their responsibilities, and makes it explicit that they must live within the means stipulated in the contract and under no circumstances will they receive additional resources from the national government, then the situation approaches that prevailing in the United States. In this situation local spending can be increased mostly by increasing locally controlled taxes. This constraint forces the subnational governments to behave responsibly in a macroeconomic sense and efficiently in an allocative sense. In the absence of "tax exporting," an extrajurisdictional externality would not arise on the revenue side, and the responsibility for any sustained national fiscal imbalance would fall squarely on the central government.

In many countries, however:

- There is no such contract (explicit or implicit).
- The assignment of spending responsibilities is vague and subject to change by new, unfunded mandates.
- The incentives for local policymakers and officials may induce them to overspend or undertax.
- The budgets for subnational governments tend to be relatively soft.
- The information needed to guide local policies is often missing, of poor quality, or not timely.
- Public expenditure management systems are not developed or sophisticated enough to support the needed accounting and managerial controls.

When clear and firm constitutional or legal guidelines are missing, decentralization may create a situation in which local governments can gain by increasing spending while shifting the financing cost to the whole country. The possibility that the financing for the extra spending will be provided mostly by those outside the jurisdiction creates an important externality that gives each local government a strong incentive to push for additional resources and to increase spending. When the resources are not available ex ante from the national government, they may become available ex post, after the spending has taken place and the debt has accumulated.[5] The political power of many local governments and the systemic and political implications of letting them go broke make it difficult for the national government to resist these pressures.

In addition to the revenue they raise from their own tax bases, fees, resources, and shared revenue, subnational governments often depend on grants from the central government. They often can make a strong case for these grants because the national government may require them to perform certain functions or to comply with certain standards without directly providing funds for them. Such unfunded mandates create implicit claims for future grants or for soft budgets. Designing an optimal grant structure is very difficult, however (Bahl and Linn 1992; Ahmad forthcoming). Thus, grants may introduce inefficiencies and create political pressures to increase their size.

There are many channels through which fiscal decentralization may aggravate structural fiscal problems. Here we discuss three: the assignment of major tax bases to subnational governments, the sharing of major tax bases, and the ex post, implicit servicing of debt incurred by subnational governments.

Assignment of Major Tax Bases

A number of decentralized countries (Brazil, India, Russia) have assigned major tax bases to subnational governments for their exclusive use. In Brazil the general value-added tax is assigned to the states. In India the sales tax is assigned to the states. In Russia the individual income tax and many excise taxes have been assigned to the subnational governments (Bahl 1994).

In India the central government has been left mainly with income taxes (which have never been very productive), foreign trade taxes (which ought to fall or even disappear over time), and highly distortive excise taxes (which are in need of reform). At the same time, the central government is responsible for servicing a progressively more burdensome public debt. Thus central government spending has tended to grow as its share of total tax revenue has been falling.

In Brazil the share of total taxes received by the central government fell from 69.2 percent in 1980 to 57.5 percent in 1990. The states' share rose from 22.2 percent to 27.9 percent during the same period, while that of the municipalities rose from 6.6 percent to 14.6 percent. The 1988 Brazilian Constitution accelerated the decline in centrally retained tax revenue, contributing to larger fiscal deficits and macroeconomic problems.

If the tax bases that are assigned exclusively to subnational governments are large and dynamic, and if the spending responsibilities of central governments (debt servicing, pensions, national public goods) cannot be easily compressed, macroeconomic problems are often inevitable. Brazil, India, and Russia have experienced macroeconomic difficulties that were caused or worsened by tax assignments. Similar difficulties may arise in China. When macroeconomic adjustment requires that a central government increase its tax levels, it will find it difficult to do so if important tax bases are not available to it. (This has been the experience in Brazil and India.) In this situation the central government will be forced to rely on less efficient or less productive tax bases. Thus either the level of taxation will be lower than desired or the structure of taxation will be less efficient than it could be.

Sharing of Major Tax Bases

While some tax bases are assigned to the exclusive use of particular levels of government, other tax bases may be shared. The sharing may be of (at least) two kinds. Different levels of government may tax the same base, or one level may collect the tax from a given base and share the revenue with other levels.

Examples of the first kind are the taxing of personal income in the United States and the taxing of sales in Argentina. In the United States personal income is taxed by both the federal government and by most states. Counties and municipalities piggy-back on states' income taxes. In Argentina sales are taxed with a value-added tax at the national level and with a cascading turnover tax at the provincial level.

When two government levels tax the same tax base, each retains its independence of action even though an increase by one level in its dependence on that base may limit the scope for the other level to tax the same base. At the subnational level the limits on effective tax rates on a given tax base are generally imposed by tax competition and by the potential mobility of the tax base.

Examples of the second kind of tax sharing are quite common. They exist in Argentina, Brazil, Colombia, Pakistan, Russia, and other countries. In Argentina the federal government collects the income tax, the value-added tax, excise taxes, foreign trade taxes, liquid fuel and energy taxes, the gross assets tax (levied on companies), the personal assets tax (levied on individuals), social security taxes, and some minor taxes. Of these, the income tax, the value-added tax, the excise taxes, the gross assets tax, and the personal assets tax are subject to sharing arrangements with other parts of the public sector. In 1993 federal government revenue, before sharing and transfers, accounted for 81 percent of all tax revenue. After revenue sharing and transfers it accounted for 54 percent.[6]

The Argentine experience captures the essence of the problem with these arrangements. When faced with the need to correct large macroeconomic imbalances, the Argentine authorities introduced major tax reforms and made highly successful administrative reforms. These policies sharply raised the share of taxes in gross domestic product (GDP). But the potential impact of this effort on reducing the public sector's fiscal deficit was dissipated by the revenue-sharing arrangement, which required that 57 percent of any additional tax revenue coming from the central government's effort be shared with the provincial governments, which immediately spent the additional revenue. The subnational governments view economic stabilization as a national public good and thus as the responsibility of the national government.

The Argentine central government also tried to reduce its spending through privatization, employment reductions, and other ways. But at the same time, partly as a result of the additional tax revenue received, provincial governments were increasing their employment and spending. Furthermore, the provinces with the lowest revenue mobilization were those that increased the size of their civil services the most. At the margin, the benefits lost by reducing central government employment probably exceeded the benefit gained by increasing provincial-level employment. The Argentine sharing arrangements ultimately magnified the effort necessary at the central level to reduce the country's fiscal deficit and have probably reduced the efficiency of public spending.

These tax-sharing arrangements, which are limited to specific taxes rather than to the entire tax revenue, also have important efficiency implications on the revenue side. The central government that finds itself in great need of raising revenue but that also has to share some tax revenue with subnational governments will have a strong incentive to raise revenue from the taxes that are not shared or from taxes that will go mostly to the central government. As a result the structure of the tax system will be distorted, and unshared taxes will acquire a greater weight in the tax system even when they are less efficient.

There is another side to this problem. A federal government that finds itself in the situation described above is prone to grant exemptions from the taxes from which it retains only a small share of the revenue raised. This seems to have happened in Pakistan in connection with the general sales tax. The central government has full legislative authority over this tax, but transfers 80 percent of its revenue to the provinces. In other words, the federal government's direct revenue cost of providing incentives is very low. Perverse incentives also occur when subnational governments are able to grant exemptions from national taxes, thus passing on the cost of the lost revenue to the nation. This problem is common in China and existed in Argentina when four provinces had the legal authority to grant exemptions from the national value-added tax. In Argentina this led to a considerable erosion of the revenue from the value-added tax, thus aggravating the fiscal crisis. In the above examples, revenue losses—and thus stabilization problems—compounded the efficiency problems. When tax sharing applies to total tax revenue, rather than to specific taxes, these problems tend to become less serious.

Borrowing by Local Governments

If strictly applied constitutional limitations prevent subnational governments from borrowing, if the market is able to impose discipline on borrowing by subnational governments, or if national governments never intervene when subnational governments get into trouble, then borrowing by subnational jurisdictions does not contribute to a country's macroeconomic difficulties. But few countries have such strict constitutional limitations, markets have proven unable to discipline borrowing (in part because of informational deficiencies; Lane 1993), and central governments are often unable to refuse assistance to subnational governments that get into trouble.

There is a lot of variety in subnational governments' borrowing experience. In Argentina, for example, all levels of government can borrow both domestically and abroad. In 1994 the Argentine provinces were able to finance a deficit of about 0.7 percent of GDP. In Brazil the states can borrow from many sources. São Paulo alone is reported to have accumulated a debt of some $40 billion (*Financial Times*, 25 March 1995, p. 4). In India the states and the center can both borrow domestically (Chelliah 1991). In Pakistan constitutional controls over provincial borrowing do not seem to have been effective. In Mexico the finances of its thirty-two states have been described as "precarious," and some states as "bankrupt" (*Financial Times*, 7 April 1995, p. 7). In Italy borrowing by subnational jurisdictions has contributed to a deterioration in the fiscal situation and has led to the emergence of "hidden" debt. Some municipalities and regions (Naples, Puglie) have encountered major financial difficulties.

There are several complex reasons for this state of affairs. In some cases they may have to do with revenue assignments that do not match expenditure assignments. More often, however, there are more proximate reasons:

- An absence of good public expenditure management systems within the subnational jurisdictions to monitor and register debt obligations and commitments.
- A lack of incentives for local policymakers not to borrow. The borrowing often gives immediate benefits to those in power while the costs are paid later, perhaps by a different administration.
- An implicit assumption that the central government will ultimately foot the bill. As long as those who lend to the governments and the officials who do

the borrowing believe that the central government will eventually come in, the budget will be soft and borrowing will be excessive.

- A lack of good subnational budgetary systems to prepare competent projections for revenue and expenditure.
- A multitude of ways in which "loans" can be obtained. Loans have come from the national government, the central bank, national or foreign banks, provincial banks, suppliers, the capital market, pension funds, arrears on civil servants' salaries, arrears on payments to utilities, and so on. At times these "loans" are voluntary; at other times they are compulsory.

As long as all these possibilities of borrowing exist, as long as there is the belief that the central government will honor subnational governments' obligations, and as long as the incentives for these governments encourage higher spending, decentralization will contribute to macroeconomic instability.

Financing the Activities of Local Governments

In much of the literature on decentralization the determination of the spending responsibilities—if not the precise levels of spending—of subnational governments precedes the question of how resources will be generated to pay for the spending. The financing of the spending is often almost an afterthought. Yet for decentralization to be successful, it must include the decentralization of both spending and revenue, and these decisions must be made at the same time.

It has generally been argued that local governments should finance their spending through "benefit pricing" or benefit taxation. For example, Musgrave and Musgrave (1984, p. 517) write that "the choice of tax instruments to be used by 'local' jurisdictions . . . should conform to the rule that each jurisdiction pay for its own benefits." This is necessary because "benefit taxation—requiring as it does a balance of tax burdens and benefit gains—neutralizes the impact of fiscal operations on location choice" (p. 518). This is, of course, necessary for the result to be Pareto-optimal. Musgrave and Musgrave also recognize, however, that "the assumption of universal benefit taxation . . . is unrealistic" (p. 518).

Assigning Tax Powers

The question of tax assignments by level of government has been discussed by many authors. While such general or theoretical discussions of tax assignments are useful, in practice country-specific factors play a large role. Local jurisdictions raise whatever taxes they are capable of raising, often without worrying much about the economic distortions that these taxes may create. The search for good taxes that can be exploited by local government has not yielded very good results (Bahl and Linn 1992; Bird 1986).

The conclusion that the kind of taxes local governments often raise, especially in developing countries, tend to be of poor quality and thus to generate many economic distortions leads to the obvious question: If decentralization is defended because it improves the allocation of resources on the expenditure side, how much of this efficiency gain is lost when the financing of that expenditure is highly distorted? This is not an easy question to answer, but it is one that must be addressed when the costs and benefits of decentralization are discussed. The easier it is to assign "good" taxes to local jurisdictions, the more justified it is to assign expenditure responsibilities to them. It is also important not to create an imbalance between expenditure responsibilities and the means available to local jurisdictions to carry them out. The assignment of tax revenue to multilevel governments can follow several options.

The first option is to assign all tax bases to the local jurisdictions and ask them to transfer some of the revenue to the national government to allow it to meet its spending responsibilities. The amount transferred upward could be determined by rule, formula, or negotiation. This option is often unattractive and inefficient for a number of reasons. It is inconsistent with a national policy that aims to redistribute income through the tax system. It is inconsistent with a policy that calls on the public sector to stabilize the economy, using the tax system to achieve this objective. It may result in excessive fragmentation of the tax system, and it may provide the wrong incentives to the subnational jurisdictions if they know that part of the taxes they collect will be shared with the national government. There is also evidence from some countries (for example, China and Mexico) that this policy leads to inefficient tax administration.

The second option is for the national government to collect all taxes and transfer some of the revenue to the local jurisdictions. The transfer of funds to the local jurisdictions can be done by sharing total tax revenue or by sharing specific taxes. As argued earlier, the first approach is superior because it gives local governments a more stable revenue source and gives the national government more freedom in pursuing its tax policy options. Still, there are problems with this option. Breaking the connection between decisions to collect tax revenue and decisions to spend that revenue destroys the concept of the tax price for public spending (that is, the idea that spending decisions carry a specific cost expressed through the taxes paid). Local officials and taxpayers may not connect the benefits they derive from public spending with the taxes they pay. Therefore local officials may not exercise the required restraint on spending, and taxpayers will be less willing to pay taxes.

A third, more common option is to assign local jurisdictions some taxing power and, if necessary, to complement the revenue raised locally with grants from the national government. The taxing power can be provided to the local jurisdictions by assigning them exclusive use of some tax bases, allowing them to share some bases with the national government, or allowing local governments to piggy-back on some national taxes. All three approaches are used in some countries.

Assigning Tax Bases

If specific tax bases are assigned to local jurisdictions, the jurisdictions would, in principle, have the option of increasing their spending by raising their taxes. Their perception of the costs and benefits of this action would presumably guide their spending and taxing decisions.

The assignment of tax bases to local jurisdictions must take into account several considerations. The first is the importance of the objectives (other than raising revenue) being pursued through taxation. The more important these other objectives are, the less advantageous it is to leave these tax bases to local jurisdictions. For example, if the government assigns considerable weight to income redistribution (through progressive taxation) or stabilization (through built-in stabilizers), certain tax bases, such as the progressive income tax and the corporate income tax, should be left to the national government.

The second consideration is the mobility of the tax base. If a tax base can easily escape taxation at the local level by moving to another jurisdiction, that base is not a good candidate for local taxation. Thus, the more mobile the tax base, the more desirable that it remain at the national level.

The third consideration involves economies of scale. Depending on informational requirements (for example, the need for a national taxpayer identification number), technical requirements (the use of large computers), or other factors, economies of scale in tax administration for a given tax argue for leaving that tax to the national government. This consideration implies that the value-added tax and the global income tax should be nationally collected taxes.

Keeping in mind these premises, we can quickly survey the assignment of tax bases, starting from the simplest.

Import and export taxes. Economists generally consider import and export taxes to be inefficient and undesirable sources of revenue, but they still account for a large share of revenue in developing countries. These taxes should always be imposed by the national government to reduce the possibility of major distortions from differential foreign trade taxes imposed by different jurisdictions.

Taxes on land and real property. Land and structures (such as buildings) are among the most immobile of tax bases. Where they are used, taxes on real property are often—but not always—imposed by local jurisdictions. Of course, while land and existing structures cannot move, new structures will not be built if a jurisdiction taxes them considerably more than other jurisdictions do. Thus, while old structures cannot move out, new structures may not move in. This limits the tax rates that can be imposed. Assessments of property values to determine the tax liability often create major difficulties. Some countries assess property values nationally but let the local jurisdictions determine the tax rate.

Natural resource taxes. Because natural resources are immobile, it could be argued that, as with land and buildings, natural resources could easily be taxed by the subnational government in which they are located. But it has been argued that these taxes should be assigned to the national government because natural resources are concentrated in particular areas, revenue from them varies, and these taxes, if collected locally, could make a particular region an attractive place to move to because of its better public services (Shah and Qureshi 1994). However, the subnational governments that control resource-rich areas are often reluctant to give up their claims to these resources. Major political conflicts have developed in some federations (Canada, Nigeria, Russia) over who should benefit from these resources. Decentralization is likely to reinforce local claims over these resources. Where the political obstacles can be surmounted, however, these taxes should go to the national government.

Sales taxes. Among sales taxes, single-stage taxes (excise and retail) must be distinguished from multistage taxes (turnover and value added). Excise and retail sales taxes can be assigned to local jurisdictions, provided that neighboring jurisdictions do not use highly different rates. If a jurisdiction uses higher rates than its neighbors, its citizens will be inclined to shop in the lower-rate jurisdictions. Factors influencing these decisions are the vicinity of the other jurisdictions, the cost of travel, and the value of the goods purchased (Tanzi 1995b). Competition among jurisdictions generally limits the scope for rate differentials and thus the freedom of actions of local jurisdictions.

Excise and retail sales taxes are generally relatively simple taxes. But retail sales taxes may be difficult to administer in economies with many small sellers—as in most developing countries—especially if rates are high. For this reason retail sales taxes are not likely to generate much revenue in developing countries. Local excise taxes, however, have proved to be useful revenue sources for subnational governments. Gasoline, alcohol, cars, hotels, and public utilities may provide convenient tax bases for subnational governments.

Imposed with a credit mechanism, value-added taxes are generally rebated on exports and imposed on imports. They follow the so-called destination principle, which stipulates that, to avoid distorting trade relations, these taxes should be paid by the final consumer. The application of the destination principle requires border checks by the jurisdiction that imposes the tax. However, it is neither feasible nor desirable to impose border checks on trade within a country because this would impose excessive costs and would impede trade flows. For these reasons value-added taxes are best left to national governments, especially in developing countries.

Personal income taxes. Personal income taxes can be global—that is, imposed on the total income received by a taxpayer (wages, salaries, interest, dividends, and income from all other activities)—or schedular—imposed separately on each type of income.

Schedular income taxes can be used by the subnational jurisdictions of developing countries if the taxes on incomes such as interest, dividends, wages, and salaries are withheld at the source by those who pay these incomes and the taxes withheld become final taxes. The tax rates must be competitive, however, or individuals will invest in other jurisdictions.

For global income taxes to operate well, all the income that a taxpayer receives from different sources and jurisdictions must be combined before the tax is calculated. The tax administration of the jurisdiction where the taxpayer resides is unlikely to have information about income earned outside the jurisdiction unless this information is provided by the national government. Thus tax evasion can be significant. For this reason it is better to leave this tax base to the national government, which is in a better position to get the relevant information.[7]

Other taxes and fees. Many smaller tax bases lend themselves more easily to exploitation by local governments. These range from relatively important ones (such as those related to the use of cars) to relatively insignificant ones (such as license fees for dogs). The better application of fees for activities that require some use of social services (such as education, health, and commercial activities) can provide important resources that come in the form of benefits received and are therefore consistent with the basic principles behind decentralization.

Efficiency losses. Thus there are serious limitations to the tax revenue that local governments can raise if they limit themselves to taxes that are efficient, easy to administer, and of a benefit-received nature. Most local jurisdictions raise only a fraction—and sometimes a small fraction—of their revenue needs from own-tax sources. Furthermore, the revenue raised is often collected with taxes that are inefficient, poorly administered, and bear little relationship to the benefit received. This conclusion relates to the question raised earlier: If decentralization is defended not on political grounds, but because it improves the allocation of resources on the expenditure side, how much of that efficiency gain is lost when the financing of that expenditure imposes significant welfare costs on the economy? This question can only be answered on a case-by-case basis, but it must be considered whenever decentralization is actively pursued.

Conclusion

Decentralization is a kind of contract whose details and implications often are not precisely spelled out. Decentralization can live up to its promise—if the constitutional and legal frameworks are clearly defined and enforced, if local governments are given access to the necessary resources, if public expenditure management systems can both monitor and control the pace and allocation of spending, and if local bureaucrats and national bureaucrats are of equal quality. Otherwise, the results tend to be disappointing. The key to successful decentralization is good planning: decentralization should mean devolving both spending responsibilities and revenue sources—and determining the magnitude of both simultaneously and in advance. Despite the difficulties in implementation, the arguments for decentralization are sound and powerful. The process can and does live up to its promises. Properly implemented, it provides important economic and political benefits as local jurisdictions improve the efficiency and accountability of public spending.

Notes

1. The subnational governments in Germany and in the Scandinavian countries, for example, are probably as competently staffed as the national governments.
2. This is the case in several Latin American countries, including Colombia and Peru, and in other regions.
3. This is the case in Argentina and in Brazil, where the net debt of subnational governments is nearly $60 billion. In Canada provincial governments have run large deficits and accumulated substantial debts. The same experience is shared by Italy's subnational jurisdictions or entities.
4. In some countries a political cycle has been identified at the local level of taxes falling and expenditure rising before elections. Of course, such cycles are not limited to subnational governments.

5. Once again, the experiences of Argentina, Brazil, and Italy since 1979 provide relevant examples. In these situations there are always local suppliers available to provide the services on credit or local banks willing to extend loans.

6. A good description of the revenue sharing arrangements in Argentina is provided by Liuksila (forthcoming) and by Porto and Sanguinetti (1993); for information on tax assignments in Brazil, see Bomfim and Shah (1994); for Russia, see Bahl (1994); for Colombia, see Ferreira and Valenzuela (1993).

7. In the United States special factors allow both the states and the counties or municipalities to tax global income by using information provided by the national authorities. These special factors are often missing in developing countries.

References

Ahmad, Ehtisham, ed. Forthcoming. *Financing Decentralized Expenditure*. Aldershot, U.K.: Edgar Elgar.

Artana, Daniel, and Ricardo López Murphy. 1994. "Fiscal Decentralization: Some Lessons for Latin America." Fundación de Investigaciones Económicas Latino Americanas, Buenos Aires, Argentina.

Bahl, Roy W. 1994. "Revenue Sharing in Russia." Reprint Series 61. Georgia State University, College of Business Administration, Atlanta, Georgia.

Bahl, Roy W., and Johannes F. Linn. 1992. *Urban Public Finance in Developing Countries*. New York: Oxford University Press.

Bayoumi, Tamin A. 1992. "U.S. State and Local Government Finances over the Current Cycle." IMF Working Paper 92/112. International Monetary Fund, Washington, D.C.

Bird, Richard. 1986. *Federal Finance in Comparative Perspective*. Toronto: Canadian Tax Foundation.

———. 1994. "Decentralizing Infrastructure: For Good or for Ill?" Policy Research Working Paper 1258. World Bank, Washington, D.C.

Boadway, Robin, and David E. Wildasin. 1984. *Public Sector Economics*. Boston: Little, Brown, and Company.

Boadway, Robin, Sandra Roberts, and Anwar Shah. 1994. "The Reform of Fiscal Systems in Developing and Emerging Market Economies: A Federalism Perspective." Policy Research Working Paper 1259. World Bank, Office of the Vice President, Development Economics, Washington, D.C.

Bomfim, Antulio, and Anwar Shah. 1994. "Macroeconomic Management and the Division of Powers in Brazil: Perspectives for the 1990s." *World Development* 22 (April): 535–42.

Brennan, Geoffrey, and James M. Buchanan. 1980. *The Power to Tax: Analytical Foundations of a Fiscal Constitution*. Cambridge: Cambridge University Press.

CEPR (Centre for Economic and Policy Research). 1993. *Making Sense of Subsidiarity: How Much Centralization for Europe?* London: CEPR.

Chelliah, Raja J. 1991. "Intergovernmental Fiscal Relations and Macroeconomic Management in India." Indian Institute of Public Policy and Finance, New Delhi, India.

Commission of the European Communities. 1993. "The Economics of Community Public Finance." European Economy Reports and Studies 5. Commision of the European Communities, Brussels.

Cremer, Jacques, Antonio Estache, and Paul Seabright. 1994. "The Decentralization of Public Services: Lessons from the Theory of the Firm." Policy Research Working Paper 1345. Office of the Vice President, Development Economics, World Bank, Washington, D.C.

de Callatay, E., and F. Ribe. 1994. "How Intergovernmental Fiscal Relations Affect Macroeconomic Stabilization: An Overview." International Monetary Fund, Fiscal Affairs Department, Washington, D.C.

de la Cruz, Rafael, and Armando Barrios, eds. 1994. *Federalismo Fiscal: El Costo de la Decentralización en Venezuela*. Caracas, Venezuela: Nueva Sociedad.

Ehdaie, Jaber. 1994. "Fiscal Decentralization and the Size of Government: An Extension with Evidence From Cross-Country Data." Policy Research Working Paper 1387. World Bank, Policy Research Department, Public Economics Division, Washington, D.C.

Ferreira, Ana María, and Luis Carlos Valenzuela. 1993. *Decentralización Fiscal: El Caso Colombiano*. Serie Política Fiscal 49. Commissión Económica para America Latina, Santiago, Chile.

FIEL (Fundación de Investigaciones Económicas Latino Americanas). 1993. *Hacia Una Nueva Organización del Federalismo Fiscal en la Argentina*. Buenos Aires: FIEL.

Gramlich, Edward M. 1987. "Federalism and Federal Deficit Reduction." *National Tax Journal* 40(3): 299–313.

Hirsch, Werner. 1968. "The Supply of Urban Public Services." In Harvey S. Perloff and Lowdon Wingo, Jr., eds., *Issues in Urban Economics.* Baltimore, Md.: Johns Hopkins University Press.

Israel, Arturo. 1992. *Issues for Infrastructure Management in the 1990s.* World Bank Discussion Paper 171. Washington, D.C.

Lane, Timothy D. 1993. "Market Discipline." *IMF Staff Papers* 40(1): 53–88.

Liuksila, Claire. Forthcoming. "Argentina: Intergovernmental Fiscal Relations—A Case Study." International Monetary Fund, Fiscal Affairs Department, Washington, D.C.

Lotz, Jorgen. 1995. "Equalization Grants to Local Governments in Denmark and Other Scandinavian Countries." International Monetary Fund, Fiscal Affairs Department, Washington, D.C.

Ma, Jun. 1995. "Macroeconomic Management and Intergovernmental Relations in China." Policy Research Working Paper 1408. World Bank, Economic Development Institute, New Products and Outreach Division, Washington, D.C.

McLure, Charles E., Jr., ed. 1983. *Tax Assignment in Federal Countries.* Centre for Research on Federal Financial Relations. Canberra, Australia: Australian National University Press.

Ministry of Economics and Public Works and Services, Argentina. 1994. *Cambios Estructurales en la Relacion Nacion-Provincias.* Buenos Aires.

Murphy, Kevin M., Andrei Shleifer, and Robert W. Vishny. 1991. "The Allocation of Talent: Implications for Growth." *Quarterly Journal of Economics* 106(May): 503–30.

Musgrave, Richard A. 1959. *The Theory of Public Finance: A Study in Public Economy.* New York: McGraw-Hill.

Musgrave, Richard A., and Peggy B. Musgrave. 1984. *Public Finance in Theory and Practice.* New York: McGraw-Hill.

Oates, Wallace E. 1972. *Fiscal Federalism.* New York: Harcourt, Brace, Jovanovich.

———. 1994. "The Potential and Perils of Fiscal Decentralization." University of Maryland, Department of Economics, College Park, Md.

Porto, Alberto, and Pablo Sanguinetti. 1993. "Decentralización Fiscal en América Latina: El Caso Argentino." *Serie Política Fiscal* 45. Commissión Económica para America Latina, Santiago, Chile.

Prud'homme, Rémy. 1994. "On the Dangers of Decentralization." Policy Research Working Paper 1252. World Bank, Transportation, Water, and Urban Development Department, Transport Division, Washington, D.C.

Putnam, Robert D. 1993. *Making Democracy Work: Civic Traditions in Modern Italy.* Princeton, N.J.: Princeton University Press.

Shah, Anwar, and Zia Qureshi. 1994. *Intergovernmental Fiscal Relations in Indonesia: Issues and Reform Options.* World Bank Discussion Paper 239. Washington, D.C.

Shome, Parthasarathi. 1994. "Fiscal Federalism—Revenue, Expenditure, and Macro Management: Selected Latin American Experiences and Recent Discussions in India." International Monetary Fund, Fiscal Affairs Department, Washington, D.C.

Tanzi, Vito. 1994. "Corruption, Governmental Activities, and Markets." IMF Working Paper 94/99. International Monetary Fund, Washington, D.C.

———. 1995a. "Basic Issues of Decentralization and the Tax Assignment." In Ehtisham Ahmad, Gao Qiang, and Vito Tanzi, eds., *Reforming China's Public Finances.* Washington, D.C.: International Monetary Fund.

———. 1995b. *Taxation in An Integrating World.* Washington, D.C.: The Brookings Institution.

Tanzi, Vito, and Domenico Fanizza. 1995. "Fiscal Deficit and Public Debt in Industrial Countries." IMF Working Paper 95/49. International Monetary Fund, Washington, D.C.

Tiebout, C.M. 1956. "A Pure Theory of Local Expenditures." *Journal of Political Economy* 5(October): 416–24.

Comment on "Fiscal Federalism and Decentralization: A Review of Some Efficiency and Macroeconomic Aspects," by Vito Tanzi

Charles E. McLure, Jr.

Vito Tanzi's article is balanced, well-reasoned, and broad in coverage. My comments focus on revenue assignment, which I believe needs more elaboration (see also the references to my other work). Although this topic is rather technical, it deserves attention, because its neglect causes mistakes.

Factors behind Recent Decentralization

Tanzi's discussion of the factors driving the recent global trend toward decentralization is generally compelling, but it understates one important factor—the power of ideas. (Recall Keynes's famous quote about madmen in authority and academic scribblers.) Surely the ideas that are surveyed in the second part of the article should appear in the first part as factors contributing to the shift toward decentralized government. I was particularly surprised by the short shrift Tanzi gives to the literature on public choice, especially that inspired by Brennan and Buchanan (1980).

Ideas are often neglected during the decentralization process, most obviously in the countries of the former Soviet Union. Among the serious mistakes in tax assignment in that region that could have been avoided are using the "restricted origin principle" for the value-added tax (that is, the origin principle for internal trade and the destination principle for external trade); sharing value-added tax revenues on an origin basis (at least in Kazakstan, Russia, and Ukraine); and sharing revenues from the enterprise profits tax on an origin basis that makes no sense (for example, with the oblast where an enterprise's headquarters are located).

Academic ideas about decentralization have had little impact on defining limits on the ability of subnational governments to borrow. This partly reflects a lack of explicit ideas; little early theoretical work on decentralization recognized that governments borrow and that it is necessary to overcome the moral hazard problem that arises if politicians and bureaucrats (as well as banks, suppliers, and other lenders) believe the central governments will not allow subnational governments to default

Charles E. McLure, Jr. is senior fellow at the Hoover Institution at Stanford University.

Annual World Bank Conference on Development Economics 1995
©1996 The International Bank for Reconstruction and Development / THE WORLD BANK

on their debt. Some countries have institutional constraints on borrowing by subnational governments and make credible the threat not to bail out fiscally irresponsible governments and lenders. As Tanzi emphasizes, institutional constraints that protect against irresponsible behavior—without unduly limiting the power to borrow—and make bankruptcy of subnational governments a credible threat are essential if decentralization is to realize its full potential.

Decentralization and Tax Assignment

Subnational governments must have their own sources of revenue if true decentralization is to exist. More than revenue adequacy is at stake. These governments must truly be the masters of their own fiscal destiny, at least at the margin, if they are to be autonomous and accountable and if decentralization is to improve the allocation of resources.

Many discussions of tax assignment begin with Musgrave's (1959) three-branch view of the public household, assigning income redistribution and macroeconomic stabilization to the central government but dividing the allocation function among two or more levels of government. Taxation that is based on the household's ability to pay is needed for income redistribution, but fees, charges, and taxation that are based on benefits received are more appropriate for financing the allocation branch (for fairness as well as for economic efficiency). This implies that the taxes assigned to subnational governments should reflect benefits received to the extent possible.

The smaller a jurisdiction, the more open it tends to be; labor, capital, goods, and services move across boundaries. Taxation that is not based on benefits received tends to repel mobile factors, and tax competition between jurisdictions imposes healthy discipline on politicians, bureaucrats, and citizens looking for a free ride (by imposing taxes that exceed the benefits provided).

Methods of Revenue Assignment

Four means of revenue assignment—determining who gets the money and how—provide significantly different answers to four crucial questions: Who chooses the tax? Who defines the tax base? Who sets tax rates? And who administers the tax? The power to set tax rates is by far the most important of these. This power is necessary for fiscal autonomy and accountability, and it facilitates tax competition. However, serious problems can arise if subnational governments are given unbridled discretion over the choice of taxes, the definition of the tax base, and tax administration.

Independent legislation and administration maximize the fiscal autonomy of subnational governments, since they choose the tax, define the base, set tax rates, and administer the tax. Complexity and duplication of effort make this approach too costly for most major taxes in developing countries.

Tax sharing errs in the other direction. Under this approach the central government chooses the tax base, sets rates, administers the tax, and shares revenues with the subnational jurisdictions where revenues originate. There is no possibility of tax competition, and fiscal autonomy and accountability exist only in spending. Tax sharing is acceptable only if uniformity is more important than autonomy. A system that is based on tax sharing is more vulnerable to macroeconomic imbalance than a system that is based on surcharges. Moreover, central governments often have few incentives to collect shared taxes.

Subnational surcharges are generally the preferred means of assigning revenues to jurisdictions where taxed economic activity occurs. The national government determines the tax base and administers the tax, but allows subnational governments to add surcharges on economic activity occurring in (or attributed to) their jurisdictions. Surcharges are simpler and cheaper than independent action and provide the possibility of tax competition and more accountability and fiscal autonomy than tax sharing.

Revenue sharing may be needed to overcome horizontal fiscal disparities between subnational jurisdictions, and perhaps vertical fiscal imbalance between them and the central government. Revenue sharing channels central government revenues to subnational governments based on such factors as population, average income, incidence of poverty, tax capacity, and fiscal effort. This approach provides little subnational fiscal autonomy and can undermine macroeconomic stability. But unlike other methods of revenue assignment, it can be used to equalize the fiscal position of subnational jurisdictions.

A *synthesis* of tax surcharges and revenue sharing can help realize the benefits of both: the administrative simplicity and fiscal autonomy of surcharges and the equalization of revenue sharing.

Assignment of Particular Taxes

Conventional wisdom on tax assignment, formulated in the context of industrial countries, is often not appropriate for developing countries. For administrative reasons it is often difficult for developing countries to find adequate revenue sources that can be assigned to subnational governments.

Sales taxes. Consistent with the conventional wisdom, second-tier governments in Canada and the United States rely heavily on the retail sales tax; some U.S. local jurisdictions also levy surcharges on state sales taxes. Subnational governments in developing countries generally cannot follow this model. Because a value-added tax (VAT) has administrative and other advantages over the retail sales tax and other taxes, it has become the "revenue workhorse" throughout the world—a situation that is not likely to change. Experience in Brazil, the only country with a second-tier VAT, indicates that the VAT is not really suitable for subnational governments; experience in the former Soviet Union suggests that sharing VAT revenues with the oblasts where they originate creates both administrative problems and economic distortions; and Canada's recent experience confirms the predicted difficulties of combining a national VAT with a provincial retail sales tax. It is conceivable that a national VAT could be implemented with subnational surcharges, but that is not likely to happen soon in developing countries. In short, sales taxation is not easily assigned to subnational governments in developing countries.

Personal income tax. Personal and corporate income taxes are conventionally assigned to the central government, which is responsible for income distribution and macroeconomic stabilization. But, as Tanzi notes, the stabilization problems facing developing countries are more likely to be structural and secular than cyclical. Thus it may be appropriate that central governments in developing countries rely more heavily on sales taxes than the conventional wisdom dictates. Given the paucity of satisfactory subnational revenues, it may be appropriate for subnational governments to levy surcharges on individual income. The central government's income tax would presumably have a tax threshold and graduated rates for distributional reasons; but on benefits grounds the subnational surcharge might have a single rate—and perhaps no tax threshold.

There are problems with this approach. In the typical developing country most taxpayers should not file tax returns, making residence-based surcharges impossible. Employment-based taxes—essentially payroll taxes—are feasible; indeed, they may be the only alternative. But where taxpayers live far from their families, as well as where cross-border commuting is important, jurisdictions providing public services may not get their fair share of revenues.

Corporate income tax. The corporate income tax should be reserved for the national government if subnational revenues from other sources are adequate. Corporate profit is a poor foundation for benefit taxation. Moreover, rates that are not uniform distort the location of economic activity, but forcing rates to be uniform across jurisdictions prevents tax competition and eliminates subnational fiscal autonomy. Independent subnational legislation and administration—the practice in the United States—should be avoided. Virtually everything in the typical formula used to determine tax liability to the U.S. states—including many issues that are not even apparent—is up for grabs, varying from state to state and often subject to litigation. Subnational revenues from this tax should come from surcharges imposed on a base determined by the central government, which should administer the tax.

Natural resources taxes. Assigning subnational governments revenues from taxes on important and unequally distributed natural resources distorts the allocation of resources toward resource-rich jurisdictions and is questionable on equity grounds. The common argument that such governments should be able to tax their natural resource "heritage" begs the question of whether this is the heritage of the nation or the subnational jurisdiction. Still, subnational governments should be allowed to collect charges and taxes adequate to compensate for environmental damage and other public costs related to the exploitation of resources (for example, specialized roads and harbors).

Property tax. The property tax is among the few potentially important taxes commonly assigned to subnational governments; it can generally be implemented locally and, within limits, reflects the benefits of public services. Among the weak links in this argument is the lack of accurate cadastral surveys. But there is another problem. If land ownership is highly concentrated, as in many developing countries, the property tax is unlikely to be an important source of revenue. Land reform increases the possibility of using the property tax as a benefit tax. Owners of small plots might be willing to pay property taxes in order to secure services for themselves and their children.

A Digression on Vouchers

Sensible tax assignment puts pressure on subnational governments to provide services that people want and to do so efficiently. But that pressure is often inadequate for the reasons noted in the public choice literature, including the lack of competitive alternatives to public provision. I conclude by discussing a potentially important substitute for revenue assignment, namely, using vouchers financed by the central government to fund services traditionally provided by subnational governments.

Suppose the central government provides vouchers that can be redeemed for specific essential services (those satisfying basic needs) traditionally provided by subnational governments, even though those services are not pure public goods (joint in supply and nonexclusive). Examples include basic health care and education. Governmental units, nongovernmental organizations, and private firms are encouraged to compete in providing these services.

Vouchers give citizen-consumers a direct voice in the types and quality of services they receive. By comparison, political processes provide only an indirect voice, especially to the poor. As in the private sector, competition encourages efficiency. There is greater budgetary flexibility, a concern of Tanzi's. There is less fiscal pressure on subnational governments, which need less revenue. Besides reducing interpersonal inequality, per capita vouchers are a powerful engine of regional equalization; means-tested vouchers are even more powerful, but difficult to implement. There is less need for revenue sharing to reduce either vertical imbalance or horizontal disparities.

Conclusion

Decentralization is no panacea. It is subject to limitations, many of which Tanzi describes. Done badly, it can reduce welfare (Prud'homme 1995). But done well, it can improve welfare by increasing the participation of people in the decisions that affect them. The important question is how to do it well.

References

Brennan, Geoffrey, and James M. Buchanan. 1980. *The Power to Tax: Analytical Foundations of a Fiscal Constitution.* New York: Cambridge University Press.

McLure, Charles E., Jr. 1993a. "The Brazilian Tax Assignment Problem: Ends, Means, and Constraints." In John H.Y. Edwards, ed., *A Reforma Fiscal no Brasil,* the proceedings volume of the international symposium on fiscal reform, September 6–10, São Paulo, Brazil.

———. 1993b. "A North American View of Vertical Fiscal Imbalance and the Assignment of Taxing Powers." In D. J. Collins, ed., *Vertical Fiscal Imbalance and the Allocation of Taxing Powers.* Sydney: Australian Tax Research Foundation.

————. 1994. "The Sharing of Taxes on Natural Resources and the Future of the Russian Federation." In Christine Wallich, ed., *Russia and the Challenge of Fiscal Federalism*. Washington, D.C.: World Bank.

————. 1995a. "Revenue Assignment and Intergovernmental Fiscal Relations in Russia." In Edward Lazear, ed., *Economic Transition in Eastern Europe and Russia: Realities of Reform*. Palo Alto, Calif.: Hoover Institution Press.

————. 1995b. "The Revenue Assignment Problem: Conceptual and Administrative Considerations in Achieving Subnational Fiscal Autonomy." Institute for Policy Research, Washington, D.C.

————. Forthcoming, a. "Intergovernmental Fiscal Relations in South Africa: The Assignment of Expenditure Functions and Revenue Sources and the Design of Intergovernmental Grants and Transfers." World Bank, Southern Africa Department, Washington, D.C.

————. Forthcoming, b. "Topics in the Theory of Revenue Assignment: Gaps, Traps, and Nuances." In Mario I. Blejar and Teresa I. Ter-Minassian, eds., *Macroeconomic Dimensions of Public Finance: Essays in Honor of Vito Tanzi*. London: Routledge.

Musgrave, Richard A. 1959. *The Theory of Public Finance*. New York: McGraw Hill.

Prud'homme, Remy. 1995. "On the Dangers of Decentralization." *World Bank Research Observer* 10(2): 201–20.

Comment on "Fiscal Federalism and Decentralization: A Review of Some Efficiency and Macroeconomic Aspects," by Vito Tanzi

David Wildasin

Vito Tanzi has written a useful survey of fiscal federalism. Many of the ideas he covers will be familiar to those who grew up reading Oates (1972) and other important literature on the topic in the late 1960s and the 1970s. But issues of fiscal decentralization have attracted much new attention since then, and Tanzi's introduction to the major themes will be helpful to those needing an overview. Tanzi focuses on the issues of fiscal decentralization that arise in developing and transition economies, where many of the questions facing policymakers and scholars are distinctive and complex. Especially in this context it is difficult to escape the linkage between fiscal decentralization and macroeconomic policy, a topic unduly neglected in the literature. Tanzi devotes welcome attention to the macroeconomic implications of fiscal decentralization, which should stimulate new research in this area.

Because of its breadth of coverage, the article naturally passes lightly over certain topics. I will identify some issues that may warrant more attention, or perhaps a different emphasis, than they receive in the article. I will not belabor the many points on which I broadly agree with the author.

Some General Issues

First, because fiscal decentralization is partly about government structure, it is useful in debates about fiscal decentralization to recognize explicitly the tension between normative and public choice approaches.[1] For policy purposes we often wish to assess whether fiscal decentralization will improve allocative efficiency or distributive equity. To do this we need some predictive or positive theory of how decentralized government institutions work.

Part of the conventional wisdom, reiterated by Tanzi, is that preferences for public services are more effectively expressed through lower levels of government, thereby making fiscal decentralization conducive to allocative efficiency. But this presumption seems to depend critically on the decisionmaking mechanism of lower-

David Wildasin is professor of economics at Vanderbilt University.

Annual World Bank Conference on Development Economics 1995

level government—whether it is democratic or dictatorial, for example—and on the constraints on local decisionmakers—the ease with which households and firms can escape (exit) or enter localities in response to their fiscal attractiveness, for example. If exit is constrained and there are no channels for voicing dissatisfaction and effecting change, there is no particular reason to presume that fiscal decentralization enhances allocative efficiency. In the most general terms there is probably a fair presumption that exit or voice (or both) may be more easily attained under fiscal decentralization. But enhancing the responsiveness of local institutions, whether by democratizing them or by making them more competitive, is a task that warrants explicit consideration in the developing country context.[2]

Second, following Oates (1972), it is useful to distinguish between economic and political decentralization. By economic decentralization Oates means any geographically nonuniform policy, whether implemented through decentralized political institutions or not. Bearing this distinction in mind, we see that there is really no such thing as a truly centralized economic system since even centrally planned economies recognize interregional economic differences and take them into account in policy formulation. This is an important distinction to consider when discussing fiscal decentralization because spatially nonuniform central government policies may interact with explicitly decentralized fiscal institutions.

There are many examples. Schiff and Valdés (1995) find that many developing countries have subjected agriculture to heavy taxation, often through price controls administered by agricultural marketing boards and the like. These policies are frequently implemented by central governments, as are transportation policies that may benefit rural and urban transportation sectors unevenly. These central government policies may themselves distort the allocation of resources, for example, by contributing to excessive urbanization. If so, they need to be taken into account in the formulation of intergovernmental grant systems, the assignment of taxing authority to local governments, and other fiscal decentralization policies. In China economic decentralization involves the "localization" of state-owned enterprises, which cannot but interact with the geographical distribution of fiscal burdens and benefits. Deregulation of the labor market, in the form of a loosening of the household registration (*hukou*) system, is bound to have major implications for urbanization and thus for the public finances of lower-level governments. In South Africa the redress of inequality is a crucial and potentially explosive issue. While it is obvious that substantial pro-poor and interracial redistribution is necessary, there may be both economic and political dangers associated with excessive concentration of fiscal power. Strengthening provincial and local institutions may create a credible institutional constraint on the exercise of the redistributive powers of the public sector and thus provide some reassurance to those likely to lose from the dismantling of the apartheid regime. Examples could be multiplied, but the main point is to appreciate that fiscal decentralization does not occur in isolation from the evolution of other policies.

Third, Tanzi's article appears in some respects (though very judiciously) to be leaning against the wind of recent trends toward fiscal decentralization. Whether decentralization is "good" or "bad" is perhaps one of the grand normative questions of the day, and it is natural that policymakers would want to have a concise bottom-line answer to this question. Attempts to provide it have led to some simplistic pro- and anti-decentralization views. In fact, however, the "right" degree of decentralization depends on what it is we are considering decentralizing and on local economic, historical, and political circumstances.

Another way to say this is that the "big question" about decentralization is really poorly posed. There is a continuum of alternatives along the centralization-decentralization spectrum, with world government at the extreme centralization end and the individual at the other end. Somewhere in the middle are countries, states and provinces, and localities. A position at either extreme (all economic decisions either completely centralized or completely decentralized) is obviously untenable. Some activities clearly reside within the sphere of the individual. And for some activities—global environmental issues come to mind—uncoordinated decisionmaking by nations is probably too decentralized and some sort of global coordination is needed. Other activities fall somewhere between the two extremes. From an economic viewpoint there is nothing special about the point on the spectrum called the "nation."[3] Some activities might best be assigned to that level of government but certainly not all. The crucial issue is to identify which level of decentralization is appropriate for each kind of activity. It makes little sense to hope for some bottom-line presumption in favor of "more decentralization" or "more centralization."

Some More Specific Points

Tanzi expresses concern with "structural deficits," rightly highlighting the importance of information, control, and accountability for decentralized borrowing. In this context it is important to bear in mind the problem of the proper measurement of the net worth position of governments (Eisner 1986; Kotlikoff 1992; Boadway and Wildasin 1993). Lower-level governments often play an important role in the accumulation of public sector assets (for example, through infrastructure investment). Moreover, in addition to explicit liabilities (formal debt obligations), they can also incur implicit liabilities, such as underfunded pension obligations to public employees. It is the change in the comprehensive net worth of lower-level governments that is most important for growth, equity, and efficiency. Using only officially measured local borrowing to determine the deficit or net worth position of lower-level governments while neglecting other local government liabilities and assets is about as meaningful as trying to measure monetary growth by tracking fluctuations in the stock of $10 bills. It is part of the story, to be sure, but we had better recognize its limitations if we don't want to be seriously misled. If controlling lower-level government borrowing squeezes badly needed infrastructure investment, the net effect could be to increase rather than reduce the fiscal burden passed along to the next generation. Improving accounting systems to better track net worth positions is an important priority at all levels of government.

Second, Tanzi raises the issue of soft and hard local budget constraints. As he notes, if localities expect to be bailed out when they run a deficit, there will be an incentive or moral hazard problem that is likely to contribute to structural deficits. If a local or provincial government is "too big (or too important) to fail," central government intervention may be needed, perhaps in the form of borrowing constraints or other regulations. However, greater decentralization is a possible alternative to central government control over local borrowing. Breaking up lower-level governments along geographic or functional lines may credibly harden their budget constraints. For example, establishing independent electricity enterprises separate from the general functions of local governments or breaking up large urban governments into more fragmented system of local governments may make these bodies "small enough to fail." We generally do not bail out households and firms that get into trouble with their creditors, and this of course is why we can afford to let them have access to the capital market on whatever terms they can obtain.

An interesting question for research is to identify what sizes or types of lower-level governments can reasonably be viewed as sufficiently small that their budget constraints are "hard." To take some U.S. examples, Orange County, California, seems to be small enough to fail: there is little sympathy for a federal government aid package to bail it out. By contrast, the current fiscal crisis in Washington, D.C., has attracted higher-level government intervention, as occurred with New York City during the 1970s. One can only imagine how soft the budget constraint would be for New York City if it were also the national capital. Although this might sound fanciful, there are many capital cities throughout the world that are also leading national economic centers, a situation that can easily turn municipal financial crises into national ones. Separating major governmental and economic urban centers (functional decentralization) or breaking large municipal governments into multiple jurisdictions (spatial fragmentation) may serve to harden the budget constraints of lower-level governments. As capital market conditions permit, it might then make sense to allow more unrestrained borrowing authority to lower-level governments in order to meet infrastructure and other critical financing needs—with the explicit understanding, of course, that the central government provides no guarantee to the creditors of lower-level governments.

Third, in several places Tanzi discusses the use of "benefit taxation" in a decentralized setting. Taxes or charges that reflect the true benefits from public services (whether total or marginal benefits) need to be carefully distinguished from those that reflect the costs that households or firms impose on public service providers. To establish the "right" locational incentives, it is crucial to charge for services on the basis of marginal congestion costs, irrespective of the benefits that a household or firm may receive from public services. These congestion costs arise from the "rivalness" of public services, that is, from that fact that public services may not be "pure" in the Samuelson sense.

Congestion costs may—but need not—be related to the benefits people receive from public services. The two are often confused because the people who use public services (for instance, children in classrooms, patients in clinics) often receive benefits from them and also impose costs on them. Proper pricing and taxation require separation of the two. The fifty-person bus and the one-person *becak* may impose equal delays on other vehicles, but the benefit of one bus trip may be fifty times greater than that of one becak trip; an infant and an aged person may both require fifteen minutes of a doctor's time for treatment, but the value of the service may be drastically different; a single adult immigrant to an urban area imposes no burden on the school system whereas a couple with children does. In such cases taxes and charges based on the cost of service provision or utilization (more specifically, based on marginal cost) rather than on subjective benefits are required to avoid incentives for inefficient migration and service utilization. The optimal congestion toll on a Samuelson pure public good is zero for all users, no matter whether the benefits it provides are high or low, in total or at the margin. However, the optimal way to internalize the congestion costs associated with the provision of quasi-private public goods (goods whose cost of provision is proportional to the number of consumers) is per capita cost sharing. Again, this is true for all users whatever the benefits they receive from consuming these goods.[4]

A final comment concerns administrative capacity, corruption, and other institutional factors in fiscal decentralization. These factors are certainly important in assessing the feasibility of decentralization, and otherwise well-conceived decentralization reforms may yield disappointing results due to a lack of adequate institutional infrastructure. However, one might conjecture that a sort of "law of conservation of administrative capacity" would apply, whereby decentralization of public sector functions neither creates nor destroys administrative talent in and of itself.[5] The issue may not be so much the availability of talent and administrative skill in the public sector as the fact that they may have to be decentralized along with public sector functions. Such reallocations take time and may require a rethinking of the reward structures for administrative service at both lower and higher levels of governments. I would be reluctant to accept the notion that higher-level governments always have better administrators; for instance, it is not obvious that the United Nations or the European Parliament have better politicians or bureaucrats than some national governments. Rather, given time and incentives to adjust, we would expect administrative talent to flow to the locus of administrative responsibilities. We should be careful about letting the tail of current administrative capability wag the dog of the proper assignment of public sector functional responsibility.

As far as corruption is concerned, we have as usual fertile ground for speculation since corruption tends by its nature to be somewhat hidden. One could imagine that central government bureaucrats might be more effectively monitored and inspected and that there are numerous opportunities for local officials to get away with petty graft. However, by virtue of their more limited powers, it is difficult for local officials to engage in enormous corruption schemes, whereas a corrupt minister of a central government may be able to do massive harm. So there may be a tradeoff between local corruption on a small scale and central corruption on a large scale. It seems impossible to say a priori which would dominate the other.

Notes

1. Political economy considerations figure prominently in the literature of fiscal federalism. For discussion and references see Rubinfeld (1987) and Wildasin (1986).

2. As the example of the competitive firm shows, democratization is not always crucial for allocative efficiency. Democratic political reform may be important for the success of some types of fiscal decentralization but not necessarily for all. From an economic viewpoint the crucial issue is the linking of the costs and benefits of resource allocation in the decisionmaking process.

3. Although it is conventional to refer to national-level policies as "centralized," the country does not necessarily provide a natural unit of analysis. Parallel to Tanzi's statement that California and Delaware cannot both be optimal given their large difference in size, the same could be said about Luxembourg, Germany, the United States, and China. For many purposes of public economics, such as the analysis of tax and transfer policies, the most economically appropriate unit of analysis is the area covered by markets for the factors of production. (Krugman 1991 emphasizes that the country is often not the natural unit of analysis for trade and specialization issues.) At certain times and places capital and labor market boundaries might roughly coincide with national political boundaries, a stylization that presumably underlies the view of many writers that tax, transfer, and other redistributive policies should be undertaken by national rather than lower-level governments. But if factor markets become international in scope—as seems increasingly to be the case—national governments are no longer central governments in the relevant sense. See Tanzi (1995) and Wildasin (1992, 1994, 1995) for further discussion of factor market integration and redistribution policy.

4. These congestion-pricing rules are first-best rules. Basic principles of taxation to achieve locational efficiency, and references to relevant literature on this topic, are discussed in Wildasin (1986).

5. Decentralization or other institutional change may well destroy institution-specific human capital. Sometimes this is indeed the purpose of institutional reorganization, but of course it may also be costly.

References

Boadway, Robin, and David E. Wildasin. 1993. "Long-Term Debt Strategy: A Survey." In Frans van Winden and H.A.A. Verbon, eds., *The Political Economy of Government Debt*. Amsterdam: North-Holland.

Eisner, Robert. 1986. *How Real Is the Federal Deficit?* New York: Free Press.

Kotlikoff, Laurence. 1992. *Generational Accounting*. New York: Free Press.

Krugman, Paul. 1991. *Geography and Trade*. Cambridge, Mass.: MIT Press.

Oates, Wallace. 1972. *Fiscal Federalism*. New York: Harcourt, Brace, Jovanovich.

Rubinfeld, Daniel. 1987. "The Economics of the Local Public Sector." In Alan Auerbach and Martin Feldstein, eds., *Handbook of Public Economics*. Amsterdam: North-Holland.

Schiff, Maurice, and Alberto Valdés. 1995. "The Plundering of Agriculture in Developing Countries." *Finance & Development* 32: 44–47.

Tanzi, Vito. 1995. *Taxation in an Integrating World*. Washington, D.C.: The Brookings Institution.

Wildasin, David. 1986. *Urban Public Finance*. New York: Harwood Academic Publishers.

———. 1992. "Relaxation of Barriers to Factor Mobility and Income Redistribution." In Pierre Pestieau, ed., *Public Finance in a World of Transition*, a supplement to *Public Finance/Finances Publiques* 47: 216–30.

———. 1994. "Income Redistribution and Migration." *Canadian Journal of Economics* 27: 637–56.

———. 1995. "Factor Mobility, Risk, and Redistribution in the Welfare State." *Scandinavian Journal of Economics* 97: 527–46. An expanded version of this paper, titled "Factor Mobility, Risk, Inequality, and Redistribution," is to appear in David Pines, Efraim Sadka, and Itzhak Zilcha, eds., *Topics in Public Economics*. Cambridge: Cambridge University Press.

Floor Discussion of "Fiscal Federalism and Decentralization: A Review of Some Efficiency and Macroeconomic Aspects," by Vito Tanzi

Have there been any instances, asked a participant from Chile, in which decentralization has improved efficiency? As the participant saw it, the main disadvantages of decentralization are practical and administrative—local governments generally lack sufficient capacity and resources to assume formerly centralized duties and powers. But if regions and communities prove that they are able to perform these functions and so are granted the power to tax and spend, does decentralization then improve efficiency? Chile, for example, has implemented demand-side subsidies—distributing vouchers for education, housing, health, and so on—and they are working quite well.

Others might have better answers than he, responded Charles McLure (discussant), but South Africa's interim constitution has a nominal provision—how well it is working, he did not know—to return all services formerly provided by the four provincial administrative units to the central government and to devolve the services back to the provinces once they have demonstrated their ability to handle finances, spending, and so on. Clearly, though, it was going to be difficult for the central government to say that it was returning powers to provinces A and B but not to provinces C and D. But, McLure added, in a sense that was the process involved in becoming a state in the United States until 1912 and then later when Hawaii and Alaska joined. So there is a precedent. Vito Tanzi offered a different example. Denmark, he said, allows "free" municipalities. These municipalities volunteer to perform a certain experiment in self-governance, the national government allows the experiment, and the results are then publicized.

On the other hand, observed Wilfried Thalwitz (chair), a number of observers feel that some U.S. states are incapable of handling the block grants being proposed by Congress. Efficiency counts, according to this view, and if the state is not efficient enough and local agencies are not capable of handling block grants, such grants should not be distributed to them.

This session was chaired by Wilfried Thalwitz, vice president, Europe and Central Asia Regional Office, at the World Bank.

Annual World Bank Conference on Development Economics 1995

In connection with distributional issues, Gustav Ranis (discussant from another session) noted that Tanzi claimed to be even-handed but that he seems to support central authority in most instances. Although Ranis agreed that there is a need for the central government to ensure distributional equity, two aspects of the distribution issue were not discussed. First, it is not just a matter of how efficiently hospitals are run but of how much is invested in hospitals relative to preventive care. Ranis's research suggests that such decisions are made very differently depending on who controls the resources. Second, while corruption may be more common at the local level, there is also a transparency effect that does not exist at the central level. In Ranis's experience corruption that is hidden from view at the central level runs deeper than local corruption, even though it may not happen as frequently.

Tanzi responded that International Monetary Fund (IMF) staff were aware of a potential bias favoring centralized power. It arises, he said, because the IMF deals mainly with central governments and is concerned about potential destabilizations. But whether there are limits on local corruption, he thought, depends on the country. In many countries there is little corruption at the national level, and corruption is much more pervasive locally. Remember, he said, corruption can mean more than just appropriating money. It can manifest itself in zoning laws or political favoritism. Decentralization has the potential to increase the amount of regulation in an economy, by adding local regulations to those of the central government. And to the extent that regulation is associated with corruption, it might increase the opportunities for corruption.

A participant from the World Bank's Southern Africa Department said that one important debate in his region was whether the central government should inherit the debts from local borrowing. Making all borrowing a function of the center does not seem to be a valid approach because it leads to directed credit systems that are inefficient and prone to political manipulation. Also, central bodies that are backed by the government are more likely to be bailed out—or at least as likely as local or subnational governments to be bailed out. When you have these microeconomic problems in the financial market or in ownership structure, you must be extremely careful in saying that centralization is not the answer. The participant then asked the panelists whether macroeconomic instability was likely to be a greater problem in centralized or decentralized systems.

David Wildasin (discussant) said that he was not sure how to answer that question specifically, but that the problem of finding ways to constrain borrowing was not limited to lower-level governments. To the contrary, it often arises for central governments. For example, the issue of central bank independence is related to the issue of hard budget constraints for central governments. Central governments sometimes get themselves into borrowing or structural deficit problems and rely on inflationary finance as a way out of their problems.

Conflicts and Dilemmas of Decentralization

Rudolf Hommes

The paradox of decentralization is that it demands more central government and more sophisticated political skills at the national level to guide the process, at the same time that it requires breaking the habit of dependence on the center. This article describes the recent trend toward decentralization in Latin America—with an emphasis on Colombia—from a political, sociological, and participatory perspective. In Latin America decentralization represents a departure from more than four hundred years of centralism, a momentous institutional change that has the potential to bring about a social revolution and create a more dynamic and self-reliant society. In Colombia decentralization emerged gradually, as the national hierarchical structure of political parties began to break down, their influence eroded by the forces of regionalism and clientelism. From these examples the article assesses the regional experience and pitfalls—from patronage and the power of political elites and unelected elites—and explores constitutional issues, providing a practical counterpoint to more analytically oriented studies of decentralization.

Political decentralization has been the norm in industrial democracies for decades. Now, increasingly, Eastern European countries and developing countries are following this lead and decentralizing their public sectors. As recently observed, "the twentieth century is ending, as it began, with great aspirations for extending the benefits of democratic self-government to ever larger numbers of men and women" (Putnam, Leonardi, and Nanetti 1993, p. 181).

Sixty-three of the seventy-five transition and developing economies with populations of more than 5 million people have transferred or are in the process of transferring political power to local governments (Dillinger 1994). In Latin America—for the second time in history—most countries are trading centralism for new, decentralized institutions, transferring resources and responsibilities to lower levels of government. Although this transfer has been motivated by the desire of regional elites

Rudolf Hommes is president of the University of the Andes. The author is grateful to Armando Montenegro and Luis Alvaro Sanchez for useful comments on this article.

Annual World Bank Conference on Development Economics 1995
©1996 The International Bank for Reconstruction and Development / THE WORLD BANK

and political barons to increase their share of power, the process has had a great degree of popular support and is contributing to political and social change throughout the region.

Decentralization can be achieved in a number of ways. Fiscal and political federalism is probably the most common form, but the new wave of decentralization has adopted other strategies as well. In many countries decentralization is achieved through the transfer of power to local units (deconcentration), coupled with revenue sharing or other forms of transfers from the center to regional and local governments. Other countries achieve decentralization by transferring power to subnational political institutions above the local level (devolution), or to decentralized entities (delegation). In countries where privatization programs have been implemented, decentralization has transferred power and responsibilities to the private sector.[1]

Regardless of its form, decentralization provides an opportunity for change that also presents many political and technical risks. This article reviews these risks from the policymakers' point of view, mostly in a Latin American context.

A Process of Political Change

The trend toward decentralized government in Latin America may truly develop into what political scientists call a social revolution. Although in many cases the move originated as a grab for power by local political elites, it also evolved from grassroots dissatisfaction. The move from a highly centralized government is intended to improve government services in order to solve what North (1990) calls a gridlock crisis in the provision of basic social services and to increase community participation in the decisionmaking process.

The Political and Institutional Setting

Latin America's move toward decentralization constitutes a radical break with the past. Although during the nineteenth century many countries in the region adopted constitutions that are formally similar to the U.S. Constitution and some of the largest countries have maintained federal political organizations, most countries embraced authoritarianism during the late nineteenth and early twentieth centuries and reverted to forms of centralism whose origins can be traced to the sixteenth-century Castilian model (Veliz 1980).

This tradition of centralized power and bureaucracy determined the institutional evolution of Latin America and may be responsible for the wide gap in development between North and South America. In contrast with North America, the legal institutions that evolved in most of South America fostered monopolies and high, inefficient rates of taxation, while discouraging trade and commerce. Likewise, the social institutions that prevailed under this model encouraged individuals to pursue careers in government, the church, or the army, and to forgo other, potentially more productive activities beyond the reach of the state (North

1981, 1990). The centralist model also inhibited the development of community-based civic institutions because it created communities that were dependent on the central government and its institutions, both formal (bureaucracy) and informal (patronage).

The new process of decentralization in Latin America may appear as a "reluctant and disorderly series of concessions by central governments attempting to maintain political stability" (Dillinger 1994, p. 9)—in other words, a neo-Sicilian ruse to change some things in order to keep most other things the same. But this view is wrong. The steps that have been taken represent fundamental changes in society. They are also opening new, potentially rewarding avenues for trial and error and thus increasing the possibilities of technical and institutional progress. Additionally, it must be understood that the changes have been brewing for some time even if they appear to be an abrupt break with the past.

The centralized governments of the past failed to effectively deliver services to the communities. Moreover, they inhibited the type of experimentation in local government that makes societies more likely to solve problems over time.[2] Although belatedly, Latin American institutions have begun to change. In Colombia, for example, decentralization began during the 1980s, when Congress forced the central government to share with local jurisdictions a share of the revenues of the newly created value-added tax. In addition, municipalities were permitted to increase local taxes. This increased their capacity to respond to local needs and shifted political power and activity from the capital to the provinces, gradually at first, and more rapidly when the system was consolidated.

In hindsight, these changes seem so natural that it is surprising they did not take place earlier, especially given the tremendous failure of the preceding institutions to deliver social services and to motivate societal change. The explanation for the delayed reaction can be found in the political organization that prevailed during earlier periods.

Centralism and Political Parties

Centralism is more compatible with strong, well-organized political parties that are organized hierarchically and have national coverage (Galeotti 1993). Centralism functions even better where political systems are characterized by one-party rule—the Mexican model—or where the leading parties have formed a government coalition that resembles one party. This was the case in Colombia during 1956–74. Centralism persisted until 1986, when an alternative paradigm of government and opposition parties was formally adopted. In Peru and the Southern Cone countries (Argentina, Chile, Uruguay) military governments effectively constituted one-party rule; in Venezuela the two leading political parties were well-organized hierarchical organizations whose coverage spanned the entire country.

Under these systems the relationship between the authorities and their constituencies was conducted through the government or the party, both hierarchical organizations. Information flowed into the bureaucracies, and favors and services flowed out of them. In terms of gathering information and delivering patronage through the hierarchy, the centralized system was efficient. But information and services rarely reached the lower levels of the population. Moreover, the centralized system began to break down when politicians began acting as independent brokers of information, patronage, and services between the voters and the government. This also broke down the hierarchy and discipline of the parties.

With the region's recent move toward pluralism and political modernization, multiparty political systems are replacing the old one-party rule. In countries that were organized around two-party systems, the parties have lost the hierarchical discipline that they had in the past and are no longer capable of delivering a unified representation in Congress. Nor are they capable of rendering services to the electorate without the brokerage of local political barons.

As party organization weakened, the government no longer depended on the political system to gather and transmit information. Additionally, the government bureaucracy, although formally centralized, was no longer truly hierarchical. Political appointees at all levels—but particularly at the middle and lower levels—developed allegiances to regional or local politicians, who may or may not have shared the government's agenda. This disrupted the flow of information, which no longer moved symmetrically through the government and party bureaucracies but could be diverted to regional or local politicians who could keep it for themselves or alter it for their own purposes. A similar development occurred with the flow of services and favors, as local politicians began acting as intermediaries and demanding a share of the spoils for their political or even personal benefit.

This evolution, which can be observed in Colombia, Mexico, Venezuela, and other countries in Latin America, gave way to an organization of parties and governments more akin to a feudal system. The independence of the central government in allocating the resources it raised through a centralized tax system was greatly diminished, while local politicians played an increasingly larger role in influencing the distribution of government services and bureaucratic positions.

Despite their gains, however, local bosses still depended on the state for resources, and their influence had to be exercised through complex negotiations involving political commitments and pledges of congressional support for government programs. Their next move, therefore, was to secure a greater degree of financial independence. This was achieved by promoting legislation and constitutional amendments that increased the share of central government funds earmarked to regional and local governments for general investment. In Colombia the political bosses pushed to increase the resources earmarked to local and regional governments but never for the popular election of regional and local authorities. Nor did local barons encourage a clear transfer of responsibilities from the center to lower levels of government. Rather, those initiatives were advanced by progressive members of the executive and national party leadership.

Some of the progressives' reforms have not been in the best interest of the local political barons. The popular election of mayors and regional governors, for example, has undermined the influence of party congressional bosses. The public has demonstrated considerable independence through such elections, electing several civic and independent candidates not linked to the party machinery or to the local barons. In many cases these newly elected officials have set agendas with priorities that are truly regional.

In other cases the experience has not been positive, because the political bosses have taken over local governments or guerrillas have infiltrated them. Still, the overall balance is favorable from a political point of view, because the level and quality of community participation has increased, and from an economic point of view, because allocative efficiency has improved significantly and the provision of basic services is more efficient.

Other countries in Latin America have followed a similar path along the road toward decentralization. Most have earmarked central government funds to lower levels of government. Not all countries, however, have succeeded in transferring new functions to these levels. In other cases the responsibilities are shared by various levels of government, and there are no incentives for the lower levels to take on new spending responsibilities. A sort of crowding-out effect takes place when the higher levels of government compete with the lower levels in the provision of services.

Public Attitudes toward Decentralization

Decentralization is associated with the greater participation of local citizens in government decisionmaking. Communities perceive that they are obtaining a larger share of public resources, and decentralization is regarded as an entitlement in local and regional public opinion. For these reasons the recent reforms seem irreversible as long as the more participatory forms of government prevail. In the absence of an authoritarian backlash, it is difficult to imagine that presidents or congresses would attempt to promote a legal or formal return to more centralized forms of government. The public does not favor centralization because it has traditionally failed to deliver and because the public attaches value to the election of local and regional officials, to the possibility of public oversight of local authorities, and to the proximity of the decisionmaking process.[3] In short, the public supports decentralization.

Institutional Conflicts

Despite the progress achieved, decentralization efforts are far from consolidated. Financial, organizational, administrative, and political obstacles impede the process. Another set of problems relates to the inertia of traditional institutions. It has already been noted that centralism in Latin America dates back several centuries. Clearly, the institutions created by this tradition will not disappear overnight. Conflict also arises from the structure of the central government and from differences in outlook between a government cast in the centralist mold, emphasizing rules and authority, and local administrations, which tend to be more interested in problem solving and display a good measure of brinkmanship.

Cultural Obstacles

North (1990, p. 140) states that when "there is radical change in the formal rules that makes them inconsistent with the existing informal constraints, there is an unresolved tension between them that will lead to long-run political instability." Accordingly, perhaps the greatest obstacle to efficient decentralization is the cultural conservatism of local communities and the tradition within central government of monopolizing resources and initiatives. Communities are accustomed to obtaining services and favors from their central government, and local administrators have long depended on the center for resources, initiatives, and ideas. For their part, national-level politicians traditionally have stunted the civic development of the communities by imposing informal but hierarchical structures such as those derived from political patronage.

Of particular importance is the existence at the local level of a civic cultural tradition. Informal civic institutions—such as solidarity, cooperation, trust of fellow citizens, respect for the government, and engagement in public issues—favor good local government. In Italy, for example, the southern communities were traditionally organized under a centralist organization that viewed the bonds in society as vertical and hierarchical. By contrast, in the northern towns, which were more self-reliant, social bonds were horizontal and based on cooperation and self-government (Putnam, Leonardi, and Nanetti 1993).

Italy also demonstrates that history matters. There is a correlation between the civic engagement and community orientation of a town and its historical origins as part of an independent political organization (the north) or of a vertically oriented hierarchical state (the south). In the north communities are moved by social issues, and citizen participation in government or community affairs is highly valued. Public life in the southern towns, by contrast, is organized "hierarchically rather than horizontally. The very concept of citizen here is stunted. . . . Public affairs is the business of . . . the bosses, the politicians, but not me" (Putnam, Leonardi, and Nanetti 1993, p. 115). Towns that display the civic values associated with cooperation and engagement are also more economically advanced. The newly decentralized local governments in developing countries will likely experience the same fate as the Italian towns.

This is particularly important in Latin America, where the tradition has been one of dependency on the hierarchical state and of political patronage. But the situation is not hopeless: there are opposing traditions in Latin America that have coexisted with the centralist tradition. For example, in countries such as Colombia, divided by mountains and bad roads, the center never could have imposed its authority if the local elites had not collaborated, starting about 1903, after nearly a century of civil wars. During the nineteenth century the regional leaders were not integrated with the national political system and ran a de facto decentralized system of government. This regional power was formally recognized in 1861, when a federalist system was adopted. Although the system was abolished in 1886, the local and regional oligarchies had already consolidated as independent political forces and were able to set their own agenda for modernization: expansion of the educational system and opening of new means of communication (Melo 1992). The return to centralism was built on the shoulders of these regional groups, which acted as intermediaries between the center and the communities. This brand of centralism quickly degenerated into clientelism, but the tradition of independent civil action is still present.

The ultimate success of the decentralization reforms will probably require that formal and informal civic institutions be strengthened alongside the newly developed local government entities. This has been stressed by development specialists, particularly in the context of promoting more active local participation to increase the accountability of decentralized government systems (Winkler 1994). These tasks of promoting citizen participation and fostering civic community values normally fall to central governments. But communities are demonstrating an ability to develop local capacity autonomously. When this occurs, any central government intervention is likely to stunt home-grown capacity. Therefore government involvement must be carefully fine-tuned.

Constitutional and Bureaucratic Constraints

A pervasive problem in the decentralization process is the overlap of responsibilities among different levels of government stemming from constitutions, laws, or the structure of government bureaucracy. The overlap of functions and the lack of clarity in intergovernmental transfers create conflict between the different authorities that may discredit the system. Such overlap can also impede the delivery of social services because each level expects the others to perform. In Venezuela, for example, the decentralization of shared responsibilities has been held up by inadequate incentives, uncertainty, and national politics. Although block grants to the states have increased, the states have no incentives to take on new spending responsibilities (Winkler 1994).

In Colombia the Constitution establishes that a portion of the central government's current revenues are to be earmarked to the departments and that the departments have to share a portion of these resources with the municipalities. The law controls the use of funds by assigning fixed percentages to different functions. Some critics argue that this system's controls are excessive because they may hinder decentralization. The rigid controls may, however, prevent the misuse of funds and inhibit wasteful initiatives by inexperienced or corrupt local officials.

Even when a decentralized system is adopted, the rules and constraints imposed by the constitution, the law, or the central bureaucracy may preserve a bias that favors the preexisting tradition of centralism. In such cases programs and priorities are determined by the center, and local governments are simply expected to carry them out (Ahmad and others 1995). Although this outcome is undesirable, it is equally undesirable for local administrations to take revenues from the center and use them, for example, to increase the bureaucracy or to fund programs that have a lower priority than the provision of basic education and health services.

One way to address the problem is to earmark funds directly for community-based institutions such as parent-supervised schools or community health boards, so that local politicians are not tempted to divert the funds to other uses and so that community civic organizations are strengthened. This approach, however, runs the risk of "re-centralization through decentralization" (Campbell, Paterson, and Brakarz 1991, p. 13), whereby community organizations bypass the local government and become dependent on the central government or the ruling party, in the same way that local elites became dependent and clientelist during the centralist era. Perhaps the root of the problem is that the local governments do not have an independent source of revenue. Therefore, during the transition stage it seems necessary to subordinate local governments to conditions set by the central government until they develop their own tax base and establish control mechanisms that prevent the diversion of funds to political or frivolous endeavors.

Local Government Autonomy

In order to achieve efficient decisionmaking in a decentralized system and effective political interactions between the government and its constituencies, local government units must have a high degree of autonomy in relation to the central government (Rueschemeyer and Evans 1985). At the same time, local governments should be protected from capture by special interest groups, by the political bosses of the old order, or by any other force that is "bent on capturing the state apparatus for [its] own purposes. The state then is in danger of dissipating its own special contribution, which lies in its ability to operate on the basis of a more general and inclusive vision than is feasible for private actors embedded in the market. If decentralization destroys the ability of the state to act coherently . . . then the unique character of its contribution is lost" (Rueschemeyer and Evans 1985, p. 56).

In societies with a long history of political patronage, where guerrillas are active in several regions and where economic interests have a tradition of interfering with government, the central government may already be partly captured by such forces. But there is a great risk that decentralization will exacerbate the problem. Local governments may be more susceptible to capture by divergent forces unless there is also a strong and cohesive civic society that provides political support and a dependable national government that protects opposing economic interests.

These conditions do not exist in many developing countries. Thus countries must develop strong bureaucratic institutions at all levels of government to foster discipline, cooperation, and relative autonomy among civil servants (Rueschemeyer and Evans 1985). Strong institutions can also be a shield against outside influence—unless managers at the local level become vulnerable to external pressure through their association with local elites or guerrillas.

This is a particularly delicate problem in Colombia because of the presence of local guerrilla and mafia groups. Both organizations have attempted to take over local governments by controlling elected officials or in some cases by threatening and even murdering them when they do not cooperate. When this occurs, the central government must provide police protection for the local administrators if decentralization is to succeed. Otherwise, the local government will be captured by these forces, which will use it for their own purposes. If the central government is militarily weak, the risk of capture is very large. Similarly, decentralization is bound to fail or even backfire in regions that are dominated by criminal or subversive factions.

Political Challenges and Credibility

The weakness of the central state, the newness of decentralization, and the cultural attachment to the formal and informal institutions of centralism may conspire to create a political and social environment in which decentralized institutions are discredited. Decentralization can also be hindered by inexperienced local administrations, disaffected congressional or political bosses, inadequate civic organizations, and an unresponsive populace.

On the other hand, minority parties, special interest groups, independent civic movements, and emerging factions of the traditional parties see decentralized government as an opportunity to establish their credibility as an electoral alternative. These alternative groups are a source of tension among different levels of government and between local authorities and political parties (and with the mafia and the guerrillas, where they play a political role).

Colombia's experience shows clearly that in some regions decentralization has reduced the influence of the political bosses and guerrilla groups that act as patronage institutions. Where they have been unable to capture the local governments, politicians and guerrillas have been active in discrediting the decentralized authorities by drawing attention to their mistakes or corruption, which helps foster more effective institutions, or by blocking the actions of successful administrations, which hinders progress. The mafia is also active in several communities; its opposition can be violent, although this is usually avoided because it achieves its goals through corrupt local officials. Such activity would not be any less common if the government organization were centralized.

Guerrilla opposition to successful local administrations often has been violent. Several mayors have been kidnapped or killed because they were performing adequately or above the norm. When mayors perform poorly or are corrupt, the guerrillas attempt to gain credibility by forcing them to comply with written performance agreements or by running them out of town. Murder is thus reserved for the effective leaders, indicating that the guerrillas are trying to weaken or discredit the newly decentralized institutions in order to preserve their hegemony and patronage or to take over local administrations. The political bosses, although using less extreme procedures, have the same objectives.

New political movements have more socially beneficial objectives. For example, to demonstrate that they can run municipalities better than the traditional elites, a former guerrilla group, M19, has restructured itself as a coalition of minority parties of the middle to far left, and several newcomers have won local elections. Such efforts at decentralization have yielded some important successes. The behavior of decentralization's political rivals indicates, in fact, that it is a credible model, since their efforts are directed toward eroding this credibility. These efforts have been successfully opposed by those who have strengthened local governments, established opportunities for minority representation, and benefited themselves by becoming politically viable.

The Sequence of Reforms

In some countries, including Colombia, the move toward decentralization was initially sponsored by regional powers who sought greater control over government resources. Regional Colombian politicians began pushing for the creation of revenue-sharing mechanisms without the transfer of new responsibilities to local administrations. Progressives at the national levels used the momentum of these early reforms to enact legislation providing for the local election of governors and mayors, thus transferring political power to the communities. Some of the newly elected officials challenged the old bosses and gained greater control of resources for their communities. After this occurred, Congress passed legislation assigning additional functions to local governments to match their additional resources. Such an evolution raises questions about proper sequencing in the process of decentralization.

Prudence and conventional wisdom dictate that, in order to prevent negative macroeconomic linkages and because "finance should follow function" (Dillinger 1994, p. 26), reforms should begin by assigning responsibilities to lower-level governments. Resources to fulfill these responsibilities should follow—almost simultaneously—through revenue sharing and increased opportunities for local taxation. Finally, measures to strengthen capacity and enhance efficiency, accountability, and control should be implemented (Campbell, Paterson, and Brakarz 1991). Does this mean that Colombia put the cart before the horse? Probably. But it may not have been feasible to do otherwise with the old political bosses. From a purely political perspective, then, it is possible that Colombia's sequence of policies was correct. This path achieved change without having to face the strong opposition of traditional political forces. It may have been risky, but it was probably the only peaceful way to achieve such change.

Resources and Responsibilities

There are different approaches to defining the distinctive roles and functions of the various levels of government. These range from the notion that it does not matter whether power is decentralized to the more practical idea that functions should be assigned to higher levels of government only when the lower levels cannot perform them better (Campbell 1994).

Roles of the Different Levels of Government

One useful way of allocating government responsibilities can be derived from the classic formulation of public economics, which assigns to the central government the functions of macroeconomic management and income redistribution and foresees a role for local governments only in the context of resource allocation (Musgrave and Musgrave 1984). According to this view, "discrete public services should be assigned to the level of government whose boundaries incorporate the affected beneficiaries. That level of government should be assigned a corresponding pricing instrument ... with which to ascertain demand" (Dillinger 1994, p. 13).

In practice, local governments are assigned two types of functions: those that involve strictly local activities (trash collection, road maintenance, drinking water distribution, and so on) and those that cross jurisdictional boundaries and for which there is central or state government interest (Peterson 1994). In addition, a number of functions that would be more effectively performed by the central government—such as poverty reduction or other income distribution programs—are often assigned to local governments. In other instances poorly defined functions overlap the various levels of government, causing gaps and duplication in service provisions. In these cases decentralization requires a strong central administration that can clearly assign responsibilities, assist weak subnational entities, and ensure compliance with central government objectives such as poverty reduction, income distribution, and environmental protection (Campbell, Paterson, and Brakarz 1991). The central government should set the stage for the activities of the decentralized, lower levels of government and should be responsible for coordination when there are conflicts and overlapping functions.

There are, however, risks attached to the pattern of intervention of the central administration. These risks can be typified by three extreme forms of government organization:

- An overcontrolled local sector that is merely an administrative arm of the central administration.
- An undercontrolled local sector that is autonomous and may choose the functions that it will perform according to its assessment of local needs and demand.
- A perversely regulated local sector in which the central government acts in ways that crowd out the local government, whether permanently or occasionally.

The first pattern tends to replicate the problems of a centralized bureaucratic administration, compounded by a lack of information and an inability to exercise effective control. This form offers few opportunities for local participation and lacks the variety that makes decentralized governments attractive as adaptive systems, politically amenable to community participation and decisionmaking. The second and third patterns make it difficult for the public to hold any level of government accountable for any specific function, fostering a situation of impunity in which central and local administrators can be negligent and get away with it (Dillinger 1994).

Agency Problems

Agency problems derive from the nature of central administration responsibility. The center can delegate, deconcentrate, or devolve functions and power, but it cannot shake the ultimate responsibility for the quality of basic services like education, health, and crime prevention. A central government cannot watch impassively when local governments fail to provide these basic services because the long-run costs of these failures will be enormous. In a sense, the national government is the government of last resort.

Central revenue-sharing programs can be used to illustrate these problems. Such programs are often designed to finance local investment or spending that was previously undertaken directly by the center, often for education, health, or the maintenance of local roads. The shared revenues are distributed according to a fixed formula, and their level can be forecast by the recipients and their creditors. Compared with mechanisms that are based on more complete contracts, these formulas are weak. They do not contain incentives to provide services efficiently or to increase coverage of these services. To correct this deficiency, the revenue-sharing formulas must be accompanied by mandated levels of spending and coverage targets. But even when these complements are provided, compliance is uncertain and monitoring is costly.

This situation can easily lead to moral hazard behavior among local administrators, with hidden information and covert actions. For example, if a local administration decides to hire personnel based on patronage rather than performance criteria, the agent (the local administrator) is maximizing his or her own political benefits to the detriment of the next generation. The agent does not bear the full consequences of the action and, because of hidden information, does not bear the risk of immediate detection. Such behavior is facilitated by the mobility of the population, so that when the next set of national civil service exams takes place, the subjects of the exam will reflect the group production of several jurisdictions, making it more difficult to assign responsibility to an individual administrator. This problem is compounded if there are no regular, standardized exams. National exams do not even exist in many countries, leaving the field wide open for opportunistic behavior by local administrators.

A similar problem arises when shared revenues that are earmarked for health or education, for example, are pledged to a bank for credit that is instead spent on a different activity carrying larger political benefits for the incumbent—such as temporary employment for potential voters. The central government cannot immediately detect whether this pledge will affect the spending capacity of the local government in education and health and cannot legally prevent it unless there are legal or constitutional authorizations to that effect. This type of problem is not, however, the exclusive province of decentralized systems. The same problem can arise when an appointed official in a centralized system follows his or her own political agenda using government money. Such activity entails even greater costs and risks because local voters would not have the incentive to replace the official since they cannot choose a successor, increasing the costs of detection to the central government.

These problems are minimized when functions are well defined for all levels of government, either through legal or constitutional provisions or through contracts between different levels of government. Still, because contracts and legislation cannot foresee all possible outcomes, the central government must use performance measures (such as national exams) and provide an adequate set of incentives to induce the desired behavior and to extract information about performance and about local capacity to deliver delegated and devolved services (Cremer, Estache, and Seabright 1994).

To achieve this, the government must build a network cenetered on effective local participation, relying on the community as a source of information and as a mechanism of control. In a decentralized system the public should hold local governments accountable for the provision of services financed by the central government. Accountability requires systematic disclosure of government activities and an institutional setting that facilitates community involvement and control. It also requires that the central government create citizen supervisory boards or lay the legal foundation for community entities that are involved in decisionmaking, such as school supervisory boards. Citizens belonging to these entities must receive proper training and support in financial management and administration. The government must provide them with timely information about the resources being disbursed, quality standards, and coverage targets. The best way to induce community participation is to demand that programs financed with government grants be cofinanced with local tax revenues. By linking performance and taxation, this creates a strong incentive for community involvement (Winkler 1994).

A complementary solution would be to pass laws imposing a strict code of behavior and rigid due process on local administrators, making them personally responsible—and legally liable—when they fail to perform in the best interests of the community. In this sense public administrators would hold the trust of the community with a mandate to pursue its welfare, much as the head of a family would zealously pursue the well-being of his or her dependents.

Such laws can act as a powerful deterrent to corruption and political clientelism if civic institutions are in place to initiate court actions against local officials, when required. Alternatively, a superintendency of local administrators could be made responsible for initiating the same actions.[4] If these types of mechanisms were to succeed, a code of behavior could ensue that would contribute to what Rueschemeyer and Evans (1985, p. 56) call an "esprit de corps," giving local officials a well-defined and shared sense of purpose and identity with the larger objectives of the community.

Political Dilemmas

Decentralization entails loss of power by the central government, by political parties, and by local political bosses. These three groups constituted the governance capacity under centralized systems. Through a complex network of favors and patronage, the center maintained the loyalty of the local elites while exercising both formal and informal authority in the regions.

Governance and Power

Decentralization breaks some of the links on which centralized governance was based: resources flow to the regions and municipalities automatically, through constitutionally and legally mandated channels; the allocation of resources is increasingly a local responsibility, with a considerable degree of independence from the central government; and the authority of local elites can be effectively challenged by civic or dissident groups, who through elections can gain access to resources that are in turn a source of power in the community.

Under decentralization the center no longer has any means of manipulating local authorities when it seeks cooperation for problems of governance. For all practical purposes, once the revenue-sharing mechanisms are defined and the communities are able to raise taxes, local authorities do not have to fully cooperate with the center in a voluntary manner.

This potential loss of control poses a dilemma for central administrators. If they promote the efficient institutions that are required to effectively develop a decentralized system, the center will be loosing its traditional grip on local governments. But if they try to maintain this grip, they will probably engage in the type of government interference that creates perverse incentives at the local level and blurs the accountability of both levels of government. This is already happening in many countries—the central government has been luring mayors by supplying ad hoc grants and maintaining a soft budget restriction for regional spending. Such an approach may turn local authorities into lobbyists for the region, impeding the entire process of decentralization, with negative fiscal consequences.

Local Elites

The traditional local elites may not be strangers to the process of decentralization just described. Although they may have originally supported decentralization, challenges by competing groups at the local level may be changing their predisposition to adapt to the changes. This trend, representing a clash between the previous informal institutions and the new formal institutions, creates conflicts and slows the process of decentralization.

Fiscal Dilemmas

As decentralization spreads, subnational governments in Latin America are acquiring a larger share of public sector revenues and expenditures. In Colombia, for example, the central government must share more than 40 percent of its current revenues with lower levels of government. Local governments now account for 28.5 percent of total public spending in Latin American and the Caribbean (Winkler 1994).

Macroeconomic Control and Local Autonomy

The fiscal behavior of lower levels of government therefore has a significant macroeconomic impact on aggregate fiscal accounts. During the transition from centralized to decentralized government in Latin America, this impact has been largely negative.

Decentralization measures in a broad spectrum of countries have had adverse impacts on macroeconomic stability, at least in the short run. At the same time central governments are often uncertain how far to extend local autonomy (Campbell, Paterson, and Brakarz 1991). The problem does not lie so much with decentralization as with the absence of budget institutions for and effective controls on local government spending and debt, and with the source of the funds that are financing the process.

When state and local budget institutions and controls are weak, the autonomous spending and indebtedness of lower levels of government may contribute to greater deficit spending. This problem is now being analyzed in the literature outside the context of decentralization, under the premise that institutions have a bearing on fiscal results. There is evidence to support the view that budgetary procedures favoring a strong finance minister and giving more power to the executive improve fiscal discipline (Von Hagen 1992).

In the context of decentralization "balanced-budget restrictions are significantly associated with larger surpluses (smaller deficits)" in state fiscal accounts in the United States (Eichengreen 1992, p. 31). In addition, Poterba (1994) has observed that rules and political factors, such as the control of one party over the state legislature, help explain differences in fiscal performance among different states.

It is unlikely that strong budget institutions will develop during the early stages of the transition to decentralized forms of government. The absence of institutions may create a lack of fiscal discipline at the lower levels of government that increases macroeconomic instability by generating large deficits in the aggregate public sector budget. This is an undesirable but not improbable result of decentralization that must be corrected when it occurs.[5] In these cases it may be appropriate to subordinate local autonomy to centrally determined budgetary controls until the local governments develop institutions and rules that foster fiscal discipline. In Brazil, for example, decentralization—and the accompanying need for sound macroeconomic management—has increased the importance of fiscal policy coordination between the national capital and the state capitals. But the intergovernmental institutions and mechanisms to guide the coordination of such policies have yet to be developed (Bomfim and Shah 1994).

Of paramount importance are rules that limit the indebtedness of all levels of government, and in this case the lower levels. When borrowing by the subnational governments within a monetary union creates negative externalities, it must be restrained (Eichengreen 1992). In Latin America, until conclusive evidence proves otherwise, local governments' access to credit should be limited so that they do not have free rein to create budget deficits and finance them through debt, much less to obtain foreign credit without the authorization of the central government (Wiesner and Murphy 1994).

Central or Local Taxation

The other issue connected with the impact of decentralization on fiscal results is the local government's source of funds. Decentralization should include an increased local tax effort to raise resources for the provision of services. This local tax effort provides the price discipline that is required to efficiently produce and deliver local services and allows consumers to express their preferences. When local governments have relative budget autonomy but do not have to raise taxes to support their spending, they tend to overspend. Furthermore, the political system may induce greater fiscal irresponsibility. This has been the case with the U.S. Aid to Families with Dependent Children and food stamp programs, which are partly financed by the federal government. It was also the experience of the U.S. disability pension program until it was reformed to check the excessive generosity of local governments. In other countries, such as Italy, regional differences in the granting of disability pensions by local governments have little to do with demographics and a lot to do with political patronage at the local level (Perotti 1994). These examples suggest that when funds are centrally raised and spending is decentralized, spending is higher. In addition, centralized taxes and decentralized spending are likely to become permanent because of voter preferences. This preference may be caused in part by democratic institutions—because voters prefer centralized taxes when there is capital mobility—and in part by patronage and corruption.[6]

Financing decentralization through local taxation is an effective check against the Leviathan tendency of government to increase its size and its tax resources monotonically. Cross-country evidence indicates that the simultaneous decentralization of the national government's taxing and spending powers exerts a negative influence on the overall size of the public sector. Thus revenue-sharing and taxing decisions should be made at the center in order to eliminate the negative influence of decentralization of the spending power (Ehdaie 1994).

Despite these clear conclusions, "there has been much less action to grant new revenue-raising authority to local governments than there has been to increase centrally financed resource transfers" (Campbell, Paterson, and Brakarz 1991, p. 13). One reason for this neglect, as already discussed, is the desire of regional barons and voters to acquire a share of the central government bounty. Another reason is the existing organization of taxes. In many countries there is some sort of income tax that is monopolized by the central government. In other countries, such as Mexico, modernization of the tax structure has strengthened the centralized income tax, and the value-added tax has replaced an obsolete system of consumption taxes operated by the states. In these cases the lower-level governments must rely on property taxes, a few minor taxes, and their share of central government revenues. Quite often, these governments are not allowed to establish their own income and sales tax, nor can they impose surcharges to be collected with broadly based and more buoyant national taxes.

These restrictions on local taxing capacity create three main problems:

- Vertical imbalances develop as a result of the low capacity for tax mobilization and the higher spending demands induced by decentralization. As an example, municipal taxes in Colombia amounted to 1.1 percent of gross domestic product (GDP) in 1993, while municipal expenses amounted to 6.5 percent of GDP. The gap had to be filled by government transfers and commercial debt.

- Horizontal imbalances develop as a result of the differences in the spatial distribution of wealth and income and of the economies of scale attached to tax collection and administration.
- Local authorities are unable to increase property taxes and business taxes or to enforce the existing tax structures because of powerful property owners and business interests that have the implicit backing of the middle class. In small municipalities this creates additional vertical imbalances because there is a minimum size of government below which it is very difficult to impose new taxes and to collect them from the local elites (Ahmad and others 1995).

Thus, despite the distortions they introduce—and notwithstanding the Leviathan effect—central government transfers or grants to state and local government are required where vertical fiscal imbalances are present. And even if tax bases improve significantly, such transfers are still needed to correct horizontal imbalances. In both cases it is usually recommended that the transfers contain price incentives to induce greater spending and taxation by local governments. When these incentives are not present, conditionality is needed to induce the desired behavior (Winkler 1994).

Revenue Sharing and Fiscal Politics

As discussed earlier, revenue-sharing mechanism are linked to the delegation or devolution of new functions and responsibilities to local governments. If these new responsibilities do not impose additional financial burdens on the local governments, decentralization does not introduce any new or additional fiscal problems to those of the centralized system. The same services will be supplied and financed, but, the hope is, at a higher level of productive and allocative efficiency.

But that is not the whole story. When resources and responsibilities are transferred from one level of government to another, there is also a shift of power—and there is no guarantee that a new political equilibrium will be achieved automatically. These situations lead to political and budgetary gamesmanship and may have a negative bearing on the overall fiscal picture.

This is currently the case in Colombia. Although the different levels of government have been assigned their respective responsibilities and functions, Congress has piggybacked legislation on subsequent laws allowing the central government to spend in the same areas of competence as the lower levels of government. This was done because the central government gives Congress more access to "pork barrel" funds—mostly through negotiations on the national budget—than do the local or state governments. This political infighting has resulted in a doubling of the pressure for spending in each of these areas.

Conclusion

Decentralization is essentially a political problem. In Latin America it represents a clear break with more than four hundred years of centralism. Decentralization is therefore not a trivial development but an institutional change that has the potential to induce a true social revolution along the path to a more dynamic and self-reliant society—a society that promotes progress and technical change and plays down the traditional symbols and sources of power that typified the centralist state.

There are also practical and political arguments in favor of decentralization. By staying closer to the people, a decentralized system may have superior information channels that permit more efficient resource allocation decisions. The proximity to the public also enhances community supervision of local authorities, thereby increasing the probability of good government.

These idealized decentralization scenarios are far removed from the actual situation, which is plagued by problems that present research challenges for the social scientist interested in political economy and add to the complexity of the policymaker's task. One of these problems is the influence of tradition on the performance of the newly decentralized institutions. These institutions perform better in communities that have a tradition of self-government and civic involvement and worse in communities that have a tradition of dependency on a central administration. Since most Latin American countries and many postcolonial developing countries share a tradition of centralism, decentralization in these countries has a cultural barrier to overcome. In addition, political problems present obstacles to decentralization: the natural tendency of politicians to overspend, which is exacerbated by decentralization or by the encroachment of patronage; the conflict between the new, formal institutions and the informal political structure of congressional or regional electoral barons; and the desire of the central government to dominate local jurisdictions. Despite these problems there is evidence that local communities are capable of organizing institutions that foster good government under decentralized conditions and, more important, evidence that in many instances local constituencies have been able to wrest power from regional elites and political barons.

Two elements appear to be essential to successful decentralization. One is the capacity of local governments to raise their own revenues. The other is the ability of national governments to direct reforms and to behave in a way that does not impede decentralization, lead to recentralization, or perpetuate the clientelist organization of the state. Central governments must learn when to impinge on local autonomy for the sake of stability and when to refrain from intervention to avoid inhibiting good government at the local level.

The paradox of decentralization is that it demands more central government and more sophisticated political skills at the national level. This problem is more political than economic. If decentralization is to develop as an institutional change that enhances the economic and social progress of the countries that are experimenting with it, central governments must be able—and willing—to steer the institutional change in the direction of a more democratic and efficient society. Because this is a new function for most national governments, they are at the beginning of a long learning curve.

Notes

1. This typology is attributed to Dennis A. Rondinelli by Dillinger (1994, p. 7).

2. North (1990, p. 81) attributes this concept to Hayek. There are many examples of what local governments can do when given the opportunity; experimentation is one of them.

3. Fiszbein and others (1995) report that more than 70 percent of the citizens polled in two communities in Colombia believed that services had improved since the popular election of mayors and expressed a willingness to participate and contribute to local public programs.

4. In Colombia nongovernmental organizations initiate popular or class action processes to defend community rights. Moreover, notaries public are entrusted to record and register all property transactions. This function is regulated by a strict code of ethics that is enforced by a superintendency. The profession has evolved quite well, with high standards of performance and a shared code of behavior that is also enforced through peer pressure.

5. Eichengreen (1992, p. 31) observes that most of the legal budget restrictions that constrain U.S. states, such as balanced-budget requirements and public debt ceilings, originated in the nineteenth century, "when they were adopted in response to debt defaults. . . ."

6. Perotti (1994) and Perotti and Alesina (1994) compare two governments under centralized and decentralized regimes and conclude that there are risk and cost tradeoffs in the decentralization of social spending and taxes. Economies of scale are sacrificed in a decentralized system, but free-rider problems and the economic opportunities for patronage can be diminished. Perotti develops simple models to predict the behavior of voters in a system where expenses are redistributive and taxes may or may not be decentralized. According to these models, decentralization of taxes and spending is more likely to minimize the distortionary effects of redistribution (the Leviathan hypothesis in different clothes), but even so voters in both regions will choose the centralized taxing decision, which is more inefficient. From this it may follow that when the system starts out with centralized taxes, it will stay unchanged because of voter preferences.

References

Ahmad, Etisham, and Charles Vehorn, Giorgio Brosio, and Bernd Spahn. 1995. "Colombia: Reforming Territorial Taxation and Transfers." International Monetary Fund, Fiscal Affairs Department, Washington, D.C.

Alesina, Alberto, and Roberto Perotti. 1994a. "Budget Deficits and Institutions." Harvard University and Columbia University, Department of Economics, Cambridge, Mass., and New York.

———. 1994b. "The Political Economy of Budget Deficits." NBER Working Paper 4637. National Bureau of Economic Research, Cambridge, Mass.

Bomfim, Antulio, and Anwar Shah. 1994. "Macroeconomic Management and the Division of Powers in Brazil: Perspectives for the 1990s." Background paper prepared for *World Development Report 1994: Infrastructure for Development*. World Bank, Washington, D.C.

Campbell, Tim. 1994. "Decentralization and Reform of the State in Latin America and the Caribbean." World Bank, Latin America and the Caribbean Technical Department, Advisory Group, Washington, D.C.

Campbell, Tim, George Paterson, and Jose Brakarz. 1991. "Decentralization to Local Government in Latin America and the Caribbean: National Strategies and Local Response in Planning, Spending, and Management." World Bank, Latin America and the Caribbean Regional Studies Program, Washington, D.C.

Cremer, Jacques, Antonio Estache, and Paul Seabright. 1994. "The Decentralization of Public Services: Lessons from the Theory of the Firm." Policy Research Working Paper 1345, World Bank, Office of the Vice President, Development Economics, Washington, D.C.

Dillinger, William. 1994. "Decentralization and its Implications for Urban Service Delivery." Urban Management Programme Discussion Paper 16. World Bank, Transportation, Water, and Urban Development Department, Urban Development Division, Washington, D.C.

Ehdaie, Jaber. 1994. "Fiscal Decentralization and the Size of Government: An Extension with Evidence from Cross-Country Data." Policy Research Working Paper 1387. World Bank, Policy Research Department, Public Economics Division, Washington, D.C.

Eichengreen, Barry. 1992. *Should the Maastricht Treaty be Saved?* Princeton Studies in International Finance, Department of Economics. Princeton, N.J.: Princeton University Press.

Fiszbein, Ariel, Tim Campbell, Eduardo Wallentin, and Martha Leverde. 1995. "Colombia Local Government Capacity: Beyond Technical Assistance." Latin America and the Caribbean Regional Office, World Bank, Washington, D.C.

Galeotti, Gianluigi. 1993. "Decentralization and Political Rents." In David King, ed., *Local Government Economics in Theory and Practice*. London: Routledge.

Melo, Jorge Orlando. 1992. *Predecir el Pasado: Ensayos de Historia de Colombia*. Colección de Historia No. 4. Bogota: Fundación Lola y Simon Guberek.

Musgrave, Richard A., and Peggy B. Musgrave. 1984. *Public Finance in Theory and Practice*. New York: McGraw-Hill.

North, Douglass C. 1981. *Structure and Change in Economic History*. New York: W.W. Norton and Company.

————. 1990. *Institutions, Institutional Change, and Economic Performance*. Cambridge: Cambridge University Press.

Perotti, Roberto. 1994. "Capital Mobility and the (In)efficiency of Fiscal Unions." Columbia University, Department of Economics, New York.

Perotti, Roberto, and Alberto Alesina. 1994. "Economic Risk and Political Risk in Fiscal Unions." Harvard University and Columbia University, Department of Economics, Cambridge, Mass., and New York.

Peterson, George E. 1994. "Decentralization Experience in Latin America: An Overview of Lessons and Issues." Latin America and the Caribbean Technical Department Dissemination Note. World Bank, Washington, D.C.

Poterba, James M. 1994. "State Responses to Fiscal Crises: The Effects of Budgetary Institutions and Politics." *Journal of Political Economy* 102 (4): 799-821.

Putnam, Robert D., Robert Leonardi, and Raffaella Y. Nanetti. 1993. *Making Democracy Work: Civic Traditions in Modern Italy*. Princeton, N.J.: Princeton University Press.

Rueschemeyer, Dietrich, and Peter B. Evans. 1985. "The State and Economic Transformation: Towards an Analysis of the Conditions Underlying Effective Intervention." In Peter B. Evans, Dietrich Rueschemeyer, and Theda Skocpol, eds., *Bringing the State Back In*. Cambridge: Cambridge University Press.

Veliz, Claudio. 1980. *The Centralist Tradition in Latin America*. Princeton, N.J.: Princeton University Press.

Von Hagen, J. 1992. "A Note on the Empirical Effectiveness of Formal Fiscal Restraints." *Journal of Public Economics* 44: 99-110.

Wiesner, Eduardo, and Ricardo Lopez Murphy. 1994. "Decentralizacion Fiscal: La Busqueda de Equidad y Eficiencia." *Informe de Progreso Económicos Social en América Latina* (IPES). Washington, D.C.: Inter-American Development Bank.

Winkler, Donald R. 1994. *The Design and Administration of Intergovernmental Transfers: Fiscal Decentralization in Latin America*. Washington, D.C.: World Bank.

Comment on "Conflicts and Dilemmas of Decentralization," by Rudolf Hommes

Wallace E. Oates

Rudolf Hommes explores the political tensions inherent in the process of decentralizing decisionmaking in the public sector. This process offers real potential for breaking the grip of central planning, which has so often failed to deliver economic, social, and political progress. Moreover, decentralization has fired the imagination of political leaders in Eastern Europe, the developing countries, and many industrial nations. But decentralization does not come easily. And, as Hommes points out, it has its dangers.

Reflecting on these tensions, Hommes evinces a certain ambivalence. On the one hand he acknowledges the potential of decentralization and notes certain instances where it has improved service delivery. But at the same time Hommes clearly is not entirely comfortable with the prospect of extensive local autonomy; he would continue to ensure a major role for the central authority as a watchdog that steps in when local governments fail to produce. As Hommes concludes, the paradox of decentralization is that it demands more central government and more sophisticated political skills at the national level.

What I find troubling here is Hommes's reluctance to permit local governments the scope that they require to exercise genuine fiscal autonomy. For example, he wants the central government to supplement grant funds by mandating spending and coverage levels. But for decentralization to be meaningful, these are precisely the determinations that local governments must make. Decentralization requires the relinquishing of central control. Some critics may argue that local officials lack the expertise to manage public affairs. But as John Stuart Mill pointed out more than a century ago, decentralized political institutions play an important role in developing skilled public administrators by allowing more widespread and direct participation in the affairs of government.

Wallace E. Oates is professor of economics at the University of Maryland at College Park and university fellow at Resources for the Future.

Annual World Bank Conference on Development Economics 1995

Dividing Government Responsibilities

For decentralization to work, it is important to get the basic framework right. As an economist, I approach this issue in terms of the assignment of appropriate functions to the different levels of government and the introduction of fiscal and political institutions that provide incentives for decisionmakers to promote socially beneficial objectives. The literature on fiscal federalism provides some rough guidelines on these issues (Oates 1972, 1994). The central government's primary role involves macroeconomic stabilization, income redistribution, and the provision of certain national public goods. Decentralized (or local) government should provide local services that are tailored to the preferences and circumstances of the local jurisdiction.

The effective performance of this federal structure requires more than just an appropriate alignment of functions. The fiscal institutions that link spending and taxing decisions and that provide for intergovernmental transfers must create a system of incentives that encourages efficient fiscal choices at the various levels of government. In this regard, Hommes stresses the importance of a heavy reliance on local taxation. If local governments are to exercise real fiscal discretion, they must not be overly dependent on resource transfers from the center. Rather, they must develop their own revenue sources for two important reasons. First, central monies nearly always come with strings attached, so local fiscal autonomy is compromised if such monies are the dominant source of local revenues. Second, dependence on grants destroys incentives for efficient local fiscal decisions. Local officials, in deciding to expand or contract local programs, must weigh the benefits of adjusting these programs against their costs. If the funds come from the center, these decisions will be of limited real economic consequence for the locality. A reliance on local revenues, especially at the margin of local programs, is critical for establishing the proper fiscal incentives for efficient local choices.

Decentralization and Economic Performance

Systematic evidence on the contribution of fiscal decentralization to economic performance is scarce. It is clear, in principle, that decentralization can enhance allocative efficiency by providing a menu of local outputs that reflects the varying preferences and conditions in local jurisdictions. But, as Hommes fears, is this potential likely to go unrealized because of local political failure?

This is not an easy question to answer, but some preliminary findings from an international study of the impact of fiscal decentralization on economic growth offer some encouraging results. This work consists of ongoing dissertation research performed by Sang Loh Kim and me at the University of Maryland. Drawing on the empirical growth literature, the study extends the basic model of Barro and Sala-i-Martin (1992) to incorporate measures of fiscal decentralization and financial structure. In addition to the usual contributors to growth (investment in physical capital, education, and a measure of existing GDP to incorporate the convergence hypothesis), the model includes a measure of fiscal decentralization (the subnational government's share of public expenditure) and a measure of the self-reliance of subnational government (own revenues as a share of total revenues). The issues of particular interest here are the relationships between fiscal decentralization and self-reliance on the one hand and the rate of economic growth on the other.

Using a sample of forty countries, the study employs the expanded model to try to explain the growth in GDP per capita over the 1974–89 period. The basic results for the standard variables contain no surprises. What is interesting is the significant and robust positive correlation between fiscal decentralization and per capita economic growth. After controlling for the other standard economic determinants of growth, the study showed that countries that exhibited greater fiscal decentralization experienced significantly higher rates of economic growth. The self-reliance variable is not itself statistically significant, but its first difference is. This suggests that countries that moved toward greater revenue self-reliance by local governments over this period achieved a higher rate of growth. This is still a work in progress, and some econometric refinements and further testing remain to be done. But the initial results suggest that a greater reliance on fiscal decentralization makes a positive contribution to economic growth.

References

Barro, Robert J., and Xavier Sala-i-Martin. 1992. "Convergence." *Journal of Political Economy* 100 (April): 223–51.

Oates, Wallace E. 1972. *Fiscal Federalism*. New York: Harcourt, Brace, Jovanovich.

———. 1994. "Federalism and Government Finance." In J. Quigley and E. Smolensky, eds., *Modern Public Finance*. Cambridge, Mass.: Harvard University Press.

Comment on "Conflicts and Dilemmas of Decentralization," by Rudolf Hommes

Rémy Prud'homme

Decentralization is fashionable today. Dillinger (1995) estimates that sixty-three of the seventy-five transition and developing economies with populations of more than 5 million people have transferred or are in the process of transferring political power to local governments. The World Bank has been actively engaged in this process. Many of the discussions about centralization and decentralization remind me of the discussions we had thirty years ago about capitalism and socialism. The trick of the Marxist economists was simple: they did not compare actual capitalism with actual socialism, nor ideal capitalism with ideal socialism, but rather actual capitalism with ideal socialism—and thus they had an easy time proving socialism's superiority.

Similarly, many people today compare actual centralization with ideal decentralization. They see that in many developing countries centralization has failed to deliver. They look at theories of decentralization, mostly based on the U.S. experience. And they conclude that decentralization is highly desirable. Note that the perception of the failures of centralization is much more acute in Latin America and Africa than in East Asia. This reflects poorer economic and social results, not greater degrees of centralization. As a matter of fact, the miracle economies of East Asia—China, Hong Kong, Indonesia, the Republic of Korea, Malaysia, Singapore, Taiwan (China), and Thailand—are all highly centralized economies that are only now beginning to decentralize (World Bank 1993 overlooks this dimension). In Korea the first local elections were organized in 1995; before then all mayors were appointed by the central government, which means local governments hardly existed as autonomous entities. All this suggests that a fresher look at these issues, going beyond the conventional wisdom on the subject, is required. Rudolf Hommes's article is a welcome contribution to this effort.

Rémy Prud'homme is professor of economics at the University of Paris XII and director of L'observatoire de l'économie et des institutions locales (L'OEIL).

Annual World Bank Conference on Development Economics 1995

Some Lessons of Political Science

Hommes's article looks at decentralization from a political science perspective. This is appropriate for at least two reasons. One is that decentralization serves political objectives as much as—or more than—economic objectives. Decentralization is not only an institutional means to an economic end but an end in itself, or a means to reach political ends. When Alexis de Tocqueville visited the United States at the beginning of the nineteenth century, he was struck by its decentralized and democratic character, as opposed to the centralized and autocratic features of most European countries, particularly France. He quickly transformed this correlation into a causality and concluded that the more decentralized a country, the less autocratic it was. It seems to me that history has not disproven de Tocqueville, and that the worst dictatorships of the past two centuries have indeed been associated with totalitarian—and hence centralized—systems. This view must have been shared by the Allied forces at the end of World War II, when they injected a fair dose of federalism and decentralization into Germany and Japan, two highly centralized countries that had gone astray politically. In other words, even if decentralization is not desirable economically, it might still be worth having. The economic loss would be the premium paid for an insurance against authoritarianism.

The other reason economists should listen to a political scientist like Hommes has to do with the mechanisms of change. Institutional change can only be brought about by a political process, by the complex interplay of various groups (professional politicians, regional bosses, economic pressure groups, bureaucracies, concerned citizens, and even guerrillas) that are motivated by economic interests but also by their traditions, ideologies, and psychological investments. An understanding of these mechanisms is essential for the applied economist. Without it, his or her advice may be correct, but it will also be sterile. This is true for every kind of policy, be it privatization policy, environmental policy, or monetary policy. But it is much more the case for decentralization policy. Because decentralization policy has a higher political content than most other policies, the way it is introduced, the forms it takes, and the sequencing that is used determine its success or failure as much as or more than the substance of the policy.

The Basic Contradiction of Decentralization

The other side of this coin is that political scientists are more descriptive than normative. They are to economists what Racine is to Corneille. Racine is said to paint men (and even more so women) as they are, whereas Corneille paints them as they should be. Hommes is no exception—he is more Racinian than Corneillian. He deals only peripherally with the question of prime interest to economists, that is, is decentralization economically desirable? Will it promote efficiency, equity, and stability?

Although Hommes does not address these issues directly, he appears to favor decentralization. He views it as an institutional change capable of enhancing the economic and social prospects of the countries that are beginning to experiment with it. Yet his article includes a number of ideas, remarks, and insights that could just as easily be used to build a strong case against decentralization. The structure of this case is illustrated in figure 1.

The dual relationship illustrated by arrow 1 is widely accepted. Decentralization is defined as the joint transfer to lower levels of government of taxes and responsibilities. In principle, decentralization thus defined will improve allocative and productive efficiency. Because decisionmakers will be closer to the people, they will provide the public goods that are most needed—and at lower costs. This increased efficiency is in turn the main (economic) rationale for decentralization.

Unfortunately, as suggested by arrow 2, decentralization is likely to have negative impacts on both equity and macroeconomic management. This is also widely recognized. Hommes makes the point quite convincingly for stability. He could have done it equally well for equity. Because tax bases are unevenly distributed among jurisdictions, decentralization of taxes gives richer jurisdictions a great advantage: they enjoy lower rates or greater revenues or both and in any case will attract a larger tax base, thus perpetuating or aggravating jurisdictional inequities. Decentralization, therefore, breeds social inequity. It is also easy to show that decentralization makes it more difficult to develop interpersonal (in addition to interjurisdictional) redistribution policies. In short, there are decentralization failures just as there are market failures.

Hence the need to introduce central government grants and controls, as suggested by arrows 3 and 3a in figure 1. Like market failures, decentralization failures call for government—that is, central government—interventions. This is widely recognized on equity and stability grounds and is the main justification for grants. Grants are used to correct the vertical imbalances between different levels of governments and the horizontal imbalances between governments of the same level. In addition, Hommes, like many others, recommends rigorous central control over the borrowing of subnational governments.

Figure 1. *The Contradiction of Decentralization*

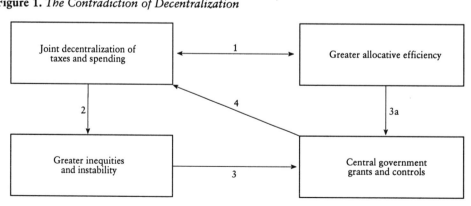

What is not so widely recognized, however, is the possibility of decentralization failures in relation to efficiency. I have shown elsewhere why and how this can happen in developing countries (Prud'homme 1994). Hommes brings a great deal of support to this view. He notes that local governments may be more susceptible to capture by divergent forces and fears that these forces will behave in an irresponsible fashion. This is why he suggests that a range of safeguards and controls be imposed by the central government. Unlike most economists, who prefer unconditional grants, Hommes want grants to be tied to incentives to efficiently provide the services involved or to provisions mandating spending levels and coverage targets. The central government, he states, is ultimately responsible for basic services like education, health, or crime prevention; it is the government of last resort.

This necessary central government intervention, however, erodes the very foundations of decentralization. The potential gains from decentralization (greater allocative efficiency) assume that local governments will be free to set their own taxes and to allocate their own expenditures. The less freedom of choice and tax autonomy there is, the smaller the gains to be expected from decentralization. If there is no freedom of choice and no tax autonomy, the benefits of decentralization disappear. To return to figure 1, arrow 4 inhibits arrow 1 and makes decentralization impossible, or at least of no use. If the assumptions on which the justification for decentralization rests are weakened or destroyed, so too is the case for decentralization.

Three Conditions for Success

Hommes sets three conditions for successful decentralization: a good, strong central government; reliance on local taxation; and well-functioning local democracy. These three conditions are in line with the preceding argument. There is no doubt that they would help make decentralization work. More precisely, they would ensure that decentralization improves allocative efficiency, but it is hard to see how they could prevent the damage done by decentralization in terms of equity and stability. But can these conditions be met? Let us ignore the third one, and focus the discussion on the first two.

Hommes's first condition asks a great deal of central governments. He does not want them to simply transfer power to subnational governments. Rather, he wants central governments to intervene actively in local governments' business—to oversee, assess, and correct—and to decide when to impinge on local autonomy for the sake of stability. This is a particularly delicate assignment. Few developing countries have a central government that is sufficiently strong, dedicated, and efficient to perform these functions. And the few that would qualify are precisely the countries that do not need decentralization. This paradox is akin to the paradox of the privatization of public monopolies: the need for complex regulation under privatization is such that countries with the skills to effectively regulate privatized monopolies also have the skills to effectively manage public monopolies. Where decentralization is needed (because central governments are corrupt and inefficient), it cannot be implemented. Where it can be implemented, it is not needed.

Hommes makes a second condition for successful decentralization, namely that a large share of subnational spending be financed by a local government's own taxes. He is right to emphasize the importance of this condition. But he is mistaken in suggesting that it can easily be met. The difficulty goes beyond what he calls the opposition (to local taxation) of powerful property owners and business interests that have the implicit backing of the middle class.

The heart of the matter is that there are very few good local taxes. Taxes that are good—or at least not too bad—at the national level become bad when used at the local level, either because they induce undesirable locational distortions or because they raise insurmountable administrative difficulties. This is a well-known problem for personal income taxes, natural resource taxes, or custom duties. Sales taxes used to be an exception and were viewed as an acceptable subnational tax base. Even these, alas, are being increasingly substituted for by value-added taxes. Although a value-added tax is indeed a better tax than a turnover tax or a retail sales tax (because it induces fewer distortions and less tax evasion), it cannot be decentralized, as Brazil has learned. To a large extent, then, there is a contradiction in the simultaneous introduction of a value-added tax and a decentralization scheme. If we are serious about decentralization, we should refrain from promoting value-added taxation. The only good local taxes are property taxes (and they are good only when they tax the pure land rent, which they never do) and internalizing taxes a la Pigou, such as congestion or pollution charges. But these taxes are difficult and costly to administer and do not produce much revenue, particularly in developing countries.

This is why, in practice, Hommes's second condition is rarely met. Published data on this issue are often misleading. The subnational share of shared taxes is usually counted as a regional or local tax, when it should be counted as a grant. The rates of these taxes are determined by national governments, who pay the political price of raising the tax rates. Subnational governments simply pocket the money, reap the political benefit of spending it, and complain that they do not receive enough. Many of the decentralization reforms undertaken recently, particularly in Latin America, have been of this nature. Local government's spending has increased, but true local taxes have not.

Conclusion

Hommes's article can therefore be read as a warning about decentralization. Decentralization is not intrinsically a good thing that should be uncritically recommended. In certain cases it can do more harm than good. A least four points have to be considered in this respect. The degree of central government efficiency is one: if the central government is inefficient or corrupt, decentralization is likely to increase inefficiency. The importance of income differentials (between households and regions) is a second criteria: the larger they are, the less desirable is decentralization. Per capita income is a third dimension: the lower the GDP per capita, the more dangerous decentralization will be. The mere functioning of local governments implies fixed costs, which in a low-income country will be increased by decentralization and will crowd out spending on goods and services. Urbanization is a fourth consideration. The possibility of having local tax bases is lower in rural areas, as is the possibility that there will be effective local political control. Therefore, the lower the degree of urbanization, the more difficult it is to decentralize. From these conditions it follows that decentralization is appropriate for countries with an efficient central government, limited income disparities, reasonably high per capita income, and large cities. Certainly, not all of the sixty-three countries engaged in decentralization reforms meet these criteria.

References

Dillinger, William. 1994. "Decentralization and Its Implications for Urban Service Delivery." Urban Management Program Discussion Paper 16. World Bank, Transportation, Water, and Urban Development Department, Urban Development Division, Washington, D.C.

Prud'homme, Rémy. 1994. "On the Dangers of Decentralization." Policy Research Working Paper 1252. World Bank, Transportation, Water, and Urban Development Department, Urban Development Division, Washington, D.C.

World Bank. 1993. *The East Asian Miracle: Economic Growth and Public Policy.* A World Bank Policy Research Report. New York: Oxford University Press.

Floor Discussion of "Conflicts and Dilemmas of Decentralization," by Rudolf Hommes

The interesting thing about the discussion was not what was said but what was not said, observed a participant from Bangladesh. It struck him that decentralization was not really an issue of inductive logic. Rather than developing from growth models of best practice, it arose from the political dynamics of particular societies at given points in time. When systems are less pluralistic and more autocratic, they make a great deal of noise about decentralization because by and large they are dealing with their own hierarchies. But those who exercise central power are reluctant to cede that power to lower levels of government. What should an international organization do in this situation, apart from advising on best practice? Should a dialogue be established with the lower levels of government, even when they are ruled by opposition parties? And if local governments come up with plausible development programs, should they be considered, or do the existing hierarchies of authority take precedence? What should be done with autocratic, centralized bureaucracies that are loathe to subordinate themselves to lower levels of government? These are the political realities of decentralization, the participant concluded, and unless they are addressed much of the discussion is academic.

What struck a participant from the Massachusetts Institute of Technology was how little seemed to be understood about decentralization and how to approach it. There was a real asymmetry to the way the issue was addressed. Almost invariably, he said, the speakers talked about the theoretical benefits of decentralization, but no one discussed whether the assumptions underlying the model of fiscal federalism—developed in an industrial context—theoretically apply to developing countries. Yet when this ideal theoretical model is attacked, it is for its practical failings. Still, after eight years of working on decentralization in developing countries, the participant could cite a number of examples where the practical problems being mentioned—such as pervasive local corruption and inadequate local skills—simply do not exist. When we think about these things, he said, we must think more analytically at the beginning, not start theoretically and then delve into anecdotal examples of why this

This session was chaired by Shahid Javed Burki, vice president, Latin America and the Caribbean Regional Office, at the World Bank.

Annual World Bank Conference on Development Economics 1995

might or might not work. Decentralization is very context-specific, and generalizations simply cannot be applied to different country circumstances.

If redistribution is the goal, said David Wildasin (discussant from another session), it helps to have all the levers of power in one place. Decentralization is inhibiting from that viewpoint, but it also has its advantages. In South Africa, for example, apartheid probably would have been unsustainable had it been implemented at the level of individual metropolitan governments. If redistribution is being done by the wrong people or is not equalizing, then decentralization may be useful. In China there is substantial inequality in the distribution of income between urban and rural workers. This situation has been sustainable largely because of tight restrictions on where people can work and live. Liberalization of the economy and dismantling of tight central controls may limit the amount of redistribution, but in any case redistribution does not always go from the rich to the poor—sometimes it goes from the poor to the rich.

Wildasin was right in saying that a centralized system does not always ensure an equitable distribution of income between households or between areas, said Remy Prud'homme (discussant). South Africa, for example, was a highly centralized country that was also probably the most unequal country in the world. Thus centralization is necessary for redistribution but it is not sufficient. In any case, most national budgets redistribute enormous amounts from richer to poorer areas. In Thailand, for example, Bangkok is losing in the budget game, since it receives less from the budget than it contributes. The same is true in many other cities and countries. Thus, Prud'homme believes, centralization is inherently more conducive to redistribution than is decentralization.

A participant from the World Bank's Europe and Central Asia Department asked if any lessons could be drawn from the reengineering taking place in large multinational institutions, which are decentralizing to nations and states. A participant from the Multilateral Investment Guarantee Agency had a similar question. One of the things happening in multinationals and states is that information technology is allowing people to access information in a very decentralized manner. How, the participant wondered, was this access to information affecting states' efforts to wield influence from the top down? It seems that the state is being subjected to the same challenges from decentralized access to information as multinational agencies that are realizing that ideas have to percolate up.

Unfortunately, said Wallace Oates (discussant), the discussion had gone down a bipolar track—centralization or decentralization—that was not appropriate. In talking about optimal fiscal federalism, he explained, the literature is trying to separate functions by level of government. Clearly, income redistribution is an important objective for central governments, but that does not mean that local governments have no role to play. Also, much of the discussion seemed to assume that decentralization would lead to macroeconomic instability. Again, the problem was one of how the argument is framed. Oates did not agree that countries with more decentralized public sectors were necessarily less stable macroeconomically, and he suggested this as an interesting area for empirical study.

Rudolf Hommes agreed. If the right controls are in place, he said, decentralization does not mean less stability. Germany, for example, has a fairly decentralized system, but with lots of controls. And Germany has a fairly stable history. Whereas in Brazil—a centralized country with no controls at all—the opposite is true. It is a matter, as Oates had said about optimal fiscal federalism, of getting the right functions in the right places.

Hommes then said that his point was not so much to make a case for decentralization as it was to acknowledge that decentralization is a political reality and that, to take advantage of it, policymakers have to be aware of the pitfalls and problems. The situation in Latin America was analogous to that of consumers who become dissatisfied with a product and so buy another brand, only to discover that the other brand is no better. In Latin America there has been tremendous dissatisfaction with centralization because it is not working. When people were offered an alternative—decentralization—they voted for it, and it will be a long time before that decision is reversed. Decentralized systems, he concluded, are fairly popular and in democratic countries will probably remain in place.

Roundtable Discussion

Second-Generation Issues in Transition

The panelists for this roundtable discussion were Stanley Fischer, first deputy managing director of the International Monetary Fund; Jana Matesová, professor of economics and research director at the Czech Management Center in Celakovice, Czech Republic; and Susan Rose-Ackerman, Henry R. Luce Professor of Jurisprudence at the Yale Law School and Political Science Department. The moderator was Michael Bruno, chief economist and senior vice president, Development Economics, at the World Bank.

Michael Bruno, Introduction

The roundtable discussion at this annual conference customarily touches on a subject at the heart of the next year's *World Development Report*. This year's topic is the transition from controlled to market-based economies. Countries have started from such different initial conditions and changed at such different tempos that stressing commonalities and distilling common lessons will be a challenge.

Not only are the countries at different stages of various aspects of reform, but they differ in political development as well. Something like half the countries of Eastern and Central Europe have gone through the initial macroeconomic shock and dislocation, and some of these countries are now among the fastest-growing economies in Europe—notably the Czech Republic, Poland, Slovenia, and Albania. But even these countries still face the difficult task of sustaining fiscal and monetary balance and of forging on with the tough restructuring and institutional and regulatory changes still ahead. In many of these countries markets—especially financial markets—are still fairly chaotic and politics are still unsettled.

The so-called first-generation issues for transition economies centered on liberalization and stabilization. These issues are still with us, and the sustainability of macroeconomic reform is still a problem for second-generation reformers. There have been debates both inside and outside the World Bank and the International Monetary Fund about whether stabilization has hurt growth—one of the issues Stan Fischer will discuss. Should we be happy about a country like Poland, which is doing

Annual World Bank Conference on Development Economics 1995
©1996 The International Bank for Reconstruction and Development / THE WORLD BANK

very well on growth but has an inflation rate still bordering on 30 percent? Cumulative research shows that inflation rates above 30 or 40 percent are harmful to growth, so should a country like Poland aim for single-digit inflation before launching other areas of reform?

What have we learned about the sequencing of stabilization and restructuring? Contrary to the common paradigm, Russia privatized first and only subsequently embarked on what looks like successful stabilization. What impact does mass privatization have on restructuring? Who controls the firms that have been privatized? Who are the real owners? Why is it that once firms are privatized, they do less restructuring than we thought they would? Jana Matesová addresses some of these questions based on the Czech experience.

One problem in the forefront lately is the threat to the rule of law, indeed, to the very existence of the state. We hear sensationalized reports of corruption and organized crime in some, though not all, the transition economies. But it is hard to find good empirical evidence of the intensity of the problem; corruption and organized crime are hardly a monopoly of economies in transition. The question is, what is it about the transition that seems to generate increased corruption? Does corruption spring from the collapse of the restraints of the old system, or is it a legacy of that system? Does it come from the transition being too rapid or too slow? Is it overstated? We know that macroeconomic reform is not sustainable without structural adjustment, so it is important that we understand the relation between property rights and adjustment for macroeconomic reasons. But corruption can also destabilize reform, can in fact delegitimize the reform process and erode political credibility—not to mention that rent seeking reduces efficiency. Susan Rose-Ackerman discusses the common problem of corruption in the transition economies, how it affects the political economy of reform, and what can be done about it.

Stanley Fischer on Stabilization and Growth

It is a mark of the success of the transition process that we are already into the second generation only five years after the first generation was born. It is another mark of success that the process is not receiving a great deal of attention. In the same week in April 1995 the International Monetary Fund's board of directors agreed to large standby loans to both Russia and Ukraine—events that even a year ago would have generated banner headlines. This time the programs received polite but almost indifferent welcomes.

There are at least two interpretations of the title of this session. We could be asking how we can assist the second generation of reformers—countries such as Cuba, the Democratic People's Republic of Korea, and Turkmenistan—based on the experiences of the first generation. Or we could be asking what problems the first-generation transition economies face as they move into the second stage of transition. I address both interpretations, focusing mainly on stabilization, inflation, and growth. The good news is that, by and large, the data support the view that stabilization is good for growth and that early stabilization is better than later stabilization. I also discuss the role of exchange rate anchors and touch on the sustainability of the reform process.

Stabilization, Inflation, and Growth

The most important news about the transition process is that, according to official data, several transition economies are already growing, among them Croatia, the Czech Republic, Estonia, Hungary, Latvia, Lithuania, Moldova, Poland, Slovakia, and Slovenia. If we include the performance of the unrecorded economy, presumably these countries started growing at least a year earlier than the official data indicate, and perhaps other countries are growing too.

One important lesson of transition—and this is certainly a lesson for the late reformers—is that stabilization is good for growth. It is almost an iron-clad law that stabilization is needed for growth and, more specifically, that no transition economy has achieved growth without first reducing inflation to the single digit per month range. (Romania is an exception; it began to grow while inflation was high.) There is also a strong relationship in the opposite direction: countries that have stabilized have generally seen growth within a year or two (de Melo, Denizer, and Gelb 1996).

There seems to be something special about the transition economies that have begun to grow: for example, they tend to be more democratic, they entered communism unwillingly, and they were in the Soviet empire for a shorter time. Still, not too much emphasis should be placed on this point, because Russia and some of the slower reformers will likely start growing within a year or two.

De Melo, Denizer, and Gelb (1996) also show that countries that reform faster experience a more rapid decline in output than those that are slow to reform. This finding is consistent with the behavior of output in the early years of transition for countries such as Belarus and Ukraine, which were slow to reform. But within three to five years the cumulative output loss for the rapid reformers is smaller than that for the slow reformers.

The data also suggest that early reformers have higher inflation as they liberalize prices, typically in the context of a monetary overhang. Whether there is a price explosion depends on the initial conditions. The Czech and Slovak Republic, for instance, did not have a price explosion, though its inflation rate was higher at the beginning of the reform process than it is in the Czech Republic now.

Does the fact that tight macroeconomic policies seem good for growth mean that it is impossible to be too tough on monetary and fiscal policy at the beginning of the transition process? Recall that just two or three years ago the Calvo-Coricelli view that output declines were caused by credit shortages was very popular. To some extent the view that tight monetary policy was responsible for output declines in transition economies confuses real and nominal rates of growth of credit: typically expanding nominal credit more rapidly does not cause real credit to grow. I do believe that it is possible to have too tight a monetary policy at the beginning of a stabilization and reform process, particularly in light of the remonetization of the economy that will take place at some point. But the political conditions in the transition economies have not permitted excessive tightening, so in most cases tighter credit and fiscal conditions would not have produced worse outcomes.

Administered prices aside, prices in the transition economies appear to be reasonably flexible. When monetary policy is tightened, the effects on inflation appear within three or four months in Russia, rather than the eighteen to twenty-four month lag that is typical in the United States.

Countries that have stabilized commonly find themselves with inflation rates in the 15–30 percent range and now face the same moderate inflation dilemma as countries such as Chile, Colombia, and Israel have faced in the past. Moderate inflation will yield to tight macroeconomic policy, supported by wage restraint and the use of an exchange rate anchor. But the last part of the journey—to inflation rates similar to those in industrial countries—is difficult, and policymakers must take advantage of every favorable price shock to try to lock in inflation reductions and make further progress.

What is needed to make the gains from stabilization and growth sustainable? Fiscal reform is a key second-generation issue for countries that have already embarked on transition. The decline in government revenues in most transition economies has been dramatic. Many governments, especially in the states of the former Soviet Union, have been able to maintain macroeconomic balance only by holding back appropriated budget funds (sequestering) or building up arrears. The unintended consequence is credit creation through the central bank or arrear creation in the private sector. Rebuilding the fiscal system (on both the expenditure and tax sides) and moving away from enterprise taxation to indirect taxes (such as customs, tariffs, value-added, and perhaps direct taxes) are priorities. So is the creation of a modern system of expenditure management and prioritization.

Another priority for countries in the second stage of transition is financial system reform. Banks are not yet playing much of a role in financing investment in most transition economies. Unfortunately, there is a real chicken and egg problem here: the banks will not be sound if they lend to companies that are not sound, but the companies cannot develop without external finance. It is likely that many transition economies will require another round of bank portfolio and capital restructuring programs. Agricultural sector reform is another priority among many of the countries of the former Soviet Union. So in many countries is the continuation and deepening of privatization, particularly in reforming corporate governance.

Among the lessons that can benefit the late reformers is how to deal with arrears. When the arrears problem first emerged, possible solutions included one-time monetization, a one-time netting operation, and complicated schemes for turning the arrears into tradable assets. But after several of these elegant one-time solutions had to be repeated it became clear that the best answer is tough-minded neglect. Firms should be left to work out interenterprise arrears on their own.

Exchange Rate Anchors

It was once accurate to say that no major stabilization program had succeeded without an exchange rate anchor. Recently, however, transition economies such as Croatia and the Kyrgyz Republic have stabilized their economies without pegging the exchange rate, and the evidence no longer unambiguously supports the need for an exchange rate nominal anchor for stabilizing rapid inflation.

I still support the use of a temporary exchange rate anchor in trying to bring down inflation quickly. Mexico's recent crisis has led many observers to believe that this approach is dangerous, but that is true only if the anchor is never moved—and the anchor analogy is precisely of something that moves and is not permanently fixed. In Poland the initial peg was held for a year; in Israel for a little longer. At some point it becomes necessary to adjust the rate, and perhaps also the exchange rate regime, because domestic inflation rarely ceases immediately. In some transition economies, including the Baltics, real appreciations at rates of 20–30 percent a year seem quite sustainable. But at some point countries that have not irrevocably fixed the rate, as in the quasi currency board monetary systems, are likely to have to start allowing it to move.

Sustainability

In my view political sustainability is the most amazing phenomenon of transition. At the outset of the transition process everybody was afraid of reversals in the postsocialist world: "If we don't support the Russians, the communists will come back, and if not the communists, then the fascists will gain the upper hand all over Eastern Europe." Five years later, despite the fact that difficulties have been more numerous and output declines have been far greater than anybody ever expected, the notion of returning to the previous system seems to be far from anybody's mind (except perhaps in some smaller, less developed formerly Soviet economies, and in the end even those economies move toward markets). [Note: from the perspective at the time of publication, in early 1996, this is no longer so clear in Russia. The results of the June presidential election will be critical in this regard.] Even when former communists have been elected, they have continued the reform process, albeit in fits and starts. That is the most remarkable feature of the first generation of reforms: the lessons learned by people who lived under the previous economic system have ensured that reform will continue despite the wrenching changes it has brought.

Jana Matesová on Mass Privatization and Restructuring

Together with decentralization and macroeconomic stabilization, the restructuring of state-owned and formerly state-owned enterprises is one of the most important steps in economic transition. Restructuring firms—changing a firm's behavior to increase its market value to investors—is a complicated and long-term process. As Michael Bruno (1994, p. 28) points out, "structural adjustment is a slow process even in the most advanced market-based economy—even when the reform is credible." Most studies dealing with regional or industrial restructuring in market economies find that the process takes ten years or more.

The breadth and depth of the restructuring required in the formerly communist economies is enormous, touching almost every former state enterprise. Changes are needed in markets, products, technologies, assets and operations, and financing, as well as in ownership. Restructuring requires firms to turn away from their exclusive focus on products and the production process and embrace markets and marketing. To reap the benefits of the greater efficiency of the private sector, firms need to face the incentive structure that comes with private ownership. And that means that privatization and the clear definition and protection of ownership rights are necessary parts of the process of changing the behavior of firms and managers.

Examples of Privatization

Unlike the experience in most Western economies, some Eastern European governments decided to privatize firms before restructuring them and to let the new, private owners lead the process of structural change. Three economies have done remarkably well in terms of the speed and scope of privatization: the former German Democratic Republic, Russia, and the Czech Republic (see Frydman, Rapaczynski, and Earle 1993 for a survey of privatization methods).

In the former German Democratic Republic a government agency, the Treuhandanstalt, acted as investment banker and sold state companies to private investors. Restructuring has been taking place in these privatized firms, so in that sense the approach is working. But there are significant risks to allowing a state agency to be so directly involved in privatization, especially the risk of backtracking if the agency extends its bureaucratic reach or yields to the temptation of rent seeking and corruption. And privatization is costly in both accounting terms and transaction costs. Further, there is always a risk that the transparency of privatization will be questioned and that privatizations will yield to political pressures. The German model, which worked under the specific conditions that applied in Germany, probably would not work in most other transition economies. Countries with lower per capita income and accumulated wealth, less stable political systems, and underdeveloped legal and ethical standards of business conduct would likely face grave problems if they tried to implement mass privatization German-style.

Russia's approach, rapid voucher-based mass privatization, resulted in firms dominated by insiders (Blasi 1994; Boycko, Shleifer, and Vishny 1993; Pistor, Frydman, and Rapaczynski 1994). According to Blasi (1994), managers of Russian privatized firms acquired an average of 65 percent of the shares in their firms. This high share of manager ownership is combined with substantial information asymmetry and with the fact that the issuers themselves—the managers of firms—are responsible for ownership registration, which does not provide enough security to other shareholders. These factors give managers almost full control over firms and substantial control over the shareholding rights of the remaining investors.

The Czech Republic provides the most successful example of mass privatization accompanied by macroeconomic stabilization. In 1989 the private sector accounted for less than 1 percent of gross domestic product (GDP), employed an estimated 1.2 percent of labor, and held 2–4 percent of registered productive assets (Dyba and Svejnar 1995; Coffee 1995). By 1995, after the second wave of voucher privatization, the private sector owned 80 percent of productive assets and accounted for more than 56 percent of GDP. Mass privatization had strong public support, with nearly 80 per-

cent of the adult population holding shares of Czech and Slovak companies and financial institutions. Unlike the case in Russia, insiders ended up with less than 10 percent
of the shares in a typical Czech firm (Earle and Estrin 1995; Kotrba 1995).

Privatization did not, however, create overly dispersed ownership structures.
Voucherholders turned over more than 70 percent of their voucher points in the
first wave and 60 percent in the second wave to investment privatization funds
(Coffee 1995; Kotrba 1995). In most privatized companies the three or four largest
private institutional investors ended up with a qualified two-thirds majority of ownership shares (Lastovicka, Marcincic, and Mejstrik 1995). If the funds joined forces
within individual companies, ownership structures would be sufficiently concentrated to facilitate restructuring. So far, however, that has not happened, usually
because of conflicting goals and incentives (Coffee 1995; Matesová and Seda 1994).
When stymied in this way, some funds have swapped blocks of shares for stakes in
other companies in which they can reach agreements with other block investors.

How Much Restructuring in Czech Firms?

The aggregate data from the Czech Republic offers little evidence of the manifestations of restructuring that are typical in market economies—bankruptcies, increasing unemployment, and mergers and acquisitions. The evidence does suggest,
however, that start-up companies rather than privatized companies are experiencing
the fastest growth in employment, assets, and production. This raises a legitimate
question about whether any restructuring is going on in privatized firms.

One reason that there is little evidence of restructuring is that privatization is so
recent—the first mass transfer of ownership to the private sector occurred in June
1993; aggregate data for 1994 are thus unlikely to show any signs of massive
restructuring. Industry-specific data, survey data from fifty privatized manufacturing firms, data collected through interviews with managers, and data on capital markets provide some information about operational restructuring in Czech firms.
These data suggest that significant changes in the structure of markets (trade with
former members of the Council for Mutual Economic Assistance shrank from 60
percent of exports in 1989 to less than 20 percent in 1994) have been followed by
much more limited changes in product structure.

There have been some changes on the asset side for privatized firms. Balance
sheet data reflect declining inventories, a shift in the structure of current assets
toward greater liquidity (primarily cash), and sales or liquidations of fixed assets—
all signs of restructuring.

The employment data are ambiguous with respect to restructuring, though much
of the data points to restructuring shifts in employment. Labor mobility has
increased significantly both within and across industries. Employment has fallen
about 10 percent during the transition (Dyba and Svejnar 1995), though unemployment is still only 3–4 percent. Even though firms are laying off employees, unemployment remains low because of decreased labor participation rates among women
and the elderly, the high labor absorption capacity of the growing services sector and

small and medium-size companies, efficient active employment policies, and cross-border employment in Austria and Germany (Svejnar, Terrell, and Muenich 1995). A 1994 World Bank survey of fifty privatized Czech manufacturing firms found that between 1991 and 1993 some 13 percent of firms had increased employment (by 0.1 to 30 percent), while 65 percent had reduced employment by 50 percent or less and 22 percent had downsized by more than 50 percent.

Most of the signs of restructuring mentioned so far seem to be independent of privatization. But in interviews, Czech managers identify the pressures of market forces as the driving power behind changes in markets and in the liquidity of assets. Second are managers' fears that they could lose their jobs if they let their companies fail. Investors keep underperforming firms in line by threatening to replace their management. Since 1993 there has been a new wave of management changes, mainly in smaller companies.

Changes in Ownership Structure and Assets

The two most significant changes since the completion of the second wave of privatization in the Czech Republic have been the substantial changes in ownership structures through private placements of shares (a "second privatization" through capital markets) and the separation of fixed assets from parent companies. Recent ownership changes in privatized firms have been quite extensive. Investors, mostly the investment privatization funds, are buying and selling large blocks of shares to attain desired liquidity levels and to concentrate their portfolios. (Because the funds acquired vouchers from their investors rather than cash, they must arrange for debt or equity financing or sell shares in order to get cash.) In many companies investment funds failed to form coalitions because of conflicting interests among institutional shareholders; now they are exchanging portfolios to avoid those conflicts. Many funds entered the voucher privatization program intending to sell part of their shares after the privatization; the funds had option contracts on selling the shares even before they started bidding for them. Domestic entrepreneurs, coalitions of smaller investment privatization funds, and foreign investors have also been engaged in takeovers of small and medium-size companies. Some re-mergers of firms that became independent in 1988–90 or as part of the mass privatization are likely to occur in the near future.

The most typical forms of operational restructuring occurring among Czech firms are sales of fixed assets and organizational restructuring. Fixed assets were removed from company balance sheets in substantial amounts in 1992 as part of the mass privatization, a process that started up again in 1994. Not all these assets have been liquidated.

Most decisions to sell assets are approved by the boards of directors of the privatized companies, typically representatives of investment privatization funds, managers, and outside directors. Which group dominates the decisionmaking process depends on the cohesiveness among the funds represented on the board, the structure of ownership in the firm, the skills of the managers and the outside directors, and agency problems between the funds and their representatives on boards.

Although there is some evidence of asset stripping, many asset sales seem rationally motivated and are likely to increase firms' viability and value for shareholders. In many cases highly depreciated fixed assets are being replaced by investment in new assets. This new investment is modest, however, and financed almost exclusively by debt. In some cases the increased financing through bank loans is the result of subsequent lending by commercial banks, which secure their loans by putting representatives of their investment subsidiaries on the boards of directors of their borrowers. What seems to determine the amount of such subsequent lending is the institutional culture of the banks, rather than any pattern based on bank size, ownership, structure, or history.

Often the most valuable and productive assets of firms are sold off, separating them from nonviable companies and their liabilities. This may represent a rational economic choice in the case of old companies with large liabilities, long-term labor contracts, and obsolete technology, products, and management systems. Such firms can be very difficult to restructure, and the future value of these assets may be higher than the future value of the firm.

Who bears the cost of the separation of viable assets from a firm's liabilities depends on what form the separation takes. Most common is a complicated organizational restructuring that establishes new limited liability subsidiaries of privatized companies. Such organizational restructuring does not affect current shareholders of the privatized company as long as the assets are sold at fair market prices, the transfer pricing between the parent company and the subsidiaries is transparent, each of the subsidiaries is financially accountable, and an external market exists for the parent company's stakes in the subsidiaries. Meeting these conditions is difficult because Czech accounting law does not require firms to produce consolidated statements, and financial flows between parent companies and their subsidiaries often lack transparency.

Does Restructuring Require Privatization?

Any obvious question is whether these changes could not as easily have occurred without mass privatization. The simple answer is probably. But the changes in the ownership structure that are now taking place would likely have been extremely costly in terms of time and political stability. Among the most important features of the voucher privatization was its strengthening of social cohesion by building a broad public constituency for privatization: as a result of its transparency the voucher privatization evoked little political opposition.

The voucher privatization promoted the restructuring of Czech firms in other important ways as well. It accelerated the creation of the institutional infrastructure needed by a market economy through the impetus it gave to the creation of financial intermediaries such as investment banks and funds, unit funds, brokerage firms, the stock exchange, and financial consultants and other services to businesses; it also provided opportunities for commercial banks to offer new financial instruments. The voucher privatization created a transparent and concentrated ownership structure that made acquisitions by real entrepreneurs and venture capitalists feasible while avoiding the kind of government intervention that leads to political speculation and incentives for perverse behavior. Finally, the voucher privatization was a tremendous learning experience for the whole population, a kind of crash course on market mechanisms and the behavior of markets.

The investment privatization funds have made significant progress in improving the financial and reporting discipline of companies. Though most funds would prefer to be portfolio managers rather than owners and directors, they all maintain long-term positions in some companies. The funds are likely to be more efficient monitors of firm management than the government would be. They provide an important counterbalance to the power of managers, whose position is strengthened by conflicts of interests among institutional shareholders of companies and the still-limited skills of directors.

One major risk in the process of mass privatization as conducted in the Czech Republic is the residual state ownership by such agencies as the National Property Fund, which involves the government in decisionmaking about individual companies. The government can better exercise its authority through regulation. Another potential risk comes from the affiliation of commercial and investment banks. The case needs to be examined separately for each transition economy, in particular the opportunity cost of restricting commercial banks from investment banking. In the Czech Republic the opportunity cost of such restrictions might have been high. Banks enjoyed relatively strong credibility, and preventing them from taking part in the voucher privatization could have threatened the credibility of the privatization itself. And later, such discrimination would likely have led to conflicts of interest between the banks, as the traditional creditors of Czech firms, and the new private owners. Still, the separation of commercial and investment banking is probably desirable even in the Czech Republic, at least until there is stronger competition among banks and proper long-term market-oriented incentives.

Obstacles to Restructuring

Three bottlenecks are slowing the restructuring of firms: information asymmetry, the lack of skills and expertise of managers and lenders, and an underdeveloped legal framework. Information assymetry constrains the efficiency of markets (including for company control and capital), increases the uncertainty in decisionmaking, and provides incentives for perverse behavior (such as insider training or rent seeking among managers, board directors, or bankers).

Thousands of Czech firms require significant restructuring or turnarounds that, in turn, require managers with strong leadership abilities, a clear vision, and relevant market economy experience. Managers possessing this set of abilities are few and far between. Although Czech managers have excellent technical skills and expertise in production management, their market experience is limited. Most managers view firms as sets of production-specific assets rather than as capital that needs to be reproduced. Many actors in the burgeoning Czech market are also naive about global competition. Few bankers, for example, are experienced with market-oriented incentives or risk management.

The underdeveloped legal framework has been another significant barrier to restructuring. Hundreds of new laws must be put in place and adjusted to support democracy and the efficient functioning of markets. Building up a judiciary that is able to enforce these laws is a long-term process that, again, depends on expertise and experience. At this point bankruptcies, ownership protection, enforcement of debt repayments, and even layoffs are significantly constrained by the underdeveloped legal system.

Creditors, for example, have no strong incentives to force debtor firms to file for bankruptcy. The bankruptcy process is slow and institutionally weak; as a result creditors are unlikely to recover their assets through the process. They prefer to rely on informal agreements outside the legal system. Debt-for-equity swaps are rare, and those that occur are debt driven rather than motivated by the potential future value of the firms, with banks swapping part of the outstanding debt for equity only as the last resort to collateralize the rest of the outstanding debt and increase their chances of repayment by taking board positions. Although the present value of the future revenues of many firms is higher than their current debts, there are few incentives for creditors to get involved in preparing or evaluating restructuring plans or overseeing the restructuring process (Dittus 1994; Dittus and Prowse 1995; Baer and Gray 1995).

Susan Rose-Ackerman on Corruption

Corruption is a commonplace of authoritarian regimes. Throughout history dictators have used their positions to extract personal fortunes and to allow loyal subordinates to enrich themselves at public expense. In states with personalized governments corruption is a function of the moral probity of their rulers, who are free to organize the state to extract payoffs if they wish.

By contrast, although the socialist states of Eastern Europe and the former Soviet Union provided special benefits to their leaders, the country houses and access to Western goods available to these officials pale by comparison with the fortunes amassed by some rulers in developing countries. Influenced by a lingering respect for Marxist ideology and recognizing the need for an efficient military, Eastern European and Soviet leaders were not pure kleptocrats. Nevertheless, although the state was not operated to maximize the wealth of the rulers, corruption was rife.

Corruption thrives in rigid systems with multiple bottlenecks and sources of monopoly power within the government. A planned economy in which prices are set below market-clearing levels provides incentives for payoffs as a way to allocate scarce goods and services. Transactions that would be legal trades in market economies are illegal payoffs in such systems. The excess demand at official prices creates perverse incentives for those with control over scarce supplies. In addition to selling goods and services to the highest bribers, the authorities in these systems have incentives to create even more bottlenecks as a way of extracting higher payoffs. Officials might, for example, create delays or introduce costly conditions in exchange for their sanction. The fundamental problem is not simply the existence of controlled prices set below the market-clearing level, but also the monopoly power of state officials who are not threatened with entry by more efficient and lower-priced competitors (Montias and Rose-Ackerman 1981; Shleifer and Vishny 1992).

Corruption and Transition

Throughout the former Soviet bloc the organization of the economy gave officials an incentive to exploit their positions for private gain and gave their customers and clients an incentive to make payoffs. Corruption was common because the rigidity of the system was not backed by an impartial legal system capable of enforcing the rules. Instead, authority was exercised by superiors in the hierarchy who often had their own reasons for bending or changing the rules. Subordinates could not appeal to the law as a reason for resisting the demands of their superiors. The system was not just rigid, but also arbitrary. Its requirements and irrationalities turned almost everyone into a law breaker. The widespread complicity of the citizenry in corrupt transactions then became a method of social control. Since everyone was guilty of something, the state could always develop a case against anyone who displeased the authorities on other grounds. Corruption cases were used to punish dissidents, not to improve the functioning of the state bureaucracy (Stern 1977).

These observations suggest that the decline of authoritarian governments and centrally planned economies ought to reduce the incidence of corruption as competitive market forces come to the fore. Illegal payoffs have been converted into legal market prices, and the level of monopoly rents should fall. The absence of such a simple association has spread gloom among free market reformers as they contemplate the corruption and lawlessness of emerging market economies in Russia and Eastern Europe and new democracies such as Argentina. Some analysts would ignore the phenomenon, arguing that it is simply one of the growing pains of the transition to a modern democratic, capitalist state. Stories of nineteenth-century U.S. robber barons are invoked to argue that "cowboy capitalism" is just a stage in the move toward market. Others argue that since some high-growth countries also have high corruption levels, corruption does not deserve much notice.

These seem to me to be overly optimistic views. Those seeking to encourage economic growth, democracy, and a fair distribution of income and wealth need to be concerned with the corruption of state officials in transition economies. Corruption has the potential to become so widespread that it could undermine and even destroy the transition process. Even if corruption is consistent with economic growth under some conditions, that does not imply that it actually facilitates growth or that it does not have negative political and social consequences. To proceed, we need to consider why corruption is not necessarily reduced by the transition to market and to democracy. Corrupt incentives are produced by the monopoly power of state officials, but the sources of this power are drastically changed by the transition to a democratic, capitalist system. If prices are permitted to reach market-clearing levels, no one need pay a bribe to get supplies. If pockets of state control remain, however, they may be the loci of payoffs. Thus the privatization process, although ultimately reducing corruption by lowering state involvement in the economy, may initially be a source of large payoffs as investors jockey for position (Manzetti and Blake forthcoming).

Short of opportunities for windfall gains in the privatization process, the basic source of corrupt incentives has changed from the bottlenecks created by an overly rigid, intrusive state to the uncertainties of one that is weak and disorganized. A society in transition implies a situation in which administrative, legal, and political structures are fragile and poorly developed. Yet people want certainty, and they may try to achieve it by paying off officials to make favorable rulings (Shleifer and Vishny 1993). The only difficulty for bribers is the lack of clear lines of authority. It may be difficult to know whether the person bribed has the authority to provide the desired benefit or whether other officials, observing the payoffs, will erect roadblocks of their own that also require payoffs. In the worst case citizens and business people simply opt out of the legal, above-ground economy and rely on organized crime to provide protection from both the state and from anyone else who seeks to interfere (Rose-Ackerman 1994; Kaufman 1994). Corruption may then be merely a device for inducing public officials to look the other way. The state has become not just weak, but irrelevant as well.

The challenge for such countries is to establish legitimate state organs operating under a rule of law without recreating the rigidities of the former state-controlled system. This is a task that must be accomplished by informed and determined reformers; the solution is unlikely to arise by spontaneous generation. In the United States, for example, the Progressive era reforms were a direct response to the excesses of late nineteenth-century capitalism and politics (Menes 1994; Bartol and Rose-Ackerman 1995). The reforms of those years were acts of political will, not the result of blind evolution.

Further, the situation in Russia suggests that spontaneous evolution in post-Soviet societies can be destructive. If profitmaking activities are viewed as "speculation" that exploits innocent consumers, then unscrupulous people will be disproportionately attracted to such activities. Such people may use violence, corruption, and intimidation to gain a competitive advantage, thus further undermining the social acceptability of market-based activities. They may enter illegal markets, such as the drug trade, contaminating the public's perception of entrepreneurial activity. Honest business people will be forced to take evasive action. They might purchase protection services from organized crime figures or organize their businesses to limit arm's length market trades because of the lack of legitimate means of contract enforcement. One study of the organization of Russian businesses, for example, found a growing trend toward vertical integration—thus recreating some features of the old system (Frye 1993). The end result of the destructive cycle could be public pressure to limit the role of the market and return to a planned economy. Schumpeter's "creative destruction" is not descriptive of the situation. There is plenty of destruction, but not much of it is creative or supportive of economic growth.

Mitigating Corruption

If stability facilitated corruption in the past and instability encourages it in the present, what can be done to control it? Despite the dramatic changes in institutional structure that have occurred in transition economies, one feature remains constant: the lack of a credible state commitment to the rule of law. These economies must introduce both substantive law reform and bureaucratic and government restructuring.

The most basic concern is the government programs that generate payoffs. Some programs serve no public purpose and should be eliminated. Some trade restrictions do little more than encourage smuggling and payoffs. Some regulatory constraints restrict market activities without correcting market failures. Other programs could be simplified to reduce official discretion or converted to legal market trades. The opportunities for corruption are reduced when the government purchases standardized products at market prices instead of writing its own specifications. Bribes become irrelevant when legal pricing mechanisms take their place.

Eliminating some bottlenecks may not be sufficient if others remain and if private agents cannot act unless a string of permissions has been received. And if a corrupt official exists at just one bureaucratic hurdle, that is sufficient to lead to high levels of bribery. The transaction costs of multiple approvals have been eliminated, but the result is simply a more efficient transfer of money from the applicant to the remaining corrupt official. This might appear to be an improvement since bribery then becomes a pure transfer from one pocket to another. The corrupt official will set the bribe just high enough to extract most of the applicant's profits without discouraging him from carrying out his project. The pure kleptocrat, however, will act like a monopolist and limit the economic activity under his control to maximize his own gain (Shleifer and Vishny 1993).

Some scholars claim that high-level corruption is less disruptive of economic growth than low-level corruption. They argue that top officials will organize payoffs to maximize their monopoly profits without discouraging the investment and economic growth that will fill their coffers. Decentralized low-level corruption introduces more bottlenecks and transactions costs because every official seeks to extract a bribe. Low-level corruption may generate not only high transaction costs, but also a decline in investment because greedy officials collectively ask for too much (Shleifer and Vishny 1993; Rodrik 1994). The result is a direct application of the result in industrial organization showing that two independent monopoly suppliers will earn higher profits if they act as a unit.

A possible policy implication of this theoretical result is that reformers should focus on low-level corruption. This conclusion appears to me to be extremely problematic. It seems unlikely that a state can foster honest behavior at low levels if top officials and politicians are corrupt. Perhaps a strong civil service tradition can produce such a result, but that is exactly what most transition economies lack.

Furthermore, reformers need to consider the distributive consequences of corruption. Bribes paid to top officials are frequently deposited outside the country, not reinvested within the country. Those concerned with economic development should not give equal weight to income gains for top officials and ordinary citizens. Finally, the relatively optimistic view of high-level corruption assumes that the menu of outside investors and trading partners is determined by underlying economic conditions. In these models corrupt demands can only discourage firms, not change the mix of potential investors and importers. A look at countries where high-level corruption is endemic suggests that this characterization is a mistake. One common pattern is for a country's rulers to contract with multinationals for excessively expensive and inappropriate investment projects as a way of extracting large bribes (Diamond 1993; Good 1994). Another possibility is the design of programs, such as those regulating business or privatizing the economy, so as to produce large payoffs. Such massive economic distortions are not open to lower-level officials. Although "death by a thousand cuts" is surely painful, beheading does not have much to recommend it either.

Another dimension of the structural analysis concerns the locus of corruption within government. It does seem possible to have, say, an honest civil service and corrupt elected politicians who accept secret payments either for their own enrichment or to finance political parties. The recent scandals in Belgium and France are of this nature, and other cases have come to light in recent years in Germany and Japan. In other cases a relatively honest set of elected politicians must deal with a corrupt bureaucracy. If politicians at the top are dependent on the information they receive from the civil service, they may have trouble penetrating a culture of corruption. Police corruption in the United States sometimes has this character (Sherman 1974). The fragility of national reform governments, even those with military backing, testifies to the need for serious administrative reform in such systems.

One place to start is with the courts and the public prosecutors. A corrupt judiciary, or one that is not independent of the executive and political branches, is a major problem because corruption cannot be reduced without credible legal sanctions. Once an honest, effective enforcement system has been established, the state can move on to the reform of political and bureaucratic institutions.

A corrupt bureaucracy could undermine an honest political regime, while a corrupt political regime need not have that effect on the bureaucracy unless it so undermines the morale of bureaucrats that the honest ones simply quit. Furthermore, if a state has established the forms of democratic government, has a relatively free press, and has not promulgated restrictive libel laws, the checks imposed by the desire for reelection will constrain elected officials but not bureaucrats (Tucker 1994).

Finally, we need to examine the complex relationship between corruption and political stability. Stability feeds corruption if the rigidity of the system creates a demand for corrupt services. Furthermore, if stability implies predictability, bribes may be paid for benefits to be delivered in the future. Corrupt payoffs can be consistent with the development of large-scale capital projects because officials can make credible commitments. Corruption that takes the form of cozy personal relationships and the exchange of favors between officials and private agents can, in turn, further the stability of the system as a dense web of relationships develops that blurs the line between public and private. Economic development in China appears to follow this pattern. Although growth has been rapid, the question for the future is whether such a highly personalized system, with its potential for arbitrariness, is consistent with large-scale capitalist development. Already, worrisome cases are arising in which local partners are able to force foreign partners out of lucrative deals because of the locals' connections with government officials (Johnston and Hao 1995; Hao and Johnston 1995).

By contrast, the stability of a system operating under a well-established legal system can reduce corruption by reducing the discretion of officials. Violations of rules can be observed and the violators disciplined. The incentives for corruption that remain concern people who want officials to violate the rules in return for a payoff.[1] The possibility of detection and punishment limits the willingness of the unscrupulous to accept and pay bribes. Stability is combined with outside checks on the actions of public officials, such as an independent judiciary, a free press, and a dense network of nongovernmental organizations. Given the necessity of a regulatory welfare state in modern capitalist economies, transition economies need to develop responsible checks on state action. At the same time they need to establish new laws governing private economic relationships and new regulatory, tax, and spending laws. They also require stronger administrative structures to deal with the regulatory and social demands that come with a liberalized economy.

Conclusion

Artificial scarcity and excessive state control are no longer the sources of corrupt incentives in formerly state-run economies. The problem is instability and unpredictability. The answer is not simply to introduce clarity and predictability into the law. The state must also investigate the operation of government and provide credible routes for those who might otherwise pay bribes to appeal official decisions. These structures impose costs, but they are costs that must be paid if corruption is to be reduced and the legitimacy of the state established in the eyes of the population. A stable government without outside checks can be a potent bribe-generating machine. A stable government with such checks is on its way to limiting corruption and in the process improving the climate for the growth of legitimate business. Aid organizations such as the World Bank and the International Monetary Fund need to focus not just on macroeconomic stabilization and privatization of state property, but also on bureaucratic and political reform.

Note

1. Shleifer and Vishny's (1993) distinction between corruption "with theft" and corruption "without theft" is relevant here. See Rose-Ackerman (1978) for recommendations for reducing corrupt incentives in such systems. The proposals include not only sanctioning strategies, but also the redesign of bureaucratic and political processes.

References

Baer, Herbert L., and Cheryl W. Gray. 1995. "Debt as a Control Device in Transitional Economies: The Experiences of Hungary and Poland." Policy Research Working Paper 1480. World Bank, Washington, D.C.

Bartol, Frederick, and Susan Rose-Ackerman. 1995. "Progressivism." In Seymour Martin Lipset, ed., *The Encyclopedia of Democracy*. Washington, D.C.: Congressional Quarterly Books.

Blanchard, Olivier, Simon Commander, and Fabrizio Coricelli. 1995. "Unemployment and Restructuring in Eastern Europe and Russia." In Simon Commander and Fabrizio Coricelli, eds., *Unemployment, Restructuring, and the Labor Market in Eastern Europe and Russia*. Economic Development Institute Development Studies. Washington, D.C.: World Bank.

Blasi, Joseph. 1994. "Corporate Governance in Russia." Paper presented at the World Bank conference on corporate governance and privatization in Central Europe and Russia, December 15–16, Washington, D.C.

Boycko, Maxim A., Andrei Shleifer, and Robert Vishny. 1993. "Privatizing Russia." *Brooking Papers on Economic Activity* 2. Washington, D.C.: The Brookings Institution.

Bruno, Michael. 1994. "Stabilization and Reform in Eastern Europe: A Preliminary Evaluation." In Olivier J. Blanchard, Kenneth A. Froot, and Jeffrey D. Sachs, eds., *The Transition in Eastern Europe*. Chicago, Ill.: University of Chicago Press.

Coffee, John C. 1995. "Institutional Investors in Transitional Economies: Lessons from the Czech Experience." Paper presented at the World Bank conference on corporate governance and privatization in Central Europe and Russia, December 15–16, Washington, D.C.

de Melo, Martha, Cevdet Denizer, and Alan Gelb. 1996. "From Plan to Market: Patterns of Transition." Policy Research Working Paper 1564. World Bank, Washington, D.C.

Diamond, Larry. 1993. "Nigeria's Perennial Struggle Against Corruption: Prospects for the Third Republic." *Corruption and Reform* 7: 215–25.

Dittus, Peter. 1994. "Corporate Governance in Central Europe: The Role of Banks." Bank for International Settlements, Monetary and Economic Department, Basle.

Dittus, Peter, and Stephen Prowse. 1995. "Corporate Governance in Central Europe and Russia: Should Banks Own Shares?" Policy Research Working Paper 1481. World Bank, Washington, D.C.

Dyba, Karel, and Jan Svejnar. 1995. "Economic Transition in the Czech Republic." In Jan Svejnar, ed., *Czech Republic and Economic Transition in Eastern Europe*. San Diego, Calif.: Academic Press.

Earle, John S., and Saul Estrin. 1995. "Worker Ownership in Transition." Paper presented at the World Bank conference on corporate governance and privatization in Central Europe and Russia, December 15–16, Washington, D.C.

Frydman, Roman, Andrzej Rapaczynski, and John Earle. 1993. *The Privatization Process in Central Europe*. London: Central European University Press.

Frye, Timothy. 1993. "Caveat Emptor: Institutions, Credible Commitment, and Commodity Exchanges in Russia." In David Weimer, ed., *Institutional Design*. Norwell, Mass.: Kluwer Academic Publishers.

Good, Kenneth. 1994. "Corruption and Mismanagement in Botswana: A Best-Case Example?" *Journal of Modern African Studies* 32: 499–521.

Hao, Yufan, and Michael Johnston. 1995. "Reform at the Crossroads: An Analysis of Chinese Corruption." *Asian Perspectives* 19: 117–49.

Johnston, Michael, and Yufan Hao, 1995. "China's Surge of Corruption." *Journal of Democracy* 6: 80–94.

Kaufman, Daniel. 1994. "Diminishing Returns to Administrative Controls and the Emergence of the Unofficial Economy: A Framework of Analysis and Applications to Ukraine." *Economic Policy* (December): 51–69.

Kotrba, Josef. 1995. "Privatization Process in the Czech Republic: Players and Winners." In Jan Svejnar, ed., *Czech Republic and Economic Transition in Eastern Europe*. San Diego, Calif.: Academic Press.

Lastovicka, Roman, Anton Marcincic, and Michal Mejstrik. 1995. "Corporate Governance and Share Prices in Voucher Privatized Companies." In Jan Svejnar, ed., *Czech Republic and Economic Transition in Eastern Europe*. San Diego, Calif.: Academic Press.

Manzetti, Luigi, and Charles Blake. Forthcoming. "Market Reforms and Corruption in Latin America: New Means for Old Ways." *Review of International Political Economy*.

Matesová, Jana. 1994. "Will the Manufacturing Heart Beat Again? Country Overview Paper." *Eastern European Economics* 31(6): 3–35.

Matesová, Jana, and Richard Seda. 1994. "Financial Markets in the Czech Republic as a Means of Corporate Governance in Voucher Privatized Companies." Working Paper 62. CERGE-EI, Prague.

Menes, Rebecca. 1994. "Bosses and Mugwumps: Economic Change and Political Reform in Urban America, 1890–1930." Harvard University and National Bureau of Economic Research, Cambridge, Mass.

Montias, J. M., and Susan Rose-Ackerman. 1981. "Corruption in a Soviet-type Economy: Theoretical Considerations." In Steven Rosefield, ed., *Economic Welfare and the Economics of Soviet Socialism: Essays in Honor of Abram Bergson.* Cambridge: Cambridge University Press.

Pistor, Katharina, Roman Frydman, and Andrzej Rapaczynski. 1994. "Investing in Insider-Dominated Firms: A Study of Russian Voucher Privatization Funds." Paper presented at the World Bank conference on corporate governance and privatization in Central Europe and Russia, December 15–16, Washington, D.C.

Rodrik, Dani. 1994. "King Kong Meets Godzilla: The World Bank and the East Asian Miracle." In Albert Fishlow, Catherine Gwin, Stephen Haggard, Dani Rodrik, and Robert Wade, eds., *Miracle or Design? Lessons from the East Asian Experience.* ODC Policy Essay 11. Washington, D.C.: Overseas Development Council.

Rose-Ackerman, Susan. 1978. *Corruption: A Study in Political Economy.* New York: Academic Press.

———. 1994. "Reducing Bribery in the Public Sector." In Duc V. Trang, ed., *Corruption and Democracy: Political Institutions, Processes, and Corruption in Transition States in East-Central Europe and in the Former Soviet Union.* Budapest: Institute for Constitutional and Legislative Policy.

Seibel, Wolfgang. 1995. "La Corruption en Allemagne." In Donatella Della Porta and Yves Mény, eds., *Démocratie et Corruption en Europe.* Paris: La Découverte.

Sherman, Lawrence W., ed. 1974. *Police Corruption: A Sociological Perspective.* New York: Anchor Books.

Shleifer, Andrei, and Robert Vishny. 1992. "Pervasive Shortages under Socialism." *Rand Journal of Economics* 23: 237–46.

———. 1993. "Corruption." *Quarterly Journal of Economics* 108: 599–617.

Stern, Mikhail. 1977. *The USSR vs. Dr. Mikhail Stern.* New York: Urizen Books.

Svejnar, Jan, Kathy Terrell, and Daniel Muenich. 1995. "Unemployment in Czech and Slovak Republics." In Jan Svejnar, ed., *Czech Republic and Economic Transition in Eastern Europe.* San Diego, Ill.: Academic Press.

Trang, Duc V., ed. 1994. *Corruption and Democracy: Political Institutions, Processes, and Corruption in Transition States in East-Central Europe and in the Former Soviet Union.* Budapest: Institute for Constitutional and Legislative Policy.

Tucker, Lee. 1994. "Censorship and Corruption: Government Self-Protection Through Control of the Media." In Duc V. Trang, ed., *Corruption and Democracy: Political Institutions, Processes, and Corruption in Transition States in East-Central Europe and in the Former Soviet Union.* Budapest: Institute for Constitutional and Legislative Policy.

Floor Discussion of "Second-Generation
Issues in Transition"

One participant asked whether developing countries would benefit if the
World Bank were to announce that it would not provide loans to a country
until the government was free of corruption, deception, and indiscipline.
Gustav Ranis (discussant from another session) asked whether part of the problem
of instability, crime, and corruption was related to going from a hidden high Gini
coefficient of power to a visible high Gini coefficient of income.

Susan Rose-Ackerman (panelist) responded that the question of when to work
from within and when to respond to a big stick from the outside was a hard one. She
found Ranis's observation interesting, that one place you see corruption—not just in
the transition economies, but elsewhere—is where strong tensions arise because of
different distributions of power in political and economic systems. It varies among
countries, she said, but centralized power has tended to disintegrate in the transition
economies in recent years, although in some countries the old nomenklatura is still
in power, which is probably an additional source of tension that leads to payoffs.

Michael Lipton (discussant from another session) asked if the panelists could
explain the sharp rise in death rates in most transition economies, especially death
rates among men between the ages of forty and fifty. Citizens were concerned about
this death rate, which had begun climbing before the transition but was accelerating
sharply. Jana Matesová (panelist), who had written a book on the subject, explained
that death rates had been increasing for men aged forty to sixty since the early 1960s
in the Czech Republic and other Eastern European countries. The main reasons
appear to be environmental: the change in lifestyle that comes with decreased
income, poor nutritional habits, low levels of physical activity, and the decreasing
efficiency of medical care under communism. These factors were even more of a
problem now because health care was one of the three sectors (at least in the Czech
economy) in which economic agents were weakest, least capable of lobbying the government, and losing the most employees. (The other two are education and social
care.) Stanley Fischer (panelist) guessed that the higher death rate for men would

This session was chaired by Michael Bruno, senior vice president, Development Economics, and chief
economist, at the World Bank.

Annual World Bank Conference on Development Economics 1995
©1996 The International Bank for Reconstruction and Development / THE WORLD BANK

continue until there was a period of sustained growth, so that the benefits from higher incomes begin to spread to the people left behind in restructuring. Every revolution hits the established people first, he said, which means men aged forty to sixty. We are only beginning to learn about the individual costs of transition, added Michael Bruno (chair), and this is one of them. Bruno had heard claims of statistical bias, but he believes that the deaths resulted from a deterioration in services combined with anxiety and disruption caused by the transition.

A participant asked Matesová whether there had been a pronounced transition involving monopolies, mergers, and regulatory mechanisms just before the Czech Republic's main transition, because such changes might hinder the main transition program. She responded that in the late 1980s and early 1990s there were a number of company splits and spinoffs and that average company size had decreased considerably. Many of the current mergers were either privatized companies merging with new startups or remergers of companies that had split before. And, of course, antimonopoly regulation was now in place to make the Czech Republic compatible with EU regulations, because the country was in the process of joining the European Union, or at least its legal system. In any case market concentration was much lower in 1995 than it had been in 1988, although there could be a problem of market concentration in the future.

A participant from Slovenia asked if restructuring first and privatizing second might not be the best approach. In his opinion the Czechs had not yet started to restructure.

A participant from the World Bank said that he was not sure, in listening to the discussion, whether "second generation" meant lessons learned from five years of experience or whether there was a natural sequence from first-generation to second-generation issues. In several countries reform had been driven by windows of opportunity rather than by any natural sequencing of events. In advising countries that were new to the process, would the panelists recommend a sequence based on lessons learned or suggest that windows of opportunity dominate the process?

Evidence suggests that it is important to aim for macroeconomic stabilization first, replied Fischer, and that is still part of conventional wisdom. More interesting is the question of when to privatize. The answer is, after macroeconomic stabilization, if possible. It is surprising how slowly privatization has advanced in most economies, and how slowly restructuring has taken place in the Czech Republic. Russia is an exception to the general rule of stabilize first and privatize later, added Bruno. For better or for worse, Russia privatized first and is only now stabilizing. It is not clear whether it is stabilizing now because there is a stronger constituency for price stability.

As for the other question—do you take opportunities as they come?—absolutely, continued Fischer. Do them in a preferred order, but do not delay enterprise sector reform while you pursue macroeconomic stabilization, and do not wait to liberalize prices, as bad as it is to liberalize and then have an outburst of inflation. Opportunities come, and you have no way of knowing how long they will last, so you cannot wait. Fischer believes that the faster an economy is privatized, the more rapidly it will see growth, but in any case much of the growth will come from new firms.

What makes this subject so interesting, concluded Bruno, is that there are surprises all along the way. Nobody knew in late 1989 and early 1990 what to expect. Only in the course of time, for example, had people realized how deeply the problems in the financial sector affected transition.

World Debt Tables 1996

This new edition of the World Bank's invaluable reference guide provides complete and up-to-date information on the external debt of and financial flows to developing countries. It works as a handy planning tool for economists, bankers, country risk analysts, financial consultants, and others involved in trade, payments, and capital flows worldwide. *World Debt Tables 1996* contains key data on the states of the former Soviet Union (FSU) and provides consolidated statistics for all developing countries, including those that do not report to the World Bank's Debtor Reporting System (DRS).

Volume I analyzes recent developments in debt and non-debt financial flows to developing countries and provides expert commentary. **Volume II** provides statistical tables for the 136 countries that report public and publicly guaranteed debt under the DRS, including the FSU countries.

March 1996.
Volume 1—Analysis and Summary Tables. Order no. 13300. $24.95.
Volume II—Country Tables (Not sold separately).
Two-volume set — Order no. 13302. $200.00.

World Bank Atlas 1996
28th edition.

The 28th edition of this handy and inexpensive atlas provides color maps, charts, and graphs representing the main social, economic, and environmental indicators for 209 countries and territories. Like other recent editions, it is organized under three development themes: The People, The Economy, and The Environment. Introductory texts explain the role each theme plays in world development.

December 1995. Order no. 13287. $7.95.

Statistical Handbook 1995: States of the Former USSR

This is the fourth annual compilation of statistical data on the rapidly evolving economies of the former Soviet Union (FSU). It is an indispensable reference, providing even more comprehensive data than the 1994 handbook for evaluating market reforms in the FSU. It converts economic data used by socialist systems to the market-based system of national accounts and incorporates new national currencies in the data. The volume contains both English and Russian versions of the text.

Decisionmakers have easy access to key statistics on the 15 independent states through the handbook's comparative tables, which provide cross-country data arranged by subject. Topics include production rates, human resources, and external trade.

Country tables give detailed information on essential statistical indicators such as public finance, monetary statistics, employment, and labor.

January 1996. Order no. 13508. $25.95.

FSU☆STARS☆
States of the Former Soviet Union 1995: Data on Diskette

The latest data for the states of the former Soviet Union are now available through the Socioeconomic Time-series Access and Retrieval System (☆STARS☆). This unique database contains more than 4,000 indicators arranged hierarchically within the World Bank Country Economic Memorandum table structure. The database covers population and labor, national accounts, foreign trade, government finance, monetary statistics, industry, agriculture, prices and wages, household budget statistics, and investment figures for the years 1980 and 1985-94, where available. The data presented in the **Statistical Handbook 1995: States of the Former USSR** is a subset of the information available in the FSU☆STARS☆ package.

☆STARS☆ allows the user to view single items, to construct and view a table on-screen, or to export the data for use in other programs such as ASCII, DBE, AREMOS, Lotus 1-2-3™, and Javelin Plus™. This package includes the complete ☆STARS☆ program and data on 3½" double-density diskettes for use on personal computers with a hard disk, at least 512K RAM, and MS-DOS 2.1 or higher. The user's manual provides a guide to getting started and viewing and extracting data.

January 1996. 3 1/2" diskettes.
Order no. 13548. $45.00.

Trends in Private Investment in Developing Countries: Statistics for 1970-94
Frederick Z. Jaspersen, Anthony A. Aylward, and Mariusz A. Sumlinski

This seventh annual statistical survey by the International Finance Corporation tracks private investment in developing countries. The current edition, which covers a 25-year period, 1970-94, contains 11 more years of data than the previous edition (1980-93).

The authors discuss foreign direct investment, determinants of private investment (domestic and foreign), and the effects of foreign direct investment, determinants of private investment (domestic and foreign), and the effects of institutional factors on investment.

Tables and graphs of updated statistics track gross domestic product, the amounts of private versus public investment, and investment shares for East Asia, Latin America, South Asia, and Sub-Saharan Africa.

December 1995. Order no. 13557. $7.95.

Managing Commodity Booms—and Busts
Panos Varangis, Takamasa Akiyama, and Donald Mitchell

Suggests guidelines by which developing countries can successfully manage the rapid surge in government revenues that occurs during a commodity boom.

The book addresses the problems associated with such booms, including long-term spending commitments, Dutch disease, and a slowdown in diversification.

December 1995. Order no. 13489. $7.95.

Order Form

Payment: Note that orders from individuals must be accompanied by payment or credit card information. Credit cards accepted only for orders addressed to the World Bank. Check with
local distributor about acceptable credit cards. Please do not send cash.

❏ Enclosed is my check
   Make check payable to the World Bank in US dollars drawn on
   a US bank unless you are ordering from your local distributor.

❏ Bill me. Institutional
   customers in the US only.
   (Please include purchase order)

❏ Charge my   ❏ **VISA**   ❏ **MasterCard**   ❏ **AMERICAN EXPRESS**

Account Number   Expiration Date   Signature (required to validate all orders)

**Note: If you are paying by check or credit card, shipping and handling charges are US$5.00 per order.
For air mail delivery outside North America, add US$8.00 for one item plus US$6.00 for each additional
item. Prices may vary by country and are subject to change without notice.**

Ship to:

Name and Title

Address

(   )

City   State   Postal Code   Country   Telephone

Please send the World Bank products listed below:

Quantity	Language	Short Title	Stock #	Price	Total Price

**Visit the World Bank's Internet Home Page!
http://www.worldbank.org**

Subtotal cost $ _____
Shipping and handling $ ___5.00___
Airmail surcharge outside USA $ _____
Total $ _____